THE RITZ

AND OTHER PLAYS

TERRENCE McNALLY

THE RITZ
AND OTHER PLAYS

INCLUDING

Bad Habits

Where Has Tommy Flowers Gone?

". . . And Things That Go Bump in the Night"

Whiskey

Bringing It All Back Home

DODD, MEAD & COMPANY
NEW YORK

Library of Congress Cataloging in Publication Data

McNally, Terrence.
  The Ritz and other plays.

  CONTENTS: The Ritz.—Bad habits.—Where has Tommy
Flowers gone? [etc.]
  I. Title.
PS3563.A323R5   812′.5′4   76-17603
ISBN 0-396-07315-8

For Robert Drivas

A FEW WORDS ABOUT THE PLAYS

Preparing the plays collected in this volume for publication presented a problem. All the plays published here are available in "acting" editions but here was the opportunity to present them as "literature." I chose literature.

Thus, what you will read are the plays I wrote, as opposed to what you may have seen in the theatre. There is a reason for this. Once a play is written and goes into rehearsal, an enormous and seemingly never-ending collaborative process begins. A playwright writes alone but once he gets into the theatre with his script he works with a director, a producer, actors, designers and finally, after the first preview, the audience itself. The result is change, sometimes for the better, but unfortunately not always. I have rewritten to accommodate an actor; I have even rewritten to accommodate a prop. In editing these plays for this edition, I have arrived at the versions that satisfy me most as the author. In the theatre, what I work for is the version that satisfies me most as a collaborator.

I see no point in being inflexible about changes when it comes to working with other people on the initial production of a new script. I have benefitted enormously from the contributions of my colleagues. So have the plays. I have F. Murray Abraham to thank for one of the funniest lines in *Bad Habits*. It comes out of an improvisation in early rehearsal. Do I thank Murray alone or do I also thank the director, Robert Drivas, for creating a work situation in which the actors felt free enough to contribute? I thank them both. I also thank my parents for teaching me the common sense to leave the line in.

I have also suffered a little at the hands of my collaborators, though not any more than is to be expected in a situation like rehearsal and a good deal less than I might have. We all make mistakes. Sometimes we are persuaded to make mistakes. Every change I have made in a play of mine was made voluntarily and I have managed to live with them—at least until now. This volume gives me the opportunity to have the last say. At the time of production, we were all wrong together; for this book I hope I'm right all by myself.

The two plays that differ most in these published versions from their New York productions are "*. . . And Things That Go Bump* *in the Night"* and *Where Has Tommy Flowers Gone?* The second is scarcely the same play. *Bump* was rewritten and rewritten because I was young and ambitious and it was my first play. I would have stopped at nothing short of murder to get it on. What was murdered, of course, was the script and it was all my doing. What you have now is the version originally performed at the Tyrone Guthrie Theatre in Minneapolis—the script I *wrote* as opposed to the patched-together play that opened on Broadway. *Tommy Flowers* was originally written for Robert Drivas and the Yale Repertory Theatre. The changes it suffered en route from New Haven to New York were made by a slightly older and a lot shrewder playwright. Yale's *Tommy* was simply too expensive a production. I tried to scale the play down. I succeeded all too well. I am really proud to see this original version in print at last.

Not all the plays here exist in these conflicting versions. Both *The Ritz* and *Bad Habits* are here presented as they were in the New York theatre. I have no regrets or second thoughts about the changes made in them during rehearsal and previews. Also, they are what I call my two "happy" plays: happy to write, happy to rehearse, happy, finally, to watch performed. Of course, they both happened to run, too.

Just about all I can tell you about *Whiskey* is that it is my least-loved play. Least loved by the people whose opinions I respect, anyway. Naturally, I'm therefore tempted to call it my favorite. It's my only remotely autobiographical work, which doesn't mean anything, except maybe that's why I'm so close to it. I'm not saying my friends are right about *Whiskey*, but I'm not saying I'm wrong about it, either.

A play is only as good as the people the playwright finds to direct and perform it. In that respect, I have been very lucky. I cannot let this opportunity pass without thanking Leueen Mac-Grath for *Bump*; everyone at Yale for *Tommy Flowers*; a totally perfect cast for *Bad Habits*; the comic genius of nearly everyone for *The Ritz* and finally Robert Drivas, to whom this book is dedicated, for everything. He has either directed or acted in most of my plays, always to my advantage. It is hard to think of these plays without him. We really do get by with a little help from our friends.

TERRENCE McNALLY

June 22, 1976

CONTENTS

vii   A Few Words About the Plays

1   The Ritz (1975)

69   Bad Habits (1974)

147   Where Has Tommy Flowers Gone? (1971)

255   "...And Things That Go Bump in the Night" (1965)

355   Whiskey (1973)

415   Bringing It All Back Home (1969)

The date listed for each play is that of the first New York City performance.

THE RITZ

(1975)

For Adela Holzer

THE RITZ was originally performed at the Yale Repertory Theatre:
It opened January 20, 1975, at the Longacre Theatre in New York
City. It was produced by Adela Holzer. It was directed by Robert
Drivas. Scenery and costumes designed by Michael H. Yeargan
and Lawrence King. Lighting designed by Martin Aronstein. The
production stage manager was Larry Forde. The assistants to the
director were Tony DeSantis and Gary Keeper.

THE CAST
(in order of appearance)

ABE	George Dzundza
CLAUDE PERKINS	Paul B. Price
GAETANO PROCLO	Jack Weston
CHRIS	F. Murray Abraham
GOOGIE GOMEZ	Rita Moreno
MAURINE	Hortensia Colorado
MICHAEL BRICK	Stephen Collins
TIGER	John Everson
DUFF	Christopher J. Brown
CARMINE VESPUCCI	Jerry Stiller
VIVIAN PROCLO	Ruth Jaroslow

THE PATRONS

PIANIST	Ron Abel
POLICEMAN	Bruce Bauer
CRISCO	Richard Boccelli
SHELDON FARENTHOLD	Tony DeSantis
PATRON IN CHAPS	John Remme
PATRON FROM SHERIDAN SQUARE	Steve Scott

The time of the play is now.

The place of the play is a men's bathhouse in New York City.

The people of the play are:

GAETANO PROCLO: He is in his early 40's, balding and stout.

CHRIS: He is in his early 30's with a big, open face and features.

MICHAEL BRICK: He is in his mid-20's, very rugged and very handsome.

CARMINE VESPUCCI: He is in his 40's, balding and stout.

CLAUDE PERKINS: He is in his 40's and quite lean.

TIGER: He is in his early 20's, wiry and has lots of curly hair.

DUFF: He too is in his early 20's, wiry and has lots of curly hair. In fact, he looks a lot like Tiger.

ABE: He is in his 50's and stocky.

THE PATRONS: They come in all sizes, shapes and ages.

GOOGIE GOMEZ: She is in her 30's and has a sensational figure.

VIVIAN PROCLO: She is in her early 40's and stout.

MAURINE: She's in her mid-40's, and very thin.

ACT ONE

The house curtain is in, the house lights are on and the overture from "Tancredi" is playing as the audience comes in. The house goes to black. In the darkness we hear the sounds of the Rosary being recited. Occasionally a stifled sob overrides the steady incantation of the prayers.

PRIESTS AND RELATIVES. Hail Mary, full of grace, the Lord is with thee. Blessed art thou amongst women and blessed is the fruit of thy womb, Jesus. Holy Mary, Mother of God, pray for us sinners now and at the hour of our death. Amen. (*Underneath all this, the funeral march from "Nabucco" is heard. The lights have revealed Old Man Vespucci's death bed. Relatives and family are grouped around him, all in silhouette. Kneeling to his right is Carmine. Kneeling to his left is Vivian. They are weeping profusely.*)

CARMINE. Poppa . . .

VIVIAN. Poppa . . . (*The death rattles are beginning. Old Man Vespucci feebly summons the others to draw close for his final words.*)

AUNT VERA. *Aspetta! Aspetta!*

COUSIN HORTENSIA. Sshh! Speak to us, Poppa!

AUNT VERA. Give us your blessing, Poppa!

COUSIN HORTENSIA. One final word, Poppa!

AUNT VERA. *Un poccita parole,* Poppa!

VIVIAN. Give us your blessing, Poppa!

OLD MAN VESPUCCI. Vivian.

VIVIAN. Yes, Poppa?

OLD MAN VESPUCCI. *Vieni qua.*

VIVIAN. Yes, Poppa.

OLD MAN VESPUCCI. Get Proclo.

VIVIAN. Get Proclo, Poppa? Yes, Poppa. He's coming. The plane was late from Cleveland. He'll be here for your blessing. (*Old Man Vespucci dismisses his daughter with a hand gesture.*)

OLD MAN VESPUCCI. Carmine, my son.

CARMINE. Yes, Poppa. I'm here, Poppa.

OLD MAN VESPUCCI. Get Proclo.

CARMINE. Get Proclo, Poppa?

OLD MAN VESPUCCI. Get Proclo. *Qui brute. Qui boce. Tha botania!* Kill him! Kill him! Kill him! Kill the son of a bitch!

VIVIAN. Proclo is my husband, Poppa!

OLD MAN VESPUCCI. (*Finally mustering all the strength he can, he raises himself up.*) GET PROCLO! ! ! (*He falls back dead.*)

RELATIVES. (*Simultaneously.*) Aaaaaiiiieeeee!

AUNT VERA. *Poppa è morto!*

PRIEST. *In nomine patris et filii et spiritu sancti requiescat in . . .* (*The lights fade on the death bed. At the same time, the sound of a pounding drum is heard. It is the opening of "One of a Kind." The lights come up, revealing activity inside The Ritz behind scrims. The main thing we see are doors. Doors and doors and doors. Each door has a number. Outside all these doors are corridors. Lots and lots of corridors. Filling these corridors are men. Lots and lots of men. They are prowling the corridors. One of the most important aspects of the production is this sense of men endlessly prowling the corridors outside the numbered doors. The same people will pass up and down the same corridors and stairways over and over again. After a while, you'll start to think some of them are on a treadmill. Most of them are dressed exactly alike; i.e., they are wearing bathrobes. A few men wear towels around their waists. Every so often we see someone in bikini underwear or an additional accoutrement, such as boots or a vest. The number of men, referred to from now on as the patrons, can vary, but each actor must be encouraged to develop a specific characterization. Even though they seldom speak, these various patrons must become specific, integral members of the cast. We also see Tiger and Duff, two attendants. They are sweeping up and making beds. Over the music, we hear announcements.*)

ABE. (*Over the loudspeaker.*) 217 coming up, Duff! . . . Tiger, they're out of soap in the showers! On the double! And check the linens and robes on the third floor . . . Just a reminder that every Monday and Thursday is Buddy Night at the Ritz. So bring a friend. Two entrances for the price of one. (*The lights dim, and the entrance area is flown in. The inner door and Abe's booth are moved on from left and right. The center scrim flies*

*as the lights come up bright, and we are in the admissions area
of The Ritz. The various patrons will pay, check their valuables,
receive a room key and then be buzzed through the inner door
adjacent to the booth. One patron has just finished checking in.
As he is buzzed through the door, we see Abe announce his room
number over a loudspeaker.)* 274! That's 274 coming up, Duff!
*(The patron disappears. The phone on Abe's desk rings, and he
answers.)* Hello. The Ritz. No, we don't take reservations! *(He
hangs up, as another patron enters.)*

PATRON. Good evening.

ABE. Yeah?

PATRON. Nasty night.

ABE. Is it?

PATRON. I'm one big puddle.

ABE. Well watch where you're dripping. I just had that floor
mopped.

PATRON. I'd like a room, please.

ABE. That's ten bucks. Sign the registration book and check in your
valuables. *(The patron begins the check-in procedure. Claude
Perkins has entered from the outside. He is wearing a raincoat
over rather ordinary clothes. He carries a bag from Zabar's Deli-
catessen and has a Valet Pack slung over one shoulder. He gets
in line behind the patron.)*

PATRON. You're dripping.

CLAUDE. What?

PATRON. I said, you're dripping.

CLAUDE. Of course I'm dripping. It's pouring out there.

PATRON. Well try not to. They don't like you dripping here. *(He
starts for the door.)* See you. *(He is buzzed through.)*

CLAUDE. I hope not.

ABE. *(Over the loudspeaker.)* 376! That's room 376! Coming up,
Duff!

CLAUDE. That's a good floor for that one. Nobody goes up there.

ABE. Well look who's back. Hello, stranger.

CLAUDE. Hello, Abe.

ABE. I thought you'd sworn off this place.

CLAUDE. I thought I had, too.

ABE. You got homesick for us, right?

CLAUDE. I didn't have much choice. I don't speak Spanish, so the

Continental is out. The Club Baths are just too far downtown, I'm boycotting the Beacon, Man's Country's had it and I've been barred from the Everard.

ABE. You've been barred from the Everard?

CLAUDE. They'll regret it.

ABE. Nobody gets barred from the Everard. How'd you manage that?

CLAUDE. There was this man there.

ABE. A fat man, right?

CLAUDE. Fat? He was the magic mountain. He drove me into one of my frenzies. I went berserk and I kicked his door in. So they threw me out and told me never to come back. I was willing to pay for it. I just wanted to talk to him.

ABE. Pick on somebody your own size, why don't you, Claude?

CLAUDE. I wouldn't like that. How much do you weigh?

ABE. Forget it.

CLAUDE. Are you up to 200 yet?

ABE. Forget it!

CLAUDE. When you get up to 200 come and knock on my door.

ABE. Forget it!

CLAUDE. Couldn't we just install a weigh-in station here?

ABE. I said forget it! You want to check that?

CLAUDE. It's my costume for the talent show. (*He is heading for the door, still carrying the Valet Pack and Zabar's shopping bag.*) It's good to be back, Abe. I'm feeling strangely optimistic this evening.

ABE. Just don't kick any doors in.

CLAUDE. I hope I don't have to. (*Claude is buzzed through the door.*)

ABE. 205! Coming up! That's 205! (*Gaetano Proclo comes dashing in. He is carrying a suitcase and a big box of Panettone, the Italian bakery specialty. He is wearing a wet raincoat, a cheap wig, a big bushy moustache and dark glasses. He goes directly to Abe.*)

PROCLO. Can you cash a check for me? It's on Ohio State National.

ABE. What do I look like? A teller in a bank?

PROCLO. You don't understand. I've got a cab waiting. I'll be right back. That's why I got into the cab in the first place, to go some-

where, and it's to here I've come. (*Sounds of a horn blowing.*)
You hear that? That's him!

ABE. You got a traveler's check?

PROCLO. No.

ABE. Travelers are supposed to have traveler's checks.

PROCLO. Well this traveler doesn't. We left Cleveland in a hurry.
Traveler's checks are for people who plan! (*More honking.*)
There he goes again!

ABE. I'm sorry.

PROCLO. Look, I've got all the identification in the world. Driver's
license, Social Security, Blue Cross, voter registration, Rotary
Club. . . . What about my business card? "Proclo Sanitation
Services, Gaetano Proclo, President." That's me.

ABE. You got a credit card?

PROCLO. I don't want credit, I want cash!

ABE. N-o, buddy.

PROCLO. Oh come on! Do I look like someone who would try to
pass a bad check? (*A realization.*) Why of course I do! (*He takes
off his dark glasses.*) There! Now can you see me? (*More honking.*) Oh all right! (*He removes his moustache.*) Now are you
satisfied?

ABE. I don't make the rules here.

PROCLO. Wait! Wait! (*He takes off his wig.*) Everything else is
real.

ABE. I'd like to help you out, mac, but—

PROCLO. The only thing that's gonna calm me down is *you* cashing
my check. My brother-in-law is a maniac and he's going to kill
me tonight. If you don't let me in there I'm going to be a dead
person. Please, mister, you are making a grown man cry. I'm begging you. It's a matter of life and death! (*More honking.*)

ABE. I shouldn't really be doing this but . . .

PROCLO. You are a good man . . .

ABE. Abe.

PROCLO. Abe. I'm gonna have a novena said for you when I get
back to Cleveland. What's your last name? Abe what?

ABE. Lefkowitz.

PROCLO. I'm *still* gonna have that novena said for you! (*More
honking. Chris has entered from the outside. He wears jeans, a
blue nylon windbreaker, and a bright purple shirt. He carries an*

overnight bag. Also, he is wearing a policeman's whistle and a "popper" holder around his neck.)

CHRIS. Does anybody have a cab waiting?

PROCLO. What?

CHRIS. Is that your cab out there?

PROCLO. Oh yes, yes, it is!

CHRIS. Well you've also got one very pissed off driver.

PROCLO. (*To Abe.*) Can you cash this for me now? (*To Chris.*) How pissed off is he?

CHRIS. On a ten scale? Ten. (*More honking.*)

PROCLO. Christ! (*Proclo is fumbling with the money and heading for the door.*) Keep an eye on those for me, will you?

CHRIS. Sure thing. (*Proclo hurries out. Chris looks at the suitcase and the Panettone.*) Planning a big night of it, honey? (*To Abe.*) I had a friend who tried moving into the baths.

ABE. What happened?

CHRIS. He died from a lack of sunshine. He died happy and blind, but he still died.

ABE. We missed you last week.

CHRIS. How do you think your customers felt? I'm a legend in my own lifetime. (*Yelling into Abe's microphone.*) Try to hold out, men! Help is on the way!

ABE. Hold your horses, Chris.

CHRIS. That's all I've been holding all week.

ABE. You wanna sign in?

CHRIS. (*While he writes.*) How's that gorgeous son of yours?

ABE. You're too late. He's getting married.

CHRIS. That's terrific. Give him my love, will you?

ABE. Sure thing, Chris.

CHRIS. Does he need anyone to practice with?

ABE. He's been practicing too much. That's why he's getting married.

CHRIS. Compared to me, Abe, she'd have to be an amateur. (*He returns the registration book.*)

ABE. Ronald Reagan! Aw, c'mon, Chris!

CHRIS. You know, he used to be lovers with John Wayne.

ABE. Sure he was.

CHRIS. Right after he broke up with Xavier Cugat.

ABE. People like you think the whole world's queer.

CHRIS. It's lucky for people like you it is. (*Proclo comes rushing back in.*)

PROCLO. He can't change a ten! Do you believe it? New York City, one of the great cities of the world, and this driver I have can't change a ten!

CHRIS. They still don't take anything over a five.

PROCLO. In Cleveland even a paper boy can change a ten!

CHRIS. Did I ever have you?

PROCLO. What?

CHRIS. I've got a rotten memory that way. You never used to live in Rego Park?

PROCLO. No!

CHRIS. 'Cause you look like someone I knew once who was from Rego Park.

PROCLO. I'm afraid not.

CHRIS. He was a large man like you and he was in ladies' shoes, I remember.

PROCLO. Well I'm from Cleveland and I'm in refuse.

CHRIS. I guess not then. Sorry.

PROCLO. That's perfectly all right. (*He hurries back out.*)

CHRIS. A gay garbageman!

ABE. You never can tell.

CHRIS. That's true. I mean, look at me. If you just saw me walking down the street, you'd think I was a queen. (*Chris blows his whistle as he is buzzed through the door.*) All right, men! Up against the wall. This is a raid!

ABE. 240! Two-four-oh. She's here, boys! (*A young man has entered from outside. His name is Michael Brick. He steps up to the admissions booth.*)

MICHAEL. I'd like a room, please. (*The first time we hear Michael's voice we are in for a shock. It is a high, boy soprano-ish treble. A timbre totally incongruous with his rugged physique.*) One of your private rooms. How much is that?

ABE. You want what?

MICHAEL. A room, please. I was told you have private rooms.

ABE. Yeah, we got rooms.

MICHAEL. Then I'd like one, sir. How much is that?

ABE. How long?

MICHAEL. Is what, sir?

ABE. How long do you want it for?

MICHAEL. Three or four hours should be sufficient for my purposes.

ABE. I don't care what your purposes are: twelve's our minimum.

MICHAEL. All right, twelve then, sir.

ABE. That's ten bucks. Sign in and I'll take your valuables.

MICHAEL. Tell me something. Has a balding, middle-aged fat man come in here recently?

ABE. I don't believe what just came in here recently.

MICHAEL. Think hard. I'll repeat his description. A balding, middle-aged fat man.

ABE. We got all kinds inside. Fat, thin, short, tall, young, old. I can't keep track.

MICHAEL. Well I guess I'll just have to go in and see for myself, sir.

ABE. I guess you will. You're not a cop, are you?

MICHAEL. I'm a detective, sir. Michael Brick. The Greybar Agency. Our client wants the goods on him and I'm just the man to get them. I've never failed a client yet. What do I do now?

ABE. Through there and up the stairs. Someone'll show you your room.

MICHAEL. Thank you, sir.

ABE. Let me give you a little tip, Brick. Stay out of the steam room.

MICHAEL. Why, sir?

ABE. It gets pretty wild in there.

MICHAEL. Oh, I can take it, sir. In my line of work I get to do a lot of wild things. This is my first seduction job. Wish me luck.

ABE. With that voice, you'll need it. (*Michael is buzzed through the door and is gone.*) 101 coming up! That's one-oh-one! Oh boy, oh boy, oh boy! (*Googie Gomez comes into the admissions area, protecting herself from the rain with a wet copy of* Variety. *She is carrying a wig box and wardrobe bag.*)

GOOGIE. No rain, he tells me! No rain, he says! No rain! That fucking Tex Antoine! That little *maricon*! I'd like to pull his little beard off! One spot on this dress and I'm finished! The biggest night of my life and it's pissing dogs and cats.

PROCLO. (*Who has entered behind Googie.*) That's cats and dogs. (*Googie has been so busy worrying about rain spots on her dress she really hasn't noticed Proclo yet. When she does, there is a marked change in her behavior and vocabulary.*)

GOOGIE. Joe Papp. Hello, Mr. Papp. It's a real pleasure to meet you. I seen all your shows. Uptown, downtown, in the park. They're all fabulous. *Fabulosa!* And I just know, in my heart of hearts, that after you see my show tonight you're going to want to give me a chance at one of your wonderful theatres. Uptown, downtown, in the park. I'll even work the mobile theatre. Thank you for coming, Mr. Papp. Excuse me, I got a little laryngitis. But the show must go on, *si?*

PROCLO. My name isn't Papp.

GOOGIE. You're not Joe Papp?

PROCLO. I'm sorry.

GOOGIE. But you are a producer?

PROCLO. No.

GOOGIE. Are you sure?

PROCLO. Yes.

GOOGIE. That's okay. I heard there was gonna be a big producer around tonight and I wasn't taking any chances. You never know. It's hard for me to speak English good like that. (*A new outburst.*) Aaaaiiieee! My God, not the hairs! *Cono!* (*Her hands are hovering in the vicinity of her head.*) Okay. Go ahead and say it. It's okay. I can take it. Tell me I look like shit.

PROCLO. Why would I want to say a thing like that to such an attractive young lady?

GOOGIE. You boys really know how to cheer a girl up when she's dumps in the down. (*She gives Proclo a kiss on the cheek.*) My boyfriend Hector see me do that: *ay! cuidado!* He hates you *maricones,* that Hector! He's a ballbreaker with me, too, mister. You know why you're not a producer? You're too nice to be a producer. But I'm gonna show them all, mister, and tonight's the night I'm gonna do it. (*Googie is moving toward the door.*) One day you gonna see the name Googie Gomez in lights and you gonna say to yourself "Was that *her?*" And you gonna answer yourself "That was her!" But you know something, mister? I was *always* her. Just nobody knows it. *Yo soy Googie Gomez, estrellita del futuro!* (*Googie is buzzed through the door and is gone.*)

PROCLO. Who the hell was that?

ABE. Googie.

PROCLO. I thought this was a bathhouse.

ABE. It is.

PROCLO. A *male* bathhouse!

ABE. It is.

PROCLO. Then what's she doing in there?

ABE. Googie sings in The Pits.

PROCLO. The pits? What pits?

ABE. The nightclub.

PROCLO. You've got a nightclub in there?

ABE. We've got a nightclub, movies, TV, swimming pool, steam room, sauna, massage table, discotheque, bridge, amateur night and free blood tests every Wednesday. . . . (*Proclo turns at the sound of Maurine entering behind him from outside. She is wearing a duffel coat with the hood up, pants and tall rubber rain boots. No chic dresser, Maurine. She seems deep in concentration and takes no notice of Proclo as she moves toward the door.*) How'd it go today, Mo? (*Maurine just shrugs. She is buzzed through the door and is gone.*)

PROCLO. I don't even want to *think* what she does.

ABE. Mo's just our accountant.

PROCLO. I asked that cab driver to bring me to the last place in the world anybody would think of looking for me.

ABE. You found it.

PROCLO. Except everybody in the world is already in there. I need calm, privacy, safety tonight.

ABE. So stay in your room and keep your door locked.

PROCLO. Don't worry. I will. How much is that?

ABE. Ten dollars. (*Proclo looks at the registration book.*)

PROCLO. Ronald Reagan!

ABE. You can write John Doe for all I care. Just so long as we get some kind of a name down there.

PROCLO. Any name at all? Oh, Abe, I'm gonna speak to the Pope about getting you canonized! (*Reads what he's written.*) "Carmine Vespucci, Bensonhurst, Brooklyn."

ABE. Who's that?

PROCLO. My maniac brother-in-law who was going to kill me tonight!

ABE. What did you do to him?

PROCLO. I got born and I married his sister.

ABE. That's all?

PROCLO. Just my whole life. (*Proclo gathers his suitcase and Panettone, ready to enter now.*)

ABE. Do you mind if I ask you a personal question?

PROCLO. The man who just saved my life can ask me anything.

ABE. You ever been in a place like this?

PROCLO. Oh sure. We got a Jack LaLanne's in Cleveland. (*The door is buzzed and Proclo goes through.*)

ABE. 196! That's one-nine-six coming up, Duff. Oh boy, oh boy, oh boy! (*While Abe is speaking, the lights will fade on the admissions area and "Just Can't Get You Out of My Mind" comes up. The admissions area and the scrims are flown. Other lights are coming up and we are in the interior of The Ritz. On the lower level we see Tiger sweeping up. Chris enters behind him.*)

TIGER. Hey, Chris.

CHRIS. Hi, Tiger.

TIGER. What took you so long? They called your number ten minutes ago.

CHRIS. I was in the boutique.

TIGER. What'd you buy?

CHRIS. A red light bulb for my room and this month's *Viva*.

TIGER. You don't need a red light bulb.

CHRIS. And I hope I don't need this month's *Viva*. Much action tonight?

TIGER. With you here I'm sure there will be.

CHRIS. Slow, hunh?

TIGER. Real dead, so far.

CHRIS. Don't worry, honey, I'll shake this place up good.

TIGER. If anybody can it's you.

CHRIS. The thing that no one understands about me is that sex is just my way of saying hello.

TIGER. Yeah, but you want to say hello to everybody you meet.

CHRIS. Don't you?

TIGER. I work here!

CHRIS. I wish I did. (*They go. Claude Perkins has come up to the wandering and lost Proclo. The love theme from "Now, Voyager" plays.*)

CLAUDE. Hello, there.

PROCLO. Hello.

CLAUDE. What seems to be the problem?

PROCLO. I can't seem to find my room.

CLAUDE. Well you just come with me.

PROCLO. Why thank you. That's very kind of you. (*They leave together. On the upper level we see Duff. Chris comes up the stairs and pokes his head into the steam room.*)

CHRIS. Guess who!

DUFF. Hey, Chris.

CHRIS. Hi, Duffie.

DUFF. 240 again?

CHRIS. And it better be clean! Last time they were having a crab race on the sheets.

DUFF. I did it myself, first thing when I came on. (*He opens the door with Chris's key.*)

CHRIS. Home sweet home! If these walls could talk . . . !

DUFF. They don't have to.

CHRIS. I've spent some of the happiest hours of my life in this room.

DUFF. I know. We've all heard you.

CHRIS. When are we gonna get together, you cute little hump?

DUFF. I don't know. Ask Tiger.

CHRIS. That means "forget it." Out! Out! I've got a busy night ahead of me. I hope. (*Calling out loudly.*) There will be an orgy beginning in room 240 in exactly four minutes! That's an orgy in room 240 in exactly four minutes! (*He goes into his room and closes the door. We have been watching Claude lead Proclo to his—that is, Claude's—room. Claude has followed Proclo in and has closed the door.*)

PROCLO. Are you sure this is 196? I think this is someone else's room. Look, see the clothes?

CLAUDE. You'll never guess what I made for dinner tonight, so I'm just going to have to tell you.

PROCLO. I beg your pardon?

CLAUDE. A nice rich ground pork meat loaf with a mozzarella cheese center, gobs of mashed potatoes swimming in gravy, carrots floating in butter and for a salad, avocado chunks smothered in Roquefort dressing. Could you just die?

PROCLO. I could just . . . ! I don't know what I could just!

CLAUDE. And then: Dutch Chocolate layer cake with two big scoops of Baskin-Robbins mocha walnut ice cream and a fudge malted.

PROCLO. It sounds delicious.

CLAUDE. You could've been there.

PROCLO. I was in Brooklyn. Now if you'll excuse me, I'll—

CLAUDE. Wait! (*He is rummaging in his shopping bag.*) You want a bagel with lox and cream cheese?

PROCLO. No, thank you. I've eaten.

CLAUDE. An eclair? Some homemade brownies? I know! A corned beef on rye with a dill pickle!

PROCLO. Really, I'm not hungry. (*Claude is blocking his way.*)

CLAUDE. How much do you weigh?

PROCLO. What?

CLAUDE. Your weight! 210? 220?

PROCLO. 226. (*Claude has started to undulate, dance almost, and move towards Proclo.*)

CLAUDE. (*Singing in a low, sexy growl.*) "Jelly Roll Baby/ You're my Jelly Roll Man . . ."

PROCLO. I think there is some confusion here.

CLAUDE. "Jelly Roll Cupcake/ I'm your Jelly Roll fan . . ."

PROCLO. In fact, I *know* there is some confusion going on in here.

CLAUDE. "You got the roll/ and I got the soul/ that strictly adores/ paying Jelly Roll toll . . ." (*Claude is still singing as he pulls Proclo toward him and they collapse heavily on the bed.*)

PROCLO. Stop it! Please! You're hurting me!

CLAUDE. I'm hurting *you*?

PROCLO. Help! Help! (*Tiger has been seen running along the corridor and uses his passkey now to come into the room. A small crowd of patrons starts forming in the corridor outside the room.*)

TIGER. (*Pulling Proclo off Claude.*) Okay, fat man! Leave the little guy alone! What are you trying to do? Pull his head off? (*He takes Proclo's key.*) Let me see your key. 196! Now get down there and don't cause any more trouble. What do you think this is? The YMCA? (*He puts Proclo's suitcase in the corridor and turns back to Claude.*) I'm sorry, sir. It won't happen again. (*Claude is moaning happily.*)

CLAUDE. I certainly hope not.

TIGER. Get down there, man! (*He goes.*)

PROCLO. He ought to be locked up! (*The crowd of patrons are all looking at Proclo.*) Hello. Whew! I just had quite a little experience in there. I think that guy's got a problem. People like that really shouldn't be allowed in a place like this. (*Stony silence from the patrons.*) What unusual pants. They look like cowboy chaps.

PATRON IN CHAPS. They are cowboy chaps.

PROCLO. I was thinking I thought they looked like cowboy chaps. Well gentlemen, if you'll excuse me, and let me get out of these clothes. Bye. Nice talking to you. (*Proclo beats an embarrassed retreat down the stairs. The group of patrons will slowly disband. Chris opens the door to his room, sticks his head out and yells.*)

CHRIS. Okay, boys, room 240! Soup's on, come and get it! (*He goes back into his room. Proclo hurries to his room. Michael Brick has appeared in the area of a pay telephone. He dials a number and waits.*)

MICHAEL. Hello, Bimbi's? Is this the bar across the street from The Ritz? There's a Mr. Carmine Vespucci there. I've got to speak to him. It's urgent.

ABE. (*Over the loudspeaker.*) Tiger! Duff! The linen people are here. On the double!

MICHAEL. Mr. Vespucci? My name is Michael Brick. I'm with the Greybar Detective Agency. You hired my partner to get something on a Mr. Gaetano Proclo, only my partner's sick so I'm taking over the case for him. I'm calling you from The Ritz. I just got here. Now let me see if I've got his description right. A balding middle-aged fat man? That's not much to go on, but I'll do my best. (*Googie enters and signals to him.*) One of those transvestites is standing right next to me. Now you just stay by the phone in that bar across the street and I'll get back to you.

GOOGIE. *Ay, que cosa linda!*

MICHAEL. I can't talk now. I think he's surrounding me for unnatural things. (*Michael hangs up, gives Googie a horrified look and hurries off.*)

GOOGIE. Hey *chico*, I was just gonna talk to you! (*Tiger enters.*) Tiger, is he here yet?

TIGER. Who?

GOOGIE. Who? What do you mean who? There is only one *who* I am interested in you telling me about! Listen, you told me there was gonna be a big producer here tonight. I dress special. I do the hairs special. If you're lying to me, Tiger. . . .

TIGER. Can't you take a little joke?

GOOGIE. My career is no joke. Nobody's career is never no joke.

TIGER. I was just trying to build you up.

GOOGIE. I tell you something and I mean this: You ever hear of instant laryngitis? No producer be out there tonight and that's what I got—instant laryngitis—and you and Duff are gonna do the show alone. Those are my words, they are from the heart and I am now officially sick!

TIGER. Googie! (*Googie rasps an answer and leaves, Tiger following her. Proclo comes wandering into view, still carrying his suitcase and still shaken from his experience with Claude.*)

PROCLO. This place is like a Chinese maze. (*Proclo is standing there when Duff comes out of one of the rooms.*)

DUFF. Are you 196?

PROCLO. Something like that.

DUFF. I meant your room.

PROCLO. So did I.

DUFF. Follow me. (*He leads Proclo to the room.*) 196. Here it is. (*Duff has opened the door for him. Proclo goes into the room. It is a shambles from the previous occupant. Duff calls out into the corridors.*) Hey, Tiger! Room 196! On the double!

PROCLO. You're kidding. Tell me you're kidding.

DUFF. What did you expect?

PROCLO. I don't know. A room maybe. A normal size room.

DUFF. You should see some of the rooms they could've put you in.

PROCLO. You're telling me they come even smaller?

DUFF. Half this size.

PROCLO. Does Mickey Rooney know about this place?

DUFF. You got far out taste, mister.

PROCLO. Vespucci. Carmine Vespucci. What's your name?

DUFF. Duff.

PROCLO. It's good to see you, Duff.

DUFF. How do you mean?

PROCLO. I was beginning to think this place was a little too esoteric for my tastes, if you know what I mean. Like that guy up there with all the food.

DUFF. I think it's something to do with the weather. Rainy nights always bring out the weirdos.

PROCLO. They shouldn't let people like that in here. It'll give this place a bad name.

DUFF. This place already has a bad name. (*Tiger has arrived with a mop and a change of linen. The room will be very crowded with the three of them and Proclo's luggage.*)

TIGER. We're both up shit creek again.

DUFF. Who with this time?

TIGER. I told Googie there'd be a producer out front tonight.

DUFF. Maybe there will be.

TIGER. I promised her. No producer, she's not going on. She's locked in her dressing room with laryngitis.

PROCLO. She told me she was feeling better.

TIGER. You know Googie?

PROCLO. I met her downstairs. She thought I was a producer. She's very colorful.

TIGER. Right now she's also very pissed off.

DUFF. Let me talk to her.

PROCLO. Not so fast, Duff. What about slippers?

DUFF. Slippers?

PROCLO. Slippers.

DUFF. Where do you think you are? Slippers! (*Duff leaves as Tiger continues to clean Proclo's room and make up his bed.*)

PROCLO. I always thought they gave you slippers in a bathhouse. I mean, you could catch athlete's foot in a place like this.

TIGER. You're lucky if that's all you catch. (*Trying to make up the bed.*) Excuse me.

PROCLO. I'm sorry. (*He stands.*) Looking at you two, I think I'm seeing double.

TIGER. He's Duff. I'm Tiger.

PROCLO. How are people supposed to tell you apart?

TIGER. They don't usually. Just try to stay out of 205 this time.

PROCLO. What's in 205?

TIGER. That room I had to pull you out of. You could hurt someone doing that.

PROCLO. Now just a minute! I thought that guy was taking me to *my* room! You don't think I went in there because I wanted to?

TIGER. (*Dawning on him.*) You trying to tell me he's a chubby chaser?

PROCLO. A chubby what?

TIGER. Someone who likes . . . (*He gestures, indicating great bulk.*)

PROCLO. You mean like me?

TIGER. You're right up his alley.

PROCLO. I knew someone like that once. I just never knew what to call him. "Get away from me, Claude!" is all I could come up with. A chubby chaser! That's kind of funny. Unless, of course, you happen to be the chubby they're chasing. Room 205. Thanks for the tip. I'll avoid it like the plague. (*Duff has returned and is knocking loudly on the door.*)

DUFF. Fifteen minutes!

PROCLO. Oh my God!

TIGER. Relax! (*He opens the door.*)

DUFF. Come on, Tiger. Show time!

TIGER. What happened?

DUFF. Googie's Mr. Big is here. He's going to be sitting ringside for the first show tonight.

TIGER. How'd you manage that?

DUFF. I didn't. But with a little help from our friend here . . . !

PROCLO. Hey, now just a minute!

DUFF. Aw, now come on, Mr. Vespucci! Give two down and out go-go boys with aspirations for higher things a break.

PROCLO. I don't want to get involved in anything.

DUFF. All you have to do is listen to her act.

PROCLO. I don't want to listen to her act.

DUFF. I don't blame you, but that's not the point.

PROCLO. I'm not a producer.

DUFF. Googie's not really a singer.

TIGER. Come on, what do you say?

PROCLO. What if she finds out?

DUFF. That's our problem.

TIGER. Leave everything to us.

PROCLO. I came here to lay low.

TIGER. Man, you can't lay any lower than Googie's nightclub act.

DUFF. Come on, we gotta change.

TIGER. You're a prince, Mr. . . .

DUFF. Vespucci.

TIGER. An honest-to-God prince.

PROCLO. Thank you, Duff.

TIGER. He's Duff. I'm Tiger. (*They run off. Proclo closes the door and shakes his head.*)

PROCLO. Seclusion! Is that asking so very much, God? Simple seclusion? I must be crazy! Allowing them to tell her I'm a producer! (*Michael Brick is seen outside Claude's door, which is ajar. He sticks his head into the room.*)

MICHAEL. Excuse me.

CLAUDE. I'm resting.

MICHAEL. May I come in?

CLAUDE. I said I'm resting.

MICHAEL. I'm looking for someone.

CLAUDE. I told you I'm resting.

MICHAEL. That's okay. I just want to ask you—

CLAUDE. What do you need? A brick wall to fall on your head? "Resting!" It's a euphemism for "not interested"! Skinny! (*Claude slams the door in Michael's face. Michael knocks on another door.*)

MICHAEL. Excuse me. May I come in? (*Michael starts into the room, then comes rushing out.*) Oh, I beg your pardon. Excuse me, may I come in? Thank you very much. (*He goes into another room. This time he comes rushing out almost at once.*) Oh, my goodness! (*Michael's mother never told him there would be nights like this. He steels himself and enters the steam room. On the swing of the door, he is back out and gone. Proclo has nearly finished changing when there is a knock on his door. He quickly puts his wig back on.*)

PROCLO. Yes?

CLAUDE. Are you there?

PROCLO. Who is it?

CLAUDE. Room service.

PROCLO. Who? (*He opens the door a crack, sees Claude and slams it.*) Go away!

CLAUDE. I've got a box of Hershey bars. (*He begins throwing bars of candy through the transom.*)

PROCLO. I said go away!

CLAUDE. Peter Paul Mounds, Milky Ways . . .

PROCLO. I know what you are now!

CLAUDE. I can make you very happy!

PROCLO. You're a chubby chaser!

CLAUDE. I know.

PROCLO. Well stop it!

CLAUDE. How?

PROCLO. I don't know! (*Proclo waits, listens.*) Are you still there?

CLAUDE. I'm never leaving.

PROCLO. You can't stand out there all night. This is my room and that's my door to it. Now go away or I'll call Tiger and Duff.

CLAUDE. I'm not doing anything.

PROCLO. You're making me nervous.

CLAUDE. (*He thinks, then sings.*) "Love your magic spell is everywhere . . ." (*He thinks.*) "Can't help loving dat man of mine . . ." (*He thinks.*) "Then along came . . ." (*He stops singing.*) Who? Then along came who?

PROCLO. Vespucci.

CLAUDE. (*An inspiration.*) Vespucci!/ I just met a boy named Vespucci!/ And suddenly that name . . . (*Proclo stops moaning and come up with a plan.*)

PROCLO. Okay, you win. What room are you in?

CLAUDE. 205.

PROCLO. All right, you go back to 205. I'll be right up.

CLAUDE. Promise?

PROCLO. On my mother's grave! (*He is crossing his fingers.*) Just get away from that door! 'Cause if you're still standing out there when I come out of this room, the deal is off.

CLAUDE. And if you're not up in my room in five minutes . . .

PROCLO. What?

CLAUDE. I'll find you.

PROCLO. And?

CLAUDE. You don't want to make me do anything rash, do you, Mr. Vespucci?

PROCLO. Oh no, oh no!

CLAUDE. Five minutes then. Room 205. If you're not up there, I'm gonna come down here and break your knees. Don't push your luck with Claude Perkins. (*He goes. His name seems to have struck a distant bell for Proclo.*)

PROCLO. Claude Perkins. It can't be the same one. Claude Perkins. That's all I need. He's dead. He has to be dead. Claude Perkins. (*Proclo opens the door and looks out. No sign of*

Claude. Without realizing it, he shuts the door behind him and locks himself out.) Oh no! Come on, will you? Open up. Damn! (*Calling off.*) Boys! Boys! You with the keys! Yoo hoo! Yoo hoo! (*Proclo is suddenly aware of a patron who is just looking at him and smiling.*) Hello. Just clearing my throat. Ahoo! Ahoo! Too many cigarettes. Ahoo! Hello there. I hear the Knicks tied it up in the last quarter.

PATRON. Crisco.

PROCLO. What?

PATRON. Crisco oil party.

PROCLO. Crisco oil party?

PATRON. Room 419. Pass it on.

PROCLO. Pass what on?

PATRON. And bring Joey.

PROCLO. Who's Joey?

PATRON. You know Joey. But not Chuck. Got that?

PROCLO. Crisco oil party. Room 419. I can bring Joey but not Chuck.

PATRON. Check.

PROCLO. What's wrong with Chuck? (*Patron whispers something in Proclo's ear. Proclo's eyes grow wide. He can't wait to get out of there.*) Chuck's definitely out! If you'll excuse me now . . . ! (*He starts moving away. The Patron leaves. Proclo starts pacing in rapid circles.*) Now wait a minute. Wait a minute. Stay calm. Be rational. Don't get hysterical. All he did was invite you to a Crisco oil party, whatever the hell that is, and told you to bring Joey. Of course, I don't know Joey, and I don't think I want to, and not to bring Chuck because Chuck—. It can't be one of those places. I mean, one or two weird people do not a you-know-what make. People are just more normal in Cleveland.

CHRIS. (*Leaning out of his room.*) Telephone call for Joe Namath in room 240. Long distance for Mr. Joe Namath in room 240!

PROCLO. Well *there!* You see? I knew I wasn't a crazy person! (*Proclo is heading toward Chris's room.*) There's just no way. . . . (*On his way, he composes a speech to himself.*) Mr. Namath? Excuse me. I wonder if I might trouble you for an autograph. It's not for me. It's for my 12-year-old, Gilda. Say, did you hear the Knicks tied it up in the last quarter? Mr. Namath?

CHRIS. (*From inside his room.*) No, don't! . . . I can't . . . Oooo! . . .

Aaaa! . . . Oh my God! . . . Do it, do it! . . . Yes! Yes! (*He puts down the magazine he was thumbing through.*) If that doesn't get those queens up here nothing will.

PROCLO. (*Knocking on Chris's door.*) Mr. Namath? (*Chris comes out of his room and sees Proclo.*) You're not Joe Namath.

CHRIS. Neither are you.

PROCLO. I thought you were Joe Namath.

CHRIS. It's the lighting.

PROCLO. I was praying you were Joe Namath.

CHRIS. I don't blame you.

PROCLO. I mean, you just had to be him!

CHRIS. Eating your heart out, honey?

PROCLO. I don't know what I'm doing.

CHRIS. Join the club. It's like some strange heterosexual gypsy curse has been put on this place tonight. How's the orgy room doing?

PROCLO. I haven't—

CHRIS. The steam room?

PROCLO. No.

CHRIS. The pool? The sauna? The dormitory?

PROCLO. Sorry.

CHRIS. Well no wonder you haven't made out.

PROCLO. I don't want to make out.

CHRIS. Who are you trying to kid? This is me, sweetheart, your Aunt Chris. (*He starts pounding on closed doors.*) Fire drill! Everybody out for fire drill! (*A door opens. A patron looks out.*) I'm sorry. I thought this was the powder room.

PATRON. We're busy.

CHRIS. (*To Proclo.*) You like this one?

PROCLO. No!

CHRIS. Neither do I!

PATRON. I said we're busy! (*He slams the door.*)

CHRIS. You've got my son in there. Tell him his mother wants to see him.

PATRON. (*From behind the door.*) Buzz off!

CHRIS. One mark on that boy's body, Wanda, and I'm calling the police! (*To Proclo.*) Well I tried.

PROCLO. Really. I don't want you to do anything for me.

CHRIS. You're not going to believe this line, but "You're new around here, aren't you?"

PROCLO. I'm afraid so.

CHRIS. I never forget a face and I've seen a lot of faces in this place. Some people think I'm a sex maniac. They're right. If I don't get laid at least twice a day I go home and beat my dog. Here's hoping for you, Jeanette! (*He offers a "popper" to Proclo, who shakes his head no.*) It's fantastic stuff. I got it from this queen I know who just got back from a hairdresser's convention in Tokyo. He does Barbra Streisand's hair, so they gave him the Gene Hersholt Humanitarian Award. (*He laughs and backslaps Proclo.*) Come on, I'll show you around.

PROCLO. That's all right. I was just going back to my room.

CHRIS. Come *on!* I don't do this for everyone. I'm an expert guide. A lesser person would charge for this sort of tour.

PROCLO. There's something I better tell you.

CHRIS. Sweetheart, relax, you're not my type. I just want to help you find yours. (*To a snooty patron who is walking by.*) Hi. (*Snooty Patron turns his back.*) We said hello. (*Snooty Patron turns his back some more. Chris turns to Proclo, gives him an eye signal and starts talking to him in a very loud voice.*) Do I know her? Darling, she is what is known as a Famous Face. She's out cruising 24 hours a day. She must live in a pup tent on Sheridan Square. If I had a nickel for every pair of shoes she's gone through . . . ! (*Snooty patron finally turns around and glares at him.*) Margaret Dumont! I thought you were dead!

SNOOTY PATRON. There's a reason some of us don't ride the subways and I'm looking right at him. (*He huffs off.*)

CHRIS. Is that supposed to mean me? (*After him.*) Screw you, honey! (*To Proclo.*) One thing I can't stand is a queen without a sense of humor. (*After him.*) You can die with your secret! (*To Proclo.*) Miserable piss-elegant fairy.

PROCLO. I have to tell you something. I'm afraid I'm not a . . . (*He will try to convey something with his hands.*)

CHRIS. You're not gay?

PROCLO. No.

CHRIS. Then what are you doing here?

PROCLO. That's what I'd like to know.

CHRIS. Baby, you're very much in the minority around here.

PROCLO. That's what I'm afraid of.

CHRIS. Or maybe you're not and that's why I'm having such rotten luck tonight. What are you? A social worker or something?

PROCLO. You mean *everybody* here is . . . ?

CHRIS. Gay. It's not such a tough word. You might try using it some time.

PROCLO. Nobody is . . . the opposite?

CHRIS. I sure as hell hope not. I didn't pay ten bucks to walk around in a towel with a bunch of Shriners.

PROCLO. What about Tiger and Duff?

CHRIS. What about them?

PROCLO. I thought they were normal.

CHRIS. They are normal. They've also been lovers for three years.

PROCLO. I'm sorry. I didn't mean it like that.

CHRIS. Yes, you did.

PROCLO. Yes, I did.

CHRIS. I'll tell you something about straight people, and sometimes I think it's the only thing worth knowing about them. They don't like gays. They never have. They never will. Anything else they say is just talk.

PROCLO. That's not true.

CHRIS. Think about it.

PROCLO. I'm sorry. I didn't know what I was getting into when I came in here tonight. I'm in trouble, I'm scared and I'm con-fused. I'm sorry.

CHRIS. That's okay.

PROCLO. You're gonna think I'm crazy but somebody is planning to kill me tonight. My own brother-in-law.

CHRIS. Are you putting me on?

PROCLO. I wish I were. And if Carmine caught me in a place like this he'd have *double* grounds for murder.

CHRIS. What do you mean?

PROCLO. My brother-in-law. For twelve years I was the butt of every sissy joke played at Our Lady of Perpetual Sorrow. It was a good name for that place. And then, when I married his only sister . . . ! They're very close, even for Italian brothers and sisters, and you know what they're like. (*He clasps his hands together.*) Cement! Except for Vivian, Vivian's my wife, that whole family's always hated me. At our wedding, her own mother had a heart attack while we were exchanging vows. Vivian said "I do" to me and Mamma Vespucci keeled right over in the front pew.

CHRIS. It's kind of funny.

PROCLO. Not when it happens to you. Yesterday, at their own father's funeral even, Carmine had all the relatives giving me that look.

CHRIS. What look?

PROCLO. That look. (*He gives a look.*)

CHRIS. I would've laid him out.

PROCLO. That's you.

CHRIS. Why didn't you?

PROCLO. The truth? I'm scared to death of him. I guess I always have been.

CHRIS. Maybe that's why he always hated you.

PROCLO. "Get Proclo." Those were their father's dying words. Do you believe it? This far from his Maker and all he can say is "Get Proclo."

CHRIS. Get Proclo?

PROCLO. That's me. With their father dead now, there's a lot of money involved that Carmine would love to screw me out of. And I'm not so sure it's particularly clean money. Carmine can chase me all over town but this is one night he's not gonna "Get Proclo."

CHRIS. And you picked a gay baths to hide out in?

PROCLO. I didn't pick it exactly. I asked my cab driver to take me to the last place in the world anybody would think of looking for me.

CHRIS. Don't worry, you found it.

PROCLO. Only now I've got a chubby chaser and someone who thinks I'm a producer after me.

CHRIS. Listen, it beats someone like your brother-in-law trying to kill you. Why don't you just stay in your room and try to get some sleep?

PROCLO. Sleep!

CHRIS. Strange as it may seem, no one's gonna attack you.

PROCLO. Someone already has.

CHRIS. Beginner's luck! Standing around out here like this, you're just asking for it. Go to your room.

PROCLO. I can't! I locked myself out!

CHRIS. Well try and find Tiger and Duff. They'll let you in. Now if you'll excuse me, darling, I want to try my luck in there. Us B-girls work better solo.

PROCLO. See you.

CHRIS. See you. (*He throws open the door to the steam room and blows the whistle.*) Hello, everybody, my name is June! What's yours? (*He is gone. Proclo is alone. He stands undecided for a moment but we can see that his curiosity is getting the better of him. He opens the door to the steam room and peers in. He goes in. The door closes. There is a long pause. The stage is empty. And at once, Proclo comes bursting out of the steam room. You have never seen anyone move as fast. He comes tearing down the stairs and runs into Duff.*)

PROCLO. The key to 196, quick!

DUFF. You're supposed to wear it.

PROCLO. I know!

DUFF. What's the matter?

PROCLO. Just let me in, please.

DUFF. Try to hang onto your key from here on out, okay?

PROCLO. Believe me, I'll make every effort. (*He is admitted.*) Thank you.

DUFF. The show's about to get started.

PROCLO. (*Puffing for breath.*) Fine, fine!

DUFF. You won't be late?

PROCLO. Of course not!

DUFF. Googie's all keyed up.

PROCLO. So am I, so am I!

DUFF. Thanks a million for helping us out like this, Mr. Vespucci.

PROCLO. Tell me something, you and Tiger are . . . lovers?

DUFF. Three years. I think that's pretty good, don't you?

PROCLO. It's terrific.

DUFF. I better get ready. See you downstairs! (*He goes, closing the door.*)

PROCLO. I wouldn't go down there and see her act for a—! *Her* act? Of course! I knew there was something funny about that Gomez woman. She's not a woman! Female impersonators . . . chubby chasers . . . B-girls . . . Baby Junes! When I grow another head is when I'm gonna leave this room! (*He sits on the bed, ex-*

hausted. Where to go now? What to do? His eyes go to the Panettone. He looks a little more cheerful. Meanwhile, Michael has raced back to the area of the telephones and dialed a number.)

MICHAEL. Bimbi's? Oh! Mr. Vespucci. Michael Brick. No one fits your description. It's pretty hard getting the goods on someone you've never seen. And you didn't tell me about that steam room. *(We see Googie entering. She sees Michael. She stops. She eavesdrops.)* If you need me I'm at 929-9929. And I'm in room 101. 101!

GOOGIE. Room 101!

MICHAEL. He's here again. *(Michael hangs up and hurries off.)*

GOOGIE. I'll be there, *chico*. Googie's gonna straighten you out between shows. *(She turns to Proclo's room. Proclo is eating his Panettone when she knocks on the door. He jumps.)* Guess who, Mr. Vespucci? *(More knocking. Proclo tries to ignore it but it is very urgent. Finally he goes to the door and opens it a crack. A fatal mistake.)*

PROCLO. Now wait a minute! *(Googie barges in and closes the door.)*

GOOGIE. I know what you're going to say.

PROCLO. You couldn't possibly!

GOOGIE. I don't believe in bugging producers just before they catch your act, so I just want to tell you one thing. In my second number, "Shine On Harvest Moon," the orchestra and me sometimes get into different keys, but if you know that it won't matter. Other than that, the act is fabulous and I just know you're gonna love it.

PROCLO. I'm sure of it!

GOOGIE. You know what *guapo* means? Handsome.

PROCLO. Oh no, I'm ugly. I'm very, very ugly.

GOOGIE. With a face like that, you could've been an actor. You still could. It's never too late. Look at Caterina Valente or Charo or Vicki Carr.

PROCLO. Of course they're *real* women.

GOOGIE. Oh no!

PROCLO. They're not?

GOOGIE. Plastic Puerto Ricans. I am the real thing. You are the real thing and I knew you were in show business.

PROCLO. Me?

GOOGIE. I knew I'd seen you someplace.

PROCLO. I was in the Cleveland Little Theatre Masque and Mum-
mer's spring production of "The Sound of Music," but I'd hardly
call that show business.

GOOGIE. Oh yeah? What part?

PROCLO. It was really more of a walk-on.

GOOGIE. I was in that show.

PROCLO. You were in "The Sound of Music"?

GOOGIE. Oh sure.

PROCLO. Where was this?

GOOGIE. Broadway, the Main Stem, where else?

PROCLO. The original cast?

GOOGIE. I was more original than anyone else in it. They fired me
the first day of rehearsal, those bastards. They said I wasn't right
for the part.

PROCLO. What part was that?

GOOGIE. One of those fucking Trapp kids. But you know what the
real reason was, mister?

PROCLO. They found out what you really were?

GOOGIE. Seymour Pippin!

PROCLO. Who?

GOOGIE. Seymour Pippin! If there's one man in this whole world I
was born to kill with my own two hands it is Seymour Pippin.
You want to hear something funny? If you didn't have all that
hair you would look a lot like him and I would probably fly
into a rage and tear all your eyes out! I never forget that face
and I never forgive. He was the company manager and if there is
one thing worse than a producer or a press agent, it is a company
manager.

PROCLO. It *is* a family show.

GOOGIE. But I fix them. I picket that show till they was crazy. I
picket, I picket, I picket. Every night! They couldn't stop me.
I picket that show every night until I got a part in "Camelot."

PROCLO. You were in "Camelot," too?

GOOGIE..Oh sure.

PROCLO. That's a wonderful show.

GOOGIE. It's a piece of shit.

PROCLO. Oh, they fired you from that one, too?

GOOGIE. Sure they fired me! What do you expect? Thanks to Seymour Pippin I get fired from everything.

PROCLO. I can't imagine why.

GOOGIE. You see this face? It's a curse! (*She is moving in for the kill. Proclo is backing off, horrified.*)

PROCLO. Keep away!

GOOGIE. Don't fight it, *chico!*

PROCLO. Believe me, you won't be happy! I won't be happy! You're making a terrible mistake.

GOOGIE. I am suddenly all woman.

PROCLO. No you're not. You're someone with a lot of problems.

GOOGIE. Make me feel like a real woman, *chico.*

PROCLO. I can't help you out in that department! It's out of my hands.

GOOGIE. Kiss me! (*Sounds of an orchestra striking up.*) Oh shit! That's my music! (*She is dragging Proclo by the hand. She throws open the door.*) Come on, my Mr. Big Producer. You're gonna love my show. I got you the best seats. I see you ringside. We save the hanky-panky for later. (*Googie hurries off.*)

PROCLO. Ringside! Hanky-panky! What am I doing here? (*Claude appears on the third level.*)

CLAUDE. Vespucci!

PROCLO. It *is* the same Claude Perkins. We were in the Army together. Compared to those two, Carmine wanting to kill me is sanity! (*He rushes off, followed by Claude.*)

CLAUDE. I warned you, Vespucci! You promised, I waited, and you didn't come! Hey, where are you? (*The music is building as the lights dim and the nightclub, complete with twinkle lights and mylar, flies in.*)

ABE. (*Over the loudspeaker.*) And now, on the great Ritz stage, direct from her record-breaking bus and truck tour with "Fiddler on the Roof," the sensational Googie Gomez! With Duff and Tiger, those amazing now you see it, now you don't golden go-go boys! (*There is a roll of drums.*) Here's Duff. (*Duff runs on. Another roll of drums.*) Here's Tiger. (*Tiger makes a great entrance. Another roll of drums.*) And here's Googie! (*Googie bursts on and launches into her first number. She is very bad but very funny. It's the kind of number you watch in disbelief. Sincerity is what saves her. Such a lack of talent is appalling, yes,*

but it does come straight from the heart. Tiger and Duff are doing their best, too. They dance well enough and they look pretty good up there.)
(*When the number ends, during the applause, we see Proclo run across pursued by Claude. Googie, followed by Tiger and Duff, goes after them.*) Hey, wait a minute! Where are you going? I was just gonna introduce you! (*They are gone. Suddenly the figure of a very wet, very angry balding middle-aged fat man comes storming through the mylar into Googie's spotlight.*)

CARMINE. I'm Carmine Vespucci of the Bensonhurst Vespuccis. I want a room in this here whorehouse and I don't want any shit.
(*There is a mighty roll of drums as Scarpia's Theme from "Tosca" is heard. A crack of cymbals. Curtain.*)

ACT TWO

Carmine is seen coming along the corridor. He is still in street clothes. He looks all around and then knocks softly on the door of Michael Brick's room.

CARMINE. Brick? Are you in there, Brick? It's Vespucci. Don't open. I don't want anyone to see us. If you can hear me, knock once. If you can't, knock twice. Are you there, Brick? (*Michael knocks once.*) Good. Our signals are working. Now listen to me, have you seen that balding fat brother-in-law of mine yet? (*Michael knocks twice.*) What does that mean? No? (*Michael knocks once.*) Okay, I think I read you. Now I know he's in here somewhere. What I don't know is how you could miss him. He's a house. Listen, Brick, none of these fruits tried to pull anything with you, did they? (*Michael knocks twice.*) You can thank Our Blessed Lady for that. Meet me in 102 in fifteen minutes. Knock three times. Got that? (*Michael knocks three times.*) Not now, stupid, *then.* And you don't have to worry about him leaving this place. Leaving it in one piece I should say. I got all my men outside. Ain't that great, Brick? Hunh? (*Michael knocks once.*) I knew you'd like that. Keep looking. (*Carmine goes into his room, starts to undress. We will see him take out a revolver, a stiletto, and a pair of brass knuckles. From offstage, Claude calls.*)

CLAUDE. Vespucci! (*Proclo appears on the third level and races into a room. Claude runs past the room and sees a patron.*) Say, have you seen a Vespucci go by? (*Proclo leaves his hiding place and heads down to the second level. Claude yells as he follows him down the stairs and they disappear.*) Vespucci! Vespucci! (*Googie appears and pokes her head into Proclo's room.*)

GOOGIE. Where are you hiding, Mr. Vespucci? (*She disappears. Proclo appears and starts down the stairs to his own room on the first level. Midway he crosses paths with Tiger and Duff.*)

TIGER. There you are!

DUFF. Why did you run away? (*Proclo escapes and continues down to his room. Tiger and Duff disappear, looking for Googie. Meanwhile Googie appears in a corridor, now looking for Claude.)*

GOOGIE. Where is this person who ruin my act? Where is this skinny little man? I kill him! *(She disappears. Tiger and Duff appear and criss-cross again.)*

TIGER. Googie! Googie!

DUFF. Googie! Googie! *(They are gone. As soon as Proclo reaches his room, Claude comes down the corridor looking for him. He opens the door, but Proclo has hidden behind it.)*

CLAUDE. Vespucci! *(As he leaves, he shuts the door, revealing Proclo, who quickly makes the sign of the cross and starts gathering his things. Meanwhile Googie has appeared down a corridor. She sneaks up on Claude and tears his robe off.)*

GOOGIE. Ah hah! *Cabron!* *(Claude races off, pursued by Googie, who is in turn pursued by Tiger and Duff.)*

TIGER. Googie!

DUFF. Googie! *(They are all gone. Proclo is in a terrific hurry. We can hear him muttering to himself as he frantically packs his bag.)*

PROCLO. I'd rather spend the night in Central Park in the rain than spend another minute in this place! They're all mad! I thought *I* had problems! If I ever get my hands on that cab driver, he's finished! So long, room, I won't miss you. *(He comes out of the room carrying his clothes, his suitcase and the box of Panettone. He slams the door.)* Hello, Cleveland! *(He sees a patron walking by.)* Which is the way out of here?

PATRON. That way. *(Proclo goes up the stairs to the second level, looking for an exit. Claude appears on a side balcony.)*

CLAUDE. Vespucci! Vespucci! *(Proclo has made his decision: it's the steam room or else. He goes rushing in with his clothes, his suitcase and the Panettone. Claude leaps over the balcony in hot pursuit.)*

CLAUDE. I hope you know what a cul-de-sac is, because you're in one. *(He goes into the steam room. Now Googie enters on the rampage. We see her tearing up and down the corridors, Tiger and Duff following, trying to calm her down.)*

GOOGIE. Where is this skinny little man who chase a producer out of my number? No one chases no producer out of Googie

Gomez' number! (*She is pounding on doors. One of them is opened by the patron in chaps.*)

PATRON IN CHAPS. Howdy, pardner.

GOOGIE. Don't howdy me, you big leather sissy! (*She pushes him back into the room.*) You think I don't know what goes on around this place? All you men going hee-hee-hee, poo-poo-poo, hah-hah-hah! I get my boyfriend Hector in here with his hombres and he kill you all! (*She is heading for the steam room.*)

DUFF. You can't go in there!

TIGER. Googie, no! (*Googie storms into the steam room, Tiger and Duff following. The door closes behind them. A moment later, Googie lets out a muffled yell.*)

GOOGIE. Pendego! (*Patrons start streaming out. Googie comes right after them. She has Claude firmly in tow.*) There will be no more hee-hee-hee, poo-poo-poo, hah-hah-hah around this place tonight! (*She slings Claude across the hall.*)

CLAUDE. You're hurting me!

GOOGIE. I'm just getting started! (*Tiger and Duff attempt to subdue her.*)

CLAUDE. You could use a good psychiatrist, mister!

GOOGIE. What you call me?

TIGER. He didn't mean it!

GOOGIE. What you call me?

TIGER. Tell her you're sorry!

CLAUDE. I havn't seen such tacky drag since the Princeton Varsity Show!

GOOGIE. Tacky drag?

CLAUDE. Thirty years ago, sonny! (*Googie has gotten herself into good street-fighting position by now. With a bloodcurdling yell she leaps for Claude and chases him off, Tiger and Duff close behind. The stage is bare for a moment. We hear Claude.*)

CLAUDE. Help! (*From the yell, it sounds as if Googie's got him. The steam room door opens and Chris comes out.*)

CHRIS. I'm going straight. (*Suddenly the steam room door slams open and Proclo, or what's left of him, staggers out. He is fully dressed, wearing the wig, dark glasses and moustache from his first entrance, and carrying his suitcase. He has visibly wilted. He doesn't seem to know where he is.*)

PROCLO. I don't believe this whole night.

CHRIS. Were you in there for all that? (*Proclo just nods.*) Where? (*Proclo just shrugs.*) You don't want to talk about it? (*Proclo just shakes his head.*) Why are you wearing your clothes?

PROCLO. I'm going to Central Park.

CHRIS. I thought you were going to stay in your room.

PROCLO. (*Blindly walking downstairs.*) I can't. I told Googie I was Carmine Vespucci. Claude thinks I'm Carmine Vespucci. Everybody thinks I'm Carmine Vespucci.

CHRIS. Well who are you?

PROCLO. Tonight I'm Carmine Vespucci.

CHRIS. I give up! (*Chris sees Michael Brick coming along a corridor.*) What have we here? Now this is a little more like it. Play it cool, Chris. (*He arranges himself attractively.*) If you don't mind, Mr. Vespucci, I'd like to try my luck with this one. Hey, Vespucci, I'm talking to you. Snap out of it!

MICHAEL. Are you Mr. Carmine Vespucci, sir?

CHRIS. You live around here, kid?

MICHAEL. No, I came in from Astoria. Are you Mr. Vespucci?

CHRIS. Say yes, say yes!

PROCLO. Yes!

MICHAEL. I'm Michael Brick. My room's right over here. (*He will start leading Proclo to his room.*)

CHRIS. Hi, I'm Chris. My room's right up there.

MICHAEL. Hi, Chris. (*Michael and Proclo have gone into Michael's room and closed the door.*) Am I glad to see you, Mr. Vespucci. (*Chris has been watching their encounter in envy and disbelief.*)

CHRIS. I don't date out-of-towners. (*He starts to exit, but is stopped by the ring of the pay phone. He answers it with an enormous scream of frustration. He hangs up and disappears. A somewhat still dazed Proclo is sitting in Michael's room.*)

MICHAEL. Now this is what I thought we'd do. Get under the bed.

PROCLO. (*Beginning to cry.*) Another one!

MICHAEL. All right, stay there. We'll pretend you're him and I'm me and the real you is under the bed.

PROCLO. (*Tears are really flowing.*) Only this one's the worst.

MICHAEL. Now get the picture. The lights are low, he's moving down the hallway and he sees me leaning against the door. I flex for him. Pecks and biceps are supposed to be a turn on. Don't ask me why. I catch his eye. I've got a cigarette dangling from my lips, I put one knee up, I wink, I kind of beckon with my head and finally I speak. "See something you like, buddy?" That's the tough guy approach.

PROCLO. Is that your own voice?

MICHAEL. Yes.

PROCLO. I mean, your real voice?

MICHAEL. Yes.

PROCLO. Your natural speaking one?

MICHAEL. Yes.

PROCLO. Thank you.

MICHAEL. Why? Does it bother you?

PROCLO. Oh no, no, no!

MICHAEL. Some people find it very irritating.

PROCLO. I can't see why.

MICHAEL. Me either. But of course I'm used to it. I've had it ever since I was a kid. I mean, I grew up and matured, only my voice didn't. Where was I?

PROCLO. The tough guy approach.

MICHAEL. Oh! And *then* . . . and this is where you're going to have to jump out—

PROCLO. I am having a nightmare.

MICHAEL. Very, very, very casually . . .

PROCLO. I can hardly wait.

MICHAEL. I thought I'd let my hand just kind of graze against my . . . (*He hesitates, then whispers in Proclo's ear.*)

PROCLO. I'm getting out of here!

MICHAEL (*Pulling him down.*) But you're going to have to help me catch your brother-in-law, Mr. Vespucci.

PROCLO. My brother-in-law?

MICHAEL. I haven't seen anyone who fits Mr. Proclo's description.

PROCLO. Proclo? My brother-in-law?

MICHAEL. The balding middle-aged fat man you hired me to catch.

PROCLO. Where do you know my brother-in-law from?

MICHAEL. I don't yet. That's why I called you at that bar across the street.

PROCLO. What bar?

MICHAEL. Where you and your men have this place surrounded so Mr. Proclo can't leave in one piece.

PROCLO. Who are you?

MICHAEL. Michael Brick, sir.

PROCLO. What are you?

MICHAEL. A detective. (*Michael is suddenly alerted by the alarm on his wristwatch.*) It's time!

PROCLO. For what?

MICHAEL. Get under the bed. He'll see you.

PROCLO. Who will?

MICHAEL. Your brother-in-law. He'll be here any second. Since I couldn't find Mr. Proclo I'm making him find me. I left a note by the coke machines saying "Any middle-aged balding fat man whose initials are G.P. interested in a good time should meet me in Room 101 at midnight sharp." When he gets here you're gonna have to help me. You see, I'm not queer.

PROCLO. (*Already climbing under the bed.*) You could've fooled me.

MICHAEL. I'm right on top of you.

PROCLO. I can't tell you how comforting that is. (*Chris is seen moving along the corridors, playing "The Lady or the Tiger." He knocks softly at different doors, and finally on Carmine's.*)

CARMINE. I said knock three times!

CHRIS. He's being masterful with me already, the brute. (*He knocks three times.*)

CARMINE. That's more like it.

CHRIS. I think I'm in love. (*Carmine opens the door and pulls Chris violently into the room, slamming the door behind them.*)

CARMINE. Quick. Don't let anyone see you. Now let me get a look at you. (*He circles Chris appraisingly.*) I'm not a judge of fruit bait, but I guess you'll do.

CHRIS. Just cool it, sweetheart. This isn't the meat rack.

CARMINE. You can can the fag act with me, Brick. Now listen, I think I've come up with something. I know this sounds like the oldest stunt in the book, but I'm going to hide under your bed.

CHRIS. On the contrary, it's a first.

CARMINE. You never tried the old under-the-bed technique?

CHRIS. Not recently.

CARMINE. What kind of a detective are you?

CHRIS. That's a good question, honey.

CARMINE. Can it, Brick, just can it. One thing I don't like is a wise guy. The only thing I don't like more is a queer wise guy. I'm calling the shots now and I'm getting under your bed.

CHRIS. Where am I supposed to be?

CARMINE. On top of it, stupid!

CHRIS. It sounds fabulous. Then what?

CARMINE. You know, do what you have to do.

CHRIS. What's that?

CARMINE. How should I know? Wiggle your fanny, shake your towel in his face.

CHRIS. Whose face?

CARMINE. My brother-in-law's, you dummy! The guy I hired you to catch. And then I pop out, catching you both in the act of fragrant delicto and whammo! I got him.

CHRIS. Your brother-in-law?

CARMINE. Who else? Jesus, you're like talking to a yo-yo.

CHRIS. Dumb and dizzy, that's me, darling! (*In a very "butch" voice.*) Just a little more of that gay humor. Ho ho ho!

CARMINE. All right, now you go back to 101. (*Chris desperately starts to leave.*) Not yet! If the coast is clear, whistle like this. . . . (*He whistles with two fingers.*) . . . and I'll high tail it to your room and slide right under and we're in business. Got that?

CHRIS. Check.

CARMINE. It's about time.

CHRIS. Only I can't whistle.

CARMINE. Goddamnit, you can't whistle either?

CHRIS. Tell you what, Mr. . . .

CARMINE. Vespucci, Carmine Vespucci. Only don't call me that! He might hear us. I need a code name.

CHRIS. Evelyn.

CARMINE. Naw, I don't like Evelyn. Sounds effeminate.

CHRIS. How about Bunny?

CARMINE. Okay, Bunny.

CHRIS. All right then, Bunny, you get under *this* bed. That way I won't have to whistle and you won't have to high tail it to 101.

CARMINE. Maybe you're not so dumb after all, Brick.

CHRIS. Just to refresh my memory, give me his name again.

CARMINE. It's Proclo, Gaetano Proclo.

CHRIS. What did he do?

CARMINE. He married my sister. I told her. I pleaded with her. I was on my knees to her. "Viv, honey, marry this Proclo character and you're marrying to stick a knife in me." She loves him, she tells me. Well I hate him, I tell her. I've always hated him. He's not of the family. He's not like us. He don't belong in Poppa's business. But she wouldn't listen to me. And so what happens? Twenty years she thinks she's happily married, my sister, but the truth is it's twenty years she's been a martyr, that woman. My sister is a saint and she don't even know it. I'll tell you one thing: with Poppa gone now . . . (*He breaks into uncontrollable sobs.*). . . Poppa, God bless him . . . I ain't sharing Vespucci Sanitation Services and Enterprises, Inc., with no fairy!

CHRIS. Your brother-in-law is a fairy?

CARMINE. He's gonna be when I get through with him.

CHRIS. What are you going to do to him?

CARMINE. I'm gonna kill him!

CHRIS. Good!

CARMINE. You know what a *delitto di passione* is, Brick? 'Cause you're gonna see one tonight. A crime of passion. An enraged brother catching his dear sweet sister's balding fat slob husband in an unnatural act with one of these these fruitcakes around here! There's no court in the country that would convict me. Twenty years I waited for this night. You're looking at a man of great and terrible Italian passions, Brick.

CHRIS. I can see that, Bunny. (*He turns off the room lights.*)

CARMINE. What happened?

CHRIS. That's how they do it here. Now get under the bed. I'm leaving the door open so he can come in. Once he gets here, you take it from there. I'm right on top of you. Now don't say another word. (*Chris has tiptoed out of the room, leaving the door ajar and Carmine under the bed. He knocks on Michael's door.*)

MICHAEL. That must be your brother-in-law, Mr. Vespucci!

PROCLO (*Ready to meet his Maker.*) I'm sure it is.

MICHAEL. (*Unlocking the closed door.*) Hold your horses, stud! (*He stretches out on the bed. We see Proclo's face looking out from the foot of the bed.*) It's open! (*Chris enters.*) See something you like, buddy?

CHRIS. You've got to be kidding.

MICHAEL. False alarm, Mr. Vespucci.

CHRIS. Where's your friend?

MICHAEL. He's under the bed.

CHRIS. Why not? Everybody else is. I always wondered what you straight guys did together. Now that I know, I'm glad I'm gay. If you didn't have all that hair, I'd ask you if your name was Guy something.

PROCLO. (*Crawling out from under the bed.*) It is.

CHRIS. And you really do have a garbageman brother-in-law who's out looking for you, don't you?

PROCLO. Unh-hunh!

CHRIS. Well, the maniac is right across the hall and he's got a gun. I just thought I'd mention it.

MICHAEL. Now he's after you, Mr. Vespucci! And you didn't mention anything about a gun. (*Googie appears in the corridor and knocks on the door.*) I'm scared! (*Chris dives under the bed.*)

PROCLO. You're scared? Move over!

CHRIS. There's not enough room.

PROCLO. I can fit.

CHRIS. I was here first.

PROCLO. It's my brother-in-law!

CHRIS. It's my ass! (*Michael has opened the door a crack and peeked out. Now he slams it shut and dives under the bed from the other side. Proclo still hasn't managed to get under.*)

PROCLO. Where do you think you're going?

MICHAEL. It's not him, Mr. Vespucci!

PROCLO. Well who is it then?

MICHAEL. It's that transvestite again!

PROCLO. What are you talking about? (*The knocking is getting louder.*) Who's there?

GOOGIE. I know you're in there, *chico!*

PROCLO. Oh, no! (*He goes to the door and opens it. Googie comes flying in, closing the door behind her and clapping one hand over Proclo's mouth.*) Now, look—!

GOOGIE. Don't speak. Don't say nothing. Say one word and Googie's out on her ass. She's breaking every book in the rule doing this. (*She has pushed Proclo onto the bed and is lying on top of him.*) You know why you don't like women? Because you never tried it, that's all. Or maybe you did and that's why. She was a bad woman. Forget her. Believe me, *chico*, it don't hurt. It's nice. It's very nice. Just lie back and Googie's gonna show you how nice.

PROCLO. Look, I'd like to help you out—!

GOOGIE. Think of a tropical night! A beach.

PROCLO. What beach?

GOOGIE. The moon is shining on the sea and in the distance, over the waves, you hear music. . . . (*She sings.*) "Besame, besame mucho!" (*Proclo is terrified. Almost involuntarily, under the bed, Michael and Chris join in singing. For several moments, there is almost a trio going between them, as Googie tries to take off Proclo's clothes.*)

GOOGIE, MICHAEL and CHRIS. Como si fuera esta noche/ La ultima vez/ Besame, besame mucho/ Piensa que tal vez mañana/ Estare lejos muy lejos/ De ti. (*Suddenly, Proclo comes back to his senses.*)

PROCLO. This isn't going to work out, Mr. Googie!

GOOGIE. Mister?

PROCLO. There's just no way!

GOOGIE. Mister? You thought I was a drag queen? No such luck, *chico!*

PROCLO. You really are a miss?

GOOGIE. This is all real. (*She has clasped his hands to her breasts. Proclo can't believe what he is feeling. His voice goes up at least an octave.*)

PROCLO. It feels real, it feels real!

GOOGIE. I just hope I'm gonna find me some *huevitos*.

PROCLO. What are *huevitos*?

GOOGIE. (*Finding them under his raincoat.*) Ay ay ay!

PROCLO. They're real, too!

GOOGIE. We're gonna make such a whoopee, *chico!*

PROCLO. Thank you.

GOOGIE. Thank you? You're gonna thank me.

PROCLO. The trouble is my brother-in-law is trying to kill me and there's someone under this bed.

GOOGIE. Oh no you don't! I'm not falling for that old hat and dance routine. You're not pulling no wool over my ears so easy.

PROCLO. I swear to God there is!

GOOGIE. Never try to shit an old pro, *chico*.

MICHAEL. He's not! There is someone under this bed.

CHRIS. Us! And if you two want to bounce around like that I'll gladly go back to my own room.

GOOGIE. (*Leaping off the bed.*) That's a rotten stunt, mister. I could lose my job for this. I told you: I threw wind in caution coming down here!

PROCLO. It's really very simple.

GOOGIE. I don't need no explaining. You rather make hee-hee-hee, poo-poo-poo, hah-hah-hah with that *maricon* you got hiding under the bed!

CHRIS. Two *maricons*, Googie!

GOOGIE. Who's that down there?

CHRIS. It's me, Chris.

GOOGIE. Hi, Chris. What are you doing down there?

CHRIS. I wish I knew.

MICHAEL. (*Poking his head out now.*) The reason we're under this bed—

GOOGIE. You!

MICHAEL. Now wait!

GOOGIE. Not only you got a fat boyfriend, you *maricon* hump—you got a mean one! (*She is hitting Michael with the pillow.*)

MICHAEL. I'm not his boyfriend!

PROCLO. He's not!

MICHAEL. And I'm not gay!

GOOGIE. With a voice like that you're no straight arrow either.

MICHAEL. I was born with this voice.

GOOGIE. So was Yma Sumac. I saw you talking on the telephone and I said, "Googie, that boy could make your blood go boil."

PROCLO. I thought you said that about me.

GOOGIE. I say that about everyone. (*Proclo is making an escape.*) Where are you going?

PROCLO. Look, I'm just someone who's in a lot of trouble, lady.

GOOGIE. You're not staying for my second show?

PROCLO. I'm not a producer. It was all your two friends' idea. Now if you'd just let me get out of here—.

GOOGIE. Hey, now wait a minute!

PROCLO. Now what?

GOOGIE. Wait just one big fat minute! (*She grabs for Proclo's wig. It comes off.*)

PROCLO. Hey!

GOOGIE. I thought maybe it was you!

PROCLO. Who are you talking about?

GOOGIE. Seymour Pippin! You don't fire Googie Gomez from no show and get away with it. (*She is trying to kill Proclo.*) You think I forget a face like yours, you bastard? I'm gonna tear your eyes out! (*Chris and Michael will eventually subdue her.*)

CHRIS. It's not him, Googie.

MICHAEL. That's Mr. Vespucci.

GOOGIE. You promise?

PROCLO. I promise.

GOOGIE. I thought you was Seymour Pippin.

PROCLO. I wish I were.

GOOGIE. What do you know? I thought he was Seymour Pippin!

MICHAEL. Seymour Pippin! (*Carmine has come out of his room and knocks on the door.*)

PROCLO. Oh my God! (*They all start scrambling for a place under the bed.*)

GOOGIE. What about me?

CHRIS. That's my place!

MICHAEL. Hurry up!

GOOGIE. Suck your gut in!

PROCLO. I am!

GOOGIE. More!

PROCLO. Who is that?

CHRIS. Relax, mister. I told you: you're not my type.

PROCLO. Well just get your hand off my—.

GOOGIE. It's okay! It's my hand.

MICHAEL. If it's him, Mr. Vespucci, just give me the word. (*Proclo, Chris and Googie have somehow all managed to squeeze under the bed. Michael opens the door. Carmine storms in.*)

CARMINE. What the hell happened to you? You said you'd be on top! I've been under that damn bed so long I can hardly walk! (*As he turns he sees Michael, who has gone into his flexing routine.*)

MICHAEL. See something you like, buddy?

CARMINE. What the—?

MICHAEL. You new around here, mac?

CARMINE. You're not Brick! Where's Brick? What have you done to him?

MICHAEL. Lie down.

CARMINE. Get your hands off me! (*Michael shoves Carmine onto the bed. Googie cries out.*)

GOOGIE. Ow! *Ay, cono!*

PROCLO. Sshh!

CARMINE. What the—?

MICHAEL. Relax.

CARMINE. Somebody's under there!

MICHAEL. Just stretch out on the bed, now.

CARMINE. What are you doing in here?

MICHAEL. Just relax: I'm trying to seduce you.

CARMINE. Get your hands off me, you goddamn Greek, or I'll lay your head open.

MICHAEL. (*Pinning Carmine down.*) Is it him, Mr. Vespucci?

PROCLO. Yes!

CARMINE. Vespucci? I'm Vespucci.

MICHAEL. Is it?

PROCLO. Yes, yes! It's him! It's him!

CARMINE. I know that voice! (*He leans over the bed just as Googie rolls out.*) What the hell is this? One of them goddamn transvestitites, sure you are!

GOOGIE. Seymour Pippin! (*She is attacking Carmine, swatting him with a pillow.*)

CARMINE. Fight fair, you faggot! (*Michael knocks Carmine out with a karate blow.*)

MICHAEL. Hi-ya! (*Carmine falls onto the bed. Proclo groans.*)

GOOGIE. Aw, shit! Why you do that? I was gonna fix his wagon for him good!

MICHAEL. He's out cold, Mr. Vespucci!

PROCLO. Just get me out of here.

CHRIS. And we were just starting to have so much fun!

GOOGIE. You know something? This man is not Seymour Pippin either. He sure got a mean face though! I wonder who he is. (*Proclo and Chris are up from under the bed now.*)

PROCLO. It's my brother-in-law.

GOOGIE. Is he in show business?

PROCLO. He's in garbage.

GOOGIE. A gay garbageman?

MICHAEL. You're sure it's him?

PROCLO. I'm afraid so.

GOOGIE. What are you two talking about?

MICHAEL. I'm a detective. Mr. Vespucci here hired me to get something on his brother-in-law Mr. Proclo there so Mr. Proclo doesn't inherit one-half the family business.

PROCLO. So that's it. (*He tries to strangle Carmine. The others hold him back.*)

MICHAEL. Mr. Vespucci wanted to catch us together so he could commit a *delitto di passione*. What's a *delitto di passione*, Mr. Vespucci? (*Again Proclo goes for Carmine's throat.*)

PROCLO. You're about to see one!

CHRIS. Hey, now take it easy! You can't do that!

PROCLO. He was going to! (*Michael has been getting ready to photograph Carmine on the bed.*)

MICHAEL. Look out now. You'll be in the picture.

CHRIS. (*Primping his hair.*) Picture? What picture? (*Suddenly Googie grabs the camera.*)

GOOGIE. Oh no! I see what you do! If that man want to be here, let him be here. What you care? I don't stand still for no blackmail! I tell Tiger and Duff what you do and you're out on your ass, big boy! Come on, Chris! (*She goes with the camera.*)

CHRIS. Excuse me, but I promised Mark Spitz we'd do a quick ten laps around the pool. (*He goes.*)

MICHAEL. Mark Spitz comes here, Mr. Vespucci?

PROCLO. I don't care!

MICHAEL. What should I do with him?

PROCLO. Kill him.

MICHAEL. I'm a private detective, Mr. Vespucci. I'm not a hit man.

PROCLO. You got something to tie him down with?

MICHAEL. Cuffs.

PROCLO. Hurry.

MICHAEL. Give me a hand with him, will you?

PROCLO. Can't you hit him again?

MICHAEL. That wouldn't be ethical, Mr. Vespucci.

PROCLO. Ethical? Your line of work and you're telling me what's ethical? Come on, let's get out of here.

MICHAEL. If you don't need me anymore, I want to find that Googie and get my camera back.

PROCLO. Fine, fine. (*Michael goes. Proclo stands looking after him, then down at Carmine on the bed.*) You blew it, Carmine. By the time you get out of this place I'll be back in Cleveland with Vivian and the kids. (*He goes, leaving the door open. He passes into Carmine's room. We will see him gather up Carmine's clothes as he yells out.*) Fat man in 101! Come and get it. Fat man in 101! He's all yours. Fat man in 101! (*As Proclo comes out of Carmine's room, he sees Tiger in the corridor.*)

PROCLO. Duff.

TIGER. I'm Tiger.

PROCLO. Whatever! Burn these for me, will you?

TIGER. Burn 'em?

PROCLO. You heard me.

TIGER. (*Scooping up Carmine's clothes.*) You're sounding happy.

PROCLO. I'm close to feeling terrific!

TIGER. What happened?

PROCLO. I'm catching the next plane to Cleveland.

TIGER. Good luck.

PROCLO. You're too late. I've already got it! (*Tiger is gone. Proclo grabs his suitcase and starts to head off. The pay phone rings and Michael answers it.*)

MICHAEL. Hello? This is The Ritz. Michael Brick speaking. It's for you, Mr. Vespucci.

PROCLO. Who is it?

MICHAEL. Who is this? It's Mrs. Proclo, calling from that bar across the street.

PROCLO. Mrs. Proclo? My God, it's Vivian. Tell her I've left.

MICHAEL. I'm sorry but he just left, Mrs. Proclo. She doesn't believe me.

PROCLO. Tell her she has to believe you.

MICHAEL. He says you have to believe me. She says she's not staying there another minute. She's taking a man's hat and raincoat and coming right over here and nothing's going to stop her. Hello . . . hello? (*He hangs up.*) I didn't even get to tell her the good news.

PROCLO. What good news?

MICHAEL. That we got our man! (*Googie is coming along on her way to the nightclub.*) Miss Gomez?

GOOGIE. Don't Miss Gomez me now, *chico.* I got a show to do.

MICHAEL. I can explain about downstairs.

GOOGIE. I don't talk to no detectives.

MICHAEL. Then about my camera! (*They are gone.*)

PROCLO. He'll kill me. She'll divorce me. My children will grow up hating my memory. Oh my God! (*Tiger is passing.*)

TIGER. What happened?

PROCLO. I just ran out of luck! There's a woman trying to get in here. Keep her out.

TIGER. They don't let ladies in here.

PROCLO. It's my wife.

TIGER. Relax. She'll never get past Abe. (*He is gone.*)

PROCLO. I did! (*He runs into his room. We see Claude come in behind him. Proclo doesn't. Yet. He sits on the bed and pants.*)

CLAUDE. Your door was open.

PROCLO. What?

CLAUDE. I'm giving you one more chance. (*He starts to sing his song.*) "Jelly Roll Baby/ You're my Jelly Roll Man . . ."

PROCLO. Please, I'm too weak.

CLAUDE. "Jelly Roll cupcake/ I'm your Jelly Roll fan . . ."

PROCLO. Look, this is a lot of fun, I can't tell you! I don't know about you, Claude, but I'm in terrible trouble.

CLAUDE. Claude!

PROCLO. I didn't say that.

CLAUDE. Wait a minute! Wait a minute! Guy! It's you, Guy!

PROCLO. Absolutely no!

CLAUDE. Gaetano Proclo, the fifth division, Special Services, the Philippines.

PROCLO. I was 4-F. I never served.

CLAUDE. It's me, Claude! Claude Perkins.

PROCLO. Get away from me, Claude!

CLAUDE. That's right! "Get away from me" Claude! We had an act together. A trio with Nelson Carpenter. We pantomimed Andrews Sisters records. "Rum and Coca Cola." Remember?

PROCLO. I don't know what you're talking about. I hate the Andrews Sisters.

CLAUDE. You hate the Andrews Sisters?

PROCLO. Look, I'm in desperate, desperate trouble, mister, and I wish you'd just go away.

CLAUDE. Just wait until I write Nelson Carpenter about this!

ABE. (*Over the loudspeaker.*) 253 coming up! That's two-five-three. You're not going to believe what's coming up, boys!

PROCLO. O my God, it is Vivian!

CLAUDE. There are other fat fish in the ocean, Gaetano Proclo, and 253 just may be one of them.

PROCLO. Just don't touch 253, Claude!

CLAUDE. We'll see about that. (*He sweeps out. Proclo returns to his room, kneels beside his bed, and quietly begins to pray. The patron in chaps walks in on the awakening Carmine in Brick's room.*)

PATRON IN CHAPS. Howdy, pardner. Handcuffs? Outta sight! (*He sinks to his haunches and just stares. Tiger, Duff, Googie and Michael are running by. The three entertainers are dressed to go on.*)

GOOGIE. If I don't hit that note, cover for me.

DUFF. How?

GOOGIE. Take your clothes off! Anything!

MICHAEL. Miss Gomez! (*They are gone. Carmine is starting to come around. The patron in chaps is still staring.*)

PATRON IN CHAPS. Far out! Far out! (*Chris pokes his head into the room.*)

CHRIS. Hi, girls!

CARMINE. Brick!

CHRIS. Don't believe a word she says. She thinks she's a detective or something.

CARMINE. Who she? What she?

CHRIS. You she. And who do you think you are? Dale Evans? (*He starts to go.*)

CARMINE. Let me out of here! I'll kill you!

CHRIS. I've got a date with 253. (*He is gone.*)

CARMINE. Gaetano! Gaetano! (*The patron in chaps runs off. On the second level we see Vivian. She is wearing a man's hat and raincoat over her black pants suit. She carries a shopping bag. Chris approaches her.*)

CHRIS. I had a hunch it would be bad, but nothing like this. (*To*

Vivian.) Welcome to the city morgue. (*Vivian recoils and lets out one of her giant sobs: an unearthly sound.*)

VIVIAN. Aaaaaaaeeeeee!

CHRIS. Forget it, mister, that's not my scene! (*Opening the door to the steam room.*) Avon calling! (*He goes in. Claude has approached Vivian in the corridor, and again the strains of the "Now, Voyager" theme are heard.*)

CLAUDE. Looking for 253? (*Vivian nods, stifling her sobs.*) Right this way. (*He leads her to his own room, of course, carefully concealing the number as they enter. He slams the door and starts to sing.*) "Jelly Roll Baby/ You're my Jelly Roll Man . . ." (*Vivian really lets out a big sob as he starts moving towards her.*)

VIVIAN. Aaaaiiiieeeee! (*No sooner does she scream than Vivian faints dead away on Claude's bed. At that moment, Carmine manages to free himself from his handcuffs by banging the bed noisily on the ground. Proclo, in his room, Carmine's threats and Vivian's screams ringing in his ears, is literally quivering, as he softly calls out.*)

PROCLO. Help. Help. Help. (*Carmine is on the rampage. He shoots the lock off his own door. The door gives and he runs in.*)

CARMINE. My clothes! Somebody took my clothes! (*He runs out of the room, brandishing the revolver.*) Okay, Gaetano! I know you're in here! I'm gonna find you if it's the last thing I do! (*He disappears. Meanwhile, Claude is trying to revive Vivian.*)

CLAUDE. All right, lie there like a beached whale. (*No response from Vivian.*) Look, I'd love to stay here and play Sleeping Beauty with you but I've got to get ready for the Talent Contest. (*He starts getting his things together for his record pantomime act.*) What's in the bag? You bring your own lunch? (*He is looking in Vivian's shopping bag.*)

ABE. (*Over the loudspeaker.*) Just a reminder, boys and girls. It's amateur night at The Ritz.

CHRIS. (*Coming out of the steam room.*) You can say that again!

CLAUDE. You've got to be kidding. (*He takes a long mink coat out of Vivian's shopping bag. He can't resist putting it on.*) What becomes a legend most? (*Carmine comes storming up to Chris.*)

CHRIS. Hi, Bunny. How's tricks?

CARMINE. You! (*He points his gun.*)

CHRIS. Is that thing loaded?

CARMINE. And you're lucky I'm not using it on you. Now where is he?

CHRIS. Who?

CARMINE. My brother-in-law, you dumb dick!

CHRIS. He was just here.

CARMINE. And?

CHRIS. He went in there. (*He motions towards Claude's room.*)

CARMINE. Well why didn't you say so?

CHRIS. I just did. You're really planning to shoot him?

CARMINE. You if he's not in there! (*Carmine starts for Claude's room. Chris hurries off in another direction. Carmine starts banging on Claude's door.*)

CLAUDE. Who's that?

CARMINE. You know goddamn well who it is. (*Claude opens the door, takes one look at Carmine, and starts his song.*)

CLAUDE. "Jelly Roll Baby/ You're my Jelly Roll . . ."

CARMINE. What the—? (*He pulls his gun.*) Get out of here! (*Claude escapes, taking his clothes and Vivian's mink with him. Carmine turns at a moan from Vivian on the bed.*) Okay, Gaetano, the jig is up! (*Then, realizing who it is.*) Viv! Vivian, baby. What have they done to you? (*He tries to revive her.*) Speak to me, Viv! Viv! (*Chris has come up to Proclo's door. Proclo is slumped. He is too tired, too defeated, to call for help anymore.*)

CHRIS. It's me, Chris! Open the door! (*Proclo does.*) That brother-in-law of yours means business.

PROCLO. Why can't he just find me and get it over with?

CHRIS. You're just going to sit there?

PROCLO. What's the use?

CHRIS. Hide somewhere.

PROCLO. I came here. He found me.

CHRIS. Wear a disguise.

PROCLO. I am! (*He tears off his wig and moustache.*) I thought you were mad at me.

CHRIS. I am but I prefer you alive to dead. I'm funny that way. (*Claude, wearing the mink, comes along the corridor.*)

PROCLO. Claude!

CLAUDE. Oh, sure. Now you know me.

PROCLO. You've got to help me.

CLAUDE. I've got to get ready for the talent contest tonight.

PROCLO. My brother-in-law's here with a gun.

CLAUDE. So that's who that maniac is! (*Proclo, Claude and Chris go.*)

CARMINE. Viv! Viv! Sis!

VIVIAN. (*Reviving.*) Where am I? Carmine!

CARMINE. What are you doing here?

VIVIAN. I couldn't stand being in that bar anymore.

CARMINE. Do you know what kind of place this is?

VIVIAN. It was horrible, Carmine. He wanted me to roll on him.

CARMINE. Who?

VIVIAN. I don't know. Some little thin man.

CARMINE. I'll kill him. I'll kill 'em all.

VIVIAN. I was afraid something terrible had happened. I asked myself what Gilda would do.

CARMINE. Gilda? Gilda's twelve years old.

VIVIAN. Not my Gilda. The one in *Rigoletto*.

CARMINE. This isn't an opera, Viv.

VIVIAN. She disguised herself as a man for the man she loved and came to a place very similar to this one.

CARMINE. And then what happened?

VIVIAN. (*New sobs.*) She was stabbed to death!

CARMINE. You weren't stabbed. You were only rolled on.

VIVIAN. Take me home, Carmine, please.

CARMINE. Home? But he's here. I can prove it to you.

VIVIAN. I don't want proof. I just want to go back to Cleveland.

CARMINE. With a man like that?

VIVIAN. I don't care. He's my husband.

CARMINE. I'm gonna kill the son of a bitch when I find him.

VIVIAN. No killing, Carmine. I don't want killing.

CARMINE. All he's done to you.

VIVIAN. He hasn't done anything to me.

CARMINE. That's what you think. Now I want you to get out of here and take a cab back to Brooklyn. Leave that husband of yours to me.

VIVIAN. I'm not going!

CARMINE. Then stay in here and don't let anyone in.

VIVIAN. No!

CARMINE. This is between him and me, Viv!

VIVIAN. If you hurt him, I'll never speak to you again!

CARMINE. It's Poppa's honor that's at stake!

VIVIAN. Poppa's dead! (*This statement causes them both to collapse into sobs.*)

CARMINE. Poppa! He's stained the Vespucci honor!

VIVIAN. Carmine, please!

CARMINE. It's like he peed on Poppa's grave!

VIVIAN. Aaaaaiiiiieee!

CARMINE. I'm thinking about Poppa, Viv. Believe me, it's not for me.

VIVIAN. What about me?

CARMINE. You, too. He peed on you, too, You've been dishonored, too, sister.

VIVIAN. Give me the gun.

CARMINE. What?

VIVIAN. Give me the gun. I'm going to kill myself.

CARMINE. Are you crazy?

VIVIAN. I want to die, Carmine. You've made me so crazy I want to kill myself.

CARMINE. It's him I'm going to kill. (*By this time, Vivian will have the gun. Suddenly, she becomes aware that her mink is missing.*)

VIVIAN. Carmine! No, no!

CARMINE. What is it!

VIVIAN. No! . . . No! . . . No! . . .

CARMINE. What is it?

VIVIAN. My mink!

CARMINE. Your mink?

VIVIAN. It's gone. They've taken it. It was in here.

CARMINE. Why weren't you wearing it?

VIVIAN. I didn't want to get it wet. It cost 900 dollars.

CARMINE. I'll get your mink back, too.

VIVIAN. He gave it to me for our anniversary. Now I really want to kill myself.

CARMINE. I'll get your goddamn mink. Now let go of me.

VIVIAN. I'm coming with you.

CARMINE. You're staying here.

VIVIAN. I don't want him dead, Carmine.

CARMINE. It's not up to you. This is for Poppa! (*He starts off.*) Gaetano! Gaetano!

VIVIAN. Carmine! (*But he is gone. Vivian runs out of the room and sees the snooty patron.*) Stop him.

SNOOTY PATRON. Who?

VIVIAN. My brother. He'll kill him. You heard him. He's a violent man.

SNOOTY PATRON. Kill who?

VIVIAN. My husband. And my mink! They took my mink! (*Vivian and the snooty patron disappear up a corridor. Proclo, Claude and Chris go running by on their way to the nightclub.*)

CHRIS. I don't know any Andrews Sisters numbers!

CLAUDE. Well fake it!

PROCLO. This will never work!

CLAUDE. He never really knew any either. Nelson and I carried you for years. (*Carmine enters and comes face to face with Chris and the others. Proclo hides behind the mink coat as Chris blows his whistle.*)

CHRIS. He went up to the steam room, boss.

CARMINE. Thanks. (*He heads upstairs. Claude, Proclo and Chris turn on their heels and run in the opposite direction. Vivian appears on the first level.*)

VIVIAN. Carmine, wait!

CARMINE. I said stay in there! (*He continues toward the steam room. Vivian sees Proclo and his group just exiting.*)

VIVIAN. My mink! Stop, thief! (*They are gone, Vivian in pursuit. Carmine runs into the steam room. This time all the patrons come flying out. Carmine follows, brandishing his gun. They all run off. Music is heard. It is a bad baritone singing the end of an operatic aria.*)

BAD BARITONE. (*Singing over the loudspeaker.*) Il concetto vidisi/ Or ascoltate/ Comeglie svolto,/ Andiam./ Incominciate! (*This is the transition to the nightclub. The talent show is in progress. There is applause as Googie steps onto the stage.*)

GOOGIE. That was Tiny Naylor singing "The Prologue" from *Pagliacci*. Bravo, Tiny, bravo. It's gonna be a close race tonight. (*She consults a card.*) Our next contestant is Sheldon Farenthold, song stylist. Take it away, Sheldon! (*Sheldon enters, encased in red balloons. He plays directly out front, thus making*

*the audience in the theatre the audience in The Pits. During the
number he will pop his balloons and do bumps and grinds.*)
SHELDON. (*Singing.*)
Why are we here? What are we doing?
It's time we all found out.
We're not here to stay,
We're on a short holiday,
'Cause . . .
Life is just a bowl of cherries,
Don't take it serious,
Life's too mysterious.
You work, you slave, you worry so,
But you can't take your dough when you go, go, go,
So keep repeating it's the berries,
The strongest oak must fall . . .
(*Suddenly, two groups of patrons, one chased by Carmine, the
other by Vivian, crisscross and disappear into the "backstage"
area of the nightclub. Sheldon shoots them a blinder but goes on
performing like the good little trouper that he is. Spoken.*)
Thanks a lot! (*Sung.*)
The sweet things in life,
To you were just loaned,
How can you lose what you've never owned.
Life is just a bowl of cherries,
So live and laugh at it all.
C'mon . . .
Live
And laugh at it all!
(*When the number ends, Sheldon takes his bows and goes.
Googie steps forward.*)
GOOGIE. Thank you. You know, it gives me a real pleasure to emcee
these amateur shows because I began as an amateur. (*Sounds of
disbelief from the offstage band members.*) It's true! I didn't
get where I am over night. Oh no, *chicos!* It took a long, long
time. A star is born, that's true, I mean, you have "it" in the
cradle or you don't, but she doesn't twinkle over no one night.
(*She laughs at her own joke, then regains herself.*) Okay. (*Suddenly a group of patrons, led by Sheldon and his balloons, races
across, chased by Carmine. Googie chooses to continue unflus-*

tered.) Our last contestant is Mr. Claude Perkins and partners recreating their famous Army act. Hit it, boys! (*Music is heard. It is a '40s sounding swing orchestra. A spotlight picks up Claude in his WAC uniform, Proclo in his wife's mink coat and a long blonde wig, and Chris in an elaborate makeshift gown made from sheets. The Andrews Sisters are heard singing one of their big hits, "The Three Caballeros." Claude, Chris and Proclo begin to pantomime to the record and jitterbug. At first, Proclo is all nerves and Claude does a Herculean job of covering for him. But as the number progresses, we see Proclo getting better and better as the act comes back to him. After a while, he's close to enjoying himself.*)

CHE ANDREWS SISTERS. (Prerecorded.)
We're three caballeros, three gay caballeros,
They say we are birds of a feather,
We're happy amigos,
No matter where he goes,
The one, two and three goes,
We're always together.
(*Suddenly all of the patrons, including poor Sheldon, balloons and all, with Tiger and Duff, are chased across the stage and into the house by Carmine and Vivian.*)
We're three happy chappies, with snappy serapes,
You'll find us beneath our sombreros;
We're brave and we'll stay so,
We're bright as a peso,
Who sez so, we say so,
The three caballeros.
(*Chris accidentally steps on Proclo's foot, but the number continues.*)
Oh, we have the stars to guide us,
Guitars here beside us,
To play as we go;
We sing and we samba;
We shout "Ay, Caramba."
What means Ay, Caramba?
Oh yes, I don't know . . .
(*The number is really building now. Proclo is boogying away like crazy. Suddenly Carmine fires a shot in the air. There is*

*total pandemonium as the group of patrons returns to the stage
from the back of the house. They run into a big huddle. Proclo
and Claude manage to lose themselves somewhere in the middle
of the crowd.*)

CARMINE. Now everybody slow down! Nobody's going nowhere.
And get some lights on. I want to see who I'm talking to. (*The
follow-spot hits Carmine.*) Not on me! I want the room lights,
you dumb fruit! (*All the lights come on.*) Okay, I want all the
fairies in a line.

CHRIS. What about us butch types, boss?

CARMINE. Shut up, you.

CHRIS. It's me, Bunny, Brick.

CARMINE. You're fired. Get over there! (*He motions with his gun
for Chris to form a line. He turns and see Michael.*) I can't
believe it. A good-looking, rugged boy like you.

MICHAEL. Believe what, sir?

CARMINE. I believe it. Get going.

GOOGIE. Wait a minute. All of this because some fat woman who
lost her mink?

CARMINE. One more word out of you, you goddamn transvestitite
and—.

GOOGIE. What you call me?

SHELDON. Careful, Googie.

GOOGIE. You make me see red, mister, and when I see red I tear
you apart. Shit! You think I'm scared of a little gun? (*Carmine
fires in the air again.*) That's okay, mister. You don't bother me,
I don't bother you. (*She backs into the main group of patrons.*)

CARMINE. Okay, Cowboy. Your turn.

PATRON IN CHAPS. I don't know what your name is but you belong
in Bellevue.

CARMINE. Who says?

PATRON IN CHAPS. A trained psychiatrist.

CARMINE. Get outta here! (*Duff and Tiger try to sneak up on Carmine.*) What are you two? The Cherry Sisters?

DUFF. Up yours, mister.

CARMINE. Get over there. All right. The rest of you! (*The group
crosses the stage, revealing Claude and Proclo, whose face is
turned. Claude approaches Carmine.*)

CLAUDE. You really know how to mess up an act, you know that, mister?

CARMINE. Christ, another one!

CLAUDE. I'm an entertainer. Pantomime acts are coming back, you'll see.

CARMINE. In the meantime, you're still a transvestitite. Move! (*Only Proclo remains now. Carmine is savoring every moment of his humiliation.*) I guess that makes it you. Look at you. I could vomit. Jesus, Mary and Joseph! Is that her mink? (*Proclo turns around. Not only is he wearing the mink and the Patty Andrews wig, he has added the dark glasses and the moustache. He nods.*) Give it back to her. (*Proclo shakes his head.*)

VIVIAN. I don't want it now. That's not Gaetano. I just want to go home.

CARMINE. Okay, Gaetano, the jig's up. Take that crap off. The wig, the glasses, the moustache, the mink. Everything. I'm giving you three. (*To the others.*) I want you all to meet my splendid brother-in-law, Gaetano Proclo.

MICHAEL. That's not Mr. Proclo! He is!

CARMINE. Who is?

MICHAEL. You are! (*Carmine spins around. Proclo bites his wrist and grabs the gun. The others subdue Carmine. For a few moments he is buried as they swirl about him. Vivian just sobs hysterically.*)

CARMINE. Get your hands off me! This time you've really done it, Gaetano!

PROCLO. Shut up, Carmine.

CARMINE. Sure, you got some balls now, you're holding a gun.

PROCLO. Don't worry about my balls, Carmine.

CARMINE. I'm gonna kill you!

PROCLO. Keep him quiet. Sit on him. I don't want to hear that voice. (*Tiger, Duff and Chris hold Carmine down and muffle his mouth, though Carmine will try to get his two cents in during the conversation that follows. Proclo has approached Vivian.*)

PROCLO. Don't cry, Viv.

VIVIAN. Don't cry, he says. Look at him like that, telling me not to cry!

PROCLO. You want your coat back?

VIVIAN. I want to know what you're doing in it!

PROCLO. It was the only thing that fit.

VIVIAN. Aaaaiiiieeee!

PROCLO. Carmine was going to kill me!

VIVIAN. AAAAIIIIEEEE!

PROCLO. Vivian, please!

VIVIAN. My husband, the man in the mink coat! I can't wait to go
to Bingo with you like that next week but I won't be there if
God is merciful because I'm going to have a heart attack right
here.

CARMINE. This is grounds for annulment, sis. I asked Father Catini.

VIVIAN. I don't want an annulment. I want to die. *Mi fa morire,
Dio, mi fa morire!*

PROCLO. Is this what you wanted, Carmine?

CARMINE. You're finished, Gaetano.

PROCLO. I can understand you hating me as a brother-in-law but
killing someone over a garbage company?

VIVIAN. *Un delitto di passione,* Carmine?

CARMINE. *Si! Un delitto di passione!*

VIVIAN. *Ma perchè?*

CARMINE. *Perchè* you're married to a flaming homo, that's *perchè!*

VIVIAN. Aaaaiiiieeee!

CARMINE. He came here tonight, didn't he?

PROCLO. A cab driver brought me here.

CARMINE. Because you told him to.

PROCLO. I never heard of this place.

CARMINE. You see that Vivian? Even a cab driver knows what a
fata he is!

VIVIAN. I just hope you're not going to insist on mentioning this in
confession.

PROCLO. Mention what?

VIVIAN. He knows your voice, Guy.

PROCLO. Who knows my voice?

VIVIAN. Father Bonnelli. He knows everyone's voice. For my sake,
Guy, for the children's, don't tell him about this.

PROCLO. I wasn't planning to!

VIVIAN. You're going through a stage. Last year it was miniature
golf.

CARMINE. This ain't like no miniature golf, Viv.

VIVIAN. I'll get over this. I get over everything. It's my greatest strength.

PROCLO. There's nothing to get over, then or now!

VIVIAN. Aaaaiiiieee!

PROCLO. Vivian, what do I have to do to convince you?

CARMINE. She is convinced! Cry your heart out, sis, it's all right. Carmine's here.

PROCLO. How the hell do you prove something like that to your wife? I give up. You win, Carmine. Let him go. (*Tiger, Duff and Chris reluctantly release Carmine, look at Proclo, and then leave.*)

CARMINE. Come on, sis, let's get out of here.

PROCLO. Vivian, wait!

CARMINE. Don't you even speak to my sister! (*Proclo stands there helpless. Maurine has appeared. She goes directly to Carmine and hands him a long sheet of figures.*)

MAURINE. Thirty seven thousand five hundred on the week. The rain killed us tonight. And next week we got the Jewish holidays coming up. Good night, boss. (*She goes.*)

VIVIAN. Who was that?

CARMINE. Just a person.

VIVIAN. She called you boss.

CARMINE. A lot of people call me boss. (*He starts to eat the sheet of figures.*)

VIVIAN. Give me that.

CARMINE. It's not what you're going to think, Vivian.

VIVIAN. "Vespucci Enterprises, Inc. Carmine Vespucci, President." This is a statement!

CARMINE. I was going to tell you about it.

VIVIAN. We own this place?

CARMINE. Poppa'd done a lot of expanding while you were in Cleveland.

VIVIAN. We own this place, Guy!

CARMINE. He doesn't have to know the family business, Viv! Now come on, this isn't the place to talk about it.

VIVIAN. So you knew what kind of place this was.

CARMINE. So did he obviously. That's why he came here. I can't help it if we own it. It's just a coincidence.

VIVIAN. What kind of cab was it, Guy?

PROCLO. What?

VIVIAN. The one that brought you here.

PROCLO. I don't remember.

CARMINE. A fairy cab!

VIVIAN. Do you remember the name of the company?

CARMINE. The Fairy Cab Company! Fairy cabs for fairy passengers! Now come on, Vivian, let's get out of here. What do you care what kind of cab it was?

VIVIAN. Think hard, Guy. It's important.

PROCLO. It was an opera . . . Aida Cab!

VIVIAN. Aida Cab! We own that company!

PROCLO. We do?

VIVIAN. Carmine, did you tell that driver to bring Guy here?

CARMINE. Of course I didn't!

VIVIAN. What did the driver look like, Guy?

PROCLO. All I remember about him is his stutter.

VIVIAN. His stutter?

PROCLO. He stuttered and smoked pot.

VIVIAN. Cousin Tito! I should've guessed. It's going to be very hard to forgive you for this, Carmine.

CARMINE. What's to forgive! I don't want no forgiving!

VIVIAN. Now take the hit off him, Carmine.

CARMINE. Vivian!

VIVIAN. Take it off!

CARMINE. No!

VIVIAN. If you don't take it off, Carmine, I am gonna tell Frankie di Lucca about you muscling into the Bingo concessions at the Feast of St. Anthony and then Frankie di Lucca is gonna put a hit out on you and you are gonna end up wearing cement shoes at the bottom of the East River and then there will be even more grief and less peace in our fucking family than there already is!

PROCLO. I am married to an extraordinary woman!

CARMINE. You wouldn't do this to me, sis!

VIVIAN. You know me, Carmine.

CARMINE. Vivian!

VIVIAN. I swear it, Carmine. *Lo giuro.*

CARMINE. *Non giura,* sis!

VIVIAN. *Lo giuro,* Carmine. *Lo giuro,* the Bingo and the cement shoes.

CARMINE. "Get Proclo." You heard Poppa.

VIVIAN. I've got Proclo, Carmine. Now take the hit off!

CARMINE. I'll lose face.

VIVIAN. Not under the East River!

CARMINE. (*Writhing in defeat.*) Aaaaiiieee!

VIVIAN. Now take the hit off him, Carmine! Is it off? (*He nods.*) On Poppa's grave? (*He shakes his head.*) I want it on Poppa's grave and I want it forever! (*He shakes his head.*) I'm calling Frankie di Lucca.

CARMINE. It's off on Poppa's grave!

VIVIAN. (*Finally breaking down.*) Poppa! All right, now I forgive you.

CARMINE. I told you: I don't want no forgiving.

VIVIAN. You already have it. And now I want to see you two forgive each other. *Il bacio del pace,* Carmine.

CARMINE. You gotta be kidding!

PROCLO. Over my dead body!

VIVIAN. I want you to kiss each other as brothers.

PROCLO. I wouldn't kiss him for a million dollars.

VIVIAN. That's exactly what it's worth, Guy.

PROCLO. I wouldn't kiss him, period.

VIVIAN. I want you to make your peace with Carmine.

PROCLO. Vivian!

VIVIAN. For me, Guy, for me.

PROCLO. I forgive you, Carmine. With a little luck nobody's gonna die in your family for a long, long time and we won't have to see each other for another twenty years. Just be sure to send the checks. *Andiamo!* (*By this time, all the patrons will have gathered as an audience to the proceedings. Proclo opens his arms and moves towards Carmine for the kiss of peace.*) Hey!

CARMINE. Hey! (*They make a slow, ritual-like circle. Of course, both men do look rather ludicrous as they circle one another: Proclo in his wife's mink coat; Carmine in his bathrobe. Carmine hesitates.*)

VIVIAN. Frankie di Lucca! (*The circling resumes. Just as they are about to kiss, Carmine gives Proclo a good punch in the stomach. But as Proclo bends over in pain, he knees Carmine in the groin.*)

Carmine goes down. The others give a mighty cheer and con-
gratulate Proclo.)

PROCLO. (*Amazed.*) I did it. I did it. (*Now jubilant.*) I won. I
didn't fight fair but I won! (*To Carmine.*) You can go *va fan-*
gool yourself, Carmine. People like you really do belong in garbage. People like me just marry into it. Get him out of here,
men!

CHRIS. Bring her up to the steam room, girls! (*The others pounce*
on Carmine, who is protesting mightily, and drag him off.)

CARMINE. I'm coming back here and I'm gonna kill every last one
of you fairies!

CHRIS. Sure you are, Nancy! (*It is a gleeful, noisy massed exit. All*
the patrons sing "La Marseillaise." For several moments we can
still hear Carmine yelling and the others cheering. Vivian has
been following them in concern. Proclo stops her.)

PROCLO. Vivian!

VIVIAN. Where are your clothes? I want to go home.

PROCLO. I'm not leaving.

VIVIAN. Don't make any more waves in the family now, Guy.

PROCLO. It's the perfect time. If I don't do it now I never will. Your
family's run herd on me since the day I met you. I'm sick of it.
I'm sick of Carmine and Connie and Tony and Tommy and
Sonny and Pipo and Silva and Beppe and Gina and your Aunt
Rosa and Cousin Tito! I'm sick of all of them. The living and
the dead. What am I? Some curse on a family? "Get Proclo."
Those were your father's dying words!

VIVIAN. He was my father. I was his only girl. You expected him to
like you?

PROCLO. Yes! Yes, I expect people to like me. I want people to like
me. It's called self-esteem, Vivian.

VIVIAN. I think we have a wonderful marriage.

PROCLO. I do, too. It's nothing personal, Viv.

VIVIAN. A beautiful home, all paid for.

PROCLO. I'm not talking about that. I'm talking about me. I'm talking about wanting things. And I do want things. I've always
wanted things. I wanted so many things I didn't get I can't even
remember them. I wanted to send Momma back to Italy before
she died. I didn't have the money in those days.

VIVIAN. Not many eight-year-old boys do, Guy.

PROCLO. I want us to be terrific forever. I want to go on a diet. No, I want to *stay* on one. I want a boat. I want a brand new fleet of trucks. I want Proclo Sanitation services to be number *one* in Cleveland. I want people to stop calling me a garbageman. I want to be known as a sanitary engineer. I want to be honored as an ecologist! I want changes! I want changes! I want changes! (*He has exhausted himself.*)

VIVIAN. I want to go back to Cleveland.

PROCLO. You know something? So do I. (*She goes to him and kisses his cheek. Claude enters with three trophies.*)

CLAUDE. We won! We won! (*He hands one of the trophies to Proclo and heads upstairs.*) We won the talent contest! We won! God bless the Andrews Sisters! Chris! Chris, where are you?

CHRIS. In the steam room!

CLAUDE. We won!

CHRIS. We won? (*Claude meets Chris in the steam room with screams of joy.*)

PROCLO. You see that, Viv? I never won anything in my whole life. That was Claude Perkins. We were in Special Services together.

VIVIAN. He seems like a nice person.

PROCLO. I wouldn't go that far, Vivian. To him I look like Tyrone Power.

VIVIAN. So did I. Now where are your things? (*They return to Proclo's room, where he will dress and pack. Googie comes storming on, followed by Tiger and Duff. She is dressed in street clothes and carrying all her belongings.*)

TIGER. We're sorry, Googie.

GOOGIE. You build someone up like that and it's all a lie. Ay, that's a low-down dirty trick to play.

TIGER. Look at it this way: one night there will be a Mr. Big out there and you'll be all keyed up for it.

GOOGIE. There ain't never gonna be no Mr. Big in this place. There ain't never gonna be me no more in this place neither. I quit.

DUFF. Come on, Googie, we adore you.

GOOGIE. You adore yourself. (*Michael appears.*) Would you believe it? They told me that Mr. Big was gonna be here tonight.

MICHAEL. Who's Mr. Big?

GOOGIE. Only the man you wait for all your life. Only the man who opens miracles. Only the man who can make you a star over one night. A producer, who else?

MICHAEL. My uncle is a producer, Miss Gomez.

GOOGIE. Oh yeah? What's he produce?

MICHAEL. Shows.

GOOGIE. Legitimate shows? I don't do no dirty stuff.

MICHAEL. Right now I think he's casting "Oklahoma" for a dinner theatre.

GOOGIE. "Oklahoma"? It's a stretch but I could do that part. You could get me an audition with him?

MICHAEL. Sure thing.

GOOGIE. You see? I had this hunch the whole evening. I got another show to do. I meet you in Bimbi's across the street. We run into my boy friend Hector and we tell him you're my agent. (To Tiger and Duff.) I see you two skunks later.

DUFF. I thought you quit.

GOOGIE. That's show business. (She is gone.)

TIGER. You got an uncle who's in show business?

MICHAEL. Seymour Pippin. He's a producer.

DUFF. Forget it, mister.

TIGER. Come on, Duff. (Michael, Tiger and Duff leave. Chris has entered.)

PROCLO. (To Vivian.) Are you ready?

CHRIS. I suppose you're wondering what happened to Bunny. We entered her in the Zinka Milanov look-alike contest. First prize is a gay guide to Bloomingdale's. We're still awaiting the judge's decision.

VIVIAN. Who's he talking about?

PROCLO. Carmine.

VIVIAN. He said she.

CHRIS. We've called the 16th Precinct. They'll be right over for him.

VIVIAN. Oh, Guy, you've got to do something for him.

PROCLO. I will, Vivian. Thanks for the help back there.

CHRIS. Just let me know the next time you three are coming in. I want to be sure not to be here. I haven't had so much fun since the day they raided Riis Park.

PROCLO. If you're ever in Cleveland Vivian makes a great lasagna.

CHRIS. Well, that's the best offer I've had all night.

PROCLO. Goodnight, Chris.

CHRIS. So long, boss. (*He heads back up to his room. We hear Googie offstage, singing a song from her third show, "Shine On Harvest Moon."*)

ABE. (*On the loudspeaker.*) 316 coming up! That's three-one-six, Duff!

PROCLO. Let's go!

VIVIAN. Guy, promise me you'll take good care of Carmine.

PROCLO. On Poppa's grave.

VIVIAN. (*A new outburst of grief.*) Poppa! (*She exits. Proclo calls off to her.*)

PROCLO. Not your Poppa's. Mine! (*As Proclo starts off, a policeman races on. Proclo stops to watch with a contented smile. Chris blows his whistle, and the policeman runs up to the steam room, where he finds Carmine, bound and gagged and dressed in a green brocade ball gown. Claude sees Carmine, too, and sings his "Jelly Roll" song as he plays tug-o'-war with the policeman over Carmine. Patrons are filling the halls. Duff and Tiger start making fresh beds. And Proclo just smiles.*)

CHRIS. Orgy! Orgy! Orgy in 240! (*The lights are fading. The play is over.*)

BAD HABITS

(1974)

For Elaine May

BAD HABITS opened February 4, 1974, at the Astor Place Theatre, and May 5, 1974, at the Booth Theatre in New York City. It was produced by Adela Holzer. It was directed by Robert Drivas. Scenery and costumes designed by Michael H. Yeargan and Lawrence King. Lighting designed by Ken Billington. The production stage manager was Robert Vandergriff. The assistant to the director and assistant stage manager was Tony DeSantis.

THE CASTS
(in order of appearance)

For RAVENSWOOD:

OTTO	Henry Sutton
APRIL PITT	Cynthia Harris
ROY PITT	F. Murray Abraham
JASON PEPPER, M.D.	Paul Benedict
DOLLY SCUPP	Doris Roberts
HIRAM SPANE	Emory Bass
FRANCIS TEAR	J. Frank Lucas
HARRY SCUPP	Michael Lombard

For DUNELAWN:

RUTH BENSON, R.N.	Cynthia Harris
BECKY HEDGES, R.N.	Doris Roberts
BRUNO	Henry Sutton
MR. PONCE	Emory Bass
DR. TOYNBEE	J. Frank Lucas
MR. BLUM	F. Murray Abraham
MR. YAMADORO	Michael Lombard
HUGH GUMBS	Paul Benedict

RAVENSWOOD

THE PLAYERS

JASON PEPPER, M.D.

DOLLY SCUPP

HARRY SCUPP

HIRAM SPANE

FRANCIS TEAR

ROY PITT

APRIL PITT

OTTO

Bright sunlight. Lush green foliage forms a background wall. Heaven on earth. There is a table with Dom Perignon champagne, coffee service, orange juice, etc. Three chairs are at the table. A small rolling cart holds towels and suntan cream. There are two chairs and a small table, shaded by a beach umbrella.

We hear lively baroque music. When the house lights are out, and before the stage lights come up, the music changes. Now it is "Wein, Du Stadt Meiner Traume" ("Vienna, City of My Dreams"). When the lights come up we see that the music is coming from the cassette recorder that Otto carries from a shoulder strap.

He enters down the aisle through the audience carrying a bouquet of flowers. As he carefully arranges them on the table, we hear the voices of April and Roy Pitt.

APRIL. (*Offstage.*) We're here!

ROY. (*Offstage.*) Hey, where is everybody? Does somebody wanna give us a hand with these things? (*Otto exits behind the foliage wall, and returns carrying three large expensive pieces of luggage. April Pitt, carrying a makeup kit, and Roy Pitt, with a tennis bag, follow him in.*)

APRIL. So this is Ravenswood! Nice. Very nice.

ROY. What do you mean nice? It's terrific! Look at that clay court, honey. Real clay. Can you stand it? (*Otto starts off down the aisle with the luggage.*)

APRIL. That's Vuitton, Buddy.

OTTO. *Ja, Fraulein.*

APRIL. Just thought I'd mention it.

OTTO. *Ja, Fraulein.* (*He is gone.*)

APRIL. Jesus, Roy, it's the Gestapo. I just hope this Pepper fellow's all he's cracked up to be.

ROY. I told you: he's just gonna have us talk to each other.

APRIL. We talk to each other all the time. What's he gonna do?

ROY. Listen.

APRIL. Just listen? A hundred and forty-five clams a day and he just listens? I knew I should have checked this guy out first.

ROY. Look what he did for Sandy and Reg.

APRIL. Sandy and Reg are lesbians and they're not in show business. They run a pet shop in Montauk for Christ's sake!

ROY. But they're happy.

APRIL. Sure, they're in dyke heaven, those two. I'm talking about us, Roy.

ROY. So am I, April. You told the answering service where I'd be? I don't want to miss that call from the Coast. (*He starts off down the aisle. The lively baroque music is heard again very softly.*)

APRIL. I'm beginning not to like the smell of this whole setup. When's our first session? This Pepper character doesn't deliver, we're gonna blow this nickel joint and head straight for L.A. Right, Roy? (*But Roy is following Otto and the luggage.*) I said easy with the Vuitton, schmuck! (*She follows them off. The stage is empty a beat. The music has gotten louder. Jason Pepper, M.D., enters with Dolly Scupp. He is in an electric wheelchair with a blanket on his lap. The music is coming from a cassette recorder built into the chair. Also, the chair has an ashtray, a small shelf on the side (for holding a book later), a holder for a martini glass, and a ship's bell for calling Otto. Dolly Scupp is carrying a shoulder-strap-type handbag and a book. Her right foot is in an orthopedic foot covering. Dr. Pepper is drinking a martini and smoking a cigarette. He and Dolly listen to the end of the music, then he turns off the cassette.*)

DR. PEPPER. Over there's our lake. A pond you might call it, but I like to think of it as a lake. After all, it's the only body of water for miles and miles. In the winter it's frozen over and quite covered with snow. And now look at it. Ah, the seasons, the seasons! I do love the seasons! What would we do without them? (*Thunder. Dr. Pepper puts both hands to his head and gingerly fingers his skull.*) Don't tell me that's not the music of the spheres. It's a day like this that makes you think the world is coming to an end. Only the real joke is, it's not going to rain. Oh don't get me wrong, I don't enjoy playing God *or* the weatherman, but I don't have this porous platinum plate in my head for nothing, either.

DOLLY. You look different on your book jacket.

DR. PEPPER. I know. Taller. May I? (*Dolly gives him the book she*

has been carrying under her arm.) *Marriage for the Fun of It!*
Oh God, are people still reading this old thing?
DOLLY. Everybody who's still married.
DR. PEPPER. I thought I knew something in those days.
DOLLY. You're being modest.
DR. PEPPER. It's my only virtue.
DOLLY. That's one more than me.
DR. PEPPER. Harry didn't tell me you were coming.
DOLLY. He didn't know. I woke up this morning and said to myself,
"I'm driving up to Ravenswood today." Don't ask me why. I just
had this sudden urge to see you.
DR. PEPPER. It's a delightful surprise.
DOLLY. I hope so.
DR. PEPPER. Your absence has made Harry's rehabilitation some-
what more difficult, you understand. I prefer to treat couples
who are having difficulties *as* couples.
DOLLY. There's nothing wrong with me, if that's what you're driv-
ing at.
DR. PEPPER. Should I be?
DOLLY. Is my husband getting any better, Dr. Pepper?
DR. PEPPER. It's Jason, Mrs. Scupp. Please, I insist on it. Until
we're over that little hurdle we're nowhere. And you're right, it's
high time we had a little chat. Coffee?
DOLLY. Thank you. (*She crosses to the table and helps herself.*)
DR. PEPPER. Cigarette?
DOLLY. No, thanks.
DR. PEPPER. It's a special tobacco, imported from Panama, that's
been fertilized with hen feces. I don't think you'll find them at
your A&P in Scarsdale.
DOLLY. I wouldn't think so.
DR. PEPPER. They have an extraordinarily . . . *pungent* taste.
DOLLY. I don't smoke.
DR. PEPPER. You're joking.
DOLLY. I gave them up years ago.
DR. PEPPER. During the big scare, huh? So many of you poor bas-
tards did. Will it bother you if I . . . ? (*He is lighting his ciga-
rette.*)
DOLLY. Not at all. My doctor insisted.
DR. PEPPER. And who might that be?

DOLLY. Dr. Fernald.

DR. PEPPER. Helmut Fernald up at Grassyview? I might've known he'd jump on the bandwagon.

DOLLY. No, George Fernald in White Plains, the County Medical Center.

DR. PEPPER. He wouldn't drive a white Buick station wagon, usually there's a couple of dalmatians yapping around in the back, and be married to one of the McIntyre sisters, would he?

DOLLY. I don't think so. Our Dr. Fernald's married to a Korean girl and I'm pretty sure they have a dachshund. I don't know what he drives. He's just our family doctor.

DR. PEPPER. Well that explains it. The curse of modern medicine, that lot.

DOLLY. Dr. Fernald?

DR. PEPPER. Your friendly, neighborhood, family G.P. Now don't get me started on *that*, Mrs. Scupp.

DOLLY. I thought the majority of doctors had stopped smoking, too.

DR. PEPPER. (*Exhaling.*) And doesn't that just sound like something the majority of doctors would do? Fortunately, there remain a few of us who refuse to be stampeded along with the common herd. I'm referring to men like Peabody Fowler of the Heltzel Foundation and Otis Strunk of the Merton Institute, of course. (*Dolly shakes her head.*) Rand Baskerville out at Las Palmetas? Claude Kittredge up at Nag's Head?

DOLLY. I'm sorry, but I'm not familiar with them.

DR. PEPPER. Who is? I can't discuss colors with a blind person, Mrs. Scupp.

DOLLY. But surely, Doctor, you're not suggesting that smoking is good for you?

DR. PEPPER. Of course not.

DOLLY. I didn't think so.

DR. PEPPER. What I *am* suggesting is that *not* smoking is conceivably worse.

DOLLY. I don't follow.

DR. PEPPER. Do you want to talk turkey or not, Mrs. Scupp?

DOLLY. Of course I do! And please, call me Dolly.

DR. PEPPER. Hello, Dolly.

DOLLY. Hello.

DR. PEPPER. Well, hello, Dolly.

DOLLY. It's my curse.

DR. PEPPER. You think Dr. Pepper is easy? Now let's start at the beginning and I'll try to keep it in layman's terms.

DOLLY. Thank you.

DR. PEPPER. Everything in life is bad for you. The air, the sun, the force of gravity, butter, eggs, this cigarette . . .

DOLLY. That drink.

DR. PEPPER. That coffee! Canned tuna fish.

DOLLY. No.

DR. PEPPER. It's true! It's loaded with dolphin meat. There's an article on canned tuna fish in this month's *Food Facts* that will stand your hair on end.

DOLLY. I love tuna fish.

DR. PEPPER. Don't we all?

DOLLY. I don't care what they put in it.

DR. PEPPER. Neither do I. Right now, this very moment, as I speak these words, you're ten seconds closer to death than when I started. Eleven seconds, twelve seconds, thirteen. Have I made my point? Now, how would an ice-cold, extra-dry, straight-up Gordon's gin martini grab you? (*He rings the service bell.*)

DOLLY. I'm afraid it wouldn't.

DR. PEPPER. Ah, vodka is the lovely lady from Scarsdale's poison. (*He rings again.*)

DOLLY. I'm on the wagon.

DR. PEPPER. You don't smoke, you don't drink . . .

DOLLY. And it's Larchmont. And I would like to talk about my husband. (*Otto appears from the aisle.*)

OTTO. Ze newlyweds have arrived.

DR. PEPPER. Ze newlyweds Pitt?

OTTO. *Ja, Herr Doktor.* I put zem in ze little honeymoon cabin.

DR. PEPPER. Good, Otto, good. Tell them we'll have our first session after lunch. Show them the lake, the stables, the tennis courts. The grand tour, Otto.

OTTO. I could give Mrs. Pitt a rubdown, maybe?

DR. PEPPER. No, Otto.

OTTO. Whirlpool?

DR. PEPPER. Nothing, Otto. Just the tour.

OTTO. (*Seeing that Dr. Pepper's glass is empty.*) Ze usual?

DR. PEPPER. Last call, Mrs. Scupp.

DOLLY. I'll have a Tab, maybe.

OTTO. *Nein* Tab.

DOLLY. A Fresca?

OTTO. *Nein* Fresca.

DOLLY. Anything dietetic.

OTTO. *Nichts* dietetic, *nichts!*

DOLLY. Water, then.

OTTO. *Wasser?*

DR. PEPPER. *Wasser fur das frau!*

OTTO. *Jawohl, Herr Doktor.*

DR. PEPPER. (*Otto has turned to go.*) *Und Otto! Dry-lich! Dry-lich! Dry-lich fur ze martini!* (*Otto exits.*) It's an extraordinary race. Is Scupp German?

DOLLY. We don't know what it is.

DR. PEPPER. Then I can say it: I can't stand them. It was a German who incapacitated me.

DOLLY. The war?

DR. PEPPER. My wife. She pushed me down a short but lethal flight of stairs backstage at the Academy of Music in Philadelphia.

DOLLY. How horrible!

DR. PEPPER. It was the single most electrifying experience of my life.

DOLLY. But why would anyone do such a thing?

DR. PEPPER. In my wife's case it was self-defense.

DOLLY. You mean you tried to kill her?

DR. PEPPER. Symbolically. It's funny how no one ever asks why it was a flight of stairs backstage at the Academy of Music; you must admit, it's not your usual place for an attempted homicide. My wife was a lieder singer. She'd just given an all-Hugo Wolf recital. She asked me how I thought it went and I said, "Maybe the only thing in the world more boring than an all-Hugo Wolf recital is your singing of an all-Hugo Wolf recital." The remark just kind of popped out of me. And when it popped, she pushed and down I went. Four short steps and here I am. Don't look so tragic, Mrs. Scupp. No Anita Wertmuller and her all-Hugo Wolf recital and no Ravenswood. We divorced, of course, and she remarried some California grape-grower. Otto used to accompany her. Now Otto accompanies me. Having been unhappy in marriage, hopefully I can help others to solve their marital difficulties. Look for the silver lining, yes?

DOLLY. You never remarried?

DR. PEPPER. What on earth for? The third and fourth toes of your left foot, wasn't it?

DOLLY. The second and third of the right.

DR. PEPPER. Accidents will happen.

DOLLY. Not with a remote-control power lawnmower, Doctor.

DR. PEPPER. Those things are devils.

DOLLY. Harry was sitting on the porch controlling it. I was sunbathing.

DR. PEPPER. He didn't go into the details.

DOLLY. Of course he didn't. That's why he's here.

DR. PEPPER. He said there'd been an accident and that was why you hadn't come here with him.

DOLLY. I wouldn't have come with him even if it hadn't happened. I'm sorry, but I can't afford to take any more chances with a man like that.

DR. PEPPER. That's what marriage is, Mrs. Scupp.

DOLLY. Not with a husband who tried to kill you, it isn't! Two toes, Doctor.

DR. PEPPER. Two legs, Dolly. (*Thunder. Dr. Pepper feels his head again.*)

DOLLY. Is my husband getting any better yet, Doctor?

DR. PEPPER. I think Harry's about ready to leave Ravenswood. (*Hiram Spane enters. He is in a long bathrobe, beach sandals, and wearing sunglasses. He goes to the table and pours champagne and orange juice into the same glass.*)

DOLLY. I hope you're right.

DR. PEPPER. He'll be along shortly. You can see for yourself. Good morning, Hiram!

HIRAM. Morning? I was hoping it was late afternoon. I haven't been up this early since I saw Mother off on the Graf Zeppelin.

DR. PEPPER. I'm sure you never saw anyone off on the Graf Zeppelin, Hiram.

HIRAM. Well it was something that moved and I was there to see her off! Now I remember. Of course! It was the *Andrea Doria*.

DOLLY. Did she go down with it?

HIRAM. Cornelia Margaret Spane, my mother, never went down with or on anything. I don't believe we've been introduced. Bitch.

DR. PEPPER. This is Mrs. Scupp, Hiram.

HIRAM. I don't care who she is.

DR. PEPPER. Harry's wife.

HIRAM. Well why didn't you say so? How do you do, Mrs. Scupp? I'm sorry, you're not a bitch. And I'm only a bitch when I've got a head on me like this one. I thought I mixed a wicked vodka stinger! What did your husband do? Study alchemy?

DOLLY. Harry? Drinking? My Harry? Harry Scupp?

HIRAM. I understand the A.A. has a warrant out for his arrest.

DOLLY. I don't think we're talking about the same man.

HIRAM. The way I feel this morning we're probably not.

DR. PEPPER. Why don't you take that dip now, Hiram?

HIRAM. Good idea, Jason. With my luck, maybe I'll drown. You like to swim, Mrs. Scupp?

DOLLY. I love to, but . . . (*She indicates her injured foot.*)

HIRAM. Come on, I believe in the buddy system: you start to drown, I'll save you. I start to drown, forget it.

DOLLY. I didn't bring a suit.

HIRAM. That never stopped anyone around this place. What do you think I've got on under here?

DOLLY. I blush to think.

HIRAM. You blush to think? I've got to live with it! If that god-damn snapping turtle doesn't attack me again, Doctor, you can tell Otto I'll be joining you here shortly for my Bullshot. (*He goes down the aisle.*)

DR. PEPPER. Hiram Spane of the Newport Spanes. They own every-thing. (*Francis Tear enters. He is wearing a bathing cap, a bath-robe and rubber bathing shoes. He pours himself a glass of orange juice.*)

DOLLY. (*Still staring down the aisle.*) Is he a patient here?

DR. PEPPER. Hiram's been a patient here since I founded Ravens-wood.

DOLLY. What's his problem?

DR. PEPPER. You're looking at him.

DOLLY. (*Finally seeing Francis.*) Oh my God!

DR. PEPPER. Francis Tear of the Baltimore Tears. They made their fortune in plumbing. Good morning, Francis! You just missed each other.

FRANCIS. We're not speaking today.

DR. PEPPER. You and I?

FRANCIS. Hiram and me. He said something very cutting to me last night. Hurt me to the quick, he did. I don't think I'm ready to forgive him yet.

DR. PEPPER. Fine, fine, there's no point in rushing it.

FRANCIS. (*To Dolly.*) Do you think I look like an embryo, madam?

DOLLY. Not at all.

FRANCIS. Thank you.

DR. PEPPER. This is Mrs. Scupp, Francis.

FRANCIS. Hello.

DR. PEPPER. Harry Scupp's wife.

FRANCIS. Well I didn't think it was his mother. I'm Francis Tear of the Baltimore Tears. We made our fortune in plumbing!

DOLLY. Yes, I know.

FRANCIS. Somebody had to do it.

DOLLY. I suppose so.

FRANCIS. What are you in?

DOLLY. I'm just a housewife.

FRANCIS. So's Hiram! He's also in distress. Psychic distress, Doctor!

DR. PEPPER. Not now, Francis, please. I like your new bathing slippers.

FRANCIS. Do you? Hiram's mother had them sent. Hiram's mother has everything sent.

DOLLY. How nice for you.

FRANCIS. You never met Hiram's mother. You don't think I look silly in these, Jason?

DR. PEPPER. Not at all. There may be fairies at the bottom of somebody's garden but there are very sharp rocks at the bottom of my lake.

FRANCIS. Do you, Mrs. Scupp?

DOLLY. They go with the cap.

FRANCIS. That's what I was hoping. I think it's important to look your best at all times. You never know. It must be Jewish, Scupp.

DOLLY. I was telling Jason, we don't know what it is.

FRANCIS. It's Jewish. It was a pleasure, Mrs. Scupp. (*He turns to go.*)

DOLLY. Likewise, Mr. Tear.

FRANCIS. Call me Francis. Everyone else does. Except Hiram. You should hear some of the things he calls me. (*Exiting down the aisle.*) Oh, no, Hiram! I get the raft today! You had it yesterday! And this doesn't mean I'm speaking to you yet! (*He is gone.*)

DR. PEPPER. Eighteen years they've been together.

DOLLY. Are they . . . ?

DR. PEPPER. I don't think so, but if they are, I'd like to be a fly on that wall. No, I think they're just old, old friends.

DOLLY. I didn't know you treated male couples at Ravenswood.

DR. PEPPER. A male couple is better than no couple at all. Love is where you find it.

DOLLY. That's true.

DR. PEPPER. Don't be blind, it's all around you, everywhere. (*Otto returns with the martini and glass of water.*)

DOLLY. Thank you.

DR. PEPPER. *Danke*, Otto.

OTTO. Ze Fraulein would like a rubdown, maybe?

DOLLY. I don't think so.

OTTO. (*Shrugging.*) Okay. (*He takes an* Opera News *off of the towel cart, opens it, sits and reads.*)

DR. PEPPER. Cheers! You were saying?

DOLLY. Doctor . . . (*She fidgets.*)

DR. PEPPER. Don't mind Otto. It would take a lot more than your lawnmower to get his nose out of that magazine.

DOLLY. Why did Harry try to kill me?

DR. PEPPER. Do you still want to talk turkey, Mrs. Scupp?

DOLLY. About Harry? Of course I do.

DR. PEPPER. About you.

DOLLY. What is that supposed to mean?

DR. PEPPER. Does Labor Day weekend, 1963, the parking lot outside Benny's Clam Box in Rockport, Maine, do anything for you?

DOLLY. I don't know. Should it?

DR. PEPPER. Think hard.

DOLLY. Benny's Clam Box.

DR. PEPPER. Harry was packing up the trunk of the car and you put the car into reverse.

DOLLY. Oh, that! How did you know?

DR. PEPPER. We have very complete files on our guests here, Mrs.

SCUPP. Ravenswood is a far cry from the Westchester County Medical Center and your quack G.P. with his Korean war bride and poodle!

DOLLY. Dachshund!

DR. PEPPER. Sorry!

DOLLY. Leave it to Harry to tell you about a silly accident like that.

DR. PEPPER. He was in traction for two months.

DOLLY. I didn't see him back there. What are you driving at, Doctor?

DR. PEPPER. Eight months later you tried to run him over with a golf cart at the Westchester Country Club.

DOLLY. It was an accident. My foot got stuck on the accelerator.

DR. PEPPER. Nobody drives a golf cart on the putting green.

DOLLY. I do! I did. I still do.

DR. PEPPER. That time he was in traction for three months.

DOLLY. You're making mountains out of mole hills, Doctor. My foot got stuck. I had new golf shoes. What's your point?

DR. PEPPER. A year later he asked you if there was water in the swimming pool before diving in.

DOLLY. I thought he asked me should he wash our Puli.

DR. PEPPER. Your Puli didn't end up in White Plains Hospital with a broken leg. Let's talk about the incident at the archery tournament.

DOLLY. Let's not.

DR. PEPPER. It's quite a story.

DOLLY. *His* version.

DR. PEPPER. I'd love to hear yours.

DOLLY. I didn't tell him to change the target when he did.

DR. PEPPER. How about his forced high dive in Acapulco?

DOLLY. He *fell*.

DR. PEPPER. Nearly six hundred feet.

DOLLY. I didn't push him.

DR. PEPPER. And what about your safari to East Africa last winter?

DOLLY. He didn't tell you about that, too?

DR. PEPPER. Harry's just lucky he's not the one who's stuffed and mounted over your fireplace, Mrs. Scupp.

DOLLY. I was delirious. A touch of malaria, I remember. I mistook him for something else.

DR. PEPPER. An albino orangutan? No, you didn't.

DOLLY. I don't want to hear these things!

DR. PEPPER. You said you wanted to talk turkey, Mrs. Scupp. All right, here's the real turkey: you and your husband have been trying to kill one another since Labor Day weekend, 1963. Why? (*A pause.*)

DOLLY. Has he been neat, Doctor?

DR. PEPPER. Neat?

DOLLY. Neat.

DR. PEPPER. Oh, neat! A little overfastidious when he got here, perhaps . . .

DOLLY. I'm talking about coasters, Doctor.

DR. PEPPER. Coasters?

DOLLY. Those things you put under glasses so they don't leave a ring.

DR. PEPPER. I can't stand them.

DOLLY. Neither can I.

DR. PEPPER. Always sticking to the bottom of your glass and then dropping off.

DOLLY. I loathe coasters.

DR. PEPPER. I loathe people who shove them at you.

DOLLY. Then you loathe Harry.

DR. PEPPER. I don't follow.

DOLLY. Harry is the king of coasters. He adores coasters. He lives coasters. He *is* coasters. He's even tried to crochet coasters. Doctor, he can be upstairs sound asleep and I can be downstairs in the den watching television late at night and he'll come in with a coaster for my glass. He wakes up at three a.m. worrying I'm making rings.

DR. PEPPER. I don't know how you put up with it.

DOLLY. I haven't! Doctor, he goes into my closet and straightens my shoes.

DR. PEPPER. Usually they wear them.

DOLLY. I wish he would. I wish he *would* put them on. Maybe he'd break a leg. But no, he just straightens them. I bet you put your toilet paper on wrong, too.

DR. PEPPER. I beg your pardon?

DOLLY. Did you know you could put a roll of toilet paper on the dispenser wrong? I didn't 'til I married Harry. "Dolly! How many times do I have to tell you? The paper should roll *under* from the inside out, not *over* from the outside down."

DR. PEPPER. Over from the? . . .

DOLLY. I try, but I can't remember.

DR. PEPPER. Under from the? . . .

DOLLY. He won't let me have down pillows in the house. They crush, he says. We're into total foam rubber. I hate foam rubber.

DR. PEPPER. I'm allergic to it.

DOLLY. I'm up to my ass in it. Doctor, this is a man who goes around straightening license plates in a public parking lot.

DR. PEPPER. Now honestly, Mrs. Scupp . . .

DOLLY. If they're dirty, he wipes them!

DR. PEPPER. What about in bed?

DOLLY. In bed?

DR. PEPPER. I mean, what's he like in bed?

DOLLY. I don't remember.

DR. PEPPER. Surely, Mrs. Scupp . . .

DOLLY. I never noticed.

DR. PEPPER. Never?

DOLLY. Our wedding night was terrific. From then on, it's been downhill all the way. His hobby is tropical fish. I hate tropical fish, Doctor.

DR. PEPPER. You hate tropical fish?

DOLLY. Not all tropical fish. Harry's tropical fish. There's something about them. Maybe it's the fact he talks to them. Or the names he gives them. Eric, Tony, Pinky. There's one round, mean-looking one he calls Dolly. When they die he buries them in the backyard. We're the only house in Larchmont with a tropical fish cemetery in the backyard. I know this sounds crazy, Doctor, but I hate those fish. I resent them in my living room and I resent them under my lawn. I'm a mature, sensible and, I think, rather intelligent woman and I hate those fish. How do you hate a tropical fish? (*She stands.*) You know something else I hate? Stereo equipment. Harry's got woofers, weefers, tweeters, baffles, pre-amps. He puts gloves on when he plays those records. White gloves like your friend. (*She indicates Otto.*) Don't get me started, Doctor. There's so many things about Harry I hate. I hate his black Volvo station wagon with the snow tires on in

August. He worries about early winters. He worries about everything. We're the only people in Larchmont with drought insur-
ance. (*She is pacing.*) I know it's none of my business, but I hate
the way he dresses. I hate his big, baggy boxer shorts. The only
shoes he'll wear are those big clumpy cordovans. Even on the
beach. But my favorite outfit is his "Genius At Work" barbecue
apron he wears over the pink Bermuda shorts and black, knee-
high Supp-Hose. Oh, I'm married to a snappy dresser, Doctor!
And try taking a trip with him. He reads road signs. Every road
sign. Out loud. "Soft shoulders, Dolly." "Slippery when wet,
Dolly." "Deer crossing, Dolly." "Kiwanis Club meeting at noon,
Wednesday, Dolly." Who gives a good goddamn? He's not
even a member of the Kiwanis Club! Who'd want him? A man
who puts on an apron after a bridge party and vacuums up isn't
exactly a load of laughs. Neither is a man who takes you to Ari-
zona for your anniversary. You know what's in Arizona? The
London Bridge! Don't get me wrong, Doctor. I love my husband.
I just can't stand him. So don't make too much out of that inci-
dent with the lawnmower. That was just the straw that broke the
camel's back!
DR. PEPPER. And a very attractive camel she is, too.
DOLLY. Thank you.
OTTO. (*Looking up from his magazine.*) Rubdown, Frau Scupp?
DR. PEPPER. *Nichts!* (*Turning to Dolly, as Otto resumes reading.*)
Listen to me, Mrs. Scupp. I'm not famous for saving marriages.
I'm not even certain I believe in them. I'm famous for successful
marriages for people who want to be married. I think I can help
you but you have to want me to help you. (*Harry is heard call-
ing, "Otto! Otto!" offstage.*) Harry's coming. I've done all I can
for him. It's up to you, now.
DOLLY. I'm frightened.
DR. PEPPER. Given your track record, I think Harry is the one with
cause for alarm. (*Harry enters. He, too, is dressed for swimming.
He carries a small cardboard box.*)
HARRY. Otto! Otto! Good morning, Jason.
DOLLY. Hello, Harry.
HARRY. (*Embracing Dolly.*) Dolly . . . Doll. Doll! Doll, baby! Hey,
this is terrific!
DOLLY. Harry, you're crushing me!

HARRY. I could eat you alive! You didn't tell me she was coming up.

DR. PEPPER. I didn't know.

HARRY. What a great surprise!

DOLLY. I'm beginning to wonder.

HARRY. What're you talking about? I've been up here so long even Fric and Frac down at the lake were starting to look good to me. So was Martin Borman over there. Good morning, Otto.

OTTO. *Gut morgen, Herr Scupp.* Ze usual?

HARRY. What time is it? It's early. I better stick with the Bloody Marys. Hot, Otto. Very, very hot. Lots of Tabasco and lots of the white stuff.

OTTO. *Jawohl, Herr Scupp.*

DOLLY. Harry!

HARRY. Otto makes a fantastic Bloody Mary. Takes the roof of your head off and leaves it there.

DR. PEPPER. Last call, Mrs. Scupp. (*Dolly shakes her head.*) *Bitte,* Otto . . . (*He holds up his martini glass. Otto nods and goes.*)

HARRY. You look wonderful. Doesn't she look wonderful, Jason?

DR. PEPPER. That's what I've been telling her.

DOLLY. I've lost a little weight.

HARRY. I can see that.

DOLLY. You haven't.

HARRY. It's that high-cholesterol diet they've got me on. You know, I never thought I'd get sick of Eggs Benedict and chocolate mousse!

DOLLY. You're meant to be on low-cholesterol.

HARRY. Talk to my doctor!

DR. PEPPER. Harry likes high-cholesterol. You'll excuse me for a few minutes, won't you? (*Dr. Pepper rolls offstage. Dolly composes herself.*)

HARRY. How are the kids?

DOLLY. Oh, Harry, they're just fine.

HARRY. Yeah?

DOLLY. Yeah . . . fine.

HARRY. That's great . . . that's just great.

DOLLY. I've got your *Hi-Fi Stereo Review*'s and *Popular Aquarium*'s in the car.

HARRY. Thank you.

DOLLY. And the summer pajamas you wrote for.

HARRY. The blue cottons?

DOLLY. I thought you meant the yellow drip-drys.

HARRY. That's okay.

DOLLY. I'm sorry.

HARRY. Really, it doesn't matter.

DOLLY. It's a pleasant drive up here.

HARRY. I hope you saw those warning signs on that bypass outside of Inglenook.

DOLLY. Oh, I did. I thought of you when I read them.

HARRY. An average of thirteen and a half people get killed there every year.

DOLLY. I'll be extra careful on the way back.

HARRY. When are you leaving?

DOLLY. I don't know. It depends. What's in the box?

HARRY. Oh . . . Henry.

DOLLY. Henry?

HARRY. My angel fish.

DOLLY. What happened?

HARRY. Evelyn killed him.

DOLLY. Who's Evelyn?

HARRY. My blue beta.

DOLLY. That's awful.

HARRY. It's just a fish. (*He throws the box over the wall of foliage.*)

DOLLY. You always used to give them such nice burials.

HARRY. I guess I'm getting cynical in my old age. So what's new?

DOLLY. Nothing much.

HARRY. I guess you sold the lawnmower.

DOLLY. No. It's in the garage waiting for you.

HARRY. Thanks.

DOLLY. It's broken, of course.

HARRY. I wasn't really trying to get you with it.

DOLLY. Yes, you were, Harry. Why?

HARRY. (*Exploding.*) There were a million reasons! It was hot. The refrigerator needed defrosting. The car keys were upstairs when they should have been downstairs. The house was still a mess from your bridge party. You forgot to renew my subscription to *High Fidelity* and they'd sent you three warnings already.

DOLLY. *Hi-Fi Stereo Review!*

HARRY. You knew how much I was looking forward to that comparative analysis of Dolby-ized cassette decks with ferric oxide heads! There was a new water ring on the telephone stand. Things like that.

DOLLY. Did I have the toilet paper on right?

HARRY. As a matter of fact, you did. What happened?

DOLLY. I don't know. I lost my head!

HARRY. Only someone had been playing my stereo. There were fingerprints on my Christmas album.

DOLLY. Who would be playing a Christmas album in June?

HARRY. I didn't say *when* they were put there, I just said I found them.

DOLLY. What were *you* doing playing a Christmas album in June?

HARRY. I wasn't. I just happened to be doing my six-month record cleaning that day. They weren't your fingerprints.

DOLLY. Thank you.

HARRY. They weren't the kids', either.

DOLLY. Well, at least I had the toilet paper on right.

HARRY. I conceded that point.

DOLLY. Well?

HARRY. It was blue!

DOLLY. That's all they had!

HARRY. It was blue! Our bathroom is red! Everything is red! The sink, the tub, the tile, the towels, the shower curtain! You know I don't like a clash. I like everything to match!

DOLLY. That's all they had!

HARRY. You asked me why. I'm telling you why. There were permanent press sheets on the bed.

DOLLY. Cotton's scarce.

HARRY. I can't sleep on permanent press. They're too hot. They're like flame sheets. Things like that. Like I said, it was hot. There were a million reasons. Then, when I saw you staked out on the lawn in your bathing suit, I just kind of lost control with the mower. What was it with me?

DOLLY. The coasters.

HARRY. Even that time in Acapulco?

DOLLY. It was always the coasters.

HARRY. I wasn't going to mention it, but . . . (*He motions to Dolly's glass. She picks it up from the table.*)

DOLLY. I'm sorry.

HARRY. It's okay! (*He takes the glass from her and puts it on the table without a coaster.*)

DOLLY. Dr. Pepper seems to think you're ready to go home.

HARRY. (*He takes out a cigarette.*) He's done wonders for me, Doll.

DOLLY. When did you take that up?

HARRY. A couple of months ago. You want one?

DOLLY. No, thank you.

HARRY. They're fertilized with chicken shit, honey.

DOLLY. I know. (*Otto has returned with the Bloody Mary.*)

HARRY. Thanks, Otto.

OTTO. Rubdown, Herr Scupp?

HARRY. Not just now, Otto. Maybe later, hunh?

OTTO. *Jawohl.* (*Otto exits.*)

DOLLY. You look terrible, Harry.

HARRY. I'm a little hungover.

DOLLY. From what?

HARRY. Margaritas. They're vicious, Dolly. Stay away from them.

DOLLY. What were you doing drinking margaritas?

HARRY. The Plungs.

DOLLY. Who?

HARRY. The Plungs.

DOLLY. What are the Plungs?

HARRY. Jeanine and Billy Plung. This young couple from Roanoke I got friendly with while they were up here. We had a little farewell party for them last night. Jeanine had me dancing the rhumba with her until nearly three.

DOLLY. You can't rhumba, Harry. You can't even foxtrot.

HARRY. Jeanine says I'm a natural.

DOLLY. I thought they were taking care of you up here.

HARRY. They are. I never felt better in my life.

DOLLY. Why would you start smoking at your age?

HARRY. I like to smoke.

DOLLY. That's not a good enough reason.

HARRY. I can't think of a better one.

DOLLY. Margaritas! And the rhumba, Harry! How old was this woman?

HARRY. Twenty-two, twenty-three.

DOLLY. Harry, what's gotten into you?

HARRY. I'm my old self again! It's me, Harry Scupp with the DeSoto roadster with the rumble seat and the good hooch and let's have a good time and "Beat Port Chester, Larchmont!" and Glen Island Casino and Dolly Veasey is my number one date. It's gonna be like the old times again, Doll.

DOLLY. We never had old times like that.

HARRY. It's never too late.

DOLLY. And what do you mean, "your old self"?

HARRY. I love you. I don't want to kill you anymore.

DOLLY. You never had a DeSoto roadster. We took the bus.

HARRY. I'm talking about life, Dolly. *Joie de vivre*. You want to see what I've been doing since I've been up here? Close your eyes. (*Dolly won't.*) I'm not going to hit you. Go over there and close your eyes. (*Dolly won't.*) I want to show you something. It's a surprise. (*She is still doubtful.*) Well, close your eyes! (*Dolly closes her eyes, and immediately extends her hand in front of her as a feeler. Harry takes something off the towel cart.*) It's incredible you should be here today. I just finished this last night. Okay, Doll, open.

DOLLY. What is it?

HARRY. An ashtray.

DOLLY. An ashtray?

HARRY. Isn't it pretty? I mean, did you know I had a sensitivity like that all bottled up inside me? I didn't.

DOLLY. You're sure it's an ashtray?

HARRY. It's a nude study of Jeanine.

DOLLY. Jeanine Plung?

HARRY. Isn't that pretty?

DOLLY. She's naked!

HARRY. Well, how else do you sculpt a nude? I did one of Billy Plung I'm thinking of turning into a lamp.

DOLLY. What you're suggesting, Harry, is that you were somewhat more than just friendly with these people.

HARRY. Oh, I was! You'd go crazy over them and vice-versa.

DOLLY. I wouldn't count on it.

HARRY. Now wait right there. There's something else I want to show you. Don't move. (*He runs off.*)

DOLLY. Doctor!

DR. PEPPER. (*Emerging, with Otto following.*) What do you think of the change?

DOLLY. What have you done to him?

DR. PEPPER. He's called you "honey" several times at least.

DOLLY. "They're loaded with chicken shit, honey," is what he said. You mean Harry and these Plung people . . . ?

DR. PEPPER. Just Mrs. Plung.

DOLLY. Where was Mr. Plung while all this was going on?

DR. PEPPER. Rumor has it with Otto.

DOLLY. I wouldn't be surprised. And you just allowed all this to happen?

DR. PEPPER. There are no rules at Ravenswood, Mrs. Scupp.

DOLLY. Which means that you let my husband go off into the woods with that horrid Plung woman!

DR. PEPPER. How did you know she was horrid? That's one secret I thought I'd kept to myself. She's a dreadful woman. I don't know what your husband ever saw in her. He would've been better off with Otto.

DOLLY. I'm beginning to think you made my husband do all these horrible things.

DR. PEPPER. I've never made anyone do anything, Mrs. Scupp. That's the secret of my success here, such as it is. I allow everyone to do exactly as he pleases.

DOLLY. At your prices I'd hardly call that a bargain.

DR. PEPPER. You'd be surprised how few people know what it is they want.

DOLLY. I know what I want.

DR. PEPPER. Do you, Mrs. Scupp?

DOLLY. I thought I did until I saw Harry like this.

HARRY. (*From offstage.*) I'll bet you didn't know I was a frustrated song-and-dance man, did you, Doll? (*Harry rushes back in. He has a ukelele and a tap board.*) Now you're really gonna get a kick out of this. You know how I always overdo things? That's because of my masculine insecurity coming out. I didn't even know I had masculine insecurity until Jason here got his hands on me. It turns out I've got a singing voice. And feet, too. Dolly, I got rhythm! Sit down. I want you to see this. (*Harry hands Dr. Pepper the uke. Otto produces a small foot-pedal drum and a set of cymbals from behind the towel cart. They launch into a*

lively, twenties-type popular song. It's obvious Harry's been prac-
ticing. He's still pretty terrible, but he's having fun. He tap
dances, too, and ends with a big finish.)

DOLLY. Stop it! I can't stand seeing you like this.

HARRY. You can't stand seeing me like what?

DOLLY. Singing, dancing, smoking, drinking! Making ashtrays!

HARRY. I told you it was a new me. Wait'll they see this down at
the country club! (*He launches back into the song. This time,
his big finish is even bigger than before. Finally Dolly hurls the
ashtray across the stage, smashing it.*) You broke my ashtray.

DOLLY. I'm taking you home.

HARRY. You broke my ashtray.

DOLLY. I thought you came here to get better.

HARRY. You broke my ashtray! (*He is advancing on her. Dolly is
trying to get something out of her purse.*)

DR. PEPPER. Harry!

DOLLY. (*Producing an aerosol can and pointing it at Harry.*) Harry!
(*Hiram and Francis are heard calling to Harry from the lake-
side. "Harry! Harry!"*)

HARRY. I promised Hiram and Francis I'd race them out to the
raft. They're like kids that way . . . they'll keep it up all morning
until I do. (*He runs down the aisle. Dolly is trembling.*)

DR. PEPPER. What is that?

DOLLY. Mace!

DR. PEPPER. It's too bad my wife didn't carry one of those. Too bad
for me, that is.

DOLLY. You said he was better!

DR. PEPPER. You still don't see the change?

DOLLY. Not the change I wanted!

DR. PEPPER. Harry loved that piece of sculpture.

DOLLY. What have you done to him?

DR. PEPPER. No, Harry's done it to himself. Maybe it's your turn
now.

DOLLY. Maybe it isn't!

DR. PEPPER. Know what you want, Mrs. Scupp. That's the first step.

DOLLY. I want a good marriage.

DR. PEPPER. Then give me three months.

DOLLY. And I want to be happy.

DR. PEPPER. Make it three and a half.

DOLLY. That's not much, is it?

DR. PEPPER. Sometimes it's everything. Now: it's a beautiful summer's day, God's in his heaven and all's right with the world. Harry will be waiting for you down by the lake. I'd go to him if I were you.

DOLLY. I'm still a little frightened to be with him. With my foot like this, I can't go swimming. Maybe I could ask him to take me boating.

DR. PEPPER. I wouldn't push my luck. Try skimming stones, Mrs. Scupp.

DOLLY. It's Dolly. Please. Call me Dolly?

DR. PEPPER. Okay, Dolly.

DOLLY. It always happens.

DR. PEPPER. I know what you're going to say.

DOLLY. I always get a crush on doctors! (*Dolly exits down the aisle. Dr. Pepper sits sipping his martini and smoking. Otto starts his tape machine. We hear* "Wein, Du Stadt Meiner Traume." *Otto picks up Harry's tap board, takes it to the towel table, and begins clearing the breakfast things.*)

DR. PEPPER. That's not at all what I thought she was going to say.

OTTO. Crush? *Was ist* crush?

DR. PEPPER. Mrs. Scupp thinks she likes me.

OTTO. Everyone likes Herr Doktor.

DR. PEPPER. That's because everyone thinks Herr Doktor likes them. You're playing your favorite song again, Otto.

OTTO. *Ja.* My mother used to sing this song.

DR. PEPPER. It's a beauty.

OTTO. My mother was a pig. Herr Doktor would like something?

DR. PEPPER. Herr Doktor just wants everyone to be happy. (*Just then a tennis ball bounces on stage. Roy and April Pitt, dressed for tennis and carrying their racquets, appear briefly down the aisle.*)

ROY. Hey, Mac, you want to send that back?

APRIL. What's the matter with you? Throw the ball back, you creep!

DR. PEPPER. Otto. (*He points to the ball. Otto returns the ball to Roy.*)

APRIL. Thanks a lot.

ROY. Yeah, thanks loads. (*They disappear up the aisle.*)

DR. PEPPER. *Das ists ze* newlyweds Pitt?

OTTO. *Ja.*

DR. PEPPER. (*Holding out his empty glass.*) *Bitte,* Otto. (*Hiram and Francis are returning down the aisle. We hear Francis yelling, "We beat you!"*) Better make that three. Make that *drei* cocktails, Otto.

OTTO. *Jawohl.* (*He goes.*)

DR. PEPPER. Who won?

FRANCIS. (*Singing, skipping almost.*) Harry and me! Harry and me! Harry and me!

HIRAM. They ganged up on me as usual.

FRANCIS. We beat you! We beat you! Da da da we beat you!

HIRAM. Well, Harry beat you.

FRANCIS. And we both beat you!

HIRAM. I was worried about that turtle.

FRANCIS. Even with these on, I beat him. (*Indeed, water is sloshing out of his rubber bathing slippers.*) I beat you! I beat you!

HIRAM. I am going to beat you black and blue if you keep that up, Francis!

DR. PEPPER. Boys, boys!

FRANCIS. I'm still not speaking to you!

HIRAM. That's a blessing!

FRANCIS. But . . . (*Very softly.*) I beat you! I beat you!

DR. PEPPER. Hiram, did you tell Francis he looked like an embryo?

HIRAM. If I'd seen him in that bathing cap, I'd've said he looked like a prophylactic.

FRANCIS. Hiram is a poor sport! Hiram is a poor sport!

HIRAM. If there's anything more vulgar than swimming, it's a swimming race.

FRANCIS. It was his idea.

HIRAM. Does that sound like me, Jason?

FRANCIS. It was, too!

HIRAM. You see what I have to put up with?

FRANCIS. Last night after dinner you said, "Let's challenge Harry Scupp to a swimming race tomorrow."

HIRAM. Are you sure you can't do anything for him, Doctor?

FRANCIS. You did, you did!

HIRAM. I'd suggest a lobotomy but obviously he's already had one.

FRANCIS. I cross my heart, he did!

HIRAM. Several, from the look of it!

FRANCIS. (*Getting quite hysterical.*) He lies, Doctor, he lies! He did suggest a swimming race after dinner with Harry Scupp last night! He did! He did!

DR. PEPPER. Don't hold it back, Francis.

FRANCIS. (*A real tantrum now: feet and fists pounding the ground.*) Tell him! Tell him it was your idea, Hiram! Tell him, tell him, tell him, tell him, tell him, tell him, tell him, tell him! (*He is exhausting himself as Hiram interrupts.*)

HIRAM. All right! So it *was* my idea. I don't like to lose. It's the Spane in me. A Baltimore Tear wouldn't understand that. (*Genuinely.*) Oh I'm sorry, Francis. (*Francis sulks.*) Now get up. You know I can't stand to see you grovel like that.

FRANCIS. I'm not grovelling, Hiram. I'm letting it all out for once. Right, Doctor?

DR. PEPPER. Just keep going. I think we might be getting somewhere.

FRANCIS. He always wants to compete with me. I can't help it if I always win. I don't even want to win. I just do. Backgammon, bridge, whist, Chinese checkers, Mah-jongg . . .

HIRAM. You never beat me at Mah-jongg.

FRANCIS. Yes, I did. That time in Morocco.

HIRAM. I don't count that.

FRANCIS. Why not?

HIRAM. I had dysentery.

FRANCIS. So did I!

HIRAM. I said I was sorry!

FRANCIS. I always win! At anything! Anagrams, Parcheesi, Scrabble, tennis . . .

HIRAM. That's table tennis, Francis!

FRANCIS. Well I win, don't I? Like I always do? I can't lose to him at anything! And he hates me for it! Oh he just hates me to death!

HIRAM. While you're down there crowing, Francis, why don't you tell the doctor the *real* story?

FRANCIS. What real story?

HIRAM. What real story!

FRANCIS. I don't know what you're talking about!

HIRAM. Why don't you tell him about Celine? (*A short pause.*) I didn't think so.

DR. PEPPER. Who is Celine?

HIRAM. A Welsh Corgi we had when we lived on 69th Street.

DR. PEPPER. It's a lovely little dog.

HIRAM. Francis killed her.

FRANCIS. It was an accident.

HIRAM. He threw her out of the window.

FRANCIS. I didn't throw her out the window. She jumped.

HIRAM. Of course she did!

FRANCIS. You weren't there. She jumped out!

HIRAM. Celine hadn't jumped *anywhere* since Mummy's car backed over her in New Hope three years before! You threw that dog!

FRANCIS. She'd been trying catch this big fly in her mouth when suddenly she just sailed out the window right after it.

HIRAM. Do you really expect Dr. Pepper to believe that cock and bull story?

FRANCIS. It's true. It's true!

DR. PEPPER. What floor were you on?

FRANCIS. The fourteenth.

HIRAM. The fatal fourteenth.

FRANCIS. I didn't throw her.

HIRAM. Well who left that window open?

FRANCIS. You couldn't breathe that night.

HIRAM. And you were thinking of yourself first, as usual!

DR. PEPPER. No air-conditioning?

FRANCIS. This was years ago.

HIRAM. When dog-killers could still get away with something as simple as an open window. God knows what he'd come up with today.

DR. PEPPER. What a ghastly story.

HIRAM. Most crimes of passion are. Francis was jealous of her. Celine adored me, couldn't stand him. She used to pee in his closet out of spite. So he killed her.

FRANCIS. If you say that again I'm going to smack your face for you.

HIRAM. Say what? You dog murderer! (*Francis flies at him.*)

FRANCIS. I am not a dog murderer! You take that back!

DR. PEPPER. Don't hold it back. (*They struggle. They do minor violence to each other.*)

FRANCIS. Take it back! Take it back, take it back, take it back, take it back, take it back . . . (*Dr. Pepper, watching from the sidelines, offers encouragement during the encounter.*)

DR. PEPPER. That's right, boys, let it out. Let it out. No holding back, now. That's right, that's right. Just let everything out now. (*During the struggle Otto returns with the drinks. He looks to Dr. Pepper, who motions him to let the combatants be. Otto shrugs, sits down with his magazine. Finally, Hiram overwhelms Francis and, pinning him down, lightly slaps his face and arm.*)

HIRAM. Have you lost your mind? Don't you ever lift a hand to me again as long as you live, do you hear me? Ever! Ever, ever, ever, ever, ever. (*One last little slap.*) Ever. (*Hiram and Francis collapse with exhaustion.*)

DR. PEPPER. All right now?

FRANCIS. I don't think Ravenswood is working out for us.

HIRAM. Of course Ravenswood isn't working out for us! Why should it?

DR. PEPPER. Did you ever think of getting another dog?

HIRAM. No more dogs. Celine was a terrible shedder.

FRANCIS. Another one would probably just pee in my closet, too.

HIRAM. Or maybe mine next time.

FRANCIS. No more dogs, Hiram? Promise?

HIRAM. The only reason we stay together is because no one else in the world would put up with us.

DR. PEPPER. If you can leave here having realized that much, I'll be satisfied.

HIRAM. *You'll* be satisfied?

DR. PEPPER. And so should you.

HIRAM. We are, I suppose. We are.

FRANCIS. You're the only real friend I've ever had, Hiram.

HIRAM. And I'm sure Dr. Pepper can see why. Help me up, will you? I think I twisted something. (*Francis struggles to his feet, then helps Hiram up.*)

FRANCIS. Are we dressing for lunch?

HIRAM. I don't know about the end of the Baltimore Tear line but the last remaining Newport Spane is. Otto, where's my Bullshot? (*As they move toward the drinks, another tennis ball bounds across the stage. Roy and April are heard yelling from the back of the house.*)

ROY. (*Offstage.*) Ball!

APRIL. (*Offstage.*) Ball!

ROY. *Ball!*

APRIL. *Ball!*

HIRAM. Who are those dreadful people?

DR. PEPPER. The Pitts.

FRANCIS. Pitts? What kind of name is Pitts?

HIRAM. Appropriate! (*He gulps his Bullshot.*)

APRIL. Hey, you, Mac, you wanna throw that ball back for Christ's sake?

HIRAM. (*Speaking straight out in the direction of April's voice.*) My name is not Mac, I'm not your ball boy, and why don't you try fucking yourself, madam! Come on, Francis. (*They exit. Dr. Pepper is alone with the tennis ball.*)

ROY. (*Running down the aisle.*) Hey, you can't talk to my wife like that! (*To April, who is following him.*) Will you please go back there? We'll lose our place on the court.

APRIL. I'll get the court back! I want to see you handle something for once!

ROY. (*Leaping on stage.*) I told you: I'm gonna flatten that S.O.B.! Keep the court! (*April and Roy, still carrying their racquets, search around the stage.*) Where'd he go?

DR. PEPPER. Good morning.

ROY. We saw you talking to him!! Now where is he?

DR. PEPPER. Who?

ROY. That guy who insulted my wife!

DR. PEPPER. Your wife?

APRIL. What do I look like? His dog?

DR. PEPPER. You must be Mr. and Mrs. Pitt.

ROY. Yeah, as a matter of fact, we *are.*

APRIL. And they got some nice class of people up at this place!

ROY. (*Cautioning her.*) Honey! I think we've been recognized.

DR. PEPPER. I'm afraid so.

ROY. Celebrity-time!

APRIL. Oh, Christ!

ROY. (*Taking off his sunglasses and shaking Dr. Pepper's hand.*) Hi, Roy Pitt. Nice to see you. We were hoping to be a little incognito up here! It's just as well. I think actors who wear big sunglasses are big phonies. This is my wife, April James.

APRIL. Hi, April James. Nice to see you.

DR. PEPPER. April James?

APRIL. It's my professional name.

ROY. You see that, honey? Even with these things on he recognized us.

DR. PEPPER. And what do *you* do, Mrs. Pitt?

APRIL. What do you mean, "What do I do?" I'm an actress. Thanks a lot, buddy.

ROY. She's an actress.

APRIL. I don't even know you but I really needed that little ego boost.

ROY. Honey, of course he recognized me. My movie was on the Late Show last night. *Cold Fingers.* He probably caught it.

APRIL. God knows you did.

ROY. It's the power of the medium! You know that kind of exposure.

APRIL. *Cold Fingers* should have *opened* on the Late Show.

ROY. Now don't start with me.

APRIL. Boy, I really needed that little zap.

ROY. He's a dummy.

APRIL. You must have seen me in something. How about *Journey Through Hell* for Christ's sake! You didn't see me in *Journey Through Hell?*

DR. PEPPER. Were you in that?

ROY. That was my beautiful April all right!

APRIL. You bet your sweet ass it was!

DR. PEPPER. That was a wonderful movie, Mrs. Pitt.

APRIL. You see that? Another zap?

ROY. April wasn't in the movie. She created the role off-Broadway . . . didn't get the film version!

APRIL. Boy, this is really my day!

ROY. She was brilliant in that part!

APRIL. I know. Too bad the play didn't support me.

DR. PEPPER. I enjoyed the film, too.

APRIL. I bet you did.

ROY. Hey. Try to cool it with her, will you?

APRIL. Try *Random Thoughts and Vaguer Notions,* why don't you?

ROY. That one was on Broadway. April was one of the stars.

DR. PEPPER. I wasn't able to catch it.

APRIL. It ran nearly eighty performances. You didn't exactly have to be a jackrabbit.

ROY. April!

APRIL. Before you zap me again, I didn't do the movie of that one, either.

ROY. You never read notices like she got for that one. Show 'em to him, honey.

APRIL. They're in the car. I break my balls trying to make that piece of garbage work and they sign some WASP starlet for the movie version thinking she's going to appeal to that goddamn Middle American drive-in audience.

ROY. I don't really think you can call Googie Gomez a WASP starlet.

APRIL. White bread! That's all she is, white bread!

ROY. (*Calling down the aisle.*) Hey, that court's taken, Buddy. We got it reserved.

APRIL. You heard him!

DR. PEPPER. I think that's the ground keeper.

ROY. That's okay, Mac! Sorry! Hang in there!

APRIL. Hi! April James! Nice to see you!

ROY. Hi! Roy Pitt! Nice to see you! Ssh! Sssh!

APRIL. What is it?

ROY. I thought I heard our phone.

APRIL. Way out here? What are you? The big ear?

ROY. You sure you told the service where I'd be?

APRIL. Of course I did. I might be getting a call, too, you know.

ROY. I'm expecting an important call from the coast. I'm not usually this tense.

APRIL. Hah!

ROY. This could be the big one, April.

APRIL. Almost anything would be bigger than *Cold Fingers*. (*Otto has appeared.*)

ROY. (*Starting to do push-ups.*) You got one hell of a thirsty star out here, waiter.

APRIL. Two thirsty stars.

OTTO. I am not a waiter. My name is Otto.

ROY. Hi, Otto. Roy Pitt, nice to see you.

APRIL. Hi, Otto. April James, nice to see you.

ROY. (*Now he is doing sit-ups.*) What are you having, honey?

APRIL. A screwdriver.

ROY. I'll have some Dom Perignon. The champagne.

APRIL. Roy!

ROY. It's included.

APRIL. Eighty-six the screwdriver. I'll have the same.

OTTO. The Fraulein would like a nice rubdown, maybe?

APRIL. From you?

ROY. Just bring the Dom Perignon, will you?

DR. PEPPER. Oh, and Otto! (*He holds up his glass.*)

OTTO. *Jawohl.* (*He goes.*)

APRIL. (*Sits, and looks at Dr. Pepper's wheelchair for the first time.*) I want to apologize for earlier when we yelled at you for the ball. We didn't realize you were . . . like that.

DR. PEPPER. Half the time I don't realize it myself.

APRIL. We do lots of benefits, you know.

ROY. April's been asked to do the Mental Health and Highway Safety Telethons two years straight.

APRIL. Easter Seals wanted me last month but they weren't paying expenses.

ROY. Nobody's blaming you, honey.

APRIL. I mean there's charity and then there's charity. I mean you gotta draw the line somewhere, right? What am I? Chopped liver?

ROY. Easter Seals wouldn't even send a limousine for her! Our agent told them they could take their telethon and shove it. (*Roy is opening up a sun reflector.*)

APRIL. What are you doing?

ROY. You don't mind if we don't play tennis for a while? I want to get some of the benefits.

APRIL. There's not enough sun for a tan.

ROY. That's what you think. It's a day like this you can really bake yourself. Just because the sky's grey doesn't mean those rays aren't coming through. Make love to me, *soleil*, make love to me.

APRIL. (*She is sitting near Dr. Pepper. Roy is sprawled out with his reflector under his chin. He just loves lying in the sun like this.*) What are you in for?

DR. PEPPER. The usual.

APRIL. A bad marriage, huh? That's too bad. You're probably wondering what we're doing here. I know on the surface it must look like we got a model marriage. But believe me, we got our little problems, too. Don't look so surprised. Roy's got an ego on him you could drive a Mack truck with. Show biz marriages ain't nothing to write home about. Half our friends are divorced and the other half are miserable. Naturally, they don't think we're going to make it. Think. They *hope*. But we're going to show them. Right, honey?

ROY. Right.

APRIL. Have you had a session with Dr. Pepper yet?

DR. PEPPER. Many. (*He picks up the book he took from Dolly and opens it.*)

APRIL. Is he all he's cracked up to be?

DR. PEPPER. I think so, but of course I'm prejudiced. (*He smiles at April and begins to read.*)

APRIL. He's gonna have his hands full with that one.

DR. PEPPER. (*Looking up.*) I'm sorry . . . ?

APRIL. Skip it. (*Dr. Pepper returns to his book. April silently mouths an obscenity at him and turns her attention to Roy.*)

ROY. Honey! You're blocking my sun.

APRIL. You're just gonna lie there like that?

ROY. Unh-hunh.

APRIL. So where's my reflector?

ROY. I told you to pack it if you wanted it.

APRIL. I want it.

ROY. You said you didn't want to get any darker.

APRIL. I'm starting to fade.

ROY. No, you're not.

APRIL. It's practically all gone. Look at you. You're twice as dark!

ROY. It's not a contest, honey.

APRIL. I mean what's the point of getting a tan if you don't maintain it? Roy!

ROY. (*For Dr. Pepper's benefit, but without looking up from the reflector.*) Do you believe this? I was with my agents all day and I'm supposed to be worried about a goddamn reflector!

APRIL. Just give me a couple of minutes with it.

ROY. It's the best sun time now.

APRIL. You know I've got that audition Wednesday.

ROY. No. N.O. (*April gives up, gets the tin of cocoa butter off the cart and begins applying it.*) April's up for another new musical.

They were interested in us both, actually, but I've got these film commitments.

APRIL. Tentative film commitments.

ROY. You're getting hostile, honey.

APRIL. What's hostile is you not packing my reflector.

ROY. I was busy with my agents. *You* are getting hostile.

APRIL. I've got a career, too, you know.

ROY. (*Sitting up, he drops the reflector and motions for quiet.*) Ssshh!

APRIL. (*Grabbing the reflector.*) Hello? Yes, we're checking on the availability of Roy Pitt for an Alpo commercial!

ROY. Shut up, April. (*He listens, disappointed.*) Shit. (*Then he sees April.*) Hold it. Stop it! (*He grabs the reflector and lies back.*)

APRIL. Roy!

ROY. After that? You've gotta be kidding! I wouldn't give you this reflector if you whistled "Swanee River" out of your ass.

APRIL. I can, too.

ROY. I know. I've heard you.

APRIL. Just lie there and turn into leather.

ROY. I will.

APRIL. There are other things in the world more important than your suntan, you know.

ROY. Like yours?

APRIL. For openers.

ROY. Like your career?

APRIL. Yes, as a matter of fact.

ROY. Will you stop competing with me, April? That's one of the reasons we came here. I can't help it if I'm hotter than you right now.

APRIL. That could change, Roy. Remember *Star Is Born*.

ROY. Well, until it does, love me for what I am: Roy Pitt, the man. But don't resent me for my career.

APRIL. I know, Roy.

ROY. I love you for what you are: April James, the best little actress in New York City.

APRIL. What do you mean, "best little actress"?

ROY. I'm trying to make a point, honey!

APRIL. As opposed to what? A dwarf?

ROY. If we're going to have a good marriage and, April, I want that more than anything . . . !

APRIL. More than you wanted the lead in *Lenny?*

ROY. I didn't want *Lenny.*

APRIL. He would've crawled through broken glass for that part!

ROY. I didn't want *Lenny.* Now goddamit, shut up!

APRIL. I can't talk to you when you get like that.

ROY. Get like what? You haven't laid off me since we got in the car.

APRIL. You know I'm upset.

ROY. We've all been fired from shows.

APRIL. Before they went into rehearsal? I'm thinking of slitting the *two* wrists this time, Roy!

ROY. Actually, Heather MacNamara isn't a bad choice for that part.

APRIL. She's the pits!

ROY. We're the Pitts! (*Breaking himself up, then* . . .) We liked her in *The Seagull.*

APRIL. You liked her in *The Seagull.* I'd like her in her coffin.

ROY. Obviously they're going ethnic with it.

APRIL. She isn't even ethnic. She's white bread. I'm ethnic. I want a hit, Roy. I need a hit. I'm going crazy for a hit. I mean, when's it my turn?

ROY. Honey, you're making a shadow.

APRIL. I'm sorry.

ROY. That's okay. Just stick with me, kid. We're headed straight for the top.

APRIL. Roy?

ROY. What, angel?

APRIL. Your toupe is slipping. (*Roy clutches at his hairpiece.*) Roy wears a piece.

ROY. It's no secret. I've never pretended. It's not like your nose job!

APRIL. Don't speak to me. Just lie there and turn into naugahyde like your mother!

ROY. Honey! I almost forgot. Your agent called! They're interviewing hostesses for Steak & Brew.

APRIL. Give him skin cancer, God, give him skin cancer, please!

DR. PEPPER. Excuse me, I know it's none of my business, but how long have you two been married?

APRIL. Three months.

ROY. And you were right the first time, it's none of your business.

APRIL. But we lived together a long time before we did.

ROY. Not long enough.

APRIL. Eight *centuries* it felt like!

ROY. Do you have to cry on the world's shoulder, April?

APRIL. I want us to work, Roy! I love you.

ROY. I know. I love you, too, April.

APRIL. You're the best.

ROY. *We're* the best.

APRIL. You really think this Pepper fellow can help us?

DR. PEPPER. I'm no miracle worker.

ROY. You?

DR. PEPPER. Hi, Jason Pepper. Nice to see you.

ROY. You're Dr. Pepper?

DR. PEPPER. Only to my worst enemies. Let's make it Jason, shall we?

APRIL. Oh Roy!

ROY. The least you could've done was told us!

APRIL. I'm so ashamed!

ROY. Talk about seeing people at their worst!

DR. PEPPER. I'm used to that.

ROY. Yeah, but you haven't heard the other side of the story.

DR. PEPPER. And I'm sure it's a good one, too.

APRIL. Roy, I could just die. (*Hiram and Francis enter. They wear striped blazers, ascots, and white summer flannels. They cross to the table and will begin playing cards.*)

HIRAM. You know what they say about white flannels, don't you, Jason? The devil's invention. Never out of the cleaners.

FRANCIS. I put mine on first, of course, and then he decided he was going to wear his!

HIRAM. Don't be ridiculous.

FRANCIS. We *look* ridiculous.

DR. PEPPER. I think you both look rather dashing.

HIRAM. Thank you, Jason.

FRANCIS. Monkey see, monkey do.

DR. PEPPER. This is Mr. and Mrs. Pitt.

ROY. And you owe my wife an apology.

HIRAM. I don't recall speaking to you, Mac.

ROY. Now, look, you . . .

APRIL. It doesn't matter.

ROY. To me it does. You're my wife!

APRIL. Not in front of . . . (*She motions toward Dr. Pepper.*) . . . please?

HIRAM. Hiram Spane of the Newport Spanes, Mrs. Pitt. I've got a foul temper and a vicious tongue. Someone yells "ball" at me and they start working overtime. And that's about as much of an apology as you're going to get out of me.

APRIL. Thank you.

HIRAM. This is Francis Tear of the Baltimore Tears.

APRIL. Hi. April James, nice to see you. This is my husband, Roy.

ROY. (*Pumping Francis's hand.*) Hi, Roy Pitt. Nice to see you.

FRANCIS. Do you like to swim?

HIRAM. Francis!

FRANCIS. I just asked!

ROY. (*Gesturing for silence.*) Ssshh! Sshh! Sshh!

HIRAM. I beg your pardon?

ROY. Shut up! (*He listens, hears something.*) There it is! (*He and April cross their fingers.*)

ROY AND APRIL. (*In unison.*) Baby, baby, baby! (*Roy runs off.*)

HIRAM. Is your husband mentally deranged, Mrs. Pitt?

APRIL. He's been expecting that call.

HIRAM. That wasn't my question.

APRIL. He's an actor. It might be a job. Normal people wouldn't understand. (*She sits.*) How long have you two been married?

FRANCIS. We're not married, Mrs. Pitt.

APRIL. Oh!

HIRAM. Oh?

APRIL. How nice.

FRANCIS. That's what you think.

APRIL. We have lots of friends like that in the city.

HIRAM. Like what?

APRIL. Like you two. We're both in show business. We have to, practically.

HIRAM. Well, we're not in show business, Mrs. Pitt, and we certainly don't have to have friends like you.

APRIL. Did I say something wrong?

HIRAM. And I'm sure you're just getting started. Excuse me. (*He turns back to his card game.*)

APRIL. I was just trying to make small talk. I got better things to do than yak it up with a couple of aunties, you know!

HIRAM. I don't think normal therapy is going to work with that woman, Jason. Why don't you try euthanasia?

APRIL. Look, mouth!

DR. PEPPER. Children, children! (*Harry appears down the aisle.*)

HARRY. Otto! Otto, pack my bags and put them in the car. Just leave something out for me to change into. It's the black Volvo station wagon, the one with snow tires. You can't miss it. And then how about a round for everyone?

OTTO. *Jawohl, Herr Scupp.* (*He goes.*)

HARRY. I'm leaving, Jason.

FRANCIS. Harry's leaving, Hiram!

HIRAM. I can see that, Francis.

DR. PEPPER. I haven't officially released you, Harry.

HARRY. I'll save you the trouble. I'm officially releasing myself. What were you planning on, Jason? Keeping me here 'til Doomsday?

DR. PEPPER. Where's Dolly?

HARRY. She's decided to stay. Try to help her, Jason.

DOLLY. (*Entering from the aisle.*) Harry! Harry!

DR. PEPPER. What happened down by the lake?

HARRY. What didn't happen, you mean.

DOLLY. It was like our honeymoon.

HARRY. Don't make it sound too dramatic, Dolly. We just decided that our marriage was better than no marriage at all. I do what I want and she does what she wants. It's called compromise, honey, and it's the secret of a good marriage. If I want to fool around with someone you're going to let me because that's what I want to do and you want what I want. And if you want to fool around you won't because I don't want you to and you don't want what I don't want.

DOLLY. That's called compromise?

HARRY. That's called marriage.

DR. PEPPER. That's called *your* marriage.

DOLLY. That's called divorce.

DR. PEPPER. Take it or leave it, Mrs. Scupp.

DOLLY. There's a choice? I think I'm doing the right thing, Jason.

HARRY. I think we're doing the right thing, Jason.

DOLLY. I hope so, Harry.

DR. PEPPER. Just so long as it makes you both happy. (*Dolly reaches for Harry's cigarette and takes a deep, satisfying drag.*) How is it?

DOLLY. Like honey. It's like someone just poured ten years of honey down my throat.

DR. PEPPER. This is Mrs. Pitt. She and her husband have just arrived. (*Roy, returning, steps right in.*)

ROY. Hi, Roy Pitt. Nice to see you. Hi, Roy Pitt. Nice to see you.

APRIL. Hi, April James. Nice to see you. (*To Roy.*) Did you get it?

ROY. It looks good but nothing definite.

APRIL. When would you leave?

ROY. We'll talk about it later. (*To Francis.*) Hi, Roy Pitt. Nice to see you.

DOLLY. Wait a minute! Wait a minute! The Retarded Children Telethon, right? That's her, honey! The girl we were so crazy about. You sang . . . "Do, do, do."

APRIL. That was for Leukemia, actually, the Leukemia Telethon.

DOLLY. Oh, we think you're just terrific. You're headed straight for the top. I hope your line of work keeps you busy, Mr. Pitt. You're in for a lot of lonely days and nights.

APRIL. Roy's an actor, too.

DOLLY. Are you, dear? (*She turns to Harry.*) You know something: I don't think we would've had so many problems if we'd had more in common.

APRIL. Dr. Pepper's really helped you, then?

DOLLY. Helped him. We'll see about me. (*Harry lets out a sudden, urgent scream.*)

DR. PEPPER. How was it?

HARRY. Fantastic.

DOLLY. Is he going to be doing that often?

DR. PEPPER. That depends on you.

DOLLY. If he pulls that in the middle of a board meeting he's going to be looking for a new job.

DR. PEPPER. You might try it yourself sometime.

DOLLY. Me? I'm as cool as a cucumber.

DR. PEPPER. What brought that one on, Harry?

HARRY. The truth?

DR. PEPPER. You're still at Ravenswood.

HARRY. I want to shtup Mrs. Pitt.

ROY. Hey!

HARRY. You see how her tennis outfit's all slit up the side? There's no tan line. You know how women who are tan all over drive me crazy, Jason.

ROY. What did you say?

APRIL. It's okay, Roy. He just said he *wanted* to shtup me. He didn't *do* it. (*Dolly lets out a sudden, urgent scream.*)

DR. PEPPER. How do you feel?

DOLLY. Hoarse.

HARRY. You'll get used to it. (*Otto has returned with a tray of champagne. He passes it around. Everyone takes one as Harry turns to Hiram and Francis.*) I'm really gonna miss you two guys, you know. Take good care of her for me, will you?

HIRAM. When you come back for her, God knows we'll still be here. I think we're probably permanent.

FRANCIS. We're just lucky Hiram's mother can afford it.

HIRAM. You're just lucky Hiram's mother can afford it.

FRANCIS. Goodbye, Harry. I'll miss you.

DOLLY. No! No farewell toasts. I propose a welcome toast to the new arrivals.

HARRY. You can't drink to yourself.

DOLLY. All right! Here's to new marriage and the Pitts.

HARRY. Here's to our old one, honey.

HIRAM. Here's to friendship.

FRANCIS. Here's to Hiram.

HIRAM. Why thank you, Francis.

ROY. Here's to April James.

FRANCIS. April who, Hiram?

HIRAM. Some little RKO starlet, obviously.

APRIL. Here's to Hollywood and Mr. and Mrs. Roy Pitt.

DOLLY. Doctor?

DR. PEPPER. Here's to . . . all of you.

OTTO. Here's to Ravenswood. (*They drink. Then Harry starts to sing "Auld Lang Syne" and they all join in. Much applauding, hugging, and laughing.*) Lunch ist served. (*They break apart and start making their exits.*)

HARRY. Goodbye, Jason. And thank you. She's all yours now.

DOLLY. I'll walk you to the car.

HARRY. (*To Roy.*) Hey! Now I know where I've seen you! *Lenny!* You were in *Lenny!*

ROY. (*With a sudden, urgent scream.*) LENNY!!

HARRY. What did I say?

APRIL. Nothing. It's all right. Goodbye.

DOLLY. Come on, Harry.

HARRY. So long, Jason. (*Dolly and Harry are gone.*)

APRIL. He's a dummy. What does he know? You're Roy Pitt, the best actor in the business.

ROY. What am I? Chopped liver? I'll probably get that movie but it doesn't go for three months. (*They start off down the aisle.*)

APRIL. Listen, I wasn't going to mention this, but since you brought it up: you think there's anything in it for me?

ROY. A terrific part. They want a name but I'll mention you for it first thing.

APRIL.. I'll test, but first-class, Roy. They're gonna have to fly me out there first-class. (*They are gone. There is more and more thunder. Dr. Pepper looks up at the sky.*)

FRANCIS. Hiram? (*He exits down the aisle.*)

HIRAM. Will somebody just look at these flannels? Soiled already! This time I'm sending your mother the bill. Old Bingo Money, that's all she is . . . (*He follows Francis off.*)

FRANCIS. (*From the aisle.*) Do you think Mrs. Scupp would like to play badminton after lunch?

HIRAM. If she did, she wouldn't want to play with you. (*Dr. Pepper watches everyone exit as Otto returns to wheel him in for lunch.*)

DR. PEPPER. *Lasse!*

OTTO. Herr Doktor does not want lunch today? (*Dr. Pepper shakes his head.*) Herr Doktor would like a martini? (*Dr. Pepper shakes his head.*) A little rubdown, maybe?

DR. PEPPER. Herr Doktor just wants everyone to be happy.

OTTO. Happy?

DR. PEPPER. *Du bist* happy, Otto?

OTTO. *Was ist* happy?

DR. PEPPER. A good question, Otto. (*Otto goes. Dr. Pepper lifts his glass in a toast.*) So long, Harry. (*Thunder and lightning. Dr. Pepper feels his skull. The guests are heard singing in the distance. Dr. Pepper sings along with them to himself, very quietly and slowly. His voice trails off. The curtain falls.*)

DUNELAWN

THE PLAYERS

RUTH BENSON, R.N.

BECKY HEDGES, R.N.

BRUNO

DR. TOYNBEE

MR. PONCE

MR. BLUM

MR. YAMADORO

HUGH GUMBS

The setting is outdoors. The stage is bare except for a high wall running the length of the cyclorama. Also, there is a small stone bench and scraggly tree. Nurse Benson strides on. Nurse Hedges follows, pushing a medical cart.

NURSE BENSON. Hello. Ruth Benson, R.N., here. At ease. Let's· get one thing perfectly straight before we begin. I am your friend. No matter what happens, I am your friend. So is Nurse Hedges. (*Nurse Hedges smiles.*) But you know something? You are your own best friend. Think that one over. I'll say the bell tolls. It tolls for all of us. Welcome to Dunelawn. Shall we begin? (*She claps her hands.*) Bruno! (*Bruno wheels in Mr. Ponce in a wheelchair. Bruno is a horror, Mr. Ponce is a crabby old man.*) Good morning, Bruno. Put him over there. Facing the sun! That's right, Bruno. Thank you, Bruno. Now go and get Mr. Blum.

BRUNO. (*Looking/leering/lusting at Nurse Hedges.*) I'm supposed to mow the lawn.

BENSON. After you've brought everyone out here you can do that.

BRUNO. (*Still leering at Nurse Hedges.*) Dr. Toynbee says I'm supposed to mow.

BENSON. You can mow later, Bruno, mow all day.

BRUNO. (*Taking a swig of whiskey from his hip flask.*) Mow and trim the hedges. All the hedges need trimming, Dr. Toynbee says. (*Provocatively to Hedges.*) It's going to be a hot one. A real scorcher all right.

BENSON. Bruno!

BRUNO. I'm going, Benson, don't wet your pants. (*He turns to go, then turns back to Hedges.*) Hey! (*Nurse Hedges looks at him.*) Hubba hubba! (*He winks, leers, laughs, exits.*)

BENSON. Ugh! (*Then, clapping her hands.*) Well, Mr. Ponce! Good morning, Mr. Ponce! How are we feeling today?

MR. PONCE. What do you think?

BENSON. I think you're feeling one hundred percent better, that's what I think!

MR. PONCE. Who asked you?

BENSON. Maybe you don't realize it, Mr. Ponce, but you are.

MR. PONCE. I want a drink.

BENSON. I didn't hear that.

PONCE. I want a drink!

BENSON. (*At a sound from Nurse Hedges.*) What is it, Hedges? You'll have to speak up, dear.

NURSE HEDGES. Are we using serum?

BENSON. Yes, serum! Of course, serum! (*The two nurses busy themselves at the medical cart during the following.*)

PONCE. Liquor! Liquor! I want liquor!

BENSON. Honestly, Becky, I don't know what's gotten into you lately.

HEDGES. I'm sorry.

PONCE. I want a drink, somebody!

BENSON. You're sniveling again, Hedges.

HEDGES. I am?

PONCE. Will somebody please get me a good stiff drink?

BENSON. I'll cure you of that if it's the last thing I do.

HEDGES. I don't mean to snivel. I don't want to snivel. I just do it I guess.

PONCE. I need a drink. I must have a drink!

BENSON. Well we'll soon put a stop to that.

HEDGES. You're so good to me, Ruth!

BENSON. I know. Syringe, please.

PONCE. I don't want to stop! I like to drink! It's all a terrible mistake!

HEDGES. (*Admiringly, while Benson prepares to administer the injection.*) No, I mean it. You're really interested in my welfare. I'm so used to women being catty and bitchy to one another, I can't believe I've found a friend who's deeply and truly concerned about me.

PONCE. How much do you want, Benson? How much cold, hard cash?

BENSON. It's called love, Becky.

HEDGES. I guess it is.

PONCE. Look at me, Benson, I'm making a cash offer.

BENSON. Good old-fashioned l-o-v-e.

HEDGES. Well I appreciate it.

PONCE. Where's Toynbee? Get me Toynbee!

BENSON. You're turning into a wonderful, warm, desirable woman, Hedges.

HEDGES. Thanks to you.

BENSON. Oh pooh! (*Mr. Ponce sees that she is about to stick him with the needle. He begins to yell and babble. He begins to jump up and down in the wheelchair as if he were strapped to it. His blanket falls off. He is! Also, he's wearing a straitjacket.*)

PONCE. Goddamn it, I want a drink and I want it now! I want a drink! I won't calm down until I get a drink! (*He's making quite a racket and carrying on like a wild caged beast. Benson stays in control. Hedges panics.*)

BENSON. Mr. Ponce! I'm not going to give you this injection as long as you keep that up. You're just wasting your time.

HEDGES. Do you want me to get help?

BENSON. I didn't hear that, Hedges.

HEDGES. I'm sorry.

BENSON. And don't start sniveling again.

HEDGES. So good to me!

BENSON. I'll have to report this to Dr. Toynbee, Mr. Ponce. I'm sorry, but my hands are tied. (*Dr. Toynbee strolls on. He has sad, benign eyes and a smile to match. Mr. Ponce immediately quiets down at the sight of him and bangs his head in shame.*) Good morning, Dr. Toynbee.

HEDGES. (*Almost a little curtsey.*) Good morning, Dr. Toynbee. (*Dr. Toynbee smiles, nods and looks at Mr. Ponce.*)

BENSON. Doctor, I think Mr. Ponce wants to leave Dunelawn.

PONCE. No!

BENSON. I don't think he deserves to be here. I'd say he's abused that privilege. (*Benson unfastens the straps that hold Ponce to the wheelchair.*)

PONCE. I'm sorry. I don't know what came over me.

BENSON. Get up.

PONCE. It was a temporary relapse, Doctor. I'm so ashamed, believe me, it won't happen again.

BENSON. (*Letting him out of the straitjacket.*) There's a long line of decent, honorable people waiting to get in here, Mr. Ponce. A very long line. And I think you'd better step right to the end of it. Well go ahead, you're free to leave now.

PONCE. I can't look at you, Dr. Toynbee, I'm so ashamed.

BENSON. No one asked you to come here and no one's keeping you.

PONCE. Don't look at me like that, Dr. Toynbee!

BENSON. He said he wanted a drink. He demanded one, in fact. He even tried to bribe me, Doctor. (*Toynbee, his eyes never off Ponce, sadly shakes his head.*) Naturally I refused. So did Nurse Hedges.

HEDGES. (*Almost curtseying again.*) Yes, yes I did, Dr. Toynbee.

BENSON. Fortunately he revealed his true colors before I was able to administer the syringe. I'll have Bruno pack your things at once, Mr. Ponce. You'll find your statement in the checkout office. You won't be charged for today, of course. Now should they call your wife and family to come and get you or would you prefer the limousine service?

PONCE. Benson, wait, please!

BENSON. Dr. Toynbee is a very busy man, Mr. Ponce. Your wife and family or the limousine?

PONCE. I'm not leaving. I won't let you throw me out like this. You're sending me straight back to the gin mills if you kick me out of here. I'm not ready to leave yet. I'm not strong enough.

BENSON. Dr. Toynbee's heard all this, Mr. Ponce.

PONCE. (*Putting the straitjacket back on.*) Look, look, see how much I want to stay?

BENSON. Take that off, Mr. Ponce.

PONCE. (*To Hedges.*) Fasten me up, fasten me up!

HEDGES. Dr. Toynbee?

PONCE. The straps, the straps, just fasten the straps.

HEDGES. (*Moved.*) Poor Mr. Ponce.

BENSON. I wouldn't do that, Hedges.

HEDGES. Dr. Toynbee? (*Toynbee, slowly, sadly, benignly, nods his head. Hedges buckles Mr. Ponce up in the straitjacket.*)

PONCE. Thank you, Doctor, thank you! (*He would like to thank Dr. Toynbee, but now, of course, there is no way to do it.*) I'll be good, I'll be better! You'll see, you'll see! This will never happen again. Come on, Benson, you heard the doctor!

BENSON. Surely, Doctor, you're not going to . . . ? (*Again Toynbee nods his head.*) That man is a saint.

PONCE. God bless him.

BENSON. Dr. Toynbee is a saint.

PONCE. I am so grateful and so happy.

BENSON. A saint!

PONCE. I could kiss his hand for this. (*He tries to, and can't.*)

BENSON. Should I proceed with the injection, Doctor? (*Dr. Toynbee smiles and nods.*) Hedges. (*Hedges helps her prepare another syringe as Dr. Toynbee moves to Mr. Ponce and stands directly behind him. He looks down at him, puts one hand on each shoulder and fixes him with a sad and solemn stare.*)

PONCE. I can't bear it when you look at me like that. You're so good, Doctor, so good! I know how rotten I am. But someday I'll be able to look you in the eye. I'll make you proud of me. I'll make me proud of me. I don't want to be me anymore. (*Dr. Toynbee smiles and bends down to Mr. Ponce's ear. When he does finally speak, it is totally unintelligible gibberish.*) You're so right, Doctor! Everything you say is so right! (*Toynbee turns to go.*) God bless you.

BENSON. Thank you, Dr. Toynbee!

HEDGES. Thank you, Dr. Toynbee!

BENSON. Goodbye, Dr. Toynbee!

HEDGES. Goodbye, Dr. Toynbee! (*Toynbee acknowledges them with a wave of the hand and strolls off.*) What a wonderful man he is.

BENSON. That man is a saint.

HEDGES. And so good.

BENSON. Why can't we all be like him?

HEDGES. How do you mean?

BENSON. Perfect.

PONCE. Please, Benson, hurry up.

HEDGES. I think you're perfect, Ruth.

BENSON. You're sweeet.

HEDGES. You are.

BENSON. Not really. And certainly not like Dr. Toynbee.

PONCE. Come on, Benson, before I get another attack.

BENSON. Do you realize he has absolutely no faults? Absolutely none.

HEDGES. No wonder he seems so good.

BENSON. He's perfect, Becky. I don't see why I can't get you to understand that. He has no place left to go.

PONCE. My hands, Benson, they're starting to shake!

BENSON. Dr. Toynbee wasn't born perfect. He worked on it and there he is.

HEDGES. You make it sound so easy.

BENSON. Take it from me, Becky, it isn't.

HEDGES. You're telling me.

BENSON. You're making wonderful progress.

PONCE. Oh my God, I'm starting to hallucinate.

HEDGES. Any progress I'm making is entirely thanks to you, I hope you know.

PONCE. A jeroboam of Bombay Gin!

HEDGES. I don't want to be perfect, Ruth, I know I never could be. Not like you.

BENSON. Oh pooh, Becky, just pooh!

PONCE. I'm salivating, Benson. Have you no mercy?

BENSON. Hang on there, Mr. Ponce, just hang on there another second.

PONCE. I'm going fast. I . . . I . . . I want a drink. I want a drink! *I want a drink!!! (Benson sticks him with the needle.)* I . . . I . . .

BENSON. Now what did you just say you wanted, Mr. Ponce?

PONCE. *(A beatific smile spreading across his face.)* I don't want anything!

BENSON. Let's fix your chair now, so you get the sun.

PONCE. Yes, that would be nice, miss. Thank you, thank you.

BENSON. *(As she makes Ponce more comfortable.)* I pity your type, Mr. Ponce. Two martinis before dinner, wine with, a cordial after, and a couple of scotch on the rocks nightcaps. Social drinking, you call it. Rummies, I say, every last one of you.

PONCE. *(A long, contented sigh.)* Aaaaaaaaaaah!

BENSON. All right now?

PONCE. I don't want anything. Any bad thing.

BENSON. Good for you.

PONCE. I'm going to make it, Benson. I'm going to be all right. *(His head falls over.)*

BENSON. Of course you are. And if you want anything, I'll be right over . . . *(She takes his head and points it towards the medical cart.)* . . . there.

PONCE. No, miss, I don't want a thing. *(Benson tiptoes over to Hedges.)*

BENSON. Whew!

HEDGES. I admire you so much!

BENSON. Becky Hedges!

HEDGES. You can help me to get rid of my faults until you're blue in the face, but I'll never be the beauty you are.

BENSON. You're an adorable person, Becky.

HEDGES. I'm not talking about adorable. I'm talking about beauty. No one ever told Elizabeth Taylor she was adorable.

BENSON. Do I have to say it? Beauty is skin deep. Besides, Elizabeth has a lot of faults.

HEDGES. You're changing the subject. Ruth, look at me.

BENSON. Yes?

HEDGES. Now tell me this is a beautiful woman you see.

BENSON. What are you driving at, Becky?

HEDGES. Nothing. I just wish I were beautiful like you. And I don't want you to just *say* I am.

BENSON. I wouldn't do that to you.

HEDGES. Thank you.

BENSON. I said you were adorable.

HEDGES. And I said you were beautiful.

BENSON. It's out of my hands.

HEDGES. It's out of mine, too.

BENSON. You're sniveling again.

HEDGES. I know.

BENSON. (*She pulls Hedges over to the bench and sits her down.*) Becky, listen to me. You think I'm beautiful. Thank you. I can accept a compliment. I know I'm beautiful. I can't lie to myself anymore. But what good did it do me as far as Hugh Gumbs was concerned?

HEDGES. Such a beautiful name!

BENSON. There you go again, Becky.

HEDGES. I didn't snivel that time.

BENSON. You made a stupid, flattering, self-serving, Minnie Mouse remark, which is much worse. Hugh Gumbs is not a beautiful name and you know it.

HEDGES. I'm sorry. I'll be good. I'll be better. Finish your story.

BENSON. I don't even remember where I was.

HEDGES. You were talking about your beauty and how little good it did you as far as Hugh Gumbs was concerned.

BENSON. That man wouldn't even look at me. Looks had nothing to do with it. I know that now. Ask Hugh Gumbs! And I know

I'm more beautiful than that hussy he abandoned me for. In my heart of hearts, I know that Mildred Canby is not a beautiful woman.

HEDGES. Mildred who?

BENSON. Mildred Canby.

HEDGES. What a horrible name, too.

BENSON. Attractive, yes. Beautiful, no. Now what Hugh Gumbs wanted in a woman, what every man wants in any woman, is something deeper than beauty. He wants character. He wants the traditional virtues. He wants womanly warmth.

HEDGES. You can say that again.

BENSON. Believe me, Hugh Gumbs is a very unhappy man right now. How could he not be? Mildred Canby had even less character and more faults than I did. And less beauty, too. I knew that marriage wouldn't last. (*She takes out her compact.*)

HEDGES. Don't cry, Ruth.

BENSON. Me? Cry? Why should I cry?

HEDGES. Because you lost Hugh?

BENSON. I'm grateful to him! He broke my heart, I don't deny it, but if it hadn't been for Hugh I would never have been forced into the soul-searching and self-reevaluation that ended up with the 118-pound, trim-figured woman you say is so beautiful standing in front of you. No, when I think back on Ruth Benson then and compare her to Ruth Benson now, I thank my lucky stars for Hugh.

HEDGES. (*As Benson continues to gaze at herself in the compact mirror.*) You're so wise, Ruth.

BENSON. Am I?

HEDGES. Wise about love.

BENSON. I wonder.

HEDGES. You are.

BENSON. We'll see.

HEDGES. I'm not.

BENSON. (*Still distracted.*) Hmmmmmmmm?

HEDGES. Wise about love. I'm downright dumb about it. If I weren't, I'd be married to Tim Taylor right this very minute. What I wouldn't give for another chance at him!

BENSON. (*Regaining herself.*) Buck up, Hedges.

HEDGES. Oh I will, Ruth. I'm just feeling a little sorry for myself. I don't know why. If you want to know the truth, I haven't thought of Tim Taylor one way or the other for a long time.

BENSON. I should hope not. A man who smokes is a very bad emotional risk.

HEDGES. Tim didn't smoke.

BENSON. But he drank. It's the same thing. Rummies, every last one of them.

HEDGES. Did Hugh Gumbs drink?

BENSON. Among other things.

HEDGES. It must have been awful for you.

BENSON. It was heck. Sheer unadulterated heck.

HEDGES. That sounds funny.

BENSON. Believe me, it wasn't.

HEDGES. No, what you just said. About it being heck. I'm still used to people saying the other.

BENSON. It won't seem funny after a while. You'll see. (*Dr. Toynbee strolls across the stage, smiling benignly, reading a book.*) Good morning, Dr. Toynbee!

HEDGES. Good morning, Dr. Toynbee! (*To Benson.*) That man is so good, Ruth!

BENSON. I worship the ground he walks on.

HEDGES. Oh me, too, me, too! I'd give anything to be just like him.

BENSON. Goodbye, Dr. Toynbee! And thank you!

HEDGES. Goodbye, Dr. Toynbee! And thank you! (*Dr. Toynbee exits down the aisle, waving.*) Ruth?

BENSON. What?

HEDGES. I know it's none of my business, but I've seen that look in your eyes whenever Dr. Toynbee passes.

BENSON. What look?

HEDGES. You know.

BENSON. The only look, as you put it, in my eyes when Dr. Toynbee passes is one of sheer and utter respect. Certainly not the look you're so grossly alluding to. You're out of line, don't you think, Hedges? You're certainly in extremely bad taste.

HEDGES. You're not sweet on the good doctor?

BENSON. Dr. Toynbee is above that.

HEDGES. I know but are you? (*Benson slaps her.*) Is any woman? (*Benson slaps her again and they fall into each other's arms crying.*) I'm sorry, Ruth, I didn't mean to hurt you. You've been so good to me! I'm such a different person since I've been with you! I don't even know who I am anymore and I say these silly, dreadful, awful things! I don't recognize myself in the mirror in the morning. I've changed so much it scares me.

BENSON. You haven't changed. You've improved, refined, what was already there. I always had this figure, don't you see? Even when I weighed all that weight, I still had this figure.

HEDGES. Even when you were up to 230?

BENSON. I was never 230.

HEDGES. You told me you were . . .

BENSON. I was never 230! Now shut up and listen, will you?

HEDGES. I'm sorry, Ruth.

BENSON. I didn't change anything. Mr. Ponce over there isn't changing. He's only emerging, with our help and Dr. Toynbee's, into what he really and truly was in the first place: a nondrinker.

PONCE. A rum swizzle!

BENSON. People are born without any faults, they simply fall into bad habits along life's way. Nobody's trying to *change* anybody, Becky. It's the real them coming out, that's all.

HEDGES. The real them!

BENSON. Look, face it, you've got big thighs, that's the real you. Now I've got nice thighs, as it turns out, but I didn't always know that.

HEDGES. I don't think I can get any thinner.

BENSON. I'm not talking about diets. I'm talking about the real you and your G.D. big thighs!

HEDGES. That's exactly what Tim Taylor didn't like about me. And now that I'm getting thinner they look even bigger. I *know!* I'm sniveling again! I don't know what to do about them, Ruth! (*She is desperately hitting her thighs.*)

BENSON. Wear longer skirts!

HEDGES. Now you really are cross with me!

BENSON. You can be so dense sometimes. I mean really, Hedges, I'm talking about a whole other thing and you start sniveling about diets. You can diet all you want and you're still going to end up with big thighs. That's not the point.

HEDGES. What is it, then?

BENSON. Oh there's no point in talking to you about it!

HEDGES. I'm sorry.

BENSON. And stop that horrible sniveling!

HEDGES. I'm never going to get any better. I have just as many bad habits as when I came here. We just keep pretending I'm improving when the real truth is, I'm getting worse! (*She races to the medical cart and hysterically prepares one of the syringes.*)

BENSON. What are you doing?

HEDGES. Why shouldn't I? I'm no better than any one of them and I'm supposed to work here!

BENSON. Give me that! (*They struggle.*)

HEDGES. Let me do it, Ruth!

BENSON. Have you lost your mind?

HEDGES. I wish I was dead! (*Benson topples Hedges, who falls in a heap, and takes away the syringe. Almost without realizing, she reaches inside her blouse and takes a package of cigarettes out of her bosom, puts one in her mouth and strikes a match. Hedges raises her head at the sound.*) Ruth!

BENSON. (*Realizing what she has done.*) Oh my God! I wasn't thinking!

HEDGES. You of all people!

BENSON. I wasn't going to smoke one!

HEDGES. It's a full pack.

BENSON. It's a courtesy pack. In case I run into someone. They're not mine. I've given it up. I swear to God I have. You've got to believe me.

HEDGES. I don't know what to think.

BENSON. Becky, please!

HEDGES. If you say so, Ruth. (*Bruno enters pushing Mr. Blum in a wheelchair.*)

BENSON. It took you long enough!

BRUNO. I suppose it did. Where do you want her?

BENSON. (*Pointedly.*) Him. I want *him* over there. Facing the sun, next to Mr. Ponce. That's where I want *him*, Bruno. And then when you've put him there, I want you to bring out Mr. Yamadoro. And I want you to do it quickly this time.

BRUNO. I told you I was supposed to mow.

BENSON. We know, Bruno.

BRUNO. Mow and trim me some hedges. Hey! (*He gives Hedges his hubba hubba leer.*)

BENSON. You're a beast, Bruno.

BRUNO. (*To Hedges.*) You got a light, baby?

HEDGES. No!

BRUNO. You, dog-face?

BENSON. You know I don't. Matches and all other smoking para-
phernalia are strictly forbidden here.

BRUNO. (*Taking out a hip flask.*) Yeah?

BENSON. So is alcohol.

BRUNO. No shit. (*Bruno downs a swig.*)

BENSON. The only reason Dr. Toynbee allows them to you is to set
an example to the guests here. A bad example. On a human self-
improvement ten scale, you rate about a minus fifty. You're a
walking, subhuman nightmare, Bruno.

BRUNO. (*For Hedges's benefit.*) Sure is a hot one coming on. A real
scorcher.

BENSON. Must you, Bruno?

BRUNO. Must I what?

BENSON. Stand there like that?

BRUNO. (*To Hedges.*) Now she don't like the way I stand.

BENSON. It's deliberately provocative.

BRUNO. What is that supposed to mean?

BENSON. Only you're about as provocative to a woman as a can full
of worms. Now either get Mr. Yamadoro out here or I'll report
you to Dr. Toynbee.

BRUNO. I'm going, Benson. Hold your bowels. (*He doesn't move.
He is trying to think.*) What you said about a can full of worms
. . . I got desires. That's all I know, I got desires and I like to do
'em. (*He goes. Hedges curiously starts to follow. Benson claps
her hands, and Hedges joins her.*)

BENSON. Good morning, Mr. Blum! How are we feeling today?
Doesn't that sun feel good on you? And that delicious breeze
from the ocean! And listen to those birds chirp! It's a day like
this that makes you wish summer lasted all year! (*As she chatters
away, she is preparing a syringe for Mr. Blum.*) When I was a
little girl, we spent our summers in Vermont and my brothers
and I used to go swimming in a little pond!

MR. BLUM. Your cap, Benson. (*It's a gently desperate plea.*)

BENSON. Hmmmmmmm?

BLUM. Please. Just let me wear your cap. I won't hurt it. I'll just sit
here and wear it. I won't say a word.

BENSON. Mr. Blum, I thought you were improving!

BLUM. I am, Benson, I swear to God I am! I just want to wear your cap for a little while. What's wrong with that? It doesn't mean anything. It's just a cap. I mean it's not like I asked to wear your skirt or your shoes or your stockings or anything! I'm all over that. A man could wear a cap like yours without it meaning anything.

BENSON. Does Dr. Toynbee know this?

BLUM. Are you crazy? Of course not!

BENSON. I'll have to tell him.

BLUM. It's not what you're thinking!

BENSON. We were all so proud of the progress you were making!

BLUM. As well you should be! I'm proud, too! Benson, I haven't been in full drag in six weeks! You know what I was like when Martha brought me here. You've seen how I've changed. You couldn't force me at gunpoint to put your shoes on.

BENSON. (*Immediately suspicious.*) My shoes?

BLUM. Yes, your shoes! Don't torment me like this! Your cap, Benson, it's all I'm asking for. Stop me before I want more.

BENSON. It's out of the question, Mr. Blum.

BLUM. I want that cap! I need that cap! I'm begging you for that cap!

BENSON. Forget the cap! The cap is out!

BLUM. Five minutes, Benson, have a heart!

BENSON. Five minutes with the cap and next it will be the shoes and then the skirt and you'll be right back where you started. I know your kind, Mr. Blum.

BLUM. (*Bitterly.*) Do you, Benson?

BENSON. Give them a cap and they want your panty hose!

BLUM. What of it?

BENSON. You're here to change, not get worse! Think of your wife!

BLUM. What of her? I can't wear a size eight!

BENSON. Then think of your daughters.

BLUM. They're goddamn pygmies, too! I'm surrounded by stunted women.

BENSON. Do you know what they call people like you?

BLUM. Fashionable!

BENSON. You're a man, Mr. Blum, you were meant to dress like one!

BLUM. You're not God, Benson, don't you tell me how to dress!

BENSON. (*Holding back the syringe from him.*) I don't have to take that from you, Blum!

BLUM. What do you know about it?

BENSON. If you persist in defying me . . . !

BLUM. What does any woman know about it?

BENSON. Not only will I withhold this syringe . . . !

BLUM. Garter belts, Benson.

BENSON. I will fill out a report . . . !

BLUM. Merry widows!

BENSON. And give it to Dr. Toynbee!

BLUM. Black net stockings! Red garters, strapless tops! Sequins!

BENSON. All right for you, Blum, all right for you! (*She starts out.*)

BLUM. Picture hats! That's right, Benson, you heard me, picture hats! (*Dr. Toynbee strolls on.*)

BENSON. Good morning, Dr. Toynbee.

HEDGES. Good morning, Dr. Toynbee! (*Dr. Toynbee smiles and nods.*)

BENSON. I want you to see something, Doctor.

BLUM. (*Head bowed, suddenly mortified.*) Please, Benson, don't. (*Benson begins to take off her cap. Blum watches in growing terror. Toynbee looks at Blum with such a great sadness.*) Benson, don't do this to me, not in front of him. Please. I beg of you. I'll change. I swear I'll change!

BENSON. He asked to wear my cap, Doctor. I think he should wear it. (*She puts the hat on his head. Blum writhes and twists in his straitjacket in the wheelchair as if he were on fire.*)

BLUM. No! No! Take it off! Take it off! (*As Blum writhes and screams, Toynbee takes out his handkerchief and dabs at his eyes. Even Hedges cries.*)

BENSON. You've made Dr. Toynbee cry, Mr. Blum. I just hope you're pleased with yourself.

HEDGES. I can't watch, Ruth.

BENSON. (*Shielding her.*) It's all right, Becky, it's going to be all right.

HEDGES. To see the poor doctor cry!

BENSON. Sshh, sshh! Dr. Toynbee's here now. Everything will be all right. (*Dr. Toynbee slowly dries his eyes, puts away the handkerchief, and goes to Blum.*) Look Becky! (*Toynbee takes the cap off Blum. At once, Blum is silent and hangs his head. Toyn-*

bee stands looking down at him.) That man is a saint. (*Toynbee hands the cap back to Benson, then turns and talks to Blum. Again we can't understand his gibberish.*) Dr. Toynbee has that rare spiritual quality that when he just looks at you with those clear grey eyes of his you suddenly feel so ashamed of yourself you could just vomit.

HEDGES. Such a good man! (*Now Blum is the one who is crying. Toynbee asks for the syringe with a gesture. Benson gives it to him and he injects Blum. Benson wheels Blum next to Ponce, who is beginning to stir restlessly.*)

PONCE. (*Very slurred.*) Bartender! I'll have a perfect Rob Roy on the rocks. I want a little service here, bartender!

BENSON. Doctor . . . ? (*Toynbee smiles benignly and nods his head. He motions to Hedges that she should administer the shot.*)

HEDGES. Me, Doctor . . . ? (*Toynbee smiles at her and nods his his head. Hedges approaches Ponce with a syringe.*)

PONCE. Make it a double Dewar's on the rocks and hold the ice. (*Hedges looks to Toynbee for encouragement. He smiles and nods his head. She injects Ponce.*) Ouch!

BENSON. (*Sharply.*) Hedges!

PONCE. Goddamn mosquitos!

HEDGES. He moved! (*Toynbee prevents Benson from helping Hedges out with a benign "Let her do it" gesture. Hedges administers the syringe with no little difficulty. Ponce smiles blissfully.*) I did it, Ruth!

BENSON. We saw you, Hedges.

HEDGES. I really did it, all by myself! Doctor? (*Toynbee smiles and nods and begins to stroll off.*)

BENSON. Thank you, Dr. Toynbee!

HEDGES. Thank you, Dr. Toynbee!

BENSON. Goodbye, Dr. Toynbee!

HEDGES. Goodbye, Dr. Toynbee! (*Spinning herself around.*) Oh, Ruth, Ruth, Ruth!

BENSON. Calm down, Hedges, it was only an injection.

HEDGES. (*Still spinning.*) He's so tremendously, terrifically and terribly good!

BENSON. You're not telling me anything about him I already didn't know. Now give a hand here, will you?

HEDGES. And you know something else? I'm a little sweet on the good doctor myself! (*She is still spinning and singing and dancing when Benson slaps her.*)

BENSON. Snap out of it, Hedges!

HEDGES. I'm sorry. You were right to do that. I'm not even worthy to mention his name. Who am I to think Dr. Toynbee even knows I'm alive? I'm dirt, Ruth. Next to him, I'm dirt.

BENSON. Well . . .

HEDGES. Don't deny it. I know what I am. I've got big thighs and I'm dirt.

BENSON. You're too rough on yourself, Hedges.

HEDGES. I have to be if I'm ever going to get rid of my faults and be like you!

BENSON. I won't say "Don't aim too high, Becky" . . . how could I? But I will say "Don't aim too high too soon."

HEDGES. (*Hugging her.*) Why are you so good to me? Everyone at Dunelawn is so good to me!

BENSON. Because we all love you and want to see you reach your full potential.

HEDGES. Zero defects.

BENSON. That's right, Becky, zero defects. No faults, no failings, no fantasy. It's a beautiful goal.

HEDGES. It sounds religious when you say it. With me it just sounds hopeless.

BENSON. Mark my words, Rebecca Hedges, R.N., the day you become perfect will be the most important day in your life.

HEDGES. It will?

BENSON. Mark my words. (*Bruno wheels in Mr. Yamadoro in a wheelchair. He, too, is straitjacketed and fastened down.*)

BRUNO. Okay, Benson, that's the Webster Hall lot. Where do you want him?

BENSON. Over there, Bruno.

BRUNO. Hey! (*Hedges looks at him.*) Hubba hubba!

BENSON. Thank you, Bruno. You can go now.

BRUNO. Who says I was talking to you?

BENSON. Aren't you supposed to mow now?

BRUNO. Maybe.

HEDGES. Mow and trim some hedges.

BENSON. Don't talk to that man.

BRUNO. That's right, pussycat. Mow and trim me some hedges.

BENSON. Then do it, Bruno.

BRUNO. Don't burst your bladder, Benson, I'm going. And don't think I ain't forgot that can of worms, horse-face.

BENSON. Bruno!

BRUNO. Stick around, kid. (*Hedges looks at him. He winks, leers.*) Yes sir, a good hot day to trim me some hedges. (*He saunters off.*)

HEDGES. The way he keeps saying that gives me the creeps. You'd think he meant me. (*She shudders.*) Jeepers creepers!

BENSON. Good morning, Mr. Yamadoro.

HEDGES. Ruth!

BENSON. What?

HEDGES. (*Referring to her charts.*) That's not Mr. Yamadoro . . . ! (*Benson pushes her away from Mr. Yamadoro, furious.*) But it's not. It's Mr. Luparelli. Vincenzo Luparelli, Ithaca, New York. It says so right here.

BENSON. He likes to be called Mr. Yamadoro. That's the reason he's here.

HEDGES. I'm sorry. I forgot.

BENSON. You forget everything! (*She turns back to Mr. Yamadoro.*) Good morning, Mr. Yamadoro, how are we feeling today? Any improvement?

MR. YAMADORO. Much better, thank you, Nurse.

BENSON. What about your urges?

YAMADORO. You mean . . . ? (*He lowers his eyes, blushes.*) . . . I can't say it.

BENSON. Yes or no? (*Yamadoro shakes his head no.*) Isn't that wonderful! Did you hear that, Becky? Mr. Yamadoro feels he's improving!

HEDGES. (*In all innocense.*) That's what they all say.

BENSON. Watch your step, Hedges.

HEDGES. Well, how come none of them ever seems to get any better? (*Benson slaps her and takes her aside.*)

BENSON. Don't ever say that again!

HEDGES. But they don't. (*Benson slaps her again.*)

BENSON. Don't ever even think it! (*She is shaking Hedges.*) Dr. Toynbee knows what he's doing. It's not his fault if his patients don't.

HEDGES. I'm sorry. I just never looked at it like that.

BENSON. Well maybe it's high time you did.

HEDGES. (*Still being shaken.*) Now you're really, really cross with me!

BENSON. A word against Dr. Toynbee and what he's trying to do here is a slap in my face!

YAMADORO. Slap. (*He giggles.*)

BENSON. Now look what you've done. You've excited him (*Indeed, Yamadoro has been vibrating with pleasure ever since this outbreak of violence of theirs. Benson goes to him, Hedges following.*) Now calm down, Mr. Yamadoro.

YAMADORO. You hit her. You hit her. Good for you, Benson, good for you!

BENSON. I didn't hit her, Mr. Yamadoro.

YAMADORO. You slap her then.

BENSON. No one slapped anyone.

YAMADORO. (*Calming down.*) They didn't?

BENSON. Did they, Nurse Hedges?

HEDGES. Oh no.

BENSON. What you saw may have looked like a slap but it wasn't.

HEDGES. Why would anyone want to slap me, Mr. Yamadoro?

BENSON. Sshh! You'll provoke him again!

YAMADORO. Impossible! It was nothing, nothing at all. A momentary relapse. My urges all are gone, my desires now like water.

BENSON. Pain, Mr. Yamadoro? You're not thinking about pain?

HEDGES. Now *you* are, Ruth!

BENSON. I have to find out!

YAMADORO. Pain? There is no such thing.

BENSON. But in your fantasies? Come on, you can tell Benson.

YAMADORO. I'm over all that.

BENSON. Are you? Imagine, imagine Mr. Yamadoro, a beautiful, voluptuous woman . . . blonde, why not? . . . and she is at your mercy.

HEDGES. Ruth!

BENSON. I know what I'm doing!

YAMADORO. So far nothing.

BENSON. She looks at you, the tears streaming down her cheeks, the drug you've given her has begun to wear off, she's your prisoner and she can't escape. She sees your glowing slit eyes fixed on her fingernails. You want to pull them off, don't you, Mr. Yamadoro? One by one! (*Aside to Hedges.*) The fingernails, that's what they go for, these Jap sadists.

YAMADORO. (*Nonplussed.*) Continue.

BENSON. (*More and more graphically.*) Aaaaaiiiiieeeeeeee! She screams. Aaaaaaiiiieeeeee! Again and again! But you are implacable. Your cruelty knows no bounds. Your lust is insatiable. (*Angry aside to Hedges.*) Don't just stand there, Hedges, help me out!

HEDGES. Aaaaaaiiiiieeeeee!

BENSON. But the room is soundproofed and her bonds hold fast. Every exquisite torment the Oriental mind has devised you visit upon her helpless, quivering, palpable flesh.

HEDGES. Aaaaaaiiiiieeeeee!

BENSON. There is no mercy, God is dead, and Satan reigns triumphant!

HEDGES. Aaaaaaiiiiieeeeee!

BENSON. (*Savagely.*) Well, Mr. Yamadoro?

YAMADORO. (*Quietly.*) I feel a strange calmness over me. All human desires and passions spent. I desire nothing of the flesh.

BENSON. (*Triumphantly.*) You see?

HEDGES. He really does seem better.

YAMADORO. I really am, missy.

BENSON. Of course he is. (*They start to prepare a syringe.*)

YAMADORO. Dr. Toynbee is a saint.

BENSON. Back to work, Hedges.

YAMADORO. (*To Ponce and Blum.*) Don't tell Benson, but I just had an orgasm. (*He giggles.*)

BENSON. Can you manage this one yourself, too?

HEDGES. I think so.

BENSON. Good girl.

HEDGES. Thanks to you. (*Hedges moves in close to inject Yamadoro. He tries to bite her. She screams.*) Mr. Yamadoro, I thought we were over all that!

YAMADORO. It's never over! (*He is violent in the chair.*)

BENSON. Give me that. (*She takes the syringe, grabs him in an armlock, and injects him.*) This'll hold him.

YAMADORO. (*A long moan.*) Mamma Mia! (*Benson and Hedges*

begin readjusting the wheelchairs. All three patients smile out at us seraphically.)

BENSON. Look at them. Like babies now. It's a beautiful sight.

HEDGES. Everyone should take Dr. Toynbee's serum. Then the whole world would be perfect. No wars, no greed, no sex. No nothing. (*Bruno enters with a letter from the office.*)

BENSON. Mr. Ponce, Mr. Blum and Mr. Yamadoro are going to be all right, Becky. It's only the Brunos of this world that are hopeless.

BRUNO. Hey, you in the white dress with the bird's legs!

HEDGES. I feel good just looking at them like this.

BRUNO. You want this, tight ass? (*He shows the letter.*)

BENSON. You're looking at the future, Becky.

HEDGES. In our lifetime?

BENSON. (*Sadly shaking her head.*) I'm afraid we're just the pioneers.

BRUNO. Hey, ugly-puss, I'm supposed to give you this.

HEDGES. A perfect world with perfect people.

BENSON. Someone has to do it.

BRUNO. There's a new patient, dog-face!

BENSON. Well, why didn't you just say so?

BRUNO. I did! (*Benson takes the papers from him, starts reading them over. Bruno exits, but not before a little "Hey!" and a few silent leers towards Hedges.*)

BENSON. Becky!

HEDGES. What is it, Ruth?

BENSON. I've been given another chance. Read this. I'm the luckiest woman alive. He's here. He's at Dunelawn. I've got him where I want him at last! Oh God!

HEDGES. Is it the same Hugh Gumbs?

BENSON. Do you know how many years I've waited for this moment? Hugh Gumbs wants to be a new person and I'll be the one helping him to mold his new self.

HEDGES. If I were you, I mean if this was Tim Taylor being admitted to Dunelawn, I wouldn't be standing here talking about it. I'd fly to him.

BENSON. But . . . (*Indicating the patients.*)

HEDGES. Go on. I can take care of everything.

BENSON. You're a doll.

HEDGES. Now it's my turn: oh pooh!

BENSON. What am I waiting for? Wish me luck!

BENSON. Luck! (*They kiss. Benson dashes off. Ponce, Blum and Yamadoro are smiling. Hedges goes to the cart, gets a book, and crosses to the bench. Reading:*) A *Critique of Pure Reason* by Immanuel Kant. (*Bruno sticks his head up over the wall and whistles softly.*) "To Becky, with all my love, Ruth Benson, R.N." So good to me! (*Bruno whistles again. Hedges finally sees him.*) Please, Bruno, I'm trying to concentrate. It's difficult material.

BRUNO. I thought we'd never ditch horse-face.

HEDGES. We?

BRUNO. It's just you and me now, Hedges.

HEDGES. I don't know what you're talking about.

BRUNO. I seen you.

HEDGES. Seen me what?

BRUNO. Looking at me.

HEDGES. I never looked at you.

BRUNO. I'm provocative. You heard Benson.

HEDGES. Provocative as a can full of worms is what she said.

BRUNO. (*Climbing down from the wall and approaching her.*) Only it ain't what she meant, is it now?

HEDGES. I'm not speaking to you, Bruno.

BRUNO. Benson looks at me, too.

HEDGES. Don't be ridiculous.

BRUNO. I seen her.

HEDGES. Ruth Benson wouldn't look at you if you were the last man on earth.

BRUNO. Around this place, that's exactly what I am. What do you say, Hedges?

HEDGES. You mean . . . ?

BRUNO. I got a waterbed.

HEDGES. I don't care what you got. You're supposed to be mowing!

BRUNO. I'm done mowing.

HEDGES. Then trim some hedges! No, I didn't mean that. Stay back, Bruno. Don't come near me. I'll call Dr. Toynbee.

BRUNO. Toynbee looks at me, too.

HEDGES. Mr. Ponce! Mr. Ponce!

BRUNO. They all look at me.

HEDGES. (*Freeing Mr. Ponce from his chair and jacket.*) You've got to help me, Mr. Ponce. He won't leave me alone. I'm frightened. I'll get you a case of liquor if you help me!

BRUNO. (*Exposing himself.*) Hubba, hubba, Hedges. (*Hedges screams and frees Mr. Blum.*)

HEDGES. Mr. Blum, I'll let you wear my cap or anything you want of mine if you'll just listen to me a minute. You don't understand.

BRUNO. (*Exposing himself again.*) Twenty-three skidoo. (*Hedges screams again, turns to Yamadoro and releases him, too.*)

HEDGES. Mr. Yamadoro, you've got to help me! You're the only one left. I'll let you hit me, if you'll just get up now.

YAMADORO. A strange inner peace has subdued the fires of my soul.

HEDGES. Oh shut up, you dumb Jap!

BRUNO. Your place or mine, toots? Let's go, sugar!

HEDGES. Help! Help! Help! (*She runs off. Bruno goes after her.*)

PONCE. We're free.

BLUM. I know.

YAMADORO. Yes, yes, yes, yes, yes.

PONCE. I don't want to leave, though.

BLUM. (*Draping the sleeve of his straitjacket around him like a boa.*) Neither do I.

YAMADORO. Celestial harmonies ring in my ears.

BLUM. What does that mean?

YAMADORO. I don't know.

PONCE. I once drank twelve extra-dry Gordon's gin martinis in the Monkey Bar at the Hotel Elysee.

BLUM. You should have seen me at the Beaux Arts Ball that time I took first prize. I went as Anouk Aimée.

YAMADORO. Exquisite woman.

BLUM. Yes, yes.

PONCE. Never heard of her.

YAMADORO. Wonderful fingernails. (*Hedges runs across pursued by Bruno.*)

HEDGES. Bruno the gardener is going to rape me and the three of you just sit there! Doesn't anybody care?

BRUNO. Hubba, hubba, Hedges! (*They are gone.*)

PONCE. I was so rotten when I was out there and over the wall.

.BLUM. I could never find a pair of white heels that fit.

YAMADORO. Did I ever tell you gentlemen about Monique?

PONCE. I used to love to drink on Saturday. There's something about a Saturday.

BLUM. Do either of you realize what a really good dresser Nina Foch was?

YAMADORO. Monique was from Trenton. A lovely girl. (*Hedges enters and tiptoes down to the house. Bruno suddenly appears from behind the hedge.*)

BRUNO. Hubba, hubba, Hedges! (*Hedges screams as they run out down the aisle. From the back of the house, we hear a "Help!," then the ripping of cloth.*)

PONCE. It's nice here.

BLUM. Peaceful.

YAMADORO. I desire nothing now.

PONCE. Dr. Toynbee's serum.

BLUM. That man is a saint.

YAMADORO. Dunelawn is heaven on earth.

PONCE. I am so happy right now.

BLUM. We all are, Mr. Ponce.

YAMADORO. Life is beautiful.

PONCE. I can't stop smiling.

BLUM. And the sun smiles on us.

YAMADORO. And we smile back at it. (*He starts to sing, very softly— a World War I type campaign song is suggested, e.g. "Pack Up Your Troubles." Blum joins him. It becomes a duet in close harmony. Ponce just looks at them. When they finish, he speaks.*)

PONCE. I hate that song. (*Hedges appears.*)

HEDGES. What is it exactly that you want from me, Bruno? (*Bruno, appearing, responds.*)

BRUNO. Hubba, hubba, Hedges!

HEDGES. You'll regret this, Bruno, believe me, you won't be happy! (*Hedges screams, and they both disappear.*)

PONCE. We really could leave now, you know.

BLUM. We'd just go back to what we were.

PONCE. You think so?

BLUM. I know.

YAMADORO. Oh, Monique! (*The three of them are really smiling now.*)

PONCE. A gin fizz with real New Orleans sloe gin. Disgusting.

BLUM. Fredericks of Hollywood. Revolting.

YAMADORO. Nina Foch spread-eagled. Hideous. (*This time it is Ponce who starts singing the song. The others join him for a short reprise as they each try to banish their private demon. They are just finishing when Benson wheels in Hugh Gumbs, still wearing his bedraggled street clothes.*)

HUGH GUMBS. Aaaaaaaaaaaaaaa!

BENSON. Mr. Gumbs, please!

HUGH. Aaaaa!

BENSON. You must try to control yourself.

HUGH. Aaaaaaaaaaaa!

BENSON. You're disturbing the others!

HUGH. Aaaaaaaaaaaa!

BENSON. It's obvious you're in great distress, Mr. Gumbs, but surely . . .

HUGH. I'm desperate, Nurse. You name it and I've got it, done it or used it.

BENSON. As soon as I've gone over your forms . . .

HUGH. Couldn't I just have my injection first?

BENSON. In a moment, Mr. Gumbs.

HUGH. I don't know if I can hold out.

BENSON. (*Keeping her head down, looking at her charts.*) Smoking. Three packs a day.

HUGH. That's right, Nurse.

BENSON. That's a lot, Mr. Gumbs.

HUGH. I'm not even being honest with you. It's closer to five.

BENSON. Five packs?

HUGH. Six, seven, I don't know! Some nights I set my alarm and wake up at fifteen-minute intervals and have a cigarette.

BENSON. Why?

HUGH. Why? Because that's how much I like to smoke! What kind of a question is that? Why? Why do people do anything? Because they like it! They like it!

BENSON. Even when it's bad for them?

HUGH. Yes! That's exactly why I'm here! I'm a liar. I'm a kleptomaniac. I chase women. I bite my nails. You've got to help me!

BENSON. Thank God, Hugh, thank God!

HUGH. What?

BENSON. (*Back to the forms.*) A terrible drinking problem.

HUGH. The worst.

BENSON. How much exactly?

HUGH. Bloody Marys at breakfast, martinis before lunch . . .

BENSON. How many?

HUGH. Two, and three before dinner.

BENSON. Wine with your meals?

HUGH. No.

BENSON. Well that's something.

HUGH. Aquavit. And three or four cherry herrings after dinner and hot saki nightcaps; that's in the winter.

BENSON. In the summer?

HUGH. Cold saki.

BENSON. It sounds like you still have your drinking problem all right.

HUGH. Still?

BENSON. I mean in the summer, too. (*Aside.*) Oh, Hugh, Hugh, you're breaking my heart!

HUGH. Aaaaaaaaaaaaaa!

BENSON. I want to help you, Mr. Gumbs!

HUGH. Then do it! Can't we do all this after the injection?

BENSON. I'm afraid not.

HUGH. (*Indicating the others.*) Look at them! How cured they seem!

BENSON. You will be, too, Hugh. Excuse me, I meant Mr. Gumbs.

HUGH. That's the first thing I'd like to change about me. My name. How could any woman love a Hugh Gumbs?

BENSON. You mustn't torment yourself like that!

HUGH. I can't help it. I meet a woman and it's fine about the drinking, fine about the smoking, it's even fine about the . . . never mind . . . but when I tell her my name, it's all over. Ask yourself, nurse, would you want to go through life as Mrs. Hugh Gumbs?

BENSON. Surely there was one woman, somewhere in your life, who didn't mind your name?

HUGH. One, just one.

BENSON. You see?

HUGH. My mother, for Christ's sake! Please, can't I have my first injection?

BENSON. We're nearly done. A moment ago you said when you met a woman it was "even fine about the . . ." What's your "about the," Mr. Gumbs?

HUGH. I can't tell you.

BENSON. I must have it.

HUGH. Believe me, you don't want it.

BENSON. Your worst habit, Mr. Gumbs, I've got to have it.

HUGH. What are you going to do with it? (*Toynbee enters, smiling as usual.*)

BENSON. This is Hugh Gumbs, Dr. Toynbee, a new patient. He won't tell me what his worst habit is. (*Dr. Toynbee goes to Hugh and stands, looking down at him with his hands on his shoulders, then bends and mumbles his unintelligible gibberish. Hugh bows his head, deeply ashamed, then motions Dr. Toynbee to lean forward while he whispers his worst habit into his ear, with much pantomiming. Dr. Toynbee straightens up, clearly appalled at what he has just heard, and leaves without even looking at Benson.*) In addition to all that, what really brings you to Dunelawn?

HUGH. I've told you.

BENSON. I thought perhaps there might be a somewhat more personal reason. I only meant perhaps someone else is responsible for your coming here.

HUGH. Like who?

BENSON. A woman.

HUGH. You're telling me! Say, and you're going to think I'm crazy, did you ever work for an answering service?

BENSON. No.

HUGH. Your voice sounds so familiar.

BENSON. I know.

HUGH. There was this real battle-axe on my service about five years ago. For a minute, you sounded just like her. Where was I?

BENSON. A woman.

HUGH. Oh yeah, a woman. Yes, there is one.

BENSON. Tell me about her.

HUGH. (*With a sigh.*) She was very beautiful, very feminine, very desirable. Everything a man could want. Intelligent, decisive, yet strangely yielding.

BENSON. (*Almost a murmur.*) Yet strangely yielding!

HUGH. She's probably the finest woman alive on the face of this earth.

BENSON. Her name, Mr. Gumbs?

HUGH. Char-Burger! Did you ever work part-time in Char-Burger on East 63rd Street!

BENSON. I'm afraid not.

HUGH. You sound so familiar and I never forget a voice. Eleven o'clock news weather girl, maybe?

BENSON. No. Her name, Mr. Gumbs?

HUGH. (*A tormented memory.*) Mildred Canby! Can I have my injection now?

BENSON. What about Ruth Benson?

HUGH. Ruth Benson?

BENSON. I believe that's the name on your biography here.

HUGH. I don't remember telling anyone anything about Ruth Benson.

BENSON. You were delirious when they brought you in.

HUGH. I was?

BENSON. You were raving about a Ruth Benson. That's all you said. Ruth Benson. Ruth Benson. Over and over again.

HUGH. What do you know?

BENSON. She must have been very important to you.

HUGH. Not particularly.

BENSON. I'll be the judge of that. Tell me about her.

HUGH. The main thing I could tell you about Ruth Benson is that she was fat. About 280, I'd say.

BENSON. I'm sure she was never 280, Mr. Gumbs.

HUGH. You never saw Ruth Benson.

BENSON. 230 maybe, but not 280!

HUGH. The point is she was fat, right? I mean she was circus fat.

BENSON. I know the type. Go on, Mr. Gumbs.

HUGH. What else about her? I think Ruth Benson is the only person, man, woman or child, I ever asked to take a bath. She used to smoke six packs a day, minimum. Cigarillos. Nicotine stains right up to her elbows! I don't guess she ever drew a sober breath. My main image of her is passed out on the floor like a big rancid mountain. And talk about being a slob! She had dust balls under her bed the size of watermelons. She didn't just have roaches in her kitchen. She raised them. It was like a goddamn stud farm in there. You'd light the oven and there'd be a flash-fire from all the grease.

BENSON. It sounds like Ruth Benson was a woman with a lot of bad habits.

HUGH. She was an out and out pig.

BENSON. I can't help noticing a special glow that comes into your voice every time you mention her name.

HUGH. We had a lot in common, Ruthie and I. I'll never forget the night we each caught the other at precisely the same instant picking their nose. God, she was gross.

BENSON. There's that glow again.

HUGH. Just thinking of her with all those fingers up there and I have to smile. You're bringing back a lot of bad memories, Nurse. I haven't thought of Ruth Benson and her soiled sheets in a long time. Your voice sounds so familiar. (*Benson is making a big show of raising her skirt to fix a stocking.*) You have beautiful legs, Nurse.

BENSON. Familiar voice, unfamiliar legs.

HUGH. The legs look like some movie star, the voice still sounds like that answering voice.

BENSON. (*Straightening up.*) Don't you know who I am yet, Hugh? No, don't say anything until I've finished. I'm not going to turn around until you tell me that you want me to turn around. I'm glad you don't recognize me. There's no reason that you should. I did it all for you, Hugh. Hugh Gumbs. Like your name, it wasn't easy. But I didn't mind the suffering, the self-humiliation, the incredible self-discipline. I wanted to torture myself into becoming someone a man like you could love and I have. Let me finish! I'm brutally honest with myself. That's not enough, I know, but it's a beginning. When I look in a mirror now I can say yes, yes, I like that person. I'm not smug, Hugh, I just know my own worth. For five years I've made myself thoroughly miserable so that today I could make you happy and I did it all for love. (*A pause.*) Now yes or no, Hugh, do you want me to turn around? (*A pause.*)

HUGH. Who are you?

BENSON. (*Turning to him, ecstatic.*) It's me. Ruth.

HUGH. Ruth?

BENSON. Ruth Benson.

HUGH. Fat Ruth Benson?

BENSON. Yes, yes!

HUGH. You don't look like Ruth.

BENSON. (*She is so happy.*) I know, I know!

HUGH. You don't sound like her, either.

BENSON. Voice lessons, darling.

HUGH. You don't even smell like Ruth.

BENSON. Zest, Dial, Dove, Lava!

HUGH. You have such beautiful legs.

BENSON. I worked for them.

HUGH. Your teeth.

BENSON. All caps.

HUGH. And your . . . (*He indicates her breasts.*)

BENSON. Exercises.

HUGH. Your big hairy mole.

BENSON. Cosmetic surgery.

HUGH. It's really you?

BENSON. It's really mè. The real me and it's all for you, Hugh, I did it all for you.

HUGH. You did?

BENSON. And now that I've found you again I'm not going to let you go this time.

HUGH. You didn't let me go the last time. I let you go.

BENSON. It doesn't matter. The point is you won't want to let me go this time. Oh Hugh, I'm going to make you very, very happy. You're the luckiest man alive.

HUGH. (*Shaking his head.*) No, Ruth, no.

BENSON. What's wrong?

HUGH. It would never work, Ruth.

BENSON. Of course it will work. It has to work.

HUGH. I couldn't do it to you.

BENSON. Yes, you can. You can do anything you want to me, don't you see?

HUGH. Ruth, I've committed myself to Dunelawn, I've gotten so bad.

BENSON. Do you love me?

HUGH. Love you?

BENSON. Be blunt with me, Hugh.

HUGH. I don't even recognize you, you're so terrific looking.

BENSON. Forget the way I look now and ask yourself: do you love me?

HUGH. You're so far above me now.

BENSON. From down there, do you love me?

HUGH. I didn't love you when you were fat and rotten. I can't love you now that you're beautiful and perfect and have such terrific legs.

BENSON. I'm not perfect.

HUGH. Well nearly.

BENSON. Nearly's not enough. Nearly's never enough. I still have my faults, too, darling.

HUGH. Like what? Name one.

BENSON. I can't off the top of my head but I'm sure I do somewhere.

HUGH. You see, it's hopeless. You're the sky above and I'm the mud below. Maybe someday I'll be worthy of you but right now I want to forget all about you and try to improve myself, too, and maybe, just maybe, you'll still be up there in the stratosphere, all shiny like an angel, when I poke my head up through the clouds.

BENSON. That was poetic, Hugh.

HUGH. And what does someone like me do with an angel?

BENSON. Love her.

HUGH. From a very great distance.

BENSON. Where are you going?

HUGH. I don't know.

BENSON. I'm coming with you.

HUGH. Angels fly. I've got to crawl first.

BENSON. I'm not an angel. Forget the angel.

HUGH. You're an angel!

BENSON. I'm not an angel!

HUGH. You're an angel!

BENSON. I'm not an angel!

HUGH. No, you're an angel, Ruth!

BENSON. I'm not an angel! It's the goddamn white uniform!

HUGH. You're an angel. I can't even ask you for a cigarette.

BENSON. Yes. Yes you can. Take the whole pack. I'll light it for you. You want a drink, darling, I'll get you a drink. Bruno! Go ahead, bite your nails. Do anything you want. I love you. (*She puts her fingers in her nose.*) It can be just like old times together!

HUGH. Start that up again and I'll crack your jaw open! (*He pulls her hand away. Benson dissolves in tears.*) Oh, Ruthie, Ruthie! Don't you see how I'd drag you down? Trying to please me you'd only degrade yourself. Please, let's not talk about it anymore. Just give me the injection.

BENSON. Then you don't love me?

HUGH. I can't love you right now, you're just too darn good for me.

BENSON. (*Fixing him with a new glance, all heavy-lidded and seductive.*) You think? (*She starts coming for him. She kisses him. A very long kiss. Hugh hardly responds.*)

HUGH. Can I please have that injection now?

BENSON. (*Her last resort.*) All right, Hugh, and remember, you asked for it.

HUGH. (*Indicating the others.*) I just want to be like them.

BENSON. You will, Hugh, you will. (*Hedges and Bruno enter. Hedges's uniform is askew. She looks worn-out and dazed.*)

HEDGES. Ruth! Ruth! Ruth!

BENSON. Becky!

HEDGES. I'm turning in my cap, Ruth.

BENSON. Becky, what's wrong?

BRUNO. Hubba, hubba, Benson.

BENSON. What has he done to you?

HEDGES. Bruno and I are going to be married.

BENSON. What?

BRUNO. You heard her, mutt-face.

BENSON. What happened, Becky?

HEDGES. I'm in love, Ruth!

BENSON. What has that beast done to you?

HEDGES. Bruno's been saving up for a trailer. We're moving to Fort Lauderdale. Bruno's mommy has a pizza stand down there. This is goodbye, Ruth.

BENSON. (*Slaps her.*) Snap out of it, Hedges.

HEDGES. (*Finally, at long last and it's about time: snapping out of it and slapping her back.*) You snap out of it! That's all you do is slap people. (*She slaps her again.*) Only now you'll have to find someone else to slap!

YAMADORO. (*He is vaguely interested.*) Slap! (*Instead of doing anything, Hugh just sits there and pulls his coat over his head.*)

BENSON. All the time I've invested in you.

HEDGES. Are you ready, Bruno?

BENSON. You must be crazy.

HEDGES. I'm *happy!*

BENSON. I thought you cared about improving yourself.

HEDGES. Bruno likes me the way I am.

BENSON. He's a beast.

HEDGES. And I've got goddamn big thighs! Nobody's perfect!

BENSON. What about Dunelawn?

HEDGES. I won't miss it.

BENSON. What about Dr. Toynbee?

HEDGES. That man is a saint.

BENSON. Then why would you leave him?

HEDGES. He gives me the creeps.

BENSON. Zero defects, Becky?

HEDGES. (*Glowing.*) That's Bruno.

BRUNO. (*Triumphant.*) Hubba, hubba, Benson!

BENSON. Don't even speak to me!

BRUNO. Let's go, sugar.

HEDGES. (*She turns to Ponce, Blum and Yamadoro.*) If any of you had any sense, you'd come with us. There's enough room in Bruno's microbus for everyone. (*She fastens her cap on Mr. Blum's head, then turns to Hugh.*)

BENSON. Just go, you . . . you pizza waitress!

HEDGES. Are you Hugh Gumbs?

HUGH. Yes, yes I am.

HEDGES. Are you in for it!

BRUNO. Hubba, hubba, dog-face!

HEDGES. Hubba, hubba, Ruth! (*They are gone.*)

BENSON. You'll regret this, Hedges, you'll regret this for the rest of your life! (*She turns to Hugh.*) Oh, Hugh, you see how terrible other people are! Thank God for Dunelawn and Dr. Toynbee. I'll get your injection right away. (*Hugh gets out of his wheelchair.*) Where are you going?

HUGH. I can't stay here with you, Ruth. I'm not even worthy of Dunelawn. Maybe I'll come back to you one day, a better and worthier man. If not, I know you'll find someone good enough for you.

BENSON. It's a rotten world out there. It'll destroy you.

HUGH. It already has. (*He starts to go.*)

BENSON. (*Concealing the syringe.*) One last kiss. (*They kiss. Benson has the syringe in her hand, poised to inject him. Dr. Toynbee enters. Benson is mortified.*) Dr. Toynbee! I'm so ashamed. I . . . Mr. Gumbs was just leaving.

HUGH. That woman is perfect! (*He goes up the aisle.*)

BENSON. I don't know what happened, Dr. Toynbee. I left them with Nurse Hedges and she's gone off to Florida to open a pizza stand with Bruno and the love of my life is gone again and I'm having a nervous breakdown because I don't understand people anymore. It's so good here. You're so good. Why would anyone want to leave Dunelawn when all we're trying to do is help them to be perfect? (*Benson is shattered. She is holding onto Dr. Toynbee for support. He puts his arm around her and takes her to the wheelchair left empty by Hugh Gumbs.*) You're so good, Dr. Toynbee. It's the end of summer. (*Dr. Toynbee goes to the cart to get a syringe.*) I won't cry. I refuse to cry. It's you and Dunelawn I'm thinking of. Not myself. The world is filled with men like Hugh Gumbs. But someone somewhere is the man for me. Zero defects. No faults, no failings, no fantasies. Where is he, Dr. Toynbee? (*She looks up into Dr. Toynbee's eyes as he injects her. A wonderful smile lights up her face.*) Oh yes! (*Dr. Toynbee gets a straitjacket hidden behind the wheelchair and carefully puts Benson's arms through it. Meanwhile, Blum begins to sing again, very softly, the same World War I campaign song. Ponce, Yamadoro, and even Benson join him. They are all smiling blissfully. In the distance, we hear even more voices beginning to sing. Dr. Toynbee smiles benignly at his three male patients. Then down at Nurse Benson. Then up at us. He takes a step forward and starts to address us in his unintelligible gibberish. A few leaves fall from the scraggly tree. The lights fade.*)

WHERE HAS TOMMY FLOWERS GONE?

(1971)

For my friends

WHERE HAS TOMMY FLOWERS GONE? by Terrence McNally was first presented on January 7, 1971, by the Yale Repertory Theatre, New Haven, Connecticut. It was directed by Larry Arrick. Set and costumes designed by Steven Rubin. Lighting and graphics co-ordinated by William B. Warfel. Lighting designed by Dennis G. Daluiso. Slides by Michael Shane. Music arranged by Barbara Damashek. Sound created by Eugene Kimball. The production stage managers were Frank S. Torok and Carol M. Waaser.

THE CAST

TOMMY FLOWERS	Robert Drivas
GRETA RAPP	Barbara Damashek
SHOWGIRL	Lydia Fisher
NEEDA LEMON	Sarah Albertson
BUNNY BARNUM	Katherine De Hetre
TOMMY'S MOTHER	
FIRST LADY	Elizabeth Parrish
WOMAN CUSTOMER	
TOMMY'S BROTHER	James Naughton
TOMMY'S NEPHEW	Henry Winkler
BEN DELIGHT	Jeremy Geidt
ARNOLD	Steve Van Benschoten
TAXI DRIVER	David Ackroyd
MODERATOR	

Also in the cast were: Louis Plante, Charles Turner, Peter Co-vette, James Brick, Maxime Lieberman and Lisa Carling.

Subsequently, WHERE HAS TOMMY FLOWERS GONE? was presented on August 11, 1971, at the Berkshire Theatre Festival, Stock-bridge, Massachusetts.

This same production opened in New York City on October 7, 1971, at the Eastside Playhouse. It was produced by Richard Scanga and Adela Holzer. It was directed by Jacques Levy. Sets by David Chapman. Lighting by Marc B. Weiss. Costumes by James

Berton Harris. Visuals by Ed Bowes and Bernadette Mayer. The production stage managers were Nicholas Russiyan and Kate M. Pollock.

THE CAST

TOMMY FLOWERS	Robert Drivas
BEN DELIGHT	Wallace Rooney
NEDDA LEMON	Kathleen Dabney
ARNOLD	Toppy
THE GIRLS	Barbara Worthington
THE MEN	F. Murray Abraham
THE WOMEN	Marion Paone

The time of the play is now.
  New York City.

The places of the play are here, there and everywhere.

The people of the play are:

> TOMMY FLOWERS
>
> BEN DELIGHT
>
> ARNOLD
>
> NEDDA LEMON
>
> THE MEN
>
> THE WOMEN
>
> THE GIRLS

OVERTURE

Special spotlight on the Conductor. He bows to the audience, acknowledging their applause—on tape, raps his baton on the podium for attention and waits. Special spotlight comes up center stage on a gleaming stainless steel and glass phonograph. More applause. There is a shiny black record on the changer ready to play.

The Conductor raises both arms. The record drops into the playing position and begins to spin. The tone arm hovers over the record a moment and then falls heavily onto it—but missing the lead-in groove so that what we hear is the horrible (and mightily amplified) clunking sound of the phonograph needle banging along the edge of the record. Clunk. Clunk. Clunk.

The Conductor just stands there with both arms raised. After what will seem· like an interminable length of time, the Black Stagehand comes shuffling out of the wings. You have never seen anyone shuffle more and get to where he is going less. He does the kind of vaudeville/minstrel show shuffle that takes three steps forward then two steps back. He has a portable cassette tape recorder slung over one shoulder and the music he shuffles to is Otis Redding's "(Sittin' On) The Dock of the Bay." When he finally makes it over to the clunk-clunk-clunking phonograph (he can take five minutes for all I care if he's an expert shuffler; the longer the better, in any case), he stands looking down at the spinning record. He starts moving his head and neck in a circle until they are going at 33⅓ r.p.m. and he can read the label.

BLACK STAGEHAND. Where has Tommy Flowers gone? Side one. (*He laughs hugely and looks out at the audience.*) Shee-it! (*He gives the phonograph a good hard swat and the needle drops into the proper groove.*)

The Conductor gives the downbeat and we hear the three opening chords of the overture to The Magic Flute. *What follows next is pretty much up to the imagination of a composer or a sound man but some of the songs and sounds that make up the* Where Has Tommy Flowers Gone? *Overture are:*

A baby crying.
"The Star Spangled Banner."
The Andrews Sisters' "Rum and Coca Cola."
"I'm Looking Over a Four Leaf Clover."
War sounds.
The theme music from "Let's Pretend" and the "Lone Ranger."
A voice calling "Henry! Henry Aldrich!"
"Abba Dabba Honeymoon."
Yma Sumac.
A big explosion.
Bill Hailey and the Comets' "Rock Around the Clock."
A woman's screams.
Elvis Presley's "Heartbreak Hotel."
More gunfire.
Early Dylan.
Sirens.
Many gunshots.
More sirens.
Early Beatles.
"We Shall Overcome."
The Zarathustra music from 2001.
The conclusion of the Magic Flute Overture *itself.*

During the Overture we will see many images flashed on a series of screens above the stage. Some of these images of Tommy Flowers, his life and times, will surely include:
Tommy as a baby boy.
FDR.
The baby boy getting bigger.
Truman.
As a little boy dressed in a sailor suit.
A birthday cake.
Now he's riding a pony.
Another birthday cake.
It's his first Holy Communion.
V-Day celebrations.
He's quite the little man now.
A Studebaker.
As a teenager with a crewcut.

Eisenhower.

At a high school prom with a flat top.

Then as a college graduate with somewhat longer hair.

Then as a tourist in Paris with even longer hair.

Kennedy.

Then as a soldier in front of the Berlin Wall with a crewcut again.

Johnson.

Then a series of pictures in which our hero's hair gets longer and longer and longer and his clothes become funky and hip.

Nixon.

In the final picture, Tommy is smiling broadly and looking right at us. With one hand he forms the "V," with the other he is giving us The Finger.

At this point the Overture reaches its climax, the phonograph blows up and the picture of Tommy Flowers is extinguished.

ACT ONE

DEDICATION

TOMMY. I would like to thank the following people for making me what I am today: Mom and Dad; my big brother Harry; my wonderful Nana; my beloved Grandpa; Walt Disney; The Little Engine That Could; Golden Books; American nuns; Batman and Robin and all the gang over at Dell Comics; Little Lulu; Wonder Woman; Betty and Jughead; Rossini, the Lone Ranger and Tonto, too; Cream of Wheat for Let's Pretend; all MGM musicals but especially the one with Abba Dabba Honeymoon; Ringling Brothers, Barnum and Bailey; Francis the Talking Mule; Ma and Pa Kettle and their farm; B.O. Plenty and Sparkle; Henry Aldrich in the Haunted House; Abbott and Costello; the Wolf Man; Kukla, Fran and Ollie; Uncle Miltie and my real Uncle Fred; Harry S Truman; Margaret S. Truman; Gene Autrey and his girdle (if he ever really wore one); Roy Rogers and Dale Evans; Johnny Weismuller; Johnny Sheffield; Sabu; Esther Williams; Joe Di Maggio; Pee Wee Reese; Jackie Robinson; Ralph Bunche; Trygve Lie; Miss America; Mr. America; the Weavers; Patty Page; Babe Diedrickson Zaharias; Mme. Chiang Kai-shek; Chuck Berry; the Coasters; Candy Barr; Lili St. Cyr; all strippers who worked with animals but especially snakes; Ava Gardner; Hal Wallis; Corinne Calvet; Jerry Lee and plain Jerry Lewis; Johnny Mathis; Terry Moore; ol' Marilyn up there, of course; James Dean; Elvis Presley; John F. Kennedy; Rose F. Kennedy; Fidel Castro; Bernadette Castro (hell, why not?); Che Guevara; Bob Dylan; Ho Chi Minh; the Beatles; Miss Teenage America; Mme. Nhu; Lady Bird Johnson; Lyndon Bird Johnson; Lynda Bird Johnson Robb; Luci Bird Johnson Nugent; the Rolling Stones; Janis Joplin; the Man From Glad; Richard M. Nixon; the last girl I balled and all the sisters of mercy to come *and* . . . whew! . . . we really do get by with a little help from our friends . . . Mr. Thomas Jefferson, who said something about God forbid we should ever be twenty years without a rebellion! To all of them I dedicate this act. Oh, yeah, I'm Tommy Flowers. Hi.

(*A really statuesque Showgirl has appeared. Her costume is revealing, her manner intensely sincere.*)

SHOWGIRL. Dynamite! Of all the good stuff that is the stuff! Place this in the immediate vicinity of a lot of rich loafers who live by the sweat of other people's brows, and light the fuse. A most cheerful and gratifying result will follow. A pound of this good stuff beats a bushel of ballots all hollow—and don't you forget it. Our lawmakers might as well try to sit down on the crater of a volcano or on a point of a bayonet as to endeavor to stop the manufacture and use of dynamite. Albert Parsons, 1885. Thank you. (*Showgirl exits. The stage is empty.*)

ANNOUNCER'S VOICE. May I have your attention please. A mink stole with the monogrammed initials DKR has been found on the floor of the ladies' room on the mezzanine level. Thank you.

THE LAST OF THE LINCOLN CENTER FOR THE PERFORMING ARTS

(*On the screens above the stage we see a photographic montage/mural of Lincoln Center. In the left panel is the New York State Theatre. In the center panel we see the Metropolitan Opera House. At the right are the Vivian Beaumont Theatre and Philharmonic Hall. On the stage level and in the middle of all this is the Lincoln Center fountain. It isn't working. A girl guide, Greta Rapp, enters and greets us.*)

GRETA. Hello, welcome to Lincoln Center. I'm Greta Rapp, your guide for today's tour. (*Consulting a piece of paper.*) *Bonjour, bienvenu à Lincoln Center. Je suis Greta Rapp, votre guide pour le tour d'aujoud'hui. Buon giorno, benvenuto a Lincoln Center. Io sono*—

VOICES. (*Unseen, grumbling.*) Speak English . . . yeah, lady, whadda ya think? . . . what did she say? what did she say?

GRETA. Then we're all Americans? Well that's something! Most days it's like the United Nations around here. (*She laughs.*) The

Lincoln Center for the Performing Arts is the nation's cultural capital. Naturally, it's in New York. (*She waits.*) That usually gets a laugh. (*She laughs.*) It was built *by* the people of New York City *for* the people of New York City to the tune of two hundred and thirty-five million, six hundred and seventy-eight thousand, four hundred and eighty-two dollars and eleven cents. There have been an awful lot of jokes made about where all those eleven cents went, too, let me tell you! (*She laughs.*) And just try to get a ticket for something! (*She makes one final effort to amuse her apparently stony-faced charges.*) Of course there are some people who consider themselves fortunate that they can't! (*Again nothing. She braces herself.*) Shall we begin? Once we're inside, no smoking, positively no picture taking and quiet, *s'il vous plait.* This way please and mind the construction. (*She crosses to underneath the picture of the New York State Theatre.*) The New York State Theatre is home for the brilliant New York City Ballet. The theatre boasts three hundred and forty-six miles, that's right, *miles,* of carpeting; thirty-one separate but equal rest rooms with a combined total of one hundred and eighty-six individual conveniences, and uses in excess of fifty tons of paper towels and bathroom tissues in one season. Fifty tons, ladies. Imagine. Sshh! We're in luck. They're holding auditions. Let's tiptoe in. (*Lights come up center stage on Tommy. He is disguised as a Ballerina. He wears a pink tutu and toe shoes. He carries a bright red shopping bag which he promptly sets down.*)

VOICE (Russian accent). (*Unseen, from the rear of the theatre.*) Miss Heather Begg.

TOMMY/BALLERINA. (*Thick cockney accent.*) That's Begg with two g's, ducky, but that's ain't what I'm doing. Swan Lake, guvnor. The whole bleeding thing. (*Music begins. Tommy dances an outlandish ballet. His concentration is fierce but he moves with all the grace of an elephant.*)

VOICE. (*After only a few moments of this madness.*) Thank you, Miss Begg! That will do, Miss Begg!

TOMMY/BALLERINA. (*In the middle of a pirouette.*) I can't stop now, luv! Wheeeeeeee! (*He whirls and dances to his conclusion. Stunned silence in the theatre. He looks out hopefully.*) Well, luv?

VOICE. No, luv.

TOMMY/BALLERINA. (*Eliza Doolittle.*) Caaaaaaaa!

VOICE. Thank you, Miss Begg.

TOMMY/BALLERINA. (*Smiling sweetly; it sounds like thank you.*) Fuck you, ducky, fuck you very much. Nice place you got here, guvnor. Pity. (*He exits, leaving the red shopping bag where he first placed it. Pinspot on the shopping bag. Other stage lights fade.*)

GRETA. As you can see, they don't call Lincoln Center the Boulevard of Broken Dreams for nothing. Many are called here by the Muses but few are chosen. We can't all be a Leontyne Price. Mind the scaffoldings. (*She crosses to underneath the picture of Philharmonic Hall.*) Philharmonic Hall, as you may have heard, heard, heard . . . ! (*She laughs.*) . . . has had more than its fair share of acoustical problems.

AN ECHO. . . . . fair share of acoustical problems.

GRETA. But I think you'll find they're pretty well under control by now.

AN ECHO. . . . . under control by now.

GRETA. For those of you with a more scientific bent of mind, recent tests now rank PH as the 19th most acoustically perfect concert hall to be erected since the Second World War. That's three places up since the last time and we're still climbing! And actually, the slight echo that remains has proved an interesting challenge to conductors, composers, and soloists alike. We'll go this way now. Careful on the stairs here, they're meant to be lit. Now this is strictly off the record. For those of you who were fortunate enough to catch the telecast of the historic opening concert, where you're standing right now is the famous spot where Lenny kissed Jackie much to Jack's chagrin. Remember, I didn't say that. Hmmm? Leonard Bernstein. Jacqueline Kennedy. President Kennedy. Never mind. Sshh! Someone's on stage. (*Lights come up center stage on Tommy disguised as a Musician. He has long, wild, unruly hair; a big moustache and glasses. He carries a pair of cymbals and another red shopping bag which he promptly sets down.*)

VOICE (Italian accent). Giuseppe Bonatella.

TOMMY/MUSICIAN. (*Heavy Italian accent.*) That's a me! Giuseppe Bonatella! The most a musical fella! The big a noise on Bleecker Street! What I'm a gonna play for you now, mister, is a the

Beethoven Ninth a Symphony in a C sharp a major, as arranged for a solo a cymbal. It's a my own arrangement. And a one, and a two, and a three . . . ! (*He crashes the cymbals violently for several minutes.*)

VOICE. Mr. Bonatella! *Signor* Bonatella! Ehi, Bonatella!

TOMMY/MUSICIAN. I can't a hear you! Too much a noise! (*He continues crashing the cymbals a while. Finally he stops.*)

VOICE. *Grazie.*

TOMMY/MUSICIAN. Ehi, paisano, you speak a Italian! Bravo! You want a more music? I play a more music! (*He crashes away again for several moments. Stops at last.*)

VOICE. That's enough, Signor Bonatella, *basta*, please!

TOMMY/MUSICIAN. Giuseppe Bonatella! That's a me! (*He crashes the cymbals.*) I getta the job, mister?

VOICE. We a letta you know.

TOMMY/MUSICIAN. I don't getta the job, mister, you gonna getta the boom-boom! (*He crashes the cymbals together one more time and exits, leaving the shopping bag behind again. Lights down center stage except for pin spot on the shopping bag.*)

GRETA. We can't all be a Van Cliburn either. The standards at Lincoln Center couldn't possibly be any lower than they are now. Let in one like that and pretty soon you're letting in them all. One thing about the level of performance here, it's consistent. That's two broken hearts today and it's not even noon. Lincoln Center is a bitch. Let's all stay together now in a tight little group. Watch out for the broken glass. That's the famous Henry Moore fountain those men are repairing. It was leaking right into the underground garages directly beneath, capacity 3126, and people coming out of the theatres kept walking into it and getting wet and then their cars wouldn't start and so they drained the fountain! It's people who don't look where they're going they should fix. Careful, it's a little tricky here. Are we all here? (*She has crossed to underneath the picture of the Vivian Beaumont Theatre.*) The Vivian Beaumont Theatre is the home of theatre at its best. Its actors and actresses, its directors, its plays, its scenery and costumes, its lighting effects, its fully annotated programs, its backstage facilities, everything! are without question the finest in the land. Just think of all the wonderful plays that have been done here and all the great stars of today who got their start on this very stage so that lucky audiences could later boast "We saw her when." Those who say the theatre is dying certainly ought to drop in at the Vivian Beaumont Theatre. Let's see what exciting young talent they're auditioning today for their Salute to the Polish Expressionists season. (*The lights come up center stage on Tommy disguised as an Actor. He wears tights, sunglasses and a T-shirt. He lies on the floor making strange noises and jerking convulsively. There is another red shopping bag beside him. The noises and jerking continue for a very long time.*)

VOICE (American accent). Mr. Takinas? (*Tommy makes intense, violent, waving gestures as if to say "I'm concentrating. Don't rush me." He groans. He jerks. The whole Grotowski-trained actor bit.*)

GRETA. (*Stage whisper.*) I think we're seeing one of those Method actors at work.

TOMMY/ACTOR. (*An insane, inarticulate howl in the direction of Greta.*) Aaaaaarrrrrgggggghhhhh!!!!!

GRETA. (*Covering her mouth.*) Sorry!

VOICE. We don't have all day, Mr. Takinas. (*Tommy nods violently as if to say "I know, I know! I'm almost ready." When he finally begins to speak it is with a rather pronounced speech impediment.*)

TOMMY/ACTOR. Speak the speech, I pray you, as I pronounced it to you, trippingly on the tongue. But if you mouth it, as many of our players do, I had as lief the town crier spoke my lines. Nor do not saw the air too much with your hand, thus, but use all gently, for in the very torrent, tempest, and (as I may say) whirlwind of your passion, you must acquire and beget a temperance that may give it smoothness. O, it offends me—

VOICE. Thank you, Mr. Takinas.

TOMMY/ACTOR. Tikanis. Orestes Tikanis. Greek.

VOICE. Yes, Mr. Tikanis. Don't call us, we'll call you.

TOMMY/ACTOR. I also do French farce, some musical comedy and I'll work in the nude. Wanna see?

VOICE. That's all right, Mr. Tikanis, and thank you.

TOMMY/ACTOR. How come you don't do more American plays?

VOICE. We'd like to, only there aren't enough of them.

TOMMY/ACTOR. I've got a whole shitload of 'em. Wanna hear one?

VOICE. Maybe next time. Who's next?

TOMMY/ACTOR. You know something funny? There ain't gonna be a next time. (*He laughs and exits, leaving the shopping bag behind. Lights come down center stage except for pin spot on the shopping bag.*)

GRETA. The way he bit my head off you'd think it was my fault. Actors! They're so temperamental. And for what? We'll take the tunnel here. Careful of the railings. They're loose. A woman fell and broke her hip last week and now she's suing us. Suing Lincoln Center! (*She has crossed to underneath the picture of the Metropolitan Opera House.*) The Metropolitan Opera House is the crown jewel in the Lincoln Center tiara. From the Chagall murals in the lobby to the Austrian cut-crystal chandeliers and African rosewood walls in the auditorium proper, truly it deserves its appellation as the Fountainbleau of the New World. And surely it is the dream of every great singer to lift his voice in song here. Indeed, one cannot truly say one has sung until one has sung at the Met, as it is so affectionately called. We seem to be in luck all around today. The legendary Metropolitan Auditions of the Air are in progress. Let's listen in.

VOICE (*Viennese accent*). Madame Anita Dorfmeister-Gluck. (*Lights come up center stage on Tommy disguised as a great Diva. He wears a large picture hat and a floor-length mink coat. He carries another red shopping bag which he will set down.*)

TOMMY/DIVA. (*Thick German accent.*) I am from the Stuttgart Opera. You know Stuttgart? Stuttgart is fabulous. Stuttgart looks just like Los Angeles. Los Angeles looks just like Stuttgart. New York looks like Dusseldorf.

VOICE. Madame Dorfmeister, if you please.

TOMMY/DIVA. Dorfmeister-Gluck, if *you* please. I shall sing, what I shall sing is *Tosca* by Puccini. The great aria, "Vissi d'arte, Vissi d'amore."

VOICE. Very good. Maestro.

TOMMY/DIVA. Which means—it's in Italian, *ja?*—she lived for art, she lived for love. I love this woman!

VOICE. May we begin then?

TOMMY/DIVA. (*Setting the scene.*) Act two. Napoleonic Rome. The Rome of Napoleon. Floria Tosca, the fabulous, the beautiful, the tempestuous grand diva, I *am* this woman to my tips! begs the evil Baron Scarpia on her hands and knees—

VOICE. Please, Madame Dorfmeister, there are others behind you!

TOMMY/DIVA. Dorfmeister-Gluck, *liebchen*. Where are they? (*Raucous German laugh.*) I begin. They go out of their heads when I do this in Stuttgart. (*Nods to accompanist after much throat clearing.*) Otto. Play, gypsy, play. (*He begins the aria in the most horrendous falsetto soprano imaginable. He is only a few bars into the aria when the Voice calls out.*)

VOICE. Thank you, Madame Dorfmeister-Gluck, thank you!

TOMMY/DIVA. (*Without missing a beat.*) You're welcome, you're welcome! (*He goes right on singing.*)

VOICE. Throw that woman out of here!

TOMMY/DIVA. (*Injured majesty.*) Don't touch me. Don't nobody lay a finger. I go. But you see those pretty Austrian cut-crystal chandeliers, *ja?*

GRETA. (*Stage whisper.*) I was telling you about them.

TOMMY/DIVA. Pretty soon you don't see those pretty Austrian cut-crystal chandeliers. I take this to the ambassador. Otto, my limousine! (*He sweeps out majestically, leaving the red shopping bag behind. Lights fade center stage except for pin spot on shopping bag. All four shopping bags glowing in their special pin spots now.*)

GRETA. We'll go outside now. Careful not to slip. These marble floors are murder. (*She moves downstage.*) Our tour of Lincoln Center for the Performing Arts wouldn't be complete without a stop at the famous Lincoln Center fountain with its beautiful dancing waters whose intricate patterns are programmed by an IBM computer. It's been estimated that you'd have to stand here ninety-three hours and forty-six minutes to see the fountain repeat itself. Of course when the fountain's actually working— Tuesdays, Wednesdays and alternate Saturdays—it's never been left on that long so nobody's had a chance to prove it, but I can't see any reason to doubt IBM. I thought I'd throw in a little plug there. My father's with IBM. *Are* you? Maybe you know him. Ira Rapp? Small world, isn't it? (*She laughs.*) Anyway, the fountain with its geometrically-patterned-after-a-design-by-Michelangelo-plaza is a popular gathering place at intermission *and* for some of New York City's weirdest weirdos. And believe me, this town is full of them. There's one now. (*Tommy enters disguised as a crazy, tattered Old Lady. He carries another red shopping bag and a violin. He mutters to himself as he makes ready to play.*)

TOMMY/OLD LADY. They want some of Ma Picker's mince pie, they're gonna get some of Ma Picker's mince pie. With arsenic and ground glass in it. No respect, no respect at all for an old lady anymore! Ma Picker's mince pie, that's the ticket! Those sons of bitches. (*He continues in this vein.*)

GRETA. I must say I haven't seen that one before. If any of you would care to make a donation and a request, I'm sure she'd be very happy to oblige.

TOMMY/OLD LADY. I don't do no requests, mister. I take donations but I don't do no requests. (*He accompanies himself on the violin and sings.*)
Lincoln Center falling down.
Lincoln Center falling down.
Lincoln Center falling down.
There's mice in the lobby.
(*Lunging out with his bowstick.*) Go on, get out of here! Everybody beat it! Scram! Shoo!

GRETA. (*Ignoring this.*) What did I tell you?

TOMMY/OLD LADY. And don't come back!

GRETA. That concludes our tour of Lincoln Center. I hope you've enjoyed yourself. And please, please don't litter. New York is a nice place to visit but we have to live here. Goodbye.

TOMMY/OLD LADY. Anybody make litter, I kill them! Go on, get away from here! Buzz off! Hit the road! Take a powder! Vamoose!

GRETA. Who do you think you are?

TOMMY/OLD LADY. You, too, mister, you, too!

GRETA. You can't do that to people!

TOMMY/OLD LADY. Who says, who says?

GRETA. The law for one.

TOMMY/OLD LADY. What law? Whose law? I don't see no law.

GRETA. Stop poking at me with that!

TOMMY/OLD LADY. I said you better beat it, mister!

GRETA. I don't want to beat it. It's a free country. I can't beat it.

I work here. And you're crazy. Now leave me alone or I'll call the police.

TOMMY/OLD LADY. (*Hog-calling.*) Sooowwwiiieee! Sooowwwiiieee!

GRETA. I mean it! (*But we can see she is amused.*)

TOMMY/OLD LADY. Okay, mister.

GRETA. Stop calling me that. I'm a girl.

TOMMY/OLD LADY. Okay, girl. (*He starts to play the violin.*)

GRETA. Must you?

TOMMY/OLD LADY. It's a free country, honey.

GRETA. Unfortunately. (*She turns her back to him, apparently for good.*)

TOMMY/OLD LADY. (*Sings.*)
>
> Lincoln Center falling down.
> Lincoln Center falling down.
> Lincoln Center falling down.

(*Speaks.*) You know something?

GRETA. What?

TOMMY/OLD LADY. For a girl guide you got a very nice pair of stems on you. (*Sings.*) There's a bomb in the lobby!

GRETA. (*Turning.*) Hunh?

TOMMY/OLD LADY. It wouldn't be a show without some tippy tap toe! (*He starts tap dancing. He drops coins at his own feet but pretends they were thrown.*) Thank you! Thank you! Much obliged, much obliged!

GRETA. What are you talking about? What bombs?

TOMMY/OLD LADY. Show time! Show time! God bless you, sir! Thank you, madame!

GRETA. You said something about bombs! You're not an old lady! You really are crazy! (*She quickly breaks off.*) Hello, welcome to Lincoln Center. I'm Greta Rapp, your guide for today's tour. The New York State Theatre—(*As she pronounces the words, the New York State Theatre is blown up in a terrific roar of explosives and a beautiful cloud of smoke. Its photograph on the screen above the stage is extinguished and the pin spot on that particular shopping bag goes out.*)

TOMMY/OLD LADY. (*Cockney accent.*) The New York State Theatre . . . ? Go on, ducky, finish what you was saying.

GRETA. Oh oh oh!

TOMMY/OLD LADY. How do you like them apples, guvnor?

GRETA. It's all blowing up!

TOMMY/OLD LADY. There's plenty more where that came from, luvy!

GRETA. There *was* a bomb!

TOMMY/OLD LADY. You bet your blooming arse there was!

GRETA. I thought you were kidding.

TOMMY/OLD LADY. I'm just beginning.

GRETA. Who are you?

TOMMY/OLD LADY. (*Italian accent.*) Giuseppe Bonatella; That's a me! And a one, and a two, and a three! (*And with that Philharmonic Hall goes down in a roar of explosives and a cloud of smoke. Its photograph and the pin spot on the red shopping bag beneath it both go out.*)

TOMMY/OLD LADY. That's right, pigs, you heard me. Burn, baby, burn! The fire this time!

GRETA. Look at Lincoln Center!

TOMMY/OLD LADY. Fuck Lincoln Center.

GRETA. Who are you?

TOMMY/OLD LADY. (*Thick speech impediment.*) You wanna see something, lady? (*The words are no sooner out of his mouth than the Vivian Beaumont Theatre goes up in a cloud of smoke. Its picture and the light on the shopping bag beneath go out.*)

GRETA. Oooooooooooo!

TOMMY/OLD LADY. You ain't seen nothing yet. The best for last, baby, the best for last.

GRETA. That was beautiful!

TOMMY/OLD LADY. You dig what I'm doing?

GRETA. Oh, absolutely! Do it again, do more! I just realized it: I hate Lincoln Center! This is fun!

TOMMY/OLD LADY. You know something?

GRETA. Don't talk, don't talk!

TOMMY/OLD LADY. *You're* crazy!

GRETA. I know, I know!

TOMMY/OLD LADY. And I love crazy chicks!

GRETA. Especially ones with nice pairs of stems on them!

TOMMY/OLD LADY. Right on, sister!

GRETA. Do more, do it again, do more!

TOMMY/OLD LADY. (*Thick German accent.*) *Das ist ein kleine* opera house? *Ja, ist das ein kleine* opera house! (*The Metropoli-*

*tan Opera House explodes with an enormous roar of dynamite
and lots of smoke. Its photograph fades and the pin spot on the
red shopping bag goes out. All the screens are dark now.*)

GRETA. Thank you, Madame Dorfmeister! Thank you!

TOMMY/OLD LADY. Dorfmeister-Gluck, *liebchen.*

GRETA. There go the Chagalls!

TOMMY/OLD LADY. I'm sorry.

GRETA. I hated them, too!

TOMMY/OLD LADY. Nice stems all the way up?

GRETA. Unh-hunh! I never knew how much I hated Lincoln Center until I saw it like this. Do more, do more!

TOMMY/OLD LADY. I can't. There is no more. (*Remembers.*) No,
wait a minute. (*This time there is an offstage explosion.*)

GRETA. The Walter Damrosch Band Shell, too! Fantastic! I'm
Greta Rapp. I live around here.

TOMMY/OLD LADY. Then what do you say we split?

GRETA. (*A hesitation.*) You really did all this? I mean the bombs
and everything, they were you?

TOMMY/OLD LADY. There's a connection?

GRETA. Yes or no?

TOMMY/OLD LADY. Yes! Because I—

GRETA. Don't tell me why. I don't care why. It'll just spoil it. I'll
find out you're a Communist or something. I hate political men.
Come on.

TOMMY/OLD LADY. Men? Men? I'm not men, man! Don't you
know who I am?

GRETA. No.

TOMMY/OLD LADY. Oh wow!

GRETA. Should I?

TOMMY/OLD LADY. You really mean you still don't know who I am
yet?

GRETA. I'm sorry, but no.

TOMMY/OLD LADY. Oh wow, baby, oh wow! (*There is another offstage explosion.*)

GRETA. The underground garages! Well who are you?

TOMMY. (*Taking off his wig.*) Tommy Flowers!

GRETA. (*Overcome.*) Tommy Flowers!

TOMMY. Tommy Flowers, Revolutionary! (*Greta has swooned by
now. Tommy catches her in his arms.*) Oh shit, I forgot Juilliard!

(*He carries her off Tarzan-style, letting out a jungle yell as he goes. There is one final explosion and a puff of smoke as the fountain explodes. The Showgirl appears dressed in the French tricolors.*)

SHOWGIRL. Louis XVI: Is it a revolt? Duc de la Rochefoucauld-Liancourt (*She has trouble with the name.*): No, sire, it is a revolution. When the news arrived at Versailles of the Fall of the Bastille, 1789. Thank you. (*She exits rapidly.*)

ANNOUNCER'S VOICE. May I have your attention, please. I have a correction. A mink stole with the monogrammed initials DKR has been found on the floor of the *men's* room on the mezzanine level. Thank you.

SUMMER OF '52

(*Tommy appears in a red baseball cap worn backwards and a scarf. He starts skimming stones.*)

TOMMY. In the first place, it was a dumb question. "Who are the ten most admired men in America today and why?" That's almost as dumb as when they ask you what you want to be when you grow up. And so I wrote your name ten times. Holden Caulfield. Holden Caulfield. Holden Caulfield. Holden Caulfield. Holden Caulfield. Holden Caulfield. Holden Caulfield. Holden Caulfield. Holden Caulfield. Holden Caulfield. "Because he's not a phony" and I got an F. (*To us, as he stops skimming stones.*) I always knew it would happen like this. I'd just be walking along the beach one night, skimming stones, and I'd see this kid just my age, looking just like me, and wearing the same red baseball cap and he'd just be walking and skimming, too, and when we finally got close together we'd both stop walking and start skimming together and without really saying anything—anything phony like "What school do you go to?"—we'd just kind of drift into this really natural conversation. (*Tommy starts skimming stones again.*) And then my parents had to go talk to Mr. Bartlett, our principal, and they all decided they didn't know what to do with me and then I had to go see Mr. Bartlett with them and they told me there was no way anyone anywhere could answer Holden Caulfield is even *one* of the ten most admired men in America today on his civics test and get away with it and how Miss Pearce had practically had a hemorrhage when she read my paper because she had such high hopes for me this semester and I would have to apologize to her and who the hell was Holden Caulfield anyway? and no wonder I was smoking in the boys' lavatory between classes and if I kept it up my growth would be stunted and I was short enough for my age as it was and hadn't my parents promised me a convertible if I didn't smoke until I graduated from high school? which is such a phony offer I almost puked because who wants a convertible *after* they graduate from high school, I'll probably be married by then or in the army or college maybe, and all the time we're in Bartlett's office he's scratching his balls, right in front of everyone, I was getting sick to my stomach, and my father is trying to sound stern and my mother is shaking her head, and all I'm thinking is how much I'd like to get out of there and have a Lucky Strike and maybe go over to Jan Moody's and hack around if her parents were still out of town—she is probably the most developed girl for her age in this state, 38D, I heard. You know, cup size. Sound good to you?—when Bartlett, still scratching his balls, and my mother's right in front of him, I should've called his bluff, "Stop scratching your balls, Bartlett!" when Bartlett asks if I want to take the test again and answer it properly this time and I looked at the three of them very calmly and said "okay" and went into another room and wrote "The ten most admired men in America today are Eisenhower, Truman, Acheson, etc., etc., etc., *because* etc., etc., etc." and I came back and handed it to them and Bartlett read it and smiled at my parents and then he smiled at me and said "You see, that wasn't so hard, was it now?" and I said "No, sir. It was very easy and now *I'm* a phony" and Bartlett was so shook up he even forgot to scratch his balls and said something about expelling me and they all agreed they'd talk about it later and we drove home with nobody saying a word and when we got there the phone was ringing and it was my big brother calling from California before he got shipped off to Korea and I couldn't think of much to say to him and so I said "Just don't get killed over there," which is just about the best and least phony thing I can think of to say to someone who's going off to Korea, especially your brother, and

that started a new outburst from my mother and so I walked
out of the house and went over to Jan Moody's, only her parents
were back, but I tried to peek in her window anyway, she likes to
sit around *nude* practically, and all I did was get my shoes muddy
and ruin some of her mother's goddamn prize-winning roses and
so I came down here and I'm very glad to have this opportunity
to offer you a Lucky Strike, tell you I really do consider you the
most admired man in America today because you're not a phony
and ask you about Times Square. When I finally get to New
York City I'm going to stand there for the entire first week just
looking at people. You know what they call it? The Crossroads
of the World. That's right where I want to be. There's nothing
to look at in this town except Jan Moody's knockers. Maybe we
could go together. I mean you know about subways and things.
(*Pause.*) Seventh Avenue and 42nd St. I was there. Holden
wasn't.

TOMMY'S MOTHER
OR
I AM THE WALRUS

TOMMY'S MOTHER. Your father and I certainly enjoyed your last
collect call. Tell me, don't they sell pens and writing paper up
in that neck of the woods anymore? I'm joshing, of course. It's
better than not hearing from you at all. I just worry about you.
What with all the violence and murders and bombings, etc.,
New York certainly doesn't sound like a very safe place to be
right now. I'm very glad I'm right here in St. Pete in my own
house. I don't miss it up there one second. Thank God, we don't
have those problems down here. Your father is the same as ever.
Smokes his head off, coughs all night, and smokes his head off
again all next day. I'm so worried he has emphysema. I'm fine,
of course. My back went out again last week and I was laid up
for three days but I can't complain. I think I need a psychologist
instead of an orthopedist but you even mention the word to
your father and he sees red. All my friends who have therapists
look and feel 100% better and we're all the same age, have the
same problems, etc. I'm convinced nearly everything is psycho-
somatic nowadays. The good TV is on the blink so we're back to

watching all the shows in black and white. It's like the Middle Ages. Well, I don't want to depress you with all our little problems and travails, so I'll sign off. I just missed you tonight. Say hello to Manhattan for me and have one on me while you're at it. Love you, Mom.

CHEZ GRETA

GRETA. (*In and out as she undresses.*) Tommy!

TOMMY. I'll be right in! (*To us.*) You'll have to excuse me. I'm a little bushed. At my age, it catches up with you. I'm thirty years old which is neither as young as I was nor as old as I'm going to be but still kind of late in the ball game. You know what I mean. I'm just a child of the fifties, a little seedy and the worse for wear, but who isn't lately?

GRETA. It's true what they say about girl guides!

TOMMY. I'm finding out!

GRETA. Then hurry up!

TOMMY. What else should you know about me? I've got a *summa cum* something from somewhere in my head, no prospects in mind and lots of bridges burned behind me, an honorable discharge from Uncle Sam and a three-dollar bill in my wallet, call it lead in my pencil or love in my heart, Greta Prince in the next room lusting for my perfect body, no place to live, and a terrific dog named Arnold who's staying with a terrific girl who just kicked me out, which wasn't so terrific of her.

GRETA. Tommy!

TOMMY. I'm coming! I'm coming!

GRETA. Well hurry up!

TOMMY. I don't always think about girls. I don't want you to get the wrong impression. I also think about blowing this country up so we can start all over again. I sort of dig this country, see? That's why I think about blowing it up so we can start all over again. Now we can blow it up nice or we can blow it up tough. What I'm doing now is nice. What some of my friends are doing is tough. I'd prefer nice. Wouldn't you?

GRETA. Tommy!

TOMMY. She really does have nice legs all the way up.

GRETA. Tommy!!

TOMMY. A little weak in the chest department but her heart's in the right place. Okay, Greta, here I come!

TOMMY'S NEPHEW SPEAKS HIS PIECE

TOMMY'S NEPHEW. Power to the people! Off the pigs! Right on! Peace. What are you up to these days, Uncle Tommy? Nobody ever hears from you anymore. St. Petersburg is the same as ever. I don't blame you for not coming back. They still think anybody with hair over an inch long is some kind of freak. Right now they're pissed off at me because they caught me with a little grass again. Big deal! They should see what I got stashed in the garage. My mother is a real ball-breaker when it comes to dope and I know he's your brother, but my father is a creep. You, Uncle Tommy, on the other hand, are probably the finest person I know. Where you painted your name on the big water tower when you were in high school still shows through and they just painted it again. I see it every day. I'm planning to run away. I'd like to join you in NYC. I hear it's good for kids up there. We could really tear that town apart. I'd have to get a job and help pay my own way, of course, but I bet you know a lot of people who could help me out. I know I can trust you. You're the only one in this whole family I can. I'm really serious about running away. I'm also thinking about Mexico or some places in Peru. I don't care if you think this is corny, but I have plans for a wonderful life. You'd still be my favorite uncle even if you weren't my only one. Your loving, spaced out, increasingly radicalized, funky, freaky nephew, Charles Flowers the First.

TRAVEL LIGHT

GRETA. (Off.) I love you, Tommy Flowers!!

TOMMY. I love you, too, Greta Rapp! I had two wonderful weeks. She had two wonderful weeks. Fair enough. I'm back to zero but something will turn up. I'd like you to meet someone. Come on Arnold—come here, meet some people. This is Arnold. He's my dog. I say that because some people confuse their dogs with people. I'm not one of those people, and I'd hate to meet that person Arnold could be confused with. I have him all entered in

the Westminster Dog Show as a chihuahua. Well, what can
they do? I've paid the entry fee. I'll just say he's a little large for
his breed. I'm going to tie-dye him, too, one day. I've even
bought the colors. In my book, he's right up there with Lassie
and Rin Tin Tin among your all-time major dog stars. Hello.

MAN. No.

TOMMY. No what, man?

MAN. Just no.

TOMMY. I didn't ask for anything.

MAN. I don't have any.

TOMMY. I said hello.

MAN. The answer is no.

TOMMY. Thank you. Thank you very much. (*To us.*) Travel light.
That's my first piece of advice. Yes sir, travel light. Everything
I own is right in here. A toothbrush, a change of shorts, my auto-
graphed picture of James Dean, my nun's habit. This is a true
play and already you don't believe me. That's about it from the
permanent collection. Everything else is temporary, disposable
and eminently replaceable. Everything breaks, nothing works
anymore. Hot enough for you?

MAN. Get a job.

TOMMY. I have one, thank you. Creep. (*To us.*) And don't encum-
ber yourself with a lot of junk. The only junk I take with me is
right up here. Facts about famous people, world capitals and
useless dates. Franz Liszt contracted cholera while vacationing
in Baden-Baden on July 7, 1873. It wasn't even fatal. Otherwise,
I'm as fluid as fluid can be. . . . Excuse me, sir, would you happen
to have any spare change?

MAN. It's exactly eleven after two.

TOMMY. I'm a little fast.

MAN. It happens.

TOMMY. Don't mention it.

MAN. Don't mention it.

TOMMY. You're welcome. And don't be ashamed of being a mooch.
You can't very well live out of a shopping bag if you're ashamed
of being a mooch. Like the man says, we all get by with a little
help from our friends.

BEN. Brother, can you spare a dime?

TOMMY. Listen, chief, this is sort of my corner and things are kind of slow today. So keep it down, hunh? Just sort of fade into the sidewalk. I wouldn't want to see you crowding my style, know what I mean?

BEN. Got you.

TOMMY. Thanks.

BEN. Money's tight.

TOMMY. I know, man, I know.

BEN. Tighter than a drum.

TOMMY. Boom, boom, boom! He's not a friend. Don't worry. I'll score. I'm very optimistic. What else could I be? I'm an American.

MAN. Hare Krishna.

TOMMY. Hare Krishna.

MAN. Krishna Hare.

TOGETHER. Ommmm.

TOMMY. Where are you from?

MAN. Queens.

TOMMY. You got any coins on you?

MAN. Fuck off, man.

TOGETHER. Ommm.

TOMMY. God bless you, too, asshole. (*To Ben.*) This used to be a good street for us until those goddamn fake monks started hitting it up. Some Joe Blow Betty Boop from Peoria, Illinois, shaves his head, mops a salad bowl from Prexy's and tells everybody he's a fucking Buddhist monk!

BEN. Is that your dog?

TOMMY. Yep.

BEN. I hate dogs.

TOMMY. Who asked you?

BEN. I had a dog once. He committed suicide. We were watching television, Ed Sullivan, and he got up and jumped right out the window.

TOMMY. It's been nice talking to you.

BEN. His name was Arnold.

TOMMY. Arnold's my dog.

BEN. He was a Siamese. A real thoroughbred. I'll move over there. I'm crowding your style.

TOMMY. Thanks, old timer, we'll be talking to you.

GIRL. Taxi!

TOMMY. Now that's more like it!

GIRL. Taxi!

TOMMY. Miss! Yoo hoo, miss! Aren't you Miss Subways?

GIRL. Yes!

TOMMY. You are?

GIRL. Yes, I am!

TOMMY. You're a great looking chick.

GIRL. I know!

TOMMY. My dog and I haven't eaten in twenty-four hours.

GIRL. Here.

TOMMY. Thank you, thank you very much. I hope you win many such elections. (*Sees it's a subway token she's given him.*) Hey! I don't ride the subways.

GIRL. Me either. They're too dangerous. Taxi! Yoo hoo, cab! (*She is gone.*)

TOMMY. I didn't even vote for you! Miss Subways, Miss Subways! Miss *Shitways*, Miss Subways! I thought I had her pegged. Come on, seven, come on, baby. (*To Ben.*) Here, take a subway somewhere. (*Flips Ben the token.*)

BEN. (*Flipping it back.*) I don't ride the subways, young man.

TOMMY. Then take a bus.

BEN. Them either.

TOMMY. Then take a walk.

BEN. (*He's found a movie magazine in Tommy's shopping bag.*) Is this yours?

TOMMY. Hey!

BEN. You mind if I look at it?

TOMMY. You can have it. Take it to the park with you.

BEN. I hate the park.

TOMMY. What's wrong with the park?

BEN. Too many damn dogs.

TOMMY. Buzz off, why don't you?

BEN. It's a free country, young man.

TOMMY. Unfortunately. (*He "reads" the subway token.*) The Metropolitan Transit Authority. Even the names of things in this country are literature. The Great Atlantic and Pacific Tea Company. Northwest Passage. Lorna Doone cookies. Lorna Doone, mind you! Thom with a "h," Thom McCann Shoes. The A. B. Dick Repeating Company. That's not penis fixation, lady, hell, no, it's poetry! God, how we loved that one in grammar school. To see the word "dick" on a ditto machine! "Dick."

MAN. Hi there.

TOMMY. You got any spare change, brother? I'm strapped, really and truly strapped.

MAN. That depends.

TOMMY. Can I guess what it depends on?

MAN. You're a big boy, you should be able to.

TOMMY. You're the best offer I've had all day. Thanks, but no thanks.

MAN. Hostile bitch.

TOMMY. I love talking to people. I majored in conversation in college.

BEN. "Lucille Ball's Night of Terror."

TOMMY. It's a terrific story.

BEN. "Bob Hope's Biggest Fear."

TOMMY. The whole issue's great.

BEN. "Mia Farrow's Cry for Help."

TOMMY. It's heart-breaking.

BEN. "Marlon Brando's Night of Terror."

TOMMY. Yeah, they're all scared shitless on the West Coast, too. (*To us.*) Franchot Tone once bought my mother a Singapore Sling at the bar in the Stork Club. No more Stork Club, no more Singapore Sling.

BEN. No more Franchot Tone.

TOMMY. And my father claims he spent a pretty memorable weekend with Lana Turner in Westport, Connecticut. They're nice people, my folks are. You'd like them. Just your average neighborhood star-fuckers, geriatric groupies. I don't mean that. Though actually I did meet Franchot Tone once and it just seemed kind of stupid to say, "Hello, Mr. Tone, you may not remember this but you bought my mother a Singapore Sling in the Stork Club before she married my father and I'm their son." He would have thought I was crazy. Or he might have thought it was nice.

BEN. Or he might have thought it was nice, young man.

TOMMY. You think?

BEN. I knew Mr. Tone.

TOMMY. No kidding?

BEN. I didn't like him.

TOMMY. Of course you didn't.

BEN. He didn't like me much either.

TOMMY. I'm not surprised. (*To us.*) But stories like that only seem to happen in this country. Did you ever meet a kid from La Paz, Bolivia, with a tale to tell like mine? No, sir, you did not! Where is everybody? What happens to them anymore? Whose mind hasn't been blown lately? Who hasn't freaked out? Alger Hiss sells stationery. J. D. Salinger has an unlisted number. Sabu's been busted. My high school English teacher, write-what-you-know-about McIlvey, where is she? Hit by a bolt of lightning while making a deposit at a drive-in bank. Her, the car, the money. Rumble! Zing! Pfft! Zap! Really. Only in America could your high school English teacher die like that. I mean it just wouldn't happen to a Laplander, an awful thing like that. (*A pedestrian has entered and crossed.*) Hey! Hey, come back here! No fair! I wasn't looking. Shit! See how you got me started? You gotta concentrate every second if you're gonna hustle. You get distracted and they could be handing out free money and you wouldn't score. So knock it off. I told you, this is my corner. Can I have my *Screen World* back now?

BEN. I was an actor, too, you know.

TOMMY. The magazine, chief.

BEN. Take it, it's yours. Never heard of anybody in it anyhow. I like my movies all right but give me good ol' live theatre any day of the week. That Lana Turner of yours couldn't cut the mustard up here. None of them movie personalities could. I was in the original production of *Kismet* with Otis Skinner.

TOMMY. Sorry I missed it.

BEN. Lots of feathers in that one.

TOMMY. It sounds terrific.

BEN. Me and Paul Muni were bitter rivals.

TOMMY. *The* Paul Muni?

BEN. He had my career.

TOMMY. I've seen *Fugitive from a Chain Gang* a dozen times.

BEN. I was up for that part, nearly had it, too.

TOMMY. What's your name?

BEN. My stage name was Ben Delight.

TOMMY. Ben Delight? I never heard of you.

BEN. It's the kind of name you can't forget.

TOMMY. What was your name before you changed it?

BEN. Jack Wonder.

TOMMY. You changed your name from Jack Wonder to Ben Delight?

BEN. It's a long story.

TOMMY. I bet. (*A woman passes by.*) Excuse me, madam, I'm not going to hassle you. I'm just taking a little poll for charity.

WOMAN. We already gave.

TOMMY. I'm sure you haven't. We're just getting started. And this one's fun. Now who's your favorite movie star?

WOMAN. Oh that's hard. That's very, very hard.

TOMMY. Well, think. It's for charity. (*Helping her out.*) Slim Pickens?

WOMAN. (*Shaking her head.*) No.

TOMMY. Mario Lanza? Franchot Tone? Me?

WOMAN. What's your name?

TOMMY. Tommy Flowers.

WOMAN. What have you been in?

TOMMY. Tommy Flowers.

WOMAN. I missed that one, I'm sorry.

TOMMY. It hasn't been released yet. Now come on, who?

WOMAN. (*Blushing.*) Well ...

TOMMY. Cary Grant, I knew it!

WOMAN. Charlton Heston.   ˙

TOMMY. Charlton Heston!

WOMAN. Is that all right?

TOMMY. It's terrific! I was just reading this article about him. He's a woman.

WOMAN. What a terrible thing to say about the man who played Moses!

TOMMY. Well, you know, these fan magazines.

WOMAN. Oh, I'm just sick.

TOMMY. Well I didn't say it. See? "Hollywood's best kept secret." "Charlton Heston Is A Woman" in great big letters.

WOMAN. They spoil everything nowadays.

TOMMY. Hey! (*She is gone. To us.*) Fuck Charlton Heston. Well maybe he is. Fuck him anyway. She'd like to. (*To Ben.*) I was an actor once myself. It shits. I've been a lot of things once. They all shit, too. What I am now, you see, is free. (*Sees Ben fiddling in the shopping bag.*) Do you mind?

BEN. Who is it?

TOMMY. Careful of that, will you?

BEN. Looks like some kind of an actor.

TOMMY. It's James Dean, for Christ's sake!

BEN. I've seen that face somewhere.

TOMMY. I should hope so.

BEN. Name some plays he was in.

TOMMY. *The Immoralist* and *See the Jaguar.*

BEN. That's all he was in, two plays?

TOMMY. I'm afraid so.

BEN. What's the matter? Wasn't he any good?

TOMMY. He was terrific. The best.

BEN. I don't see how terrific he could've been if all he was in was two plays.

TOMMY. You'll just have to take my word for it.

BEN. Never heard of him.

TOMMY. He was a movie star.

BEN. Not in my book.

TOMMY. *East of Eden. Rebel without a Cause. Giant.*

BEN. Go on.

TOMMY. That's it.

BEN. Two plays and three movies?

TOMMY. He died young.

BEN. No wonder you don't hear his name mentioned much.

TOMMY. May I have my picture back?

BEN. I thought I knew all the greats. But James Dean. That's a new one on me. A real star, hunh?

TOMMY. One of the biggest.

BEN. You could've fooled me.

TOMMY. (*To us.*) How can anybody not have heard of James Dean? And how do you tell somebody who hasn't what he was like? He was just like you, only he was your big brother, too. I know this for a fact: James Dean, the movie star, liked me, Thomas P. for Prospers Flowers, a high school kid with pimples.

JIMMY

(*Warner Brothers logo appears.* East of Eden *theme music is heard.*)

BARMAID. Two Schlitz. That kid shouldn't be in here, Jimmy.

TOMMY. It's okay, Lois, he's with me. (*She goes.*) Listen, Tom Flowers, I'm gonna have to split.

YOUNG TOMMY. Where you going, Jimmy?

TOMMY. Nowhere.

YOUNG TOMMY. Why don't you stay then?

TOMMY. You see the Porsche Spider out there? They told me it'll do 160. I'm gonna find out.

YOUNG TOMMY. That's too fast, Jimmy.

TOMMY. I've got to.

YOUNG TOMMY. Okay, Jimmy.

TOMMY. Hey, and listen, Tom. Your father likes you. He just don't know how to say it. Just try talking to him, man to man. He's . . . unh . . . shy, Tom. It's hard for him to tell you he loves you. Try making it easy for him, what do you say?

YOUNG TOMMY. Thanks, Jimmy.

TOMMY. And, hey, you know something else? Gretchen Selby likes you, too.

YOUNG TOMMY. I don't think so, Jimmy. Not after what I done.

TOMMY. That's not what she told me.

YOUNG TOMMY. You talked to her?

TOMMY. I said, hey, Gretchen, what's so wrong if my friend Tom Flowers drinks a few beers and raises a little hell and maybe he ain't an A+ student like you and maybe your mother thinks he's a hellion and won't let you go out with him and your father thinks he's a bad kid and wants you to go out with Buba Walsh. Buba Walsh is a square, baby. And then she started crying and saying "Tell Tommy" . . . is that what she calls you, Tom? . . . "Tell Tommy I love him and I know he's not bad."

YOUNG TOMMY. Gretchen really said that?

TOMMY. Yeah, she did.

YOUNG TOMMY. Gretchen Selby, 108 Surf Street, St. Petersburg, Florida?

TOMMY. Hey, Tom, it's me, Jimmy talking. Ain't I always been straight with you?

YOUNG TOMMY. Sure thing, Jimmy.

TOMMY. Then what are you waiting for? I gotta split now. You see that Porsche Spider out there? They told me it'll do 160. I'm gonna find out.

YOUNG TOMMY. I'll go with you.

TOMMY. I've got to find out all by myself. See you later, Tom. Hey, it's gonna be all right.

YOUNG TOMMY. Yeah?

TOMMY. It's got to.

YOUNG TOMMY. Thanks, Jimmy. Stay happy.

TOMMY. Happy! Who says I ain't. (*Car sounds, screeching of tires, a crash.*)

YOUNG TOMMY. Jimmy? Jimmy? Jimmy!!

TOMMY. If I'd've been there that never would have happened. The best friend I ever had and I wasn't with him! (*The Warner Brothers logo and music have faded.*)

BEN. *Kumquats!*

TOMMY. Kumquats?

BEN. *Kumquats!* I saw you in *Kumquats.*

TOMMY. You're putting me on now.

BEN. The Belasco Theatre. The season of . . . let's see . . .

TOMMY. Five or six years ago.

BEN. I never forget a face.

TOMMY. You don't know who Jimmy Dean is but you remember me in *Kumquats?*

BEN. I forget names but I can't shake faces.

TOMMY. I had ten lines!

BEN. There are no small parts, young man, only—

TOMMY. I know, but I had green stripes on my face and was wearing feathers!

BEN. I remember those stripes.

TOMMY. It only ran one night.

BEN. That's why I try to make most openings.

TOMMY. You really saw it?

BEN. Oh indeed I did, sir.

TOMMY. You've got to be kidding.

BEN. I was there all right.

TOMMY. That was some play, hunh?

BEN. One of your all-time super-flops, that one.

TOMMY. I told them it was ahead of its time.

BEN. That it was, sir, that it was.

TOMMY. What . . . unh . . . well what did you think of it?

BEN. That *Kumquats* show?

TOMMY. It's *Kumquat*, actually. Singular. Just one kumquat. We could never figure out why people insisted on pluralizing it.

BEN. I guess when you think of kumquats you just naturally think of more than one.

TOMMY. Yeah, I guess so.

BEN. *Kumquat*, singular, was a badly written, ill-structured, poorly motivated, humorless, pedantic, philosophically sophomoric, cliché-ridden *and* plagiarized (and that takes some doing!) three and a half hour, $5.50 from where I sat, piece of shit.

TOMMY. Oh really?

BEN. *Kumquats*, plural, would have been a double piece of shit.

TOMMY. No kidding?

BEN. You were pretty four thumbs yourself.

TOMMY. Oh?

BEN. All nerves, no style.

TOMMY. Unh-hunh!

BEN. And you tripped. I remember you tripped.

TOMMY. Oh you remember that?

BEN. You came in, said one line and fell right over your feathers!

TOMMY. Thanks for reminding me.

BEN. Tell me . . . (*He's laughing so hard he can barely speak.*) Tell me, is that your own voice you use when you act?

TOMMY. Are you through?

BEN. (*Drying his eyes.*) I guess.

TOMMY. You know what the trouble with old people like you is? Exactly what they are: they're old. Their bodies are old, their minds are old, their skin is old, their hair is old, their eyes are old, their glands are old, their cocks and cunts are old. They look old, they act old and they smell old. Everything about them is old, it's old, man, it's old. And because they're old they hate anything young and most of all they hate young people. They hate young people's clothes, they hate long hair, they hate grass and acid, they hate words like fuck but most of all they hate to fuck because they can't do it anymore. Well I'm young, mister, and I can fuck and when I'm not fucking or getting stoned or just grooving, I'm out finding out every good way I can to fuck up this whole fucking system that produces fucked up old people like you. You're dead, mister, you're already dead. You've already lost and we've already won.

BEN. (*Simply.*) All right, son.

TOMMY. Erase that. Erase everything I just said.

BEN. That's all right, too.

TOMMY. I didn't mean it and I'm truly and deeply ashamed of myself and you'll just have to take my word for it.

BEN. Okay.

TOMMY. No, really!

BEN. It's okay, son, it's okay.

TOMMY. It's not and you don't have to say it is.

BEN. Me and my friend here, we understand, don't we, boy, hunh?

(*Tommy suddenly hugs Ben and kisses him.*)

TOMMY. You know what my wonderful grandfather taught me? God, why couldn't the whole world have known him? I wanted money for the movies and he wouldn't give me any. Maybe he didn't even have it. He only worked for the post office. He said "Walk in backwards and they'll think you're coming out." Isn't that beautiful? Hunh? "Walk in backwards and they'll think you're coming out." But I was a little boy then and I never liked him after that. It took me twenty-five years to realize the almost ancient wisdom of that remark. "Walk in backwards and they'll think you're coming out." You know something? They do.

BEN. Why of course they do, son.

TOMMY. You knew about that?

BEN. How do you think I saw you in that *Kumquats* show?

TOMMY. Look at that coat. It's worse than mine. Come on, we'll go to Bloomingdale's. I'll get you a new one.

BEN. That's all right.

TOMMY. I want to.

BEN. I'm perfectly fine in this.

TOMMY. Bullshit. We'll hop a cab and have you fixed up in no time.

BEN. But you don't have that kind of money.

TOMMY. I don't have any money. Dig?

BEN. I don't know, kid.

TOMMY. You know how long it's been since anyone's called me kid?

You just got yourself an entire fall wardrobe. Now what do you say?

BEN. Well ...

TOMMY. This street's dead anyway. Bloomingdale's is loaded with easy-to-score-with chicks. I'll find myself something while I'm at it. (*Calls.*) Taxi! (*Jumping back.*) Cocksucker! (*Pretending to jot down license number.*) 4Z 5505. (*To Ben.*) I'm used to this.

BEN. So am I.

TOMMY. When I finally get one, I love to tell 'em 136th Street and Lenox Avenue. They have cardiac arrests. Taxi! He's stopped for a light. Come on, let's grab him, if the doors aren't locked. (*They approach a cab.*)

HACK. (*New York accent.*) *Bonjour, bonjour!*

TOMMY. You go uptown?

HACK. I go uptown, downtown, crosstown, Chinatown, Brooklyn, Queens, the Bronx, Jersey, all three airports and Westchester County, what can I tell you? You want to go to Grand Rapids, Michigan? I'll take you to Grand Rapids, Michigan. *Bonjour, bonjour!*

TOMMY. We're only going to Bloomingdale's today, thank you.

HACK. Bloomingdale's it is. Just thought I'd mention it. Climb in. (*Tommy, Ben and Arnold get into the cab.*) *Allons enfants de la patrie!*

TOMMY. Don't throw the meter.

HACK. Meter? What meter? I don't see no meter. As far as I'm concerned, this cab is empty. I ain't picked up a fare all day, you know what I mean? I'm gonna take 11th Avenue, just in case. I bet you two was surprised when I even stopped for you, weren't you? Hunh? Hunh?

TOMMY. We certainly were, sir.

HACK. Most drivers would rather pick up your mutt than you two and no offense.

TOMMY. We're very grateful.

HACK. I'll tell you why. See, the point is you gotta accept life. That's right, you heard me, accept it. Too many drivers don't accept life, so they're always locking their doors and refusing to pick up fares like maybe that was gonna keep 'em from getting mugged or stiffed or murdered even. But not me, mac, no sir. If some nigger wants to mug me, he's gonna mug me, know what I mean? God's will be done and all that, only I ain't religious. Figure that one out.

TOMMY. We're working on it.

HACK. I been mugged 16 times . . . 17 if you count that Spic bitch . . . but I've been pushing a hack for 20 years and if you do some long dividing you'll find that I been mugged on the average of less than once a year, which ain't so bad. 'Course all these muggings have happened in the past three years but my boss says you gotta figure it over the whole twenty. *C'est la vie, c'est la vie!* Look at the tits on that one! (*Out the window.*) That's right, honey, if you got 'em, flaunt 'em! (*Back into the cab.*) Would you mind not smoking? I'm allergic. (*Tommy has lit a joint.*)

TOMMY. This is a French cigarette.

HACK. Oh. *Parlez-vous français*, either of you two?

TOMMY. I'm afraid not.

HACK. I had one of them Indian women in here a couple of minutes ago. Right where you're sitting. Indian from the country India. She was even wearing one o' them things they wear, that's how Indian she was.

TOMMY. Sari.

HACK. That's okay.

TOMMY. No, they're called a sari, what she was wearing.

HACK. Oh! Sari, hunh? That's a terrific word. *Aimez-vous* saris? *Non, je n'aime pas* saris. Christ, it's a terrific language that French stuff. I'm teaching myself so I can talk to foreign people, too. If there's one thing I like it's exchanging views and if there's one thing this town is full of, it's foreign people. It was either French or Spanish, if you know what I mean. She spoke French. Say, either of you two gambling men?

BEN. That depends, sir.

HACK. I bet you a dollar you can't guess how old I am and I already told you I been pushing this thing 20 years. Go ahead, take a guess. I'll give you five years either side of it, too. I'm listening.

BEN. Forty-five.

TOMMY. No, much younger. Forty-one at most.

HACK. Hah! Don't I wish I'd see either of them two again. Fifty-five and me are old friends, too. I'm 63 years old this May, my friends. *Soixante-trois.*

TOMMY. That's amazing.

BEN. It's depressing.

HACK. You don't believe me.

TOMMY. We believe you.

HACK. Look at that and call me a liar.

TOMMY. You're 63 years old this May all right.

HACK. Okay, so cough it up. If there's one thing that gets me going it's people who welsh on their debts. Know what I mean?

TOMMY. Absolutely. I'm sorry, Ben, but he's got a point. (*Tommy and Ben pool their resources.*)

HACK. This one guy, this little kike bastard, he guessed I was 47 and then he wouldn't pay up and said he thought it was just a game. Ask me, what's a game anymore? I'll tell you, nothing's a game anymore. Brother, he pissed me off.

TOMMY. You've got a colorful vocabulary.

HACK. Thank you. I pride myself on it. One thing I ain't ever been accused of is boring my passengers half to death. Most drivers just yak-yak-yak and who asked 'em? Who asked 'em? Honor the passenger. Respect his intelligence. And keep your GD mouth shut. That's my philosophy. (*Out the window.*) What's the matter with you? You paraplegic or something? (*Back into cab.*) *C'est la vie! C'est la vie!* You know what my son Benedict says?

TOMMY. No, what?

HACK. He's a veterinarian up in Maine, he got out of this rat race, nice wife, nice family, nice house, nice car, nice neighborhood, so far, but like Benny says: the quality of life, pa, it's the quality of life that ain't so hot anymore.

TOMMY. That's true.

HACK. My dear dead wife, Rosa, Rosa Capri her maiden name was, how's that for a monicker? Rosa Capri, God bless her, you'da thought she was a Guinea with a handle like that, when we'd be stuck in traffic like this she'd say "What's the race, Mayo, what's the big race?" Wonderful woman. I don't know. I don't know anymore. Your friend don't say much.

BEN. I'm asleep.

HACK. God bless you, mac.

BEN. I'm old. I'm tired.

HACK. Who ain't, who ain't? V*oici* Bloomingdale's. There she is.

TOMMY. Thanks for the lift. That's all you've got, Ben?

BEN. You're the one who wanted to take a cab.

HACK. (*Last of the big spenders.*) Let's just say three dollars and call it even. Two for the ride and the buck you just lost to me.

TOMMY. Let's just say *none* for the ride and ninety-nine cents for what we lost to you.

HACK. Hey, what's this?

TOMMY. A subway token and sixty-four cents. We owe you a penny. Unless you want to wait for us.

HACK. Wait for you??

TOMMY. I didn't think so. Officer! Officer!

HACK. What are you doing?

TOMMY. This driver didn't throw his meter and I'm making a citizen's arrest!

HACK. You said you was gonna take care of me!

TOMMY. I am. Hey, officer!

HACK. Stop for you? I shoulda run over you! (*He flees.*)

TOMMY. There'll be a four-state dragnet out for you, 5Z-6022! (*To Ben.*) You're not coming in?

BEN. I hate Bloomingdale's. I'll wait out here.

TOMMY. Then keep an eye on Arnold.

BEN. One of those trench coats with a zip-in lining would be nice. An Aquascrotum.

TOMMY. You start big. Only it's Aquascutum, okay? (*He goes.*)

BEN. I thought Aquascrotum sounded funny. (*Lights down on Ben and Arnold.*)

LOVE IS WHERE YOU FIND IT

(*The lights come up on a row of pay toilets. From behind one of the closed doors we hear Tommy singing "Shenandoah." After a while, he stands up and looks down into the adjoining booth.*)

TOMMY. Beautiful song, isn't it? (*A woman screams.*) Got a match?

NEDDA. I'm trying not to get hysterical and start yelling for the cops or anything but this is the ladies' room!

TOMMY. I know.

NEEDA. Don't you think you ought to be in the men's room, sir?

TOMMY. I was in the men's room. I didn't like it. It's not so hot in here either, now that you mention it, but compared to the men's room it's Chock Full O'Nuts.

NEDDA. You're not meant to be in here!

TOMMY. I know.

NEDDA. It's against the law.

TOMMY. No, it's not. (*Nedda comes charging out of her booth carrying a cello case.*) Where are you going?

NEDDA. I'm going to call a policeman is where I'm going, you . . . you rapist!

TOMMY. You forgot your purse. (*Nedda puts down the cello case and goes back into her booth while Tommy darts out, grabs the cello case and takes it into his booth. When Nedda comes back out, she can't find her cello case.*)

NEDDA. Where's my . . . ? Give me that!

TOMMY. (*From behind the door of his booth.*) What is it?

NEDDA. (*Trying to reach over.*) Never mind! Now give it to me!

TOMMY. Tell me what it is first.

NEDDA. A cello case!

TOMMY. What's in it?

NEDDA. A cello.

TOMMY. I've always wanted to play the cello.

NEDDA. Don't open that!

TOMMY. It's so light for a cello!

NEDDA. It's a Stradivarius!

TOMMY. A real Stradivarius?

NEDDA. It's very fragile. Please don't open it!

TOMMY. I've always wanted to see a Stradivarius.

NEDDA. I said don't open that!

TOMMY. I'll be very careful! Oh! What have we here? No wonder you didn't want me to open it. (*Handing the objects mentioned up to her.*) A red-and-white umbrella. The price tag's still on it. It must be a Stradivarius. And what's this? A Westinghouse Stradivarius alarm clock out of its box. Two Stradivarius dresses. Feels like a Stradivarius cashmere sweater. No, Stradivarius vicuna. Stradivarius shoes. And a tube of Charles of the Ritz Stradivarius Rose Blush Lipstick! They're very unusual cellos, these Stradivariuses: no strings.

NEDDA. (*Her arms full now.*) I'm going to pay for it.

TOMMY. Boy, you really cleaned them out, didn't you?

NEDDA. You can't do anything to me, I haven't left the store yet!

TOMMY. (*Standing up.*) Mr. Pinkerton guard! Mr. Pinkerton guard! We've got a shoplifter in stall eleven. Help! Help!

NEDDA. It's not what you're thinking.

TOMMY. (*Nailing her.*) What is it then?

NEDDA. (*Squirming.*) I don't know but it's not what you're thinking.

TOMMY. Then about that policeman: what do you say we call a truce?

NEDDA. Okay, okay!

TOMMY. I bet you feel pretty rotten now, don't you?

NEDDA. I've never done anything like this in my life.

TOMMY. Rip off Bloomingdale's?

NEDDA. I didn't know I'd feel so guilty.

TOMMY. You didn't know you were gonna get caught.

NEDDA. I'm going to take it all back. Yes, yes! That's exactly what I'm going to do: put everything back right where I found it.

TOMMY. Relax. You should see the haul I've got down here. It's not as big as yours, of course, whose is? but . . .

NEDDA. You stole something, too?

TOMMY. Bloomingdale's runs a terrific free store. Listen to this. (*A radio is heard.*)

NEDDA. You took a radio?

TOMMY. Nice tone quality for a Jap import, don't you think? I'd have preferred a Zenith but they were all out.

NEDDA. I took the last Zenith.

TOMMY. Where?

NEDDA. It's inside the boots.

TOMMY. Hot shit, she did! Are you sure this is the first time you've ripped off Bloomingdale's?

NEDDA. First and last.

TOMMY. But you're off to such a terrific start.

NEDDA. I don't have the nerves for it. I'm shaking like a leaf. Look at me.

TOMMY. Okay. (*He gets up and looks at her.*) Hi.

NEDDA. Hi. (*Short pause.*)

TOMMY. Somebody's coming.

NEDDA. You better hide! (*Tommy and Nedda duck down in their*

respective booths. A woman enters and goes into the third booth.
Pause. We hear her sigh in relief.)

TOMMY. Hey, Mac! Did you see where the Mets are in first place again? I tell you! What a ball club! What a ball club! They should've dropped that Minny Minoza three seasons ago. (*Tommy is standing up in his booth waiting for her as the woman's head slowly appears over the top of the door.*)

WOMAN. Oh dear. I'm sorry. I'm most terribly sorry. I thought this was the . . . I had no idea . . . !

TOMMY. That's okay, lady, that's okay. Think nothing of it.

WOMAN. I could have sworn it was the ladies' room!

TOMMY. It is. Now sit down! (*Woman's head disappears as she sits.*) Now the Orioles are a whole other ball team! You see them against the Senators last week? The ninth inning, two men out, the bases loaded and they put Herlihy in against Braverman! (*The woman stands up again, runs out of her booth and is gone.*) Don't you want to know who won? (*Knocks on Nedda's door.*) Do you?

NEDDA. What am I going to do now?

TOMMY. You can come out of there for openers. (*Nedda reappears.*) Hello again.

NEDDA. What do I do with all this?

TOMMY. Pack up your Stradivarius and wait till the coast clears. You're better off in here with me. You like rock or classical?

NEDDA. Hunh?

TOMMY. A little music will calm you down. Rock or classical?

NEDDA. Classical.

TOMMY. Classical? Fancy! Classical it is. (*He turns on the radio again.*) Listen to that resonance. Must be all the tile. Hey, this is nice.

NEDDA. (*Repacking her cello case.*) Are you sure it's not against the law for you to be in here?

TOMMY. Unh-hunh.

NEDDA. I can't believe it.

TOMMY. You'd be surprised how many laws against things they haven't gotten around to thinking of yet. Did you know you can have a complete Chicken Delight dinner delivered to your seat in a movie theatre? They don't like it, they discourage it, in fact, but it's not against the law. And you know those tags on mat-

tresses that say Do Not Remove Under Penalty of Law? There's
no such law. Rip 'em off, rip 'em off. It's your fucking mattress
and you can do anything you want with it. And you can, too, return a bathing suit. They just say the Board of Health says you
can't so they don't have to be bothered. I pee in them first and
then I return them, that's how un-against the law returning a
bathing suit is.

NEDDA. Well it was nice talking to you . . .

TOMMY. It's Flowers, ma'am, Tommy Flowers.

NEDDA. It was nice talking to you, Mr. Flowers.

TOMMY. Aren't you going to wash your hands?

NEDDA. Is there some law about that, too?

TOMMY. No, but it's a nice habit.

NEDDA. I think the coast is clear now.

TOMMY. Don't go.

NEDDA. Hunh?

TOMMY. Stay.

NEDDA. I can't.

TOMMY. Okay.

NEDDA. And thanks for not turning me in.

TOMMY. It's not my store. I mean if this place were called Tommy
  Flowers then maybe I'd get a little uptight about people like you.

NEDDA. I told you! I never did anything like this in my life. I don't
  know what came over me today.

TOMMY. Yes, you do.

NEDDA. Yes, I do. Greed. Wish me luck.

TOMMY. Good luck. (*She still hesitates.*) You're scared?

NEDDA. Well aren't you when you . . . ? (*Tommy is drawing on a
  joint.*) Is that what I think it is?

TOMMY. It ain't oregano. You want some?

NEDDA. You could get in a lot of trouble doing that.

TOMMY. No worse than we're both in now. You better take some.
  It's a cold and heartless city out there, full of store detectives and
  vicious little meter maids.

NEDDA. I hate this city. I hate it, I hate it!

TOMMY. What's the matter?

NEDDA. I don't know. Everything!

TOMMY. What's your big rush anyway?

NEDDA. I wish I knew.

TOMMY. You know something? You really are better off in here with me.

NEDDA. I know! (*She takes the joint.*) My father was right Three months in New York City and I'm a fallen woman. (*She smokes.*)

TOMMY. Nice, hunh?

NEDDA. Wonderful! I'm ruining my entire life.

TOMMY. So what's your name, fallen woman?

NEDDA. (*Smoking in earnest.*) Nedda Lemon.

TOMMY. Any relation to Jack?

NEDDA. No.

TOMMY. I bet you're sick of people asking you that question?

NEDDA. Not particularly. May I ask you something? Are you trying to pick me up?

TOMMY. What do you think?

NEDDA. I just wanted to make sure.

TOMMY. So what do you do besides shoplift Bloomingdale's?

NEDDA. I told you I've never . . . !

TOMMY. I said what else.

NEDDA. (*Pointing to cello.*) This.

TOMMY. That?

NEDDA. I'm a cellist.

TOMMY. A real cellist?

NEDDA. A real cellist.

TOMMY. No shit?

NEDDA. No kidding.

TOMMY. A serious cellist?

NEDDA. Too serious.

TOMMY. I better watch my step then.

NEDDA. If you'd said you were Pablo Casals or Rostropovitch, I'd've done cartwheels.

TOMMY. I'm Pablo Casals or Rostropovitch.

NEDDA. I can't do cartwheels.

TOMMY. Are you famous?

NEDDA. A real biggy.

TOMMY. I can do cartwheels.

NEDDA. With a lot of practice and a little luck, I may one day be asked to play the Lord's Prayer at somebody's bar mitzvah in Brooklyn.

TOMMY. That would be quite a stunt if you could pull it off.

NEDDA. I'm just a nobody.

TOMMY. Don't say that, man.

NEDDA. Living in this city I feel about this big most of the time.

TOMMY. How big is that?

NEDDA. Infinitesimal.

TOMMY. That's pretty small.

NEDDA. I know.

TOMMY. Well you're not. Not to me you're not. To me, you're one of the all-time super biggy cellists.

NEDDA. Thank you.

TOMMY. I guess you're bow-legged?

NEDDA. No!

TOMMY. Where do you live?

NEDDA. The Village, where else?

TOMMY. Alone?

NEDDA. You really are trying to pick me up.

TOMMY. But wait'll you tell your father you smoked with Pablo Casals or Rostropovitch in the ladies' room at Bloomingdale's. (*They are both pretty high and giggly by now.*)

NEDDA. He'll never believe me.

TOMMY. I know.

NEDDA. I don't believe it either. My father wants me to go back home and marry this creep lawyer and be a creep music teacher until we start having creep babies and then I can become a creep housewife and maybe he's right, only I don't want to, and I just broke up with this creep oboist who all he did was suck on his reeds and now I'm a criminal and the only reason I'm telling you all this is I'm stoned and you're a stranger and no one ever tried to pick me up in the ladies' room before and I guess I'm flattered but I'm too much of a creep to let you and it was very nice talking to you, Mr. Flowers. (*There is a pause.*)

TOMMY. I need a place to stay, Miss Lemon.

NEDDA. You do?

TOMMY. Me and Arnold.

NEDDA. Who's Arnold?

TOMMY. My dog. He's very nice. You'll like him. He's beautifully housebroken and he's very unusual in that he never gets that doggy odor which can be so offensive to some people or sheds any hair. Believe me, he won't be any trouble.

NEDDA. It's not Arnold I was worrying about.

TOMMY. You mean it's me?

NEDDA. Don't get me wrong. I think I like you and everything. Only, well, you know . . .

TOMMY. You're a virgin.

NEDDA. No, it's not that.

TOMMY. Yes or no?

NEDDA. No.

TOMMY. You got a social disease?

NEDDA. That's not very funny, Mr. Flowers.

TOMMY. Tommy, please, Miss Lemon, it's Tommy! I just thought I'd ask. There's practically an epidemic.

NEDDA. I like men, I like being with someone. I'm just not terribly promiscuous that way.

TOMMY. Okay, I'll tell you what: if you don't want to make love, we won't make love.

NEDDA. What about you?

TOMMY. I always want to make love.

NEDDA. You do?

TOMMY. It's my curse. I'll tell you what: we'll pick up Arnold and this friend of mine who's out having coffee . . .

NEDDA. There's someone else?

TOMMY. Ben Delight.

NEDDA. Ben Delight?

TOMMY. But that's just his stage name. He changed it from Jack Wonder.

NEDDA. Jack Wonder?

TOMMY. Don't worry, you'll like him. He knew Paul Muni.

NEDDA. Paul Muni?

TOMMY. Paul Muni! How old are you? Ten? And then we'll all head for your place and you can cook us a spaghetti dinner. I'm crazy for Italian food. So's Arnold.

NEDDA. I don't know what to say.

TOMMY. I do. I like your name, I like your style, I like the sound of your voice. I also like what I see, I like it a lot, and I'm really desperate for a pad tonight. So come on, Nedda Lemon, no-relation-to-Jack, what do you say?

POLICEMAN. (*Off.*) All right, buddy, come out with your hands up!

TOMMY. Kill the joint! (*Tommy hides in the booth, Nedda pops the joint in her mouth.*)

POLICEMAN. (*Off.*) I know you're in there! Now are you coming out or am I coming in there after you? One, two, three. I'm coming in. (*Policeman enters with woman.*)

NEDDA. (*Indignant.*) I beg your pardon?

POLICEMAN. Step aside, miss, there's a man in there.

NEDDA. There's no one in here. You're the only man in here.

POLICEMAN. Now sshh!

NEDDA. This is the ladies' room!

POLICEMAN. And I'm going to keep it that way! All right, buddy, I know you're in there. Now come out of there. Come out I say. Now open up or I'll shoot. (*To woman.*) There better be a man in there.

NEDDA. If there is a man in there, I don't think you have to shoot him.

POLICEMAN. One.

NEDDA. You must be crazy.

POLICEMAN. Two.

NEDDA. He's got a gun!

POLICEMAN. Three!

NEDDA. No. (*The door swings open to reveal Tommy disguised in a nun's habit.*)

TOMMY. Yes, officer?

POLICEMAN. I'm terribly sorry, sister. Some nut told me there was a man in here.

TOMMY. That's perfectly all right.

POLICEMAN. I don't know what to say, sister.

TOMMY. God bless you.

POLICEMAN. Thank you, sister.

TOMMY. (*Taking Nedda's arm.*) Excuse us. She's a nun and look at her. It's the third time this month she's tried to escape. Sister Rose, control yourself! You're not even supposed to be in Bloomingdale's. (*On their way out.*) You know something? I am going to want to make love to you.

NEDDA. You know something? Me, too, Sister Rose.

TOMMY. You're Rose; I'm Mary. (*They are gone.*)

POLICEMAN. What's happening to holy mother church? I'm taking me kids out of parochial school so fast those nuns won't know what hit 'em. (*He goes. Woman sighs, goes into a booth, closes the door and sits.*)

STORE ANNOUNCER. Your attention, may I have your attention, please. For your shopping convenience, Bloomingdale's will be open until 9 p.m. this evening. I repeat, for your shopping convenience . . . what is this?

TOMMY'S VOICE. This is Tommy Flowers. For your shopping convenience Bloomingdale's is going to be bombed. Grab what you can before it's too late and split. You've got three minutes to split. (*The woman screams and comes charging out of her booth. Lights up on Tommy taking off his improvised nun's habit: he's used his white jockey shorts for the headpiece.*)

TOMMY. I haven't really put a bomb in Bloomingdale's but don't think it hasn't crossed my mind. A lot of things have crossed my mind . . . but so far I'm still playing it nice. Well why not? Somebody might get hurt. Besides, so far nice is fun. Try it some time. Try the ladies' room, try the men's room. You might be pleasantly surprised. You've got fifteen minutes. That's a lot.

ENTR'ACTE

Special spotlight on Conductor. He turns, bows to audience, accepts the rose that has been thrown to him, turns again and waits. The lights come up center stage on another gleaming stainless steel and glass phonograph. Again there is a shiny black record on the changer all ready to play. The Conductor raps for attention, then raises both arms ready to conduct.

The Black Stagehand shuffles out of the wings still playing his portable cassette, watches and waits. The record drops into the playing position and begins to spin. The tone arm hovers over the record a moment and then drops noiselessly into the spinning grooves. At once: Music! Loud! Stereophonic sound! What we hear is a luscious choral rendition of "America, The Beautiful" sung by an invisible chorus in the ripest Mormon Tabernacle Choir style. The Black Stagehand shrugs and shuffles off. What we see on the screens above the stage are images of America, The Beautiful in vibrant Kodachrome. Think of the large photographic murals in Grand Central Station. Pictures of her spacious skies, her amber waves of grain, her purple mountains majesty above her fruited plains from sea to shining sea.

After one full verse of "America, The Beautiful" there is a musical/visual transition. The lush stereophonic sound changes to the scratchy, tinnier tone of an old 78 rpm record and we will hear a medley of old popular American songs. The Conductor will turn to face the audience and lead them in a sing-along. He's suddenly sprouted a goatee and looks remarkably like Mitch Miller now. What we will see on the screens is what has become of those spacious skies, amber waves of grain, fruited plains and shining seas of America, The Beautiful. The Showgirl will help out by holding up cue cards with the song lyrics. Some of the old popular American songs we hear are: "Moonlight Bay," "Harvest Moon," "In the Good Old Summertime," "April Showers," "June Is Busting Out All Over," "This Was a Real Nice Clambake," "White Christmas," "Blue Skies," "By the Beautiful Sea," etc. Some of the images of America we see are: factories belch-

ing smoke, over-crowded beaches, littered campsites, trash-strewn streets, clogged sewers, billboard-glutted highways, the astronauts' litter on the moon, traffic jams, polluted rivers, oil slicks, mutant sealife, crops being spray-dusted, etc.

During this sing-along, old popular American music medley, the Black Stagehand appears and dances a very elegant soft shoe routine. He moves with an indefinable grace. He is elegant the way Mozart is elegant. His slow, easy, fluid dance movements evoke nostalgia for an America that was. It is almost an elegy, in fact. After his soft shoe ends, the Black Stagehand glides off into the wings, the Conductor turns his back to us and again begins to conduct his invisible forces and the beautiful stereo music returns with a reprise of "America, The Beautiful."

On the screens we now see pictures of the Stock Exchange, the Statue of Liberty, and Rockefeller Center. The music fills the theatre. The Kodachrome pictures are gorgeous.

"America, The Beautiful" hits its final chord. Then again. Then again. Then again. Clearly the record is stuck. With each repeat of the final chord, there is the sound of an explosion and one of the pictures is extinguished only to be replaced by another. Some of the places and landmarks exterminated in this fashion are: Con Edison, The Induction Center, Chase Manhattan Bank, Columbia University, Grant's Tomb, The George Washington Bridge, The Metropolitan Museum of Art, The Empire State Building, Madison Square Garden, Howard Johnson's, etc. The Conductor is powerless to do anything. Instead, he can only conduct the final chord over and over again.

The Black Stagehand comes shuffling out of the wings, taking all the time in the world, a big "I told you so" grin on his face and clearly enjoying the sound and sight of all this carnage. He stands by the phonograph, recognizing his power to stop the bombings and taking his own sweet time to do so. Several times he is about to reach down to "unstick" the record, only to stop at the last moment and let the building in question explode. Clearly, he's playing a game of Cat and Mouse and having a good time at it, too. It is only when a picture of this theatre itself, the one we are all in now, appears that he moves quickly to avert another disaster. He hits the phonograph hard and the final chord is played and this time stays played. The Black Stagehand grins triumphantly.

BLACK STAGEHAND. Where Has Tommy Flowers Gone? Side two. Shee-it! (*He is still grinning and gloating when the phonograph explodes.*)

ACT TWO

COMRADE MARILYN

The Twentieth Century Fox fanfare.
The blonde hair and pretty face of Marilyn appear in a special
light. That is all we see of her.
Tommy Flowers is Marilyn.

MARILYN. (*Fielding questions like an old pro.*) . . . which will lead
to the violent overthrow of the corrupt and decadent institutions
that control our capitalistic, materialistic, racist society. That's
what I think, comrade.

VOICE. That doesn't sound like you.

MARILYN. It wasn't. (*Piano introduction.*) Mr. President. Ladies
and gentlemen. Lennie. (*She sings.*)
> Happy birthday to you.
> Happy birthday to you.
> Happy birthday, dear America.
> Happy . . .

(*She does some quick adding.*)
> 195th birthday to you!

(*The song ends, taped applause.*)

VOICE. Hold it, Marilyn! Atta girl! (*Flashbulbs pop. Marilyn
poses.*)

MARILYN. Thanks, honey.

VOICE. How is it up there, Marilyn?

MARILYN. Oh it's just peachy! How is it down there?

VOICE. Do you have a new love interest?

MARILYN. I always have a love interest, honey.

VOICE. Who's the lucky man?

MARILYN. I think all men are lucky.

VOICE. Come on, what's his name?

MARILYN. Kay. Isn't that too much?

VOICE. Kay? His name is Kay?

MARILYN. That's what I told him. Kay Guevara. What kind of a
name for a man is that?

VOICE. You mean Che Guevara? That Che?

MARILYN. That's what I said. Shay.

VOICE. The Cuban revolutionary?

MARILYN. Cuban? He told me he was from Havana.

VOICE. Tell us, does Señor Guevara think the CIA plotted his murder?

MARILYN. Whose murder, honey?

VOICE. His. In Bolivia.

MARILYN. Oh, no, sweetie, then it's not the same Kay Guevara. This one's not dead. We're having what the French call an *affaire du coeur*. You know what I call it, honey? That Old Black Magic! Is that okay to say anymore? Everybody's so touchy these days! Can I do my number now?

VOICE. Of all the men in the world, why him?

MARILYN. That's easy. He's very nice and extremely well read and he's told me all sorts of things I didn't know before.

VOICE. Like what?

MARILYN. Also, he's kind of cute with that little beard and beret! (*More flashbulbs. Marilyn is happily posing for them.*) Oooooooo!

VOICE. Like what?

MARILYN. Aaaaaaaaa!

VOICE. Marilyn, like what?

MARILYN. Hunh?

VOICE. Skip it.

MARILYN. All these questions. All I want to do is sing, honey.

VOICE. Just one more question. If you had it all to do all over again, would you do it any differently?

MARILYN. Had what, honey?

VOICE. Life.

MARILYN. What life, sweetie?

VOICE. Yours.

MARILYN. You mean I'm not alive?

VOICE. You didn't know?

MARILYN. I told you: nobody ever tells me anything.

VOICE. I just assumed.

MARILYN. But I'll tell you something! You're morbid, mister. You think everyone's dead. And I'll tell you something else! I'm not the one who's dead. You are. I'm glad I didn't do my number for you. Why don't you try fucking yourself!

VOICE. We're sorry.

MARILYN. Sure you are.

VOICE. We all remember you.

MARILYN. I remember you, too.

VOICE. We all love you.

MARILYN. I know.

VOICE. We all need you.

MARILYN. Don't, honey, you'll make me cry.

VOICE. We all miss you.

MARILYN. I miss you, too.

VOICE. And you're still very much alive.

MARILYN. I am?

CUBAN ACCENT. (*Off.*) Marileen, *vamonos, muchacha!*

MARILYN. I've got to split, honey. He hits me when I'm late.

VOICE. Just tell us what you think of what's going on down here?

MARILYN. You mean all the bombs?

VOICE. Right.

MARILYN. From where I am they look very pretty. And that Tommy Flowers is kind of cute, *n'est-ce pas?* if you know what I mean. I'm no politician. I just think people should be nicer to one another.

CUBAN ACCENT. Marileen!

MARILYN. That's what he says, too, only it takes longer and it's more complicated.

CUBAN ACCENT. *Ay, muchacha, vamonos!*

MARILYN. Next time I'll do "Running Wild" from *Some Like It Hot* in which I had first star billing over Jack Lemmon and Tony Curtis, only it was for United Artists. Even Kay likes that one. Bye, honey! (*She starts to wiggle off, then turns and speaks over her shoulder.*) You know something? I knew I wasn't dead! (*And with a shimmy and a wiggle and a squeal, Marilyn is gone.*)

ANNOUNCER'S VOICE. This just came in. A man who the police say blamed Eastern Airlines for the death of his champion Irish wolfhound walked up to an Eastern jet today and chopped eighteen holes in its underbelly with an ax, airport officers said. Thank you. (*The Showgirl appears.*)

SHOWGIRL. Revolution is the only thing, the only power that ever worked out freedom for any people. The powers that have ruled long, and learned to love ruling, will never give up that preroga-

tive till they find they must, till they see the certainty of overthrow and destruction if they do not! To plant—to revolutionize
—those are the twin stars that have ruled our pathway. What
have we then to dread in the word *revolution?* We, the children
of rebels! We were born to be rebels—it runs in our blood!
Wendell Phillips, 1848. Thank you. (*She goes.*)

THE GREAT ATLANTIC & PACIFIC TEA PARTY

(*The lights come up on Tommy with a shopping cart. He is
eating yogurt.*)

TOMMY. I can't help smiling. Life is just too much fun lately. I've
got a fairly permanent roof over my head, Bach's Sonatas for
Unaccompanied Cello running out of both ears and two wonderful friends. Three, if you include Arnold. The health department
has a thing about dogs in supermarkets. Afraid they'll crap in the
aisles or something. I suppose they have a point. (*Nedda enters
with a shopping cart. She looks very pregnant.*) It's not what
you're thinking. Good God, no. We're doing our shopping.

NEDDA. (*Through clenched teeth.*) As soon as we get out of here,
you take the turkey. It's leaking. Now what do I do with these?

TOMMY. Find some 39¢ tops to fit the 96¢ jars and play it cool at
the check-out. (*Wrinkling his nose at what he sees.*) Mama
Lucia's Frozen Pizza?

NEDDA. Beethoven's Six Symphonies. The last three didn't fit. Anything else, maestro?

TOMMY. How are we fixed for fruit?

NEDDA. (*Nodding to her bosom.*) Apples, oranges . . . take your
pick.

TOMMY. You're catching on.

NEDDA. I've got a good teacher. (*She goes. Ben enters walking
rather stiffly.*)

BEN. I've got six eggs in my drawers.

TOMMY. I think maybe five now.

BEN. I was afraid I felt something.

TOMMY. Put the lamb chops *under* the potatoes, not on top.
They'll overcharge us. You're a novice in crime, Ben.

BEN. I can't seem to get the swing of it, Tom.

TOMMY. Hang in there, you will. And walk tall! (*An egg rolls out* of *Ben's pants as he walks off. Tommy takes out a can opener and helps himself to some food. Also, a straw for a twist-open pop bottle.*) *Bourgeois, vous n'avez rien compris.* Bourgeoise, you have understood nothing. French rebellion poster. But I look at it this way: America's a rich country. It can afford me. Of course if I really had balls I'd light a can of Sterno and rustle me up a Spanish Omelette right here in Aisle D. This is delicious!

ANNOUNCER'S VOICE. Is there a doctor in the house? We need you, man, we really need you. There's a young chick in the manager's office who's really freaked out on some bad acid. She's having a really bad trip. So help her out, hunh, man? Peace. (*The Showgirl appears. She is half out of her last costume and half into her new one.*)

SHOWGIRL. Who do they think I am with these quick changes? Plastic Woman? (*Composing herself, but still surly.*) We can't have education without revolution. We have tried peace education for nineteen hundred years and it has failed. Let us try revolution and see what it will do now. Helen Keller, 1916. (*Showgirl exits.*)

TOMMY'S OLD FLAME

TOMMY'S OLD GIRL FRIEND. Hi, Tommy. Remember me? If you said you didn't, I'd come up there and scratch whoever-she-is' eyes out for her! It's me, all right. Only it's Beverly Swantner now. You remember Norman. Just listen to him. (*We hear snoring.*) You know what I've been thinking about tonight? A pink and white Ford Fairlane with a chrome dip in the door. The back seat in particular. Sound familiar? We were just terrible together, Tommy! I bet everyone at Paine High School knew about us. You probably told them. Well don't look at me. Shelly Pape is the only girl I ever told and *she* was hardly in any position to talk.

Do you ever think about what it might've been like if we'd gotten married? I'm serious. I could've gotten you to, you know. I didn't have to make you use those things. And don't think I didn't think about it. Right at the end I practically made a scene about them. Remember? It wasn't anybody's fault. You wanted something else. I ended up wanting this. I've got it. What about you? Only, well, it was different with you. Happier, better, more different I guess. Listen to me! We were just so young then, that's all. We thought we were very, very old but all we really were was young. If you're ever back in St. Petersburg, and I wouldn't wish that on my worst enemy, please look us up. Norman would get a kick out of seeing you again, too. Oh, Tommy!

A QUIET EVENING AT HOME

(*Lights up on Nedda playing her cello. Ben is reading* Variety. *Arnold is at his side. Tommy is lying on the floor.*)

TOMMY. (*Regarding Nedda fondly.*) Hey! (*Nedda shakes her head, too busy concentrating on the music to look up even.*) You're biting your tongue again.

NEDDA. I am not! (*A moment later and she is doing it again.*)

TOMMY. That's nice.

NEDDA. It's hard.

TOMMY. Just keep your tongue in.

NEDDA. Sshh!

BEN. It says here there's twin strippers in Tulsa with identical forty-nine inch busts. They call themselves Stress N' Strain. I played Tulsa. *Shanghai Gesture.*

TOMMY. Must have been a lot of feathers in that one, too.

BEN. No feathers but a hell of a lot of fans. (*Tommy has settled back to smoke.*)

TOMMY. I like this. I like this whole evening. I even liked your lasagna tonight.

NEDDA. It was ravioli.

TOMMY. It was so good it tasted like lasagna. What do I know? Now shut up and fiddle. (*Pause. Only the cello music.*)

BEN. I like the kid. He's been good to me. I sleep over there. It's a little lumpy but I've done worse. What I can't always figure is why the kid likes *me*. I knew Eugene O'Neill. Tommy can't get over it. Hell, I toured the *Count of Monte Cristo* five straight seasons with his father! Hick towns then like Waco, Texas, or Topeka, Kansas, real flea bags, and he's impressed. I've been everywhere and seen everything and there's nothing new under the sun. But try telling Tommy that. I checked up on that Mr. James Dean of his. Seems he was pretty good. But as Tommy

says, he died young. Poor sonofabitch. Me, I want to live forever
and I nearly have. You can add ten years to what you're thinking
and you'll still be off by twenty. I like the girl, too. She's a lady.
Not too many of them around anymore either, let me tell you.
'Course I can't stand all that damn fiddling but it's nice here
with them. While it lasts. I'm even kind of fond of Arnold tonight. Not crazy about him, mind you, just fond. I'm getting
mellow. I've got to watch that. That damn spaghetti of hers is
coming up on me! (*Nedda stops playing.*)

NEDDA. Tommy?

TOMMY. I'm right here, Nedda. I'm so right here I can't believe it.

NEDDA. Me, too. Good, I'm glad.

BEN. They're making another musical out of *Peter Pan.* They're
auditioning fairies. (*Nedda resumes playing. Pause. Only the
cello music.*)

NEDDA. I'd like to ask Tommy if he loves me. I wonder what he'd
say. I'm sorry, but I'm a very conventional budding girl cellist
from Tampa, Florida, that way. Tommy's from St. Petersburg.
Small world, isn't it? I grew up thinking life could be very nice
if you just let it. I still do. It's certainly full of surprises and most
of them are good. Like my music. That happened when I was ten
years old and went to my first concert. I came home in a dream.
Or like Tommy Flowers! That happened . . . well, you *saw*
where that happened and we came home in a cab Tommy didn't
pay for. I love my music. Whenever I get the teeniest bit depressed I think about it and I'm all right again. The notes are
hard for me, I can't always play them at first, but if practice
makes perfect then I'm going to be a very good cellist one day.
That's what I want. And now there's Tommy. Someone I hadn't
counted on at all. A small world but so many different people in
it! I don't know what Tommy wants, so I have to play it by ear
with him. That's hard for me and I'm pretty smart about men.
It's not like practicing my music; Tommy has to help, too. And
which is real or which is realer? All these little, wonderful, difficult notes some man wrote once upon a time somewhere or me,
right now, in a whole other place, trying to play them and wanting to ask Tommy Flowers if he loves me and wanting him to
answer, "I love you, Nedda Lemon"? They're both real. I don't
want to change the world. I just want to be in it with someone.

For someone with such a sour name, I could be a very happy person. (*Nedda stops playing.*) Tommy?

TOMMY. You stopped.

NEDDA. Do you love me?

TOMMY. I love you, Nedda Lemon. I'm here. You're there. We're together and it's nice.

NEDDA. I know. How about another cup of coffee?

TOMMY. Only no Pream in it this time, hunh? It has cyclamates or something. (*Nedda has gone by now.*) Somebody ought to blow that place up. Maybe I will. (*The phone rings. Tommy answers it in an exaggerated Southern black accent.*) Nedda's place. Rosco speaking. I work at the Mobil station on the corner. Miss Nedda said I might come over here to use her shower when I wanted to . . . well, suh, who is *this?* . . . Oh. (*Nedda has returned.*)

NEDDA. Pream was all we had. You'll have to drink it black. Who is it?

TOMMY. It's for you.

NEDDA. Who is it?

TOMMY. It's your father.

NEDDA. (*She takes the phone from Tommy.*) Hi, daddy, how are you? . . . Hunh?

TOMMY. I should've guessed it might be him.

NEDDA. Just a friend . . . no, of course not! . . . what do you mean?

TOMMY. Nedda hasn't called home to ask for money in weeks. I'm trying to get her to be more independent.

NEDDA. (*Looking at Tommy now.*) It was just a joke, daddy.

TOMMY. You said he was a big liberal.

NEDDA. Of course I don't! . . . Well what if I did? (*Still talking she takes the phone into the other room.*)

TOMMY. Bet you can't count to ten without smiling! (*Ben is standing up.*) So what's up, Ben?

BEN. I'm going to bed. Come on, Arnold. And no snoring this time.

TOMMY. Good night, Ben.

BEN. Good night, Tommy. (*Ben and Arnold go. Tommy waits until the coast is clear.*)

TOMMY. I've been doing some interesting reading lately. I've got something I want to show you. (*He brings the makings of a homemade bomb and an instruction manual from out of a hid-*

ing place.) A cigar box. A dry cell battery. Some wire. An alarm clock. And dynamite. I know it doesn't look like much but ac-. cording to this pamphlet it packs some little wallop. *The Civilian Guide to Explosives.* It's free from the United States Army Corps of Engineers. All this talk about bombs . . . even the government wants to get in on the act. I'm up to lesson four. (*He turns on the television and settles back to work.*) Maybe there's a good revolution on.

ANNOUNCER'S VOICE. . . . told reporters today that there was no "real danger" of a black or Puerto Rican shooting the President because "they can't shoot very straight."

TOMMY. You want to bet?

ANNOUNCER'S VOICE. Mr. Hoover, who is 74, went on to deny rumors that he intends to retire this year.

TOMMY. Hang in there, you old fairy!

ANNOUNCER'S VOICE. The First Lady was in town today to officially open the Carmen Hernandez Center for Blind Child Study. The multi-million dollar center is named for the nine-year-old girl who got her wish to meet the President a few short weeks before she succumbed to leukemia. Blind at birth, Carmen was also mentally retarded. "She was the bravest little girl who ever lived," said her father, Hector Hernandez. Carmen had her big day in Washington and now there's a center named for her but her parents are still on relief. I'll be right back with Frank Cross and the weather.

INSTANT REPLAY

(*The First Lady and the interviewer have appeared.*)

FIRST LADY. I declare this center open. (*She snips the ribbon. Applause.*) Thank you.

INTERVIEWER. It's a wonderful facility, isn't it?

FIRST LADY. My, my, my, my, my!

INTERVIEWER. And you'll notice that even the water fountains are so designed that the children confined to wheelchairs can reach them without assistance.

FIRST LADY. My, my, my, my, my!

INTERVIEWER. Perhaps you'd care to comment?

FIRST LADY. It's a wonderful facility, Bob. I'm speechless. My, my, my, my, my!

INTERVIEWER. The children here at Carmen Hernandez have asked me to give you this small token of their affection that was made for you in their new crafts center with their very own little hands.

FIRST LADY. You know, Gene, it's touching when this sort of thing happens. No matter how many times it happens, I'm just completely touched. What is it?

INTERVIEWER. I believe it's a pot holder.

FIRST LADY. A pot holder, Frank! My, my, my, my, my!

INTERVIEWER. Unh, it's Flo, ma'am. The name is Flo.

FIRST LADY. Flo! Of course it's Flo! I know it's Flo! Why do I keep calling you Ted? But you see, Flo, I genuinely like poor people and minority groups and the physically handicapped. Yes, I do. I've been lucky enough to be able to sit down and have a real heart to heart with people less fortunate than myself. I'm convinced we all should. I'm sorry more people haven't. It's such an enriching experience, Gabe, let me tell you. It's because of something like this little . . . *potholder*. . . . I can say this to you today, Chet: there are no poor people . . . no, not really! . . . only poor hearts. (*Ovation.*) May I say something? Young people. That's right. You heard me. It's you young people, that's who. You kids. I think you young people in this country are pretty darn wonderful. W-o-n-d-e-r-f-u-l. I know that's a pretty unfashionable statement to make these days, Hugh, but the youth of America are number one in my book. I'm sorry, Dan, but I say exactly what's on my mind.

INTERVIEWER. It's Flo, ma'am, it's Flo.

FIRST LADY. No, I'm sorry, Flo. But I'm just crazy about today's kids. My recent tour of North Dakota college campusi really rammed that point home to me in no uncertain terms, Gabe, let me tell you!

INTERVIEWER. Perhaps you'd care to tell us about it?

FIRST LADY. I just did. (*There is an awkward moment happily broken by the appearance of Rachel Gonzalez who gropes her way uncertainly onto the stage and stands now with her back to the audience. Rachel Gonzalez is a very tall Puerto Rican girl, 10 years old, dressed in a pink satin party dress, gold cross around her neck and a religious medallion pinned to her dress, high socks and black patent leather slippers wtih taps. There is a big rose in her hair, too. Rachel Gonzalez is Tommy Flowers.*)

MODERATOR. Thank you. And now we'd like you to meet Rachel Gonzalez, our own little mentally retarded, leukemia-stricken, Fight For Sight poster girl of the year. Let's hear it for Rachel! (*Applause on tape.*)

RACHEL. (*Blowing kisses, her back to the audience.*) Hello. Hello, everybody. I wish I could see you, the way you can see me. Hello. Hello, everybody.

MODERATOR. We're over here, Rachel, that's the girl!

RACHEL. (*Facing front now, blowing more kisses.*) Hello. Hello, everybody. You gonna donate? You better donate!

MODERATOR. Rachel's a Puerto Rican, aren't we, sweetheart?

RACHEL. *Si.*

MODERATOR. My, but aren't we big for our age!

RACHEL. *Si.*

MODERATOR. *Muy, muy grande.*

RACHEL. *Si.* (*Rachel is touching the First Lady's face.*)

MODERATOR. Unh, Rachel . . . !

FIRST LADY. It's all right, Walter. It's just her way of seeing me.

RACHEL. You smell funny.

FIRST LADY. That's my perfume.

RACHEL. It smells like my neighborhood.

MODERATOR. Unh, how old are we, Rachel?

RACHEL. *Si.*

MODERATOR. We're nine years old going on ten, aren't we, sweetheart?

RACHEL. No.

MODERATOR. What are those you're carrying, Rachel?

RACHEL. Flowers.

MODERATOR. And who are those flowers for?

RACHEL. Her.

FIRST LADY. More flowers! My! What's my name, Rachel?

RACHEL. *Si.*

FIRST LADY. What is my name?

RACHEL. No.

MODERATOR. Why that's the . . .

FIRST LADY. Wait, Walter, let me do it. Rachel?

RACHEL. Don't hit me, mister, don't hit me, don't hit me!

FIRST LADY. No one's going to hurt you, Rachel. Now: *como* . . . unh, *como*, it's coming back! . . . *como, como, como* . . . *Como me!* . . . *Como me llamo?*

MODERATOR. *Muy bien*, yourself.

FIRST LADY. It's very simple. We honeymooned in San Juan and I've always had this knack for picking up foreign languages. You see, Dell, my feeling is that—

RACHEL. (*Yanking at First Lady's skirt.*) Hey! What about me?

FIRST LADY. I'm sorry, darling! Hmmm? *Como mi llamo?* (The poor thing!) *Como mi llamo?*

RACHEL. What's my name?

FIRST LADY. You understood! She understood! (*First Lady clutches Rachel to her. Studio audience applauds.*)

MODERATOR. (*Stage whisper.*) What Rachel doesn't know is that she has only six weeks to live. (*The First Lady is being pawed all over.*) Unh, Rachel!

FIRST LADY. I don't mind, David, really I don't.

RACHEL. You have big *carrangas*. This man in our slum tenement try to play with my little *carrangas* all the time and make *puñetas* with me but I stab him in the eye with an ice pick, like that! and he go to Bellevue and maybe he never get out or else he have to get a dog and sell pencils. I don't care. I been to Bellevue too. It's a big dirty place. I been there after the *raton* bit me. The *raton* was that big. It bit my *clamato*. I cried like a little devil. I cried so much my big sister the *puta* tied me to the bed and stuffed rags down my throat for five days until my father got back from San Juan and he beat the shit out of her and then he took us *both* to the hospital. I'm hungry. I want a cheeseburger and a chocolate malt and french fries and a piece of apple pie à la mode. Can I have those things, First Lady? Oh please, oh please, oh please!

FIRST LADY. Of course you can, Rachel. You can have anything you want. Just as soon as we're off the air I'm going to buy you the biggest hamburger you ever saw.

RACHEL. I can't see! And I said a cheeseburger!

FIRST LADY. Of course, Rachel, of course! How I love that fiery Latin temperament, Ray.

RACHEL. You better believe it. I have gypsy blood in my veins. I

was born with castanets in my fingers and a rose in my teeth. I
will now sing and dance *Clavelitos.*

FIRST LADY. One of my favorites!

RACHEL. No shit.

FIRST LADY. Absolutely!

RACHEL. You're a nice lady. That's too bad. (*She comes downstage.*) Hit it, chicos! (*Rachel goes into her number like a hard-
driving little professional. All traces of the shy little girl vanish
when she entertains. The full stage lights come up fast, as Rachel
socks into her grand finale. Ovation.*) Goodbye, goodbye, everyone! I love you! (*Blowing kisses, she is on her way out, stum-
bling, tripping, groping, when she suddenly whirls around to face
us and makes the clenched fist salute.*) Venceremos! (*And
Rachel/Tommy is gone.*)

FIRST LADY. (*Smiles, sighs.*) So afflicted and yet so full of life!

MODERATOR. If that isn't the cutest little Puerto Rican child I've
ever seen I'll eat my hat.

FIRST LADY. She forgot all about her cheeseburger! No, a sight like
Rachel Gonzalez really tears the heart out of you. If only she
were more retarded, then maybe it wouldn't occur to her that she
was blind. As our President is so fond of saying, "What they
don't know, won't hurt them."

MODERATOR. This is in reference to Rachel?

FIRST LADY. No. I think it's in reference to just about everyone.
(*Explosion. The bouquet of flowers Rachel has given her blows
up in her face. The First Lady and the Moderator are gone.*)

THE LAST OF THE BIG SPENDERS

(*Howard Johnson's. Nedda and Tommy are finishing dinner.*)

TOMMY. No, I think my pre-pubescent fascination with Wonder
Woman influenced my entire attitude towards women. In fact,
I know it has. I probably would have grown up a raging lesbian
if I'd been born a girl because of her. I didn't just read Wonder
Woman comic books like some of the other kids (she was never
very popular; not like Superman or Captain Marvel anyway); I
was obsessed with them. I even considered asking my mother to
run up a copy of that red, white and blue, stars and stripes, hal-
ter and panties outfit she ran around in (Wonder Woman, wise

guy, not my mother) on the old family Singer—(*Points to Nedda's plate.*) Aren't you going to finish those? (*Nedda shakes her head.*) Waitress! (*Resuming at once.*)—but I knew my father would kick *both* our asses around the block if he ever came home and caught me in that get-up. Don't laugh. At least I turned out straight. All my friends who read Batman ended up queer. (*Waitress has appeared.*)

WAITRESS. Not more clams?

TOMMY. We can't finish these. Would you put them in a guppy bag?

WAITRESS. A what?

TOMMY. Guppy bag. For our fish.

WAITRESS. We only got doggy bags.

TOMMY. I don't think they'll notice. They're piranhas. Now hop to it. (*Waitress regards him warily, quickly clears the table.*) God, she was a tough cooz, old Wonder Woman was! Remember her invisible airplane?

NEDDA. Tommy!

TOMMY. All the other characters kept talking about how invisible it was. To them it looked like she was sitting on air. But *I* could see it. To me it just looked like she was sitting in a plastic airplane. Whoever drew that comic really botched that one up. Relax will you?

NEDDA. This is all I have! (*She has a bill. Tommy takes it from her.*)

TOMMY. Remember her truth lasso? Her magic bracelets?

NEDDA. What are we going to do?

TOMMY. Jesus Christ, you don't remember anything about Wonder Woman! Didn't you read? You really are ten!

NEDDA. What are you doing?! (*Tommy has set fire to the bill with a match. Next he will light another cigarette with it.*)

TOMMY. If she got you in her truth lasso you'd confess to anything. I love you, I hate you, you've got bad breath—that sort of thing. The magic bracelets were for warding off bullets. She could move them so fast the bullets were deflected right off them. Now the same artist did a terrific job there. All these squiggly lines around her wrists to indicate how fast she was moving them. (*He demonstrates.*) You know?

NEDDA. People are looking!

TOMMY. (*Waving, the flaming bill in one hand.*) Hi! Hello there! Enjoying your meal?

NEDDA. Tommy!

TOMMY. And she had this fantastic headband she could plug into this sort of television receiver kind of thing to talk to her mother and the other chicks back home on the isle of Lesbos. They were always practicing archery or doing gymnastics or something when she'd ring up. Very dykey, the whole setup. Hey, calm down, it's just money.

NEDDA. I know!

TOMMY. Get hung up on that stuff and you're right back in the system right up to here.

NEDDA. That was all I had. There's no more.

TOMMY. Good!

NEDDA. You may like to wash dishes, I don't.

TOMMY. Nobody likes to wash dishes. How are we doing on silverware?

NEDDA. We've got a service for eight.

TOMMY. (*Gathering more.*) There's never enough. (*Waitress has appeared.*) That's just what I was telling the little lady here. What month were you born, honey?

WAITRESS. November, why?

TOMMY. A Scorpio, I knew it. I can always tell. Very passionate women, those Scorpios.

WAITRESS. November 29th. I'm a Sagittarius and I'm about as passionate as that plate. Is that it? (*She starts to total the check.*)

TOMMY. May I ask you another personal question, Jeanette?

WAITRESS. Who Jeanette? What Jeanette?

TOMMY. Your badge says Jeanette.

WAITRESS. It came with the uniform. I'm Dolores.

TOMMY. For Dolores Del Rio! What did I tell you, Nedda?

WAITRESS. Dolores Del Flushing.

TOMMY. Just between you and me, Dolores, and this won't get any further: are you getting much around here?

WAITRESS. What does it look like?

TOMMY. I meant salary.

WAITRESS. So did I. $1.30 an hour plus tips. Why?

TOMMY. That's bad, man, that's really bad.

WAITRESS. You want to make a better offer?

TOMMY. Howard Johnson should be ashamed of himself.

WAITRESS. I'll tell him you said so.

TOMMY. $1.30 an hour plus tips! Did you hear that, Nedda? If I were you, Dolores, I'd take off my apron, rip up that check and go on strike.

WAITRESS. They *are* on strike. That's why they hired me. What are you, a Communist? Pay up front. (*She leaves Tommy with the check and goes.*)

TOMMY. Fucking scab.

NEDDA. Tommy!

TOMMY. $8.68.

NEDDA. Look at me.

TOMMY. Fucking tax.

NEDDA. You said you were taking me to dinner.

TOMMY. I'm trying to.

NEDDA. By beating the check?

TOMMY. Hey, calm down, it's just Howard Johnson's. The clams weren't that good.

NEDDA. If we were married, we'd be divorced, you know that, don't you?

TOMMY. Two minutes ago you loved me.

NEDDA. Two minutes ago I thought this was going to be a nice evening.

TOMMY. It still is. Happy birthday, Nedda.

NEDDA. It's not my birthday.

TOMMY. It is now! (*Restaurant lights dim fast as manager appears with a cupcake and a candle.*)

MANAGER. (*Greek accent.*)

> Happy birthday to you.
> Happy birthday to you.
> Happy birthday . . .

(*Tommy joins in.*)

> . . . Nedda Lemon
> Happy birthday to you.

TOGETHER. Speech! Speech! Speech!

NEDDA. (*Standing.*) I want everyone in this restaurant to know I've never been unhappier in my life! (*She can't continue. She sits down.*)

MANAGER. (*Clapping happily.*) *Ella! Ella!*

TOMMY. Thank you. Thank you. Wasn't that nice of him, Nedda? She's 47 years old, would you believe it? We're expecting our first child. That was very kind of you . . . (*Manager is adding price of cupcake to bill.*)

MANAGER. Cupcake.

TOMMY. It's not on the house?

MANAGER. In Howard Johnson's nothing is on the house.

TOMMY. What happened to Greek hospitality?

MANAGER. Gone with the junta. Kaput! (*He laughs at his own joke.*)

TOMMY. I didn't want to mention this, but what about this *roach* I found in my food? Think quick, Tino, people are watching. (*Manager takes the roach from Tommy's plate, looks at it.*)

MANAGER. Tony's Novelty Shop, 46th and 8th, three for a dollar, right?

TOMMY. Two for a dollar. You handled yourself magnificently. You see, Miss Lemon here is the restaurant and food editor for an exciting new gourmet magazine, it's all very hush-hush and I shouldn't be revealing her identity but you're a nice guy and I thought I'd give you a break. How many stars did you say you were giving this place, darling? Four? Four stars! (*Handing the check to the manager.*) Take care of this, will you? Thanks, Tino.

MANAGER. What's the name of this magazine?

TOMMY. Free Eats.

MANAGER. They were already in here.

TOMMY. No kidding?

MANAGER. About five times so far today.

TOMMY. It's got a big circulation.

MANAGER. Too big. (*Handing the check to Nedda.*) Happy birthday, lady.

TOMMY. Could I have my cockroach back?

MANAGER. I'm keeping it hostage up at the register. (*He goes.*)

TOMMY. You're not Greek! You're some kind of Turk! $8.98! Thirty cents for this shit! Fucking inflation. You want some? You hate me.

NEDDA. I guess I'm in love with you in theory because in reality you give me the hives.

TOMMY. 1, 2, 3, 4. . . .

NEDDA. . . . 5, 6, 7, 8, 9, 10.

TOMMY. You're not laughing.

NEDDA. Just once I wanted to enjoy my meal, pay the check and walk out like a normal person.

TOMMY. Go ahead, I'll wait for you. Come back tomorrow with the bread and bail me out.

NEDDA. I'm thinking of it.

TOMMY. You want to call your father?

NEDDA. I'm thinking of that, too. I'm tired, Tommy. People can't live like this.

TOMMY. Like what?

NEDDA. Like we are!

TOMMY. We could always blow this place up.

NEDDA. I'm being serious!

TOMMY. So am I. Now hang on. (*He suddenly stands up and begins shouting.*) I've had it with you, Fred! I'm fed up to here with you!

NEDDA. People are looking!

TOMMY. Of course people are looking, Fred! I don't blame them, Fred! They can look all they want! The analyst told us he was over all this. Maybe you can fool these people, Fred, but you can't fool me. I wanted to be proud of you, Fred, but you're a disgrace. Pay for your own dinner. I don't take that shit from any man. Hell, you can earn it right here. (*He violently overturns the table.*) Do a little floor show for them, you . . . tatty transvestite! Out of my way, please, out of my way. I can't bear it. (*He storms out, leaving Nedda, overwhelmed to say the least, sitting alone at the table.*) The ability to improvise in my line of work can't be overemphasized. That's called the Tommy Flowers Foolproof Free Eats Plan, emergency phase three. I just thought of it. You loved that one, right, Grandpa? Let's see if Nedda did. (*The manager has escorted Nedda out of the restaurant and onto the street. Tommy watches her standing there, so thoroughly and totally wretched, and then to us.*) I didn't want this. Honest. (*Calling for her.*) Psst!

NEDDA. What?

TOMMY. Get over here.

NEDDA. I don't ever want to see you again.

TOMMY. You can take that wig off now, Fred. I beat the check, didn't I?

NEDDA. I don't care.

TOMMY. Hey, look at me.

NEDDA. No.

TOMMY. A little smile already, Fred.

NEDDA. That's what you think!

TOMMY. It's getting bigger.

NEDDA. Smiles aren't enough, Tommy. Just because you make someone happy . . .

TOMMY. I make you happy, Fred?

NEDDA. I mean smile. Just because you make someone smile doesn't mean you're making them happy. So leave me alone. Please, just go away. If you knew how unhappy I was, you wouldn't stand there trying to make me laugh. I can't stand being happy with you, it's making me miserable. I just want to be unhappy all by myself. (*This is too much, even for her.*)

TOMMY. I'm sorry I make you so happy, Fred.

NEDDA. My name's not Fred. It's Nedda Lemon and I hate you! (*She's in his arms by now.*)

TOMMY. I know.

NEDDA. I loathe you.

TOMMY. Don't stop.

NEDDA. I can't stand you.

TOMMY. Of course you can't.

NEDDA. You're not even that good in bed.

TOMMY. You go too far, Miss Lemon.

NEDDA. What am I doing with you?

TOMMY. That's the breaks.

NEDDA. I want a nice doctor with a good practice who smokes a pipe.

TOMMY. So do I.

NEDDA. I want to live in the suburbs and drive a station wagon.

TOMMY. So did Eva Braun.

NEDDA. I want a big family.

TOMMY. So lay off the pills.

NEDDA. What if I did?

TOMMY. Look, I'm not a doctor and I hate pipes. I like who I am and where I am. I like you.

NEDDA. Why does everything have to be guerilla warfare with you?

TOMMY. You're not the enemy.

NEDDA. I don't see the point.

TOMMY. The point is, get it while you can.

NEDDA. I don't see any future in it.

TOMMY. Future? The whole thing's gonna collapse.

NEDDA. What do you want?

TOMMY. I don't know.

NEDDA. That's childish.

TOMMY. It's honest.

NEDDA. What do you want from me?

TOMMY. I want to go home and make love to you.

NEDDA. Tommy!

TOMMY. Fuck the movie. Unless you want to do it right here on the street. I feel much better about it now that your name's not Fred.

NEDDA. Answer me!

TOMMY. I think maybe I want everything.

NEDDA. That's impossible.

TOMMY. I know I want you.

NEDDA. You've already got me.

TOMMY. Now do you want to make puñetas with me or go to the Waverly?

NEDDA. I don't know what I want anymore.

TOMMY. I'm giving you a choice.

NEDDA. Puñetas *and* the Waverly.

TOMMY. In which order?

NEDDA. (*Opening her purse.*) Get a paper.

TOMMY. I don't need that. I'm surprised you didn't leave it on the table for Ataturk.

NEDDA. Aren't we ever going to pay for anything?

TOMMY. Not if I can help it.

NEDDA. What about the movie?

TOMMY. We'll walk in backwards.

NEDDA. Tommy! (*He goes. Nedda stands a moment, looks at the money in her hand, makes a face, makes a decision and goes back into Howard Johnson's.*)

TOMMY. That's how Nedda Lemon ended up in the Women's House of Detention. When I came back with the *Post*, she wasn't there. I looked up and down Sixth Avenue for her, every-where, even that crummy paperback bookstore. There wasn't a trace of her. And then there was a police car in front of Howard Johnson's and there was Nedda getting into it with two police-men. No wonder I couldn't find her. The last place I would've looked for Nedda was back in Howard Johnson's. (*Calling off.*) Come on, Arnold, let's go visit Nedda.

NEDDA INCARCERATED

TOMMY. Nedda!

NEDDA. (*Off.*) Tommy!

TOMMY. Nedda.

NEDDA. Are you there?

TOMMY. Yes!

NEDDA. (*Appearing at another stage level.*) I can't see you!

TOMMY. I'm down here! On the street!

NEDDA. I can't see you!

TOMMY. It doesn't matter! I'm here! What happened?

NEDDA. I went back!

TOMMY. Why?

NEDDA. To pay him!

TOMMY. Pay him?

NEDDA. It didn't seem right!

TOMMY. It didn't seem what?

NEDDA. Right!

TOMMY. That was dumb!

NEDDA. He wouldn't even listen to me!

TOMMY. I said that was dumb!

NEDDA. He just called the police!

TOMMY. How are you?

NEDDA. I hate it here!

TOMMY. I know!

NEDDA. I hate it a lot!

TOMMY. I'm sorry!

NEDDA. I just hate it!

TOMMY. Did you hear me say I was sorry? How are you?

NEDDA. How are you?

TOMMY. I'm fine!

NEDDA. And Arnold?

TOMMY. He's right here! He says hello!

NEDDA. And Ben?

TOMMY. Unh, fine.

NEDDA. Hunh?

TOMMY. He's fine! Everybody's just fine! (*To us.*) We were just sitting in the Automat, Ben and me, having a cup of coffee, when this awful rattle sound started coming out of him. It was awful trying to get him out of there or anyone to help us. Don't ever be old and sick and poor in this town. Just don't you ever. (*The lights have come up on Ben.*)

BEN. They don't like that.

TOMMY. He was just sick, ol' Ben was, you know? And they were asking for deposits like.

BEN. Admittance fees, they're called admittance fees.

TOMMY. Jesus Christ, Jesus Christ, Jesus Christ.

BEN. Finally Tommy got me into Bellevue.

TOMMY. After I told the nurse on admissions I'd personally take that stethoscope and ram it down her fat dumb throat if she didn't let Ben in.

BEN. He meant it, too, and she knew he did.

TOMMY. He's been there ever since on the critical list. They put him in a ward with ten other old men on the critical list. Nice. I'll come again tomorrow.

BEN. That's okay.

TOMMY. You can count on it. I still want to hear about you and Paul Muni.

BEN. Tom.

TOMMY. What?

BEN. I never knew Paul Muni. Any of those people.

TOMMY. Sure you did.

BEN. No. I was a vagabond, gypsy, third-rate barnstormer. I had a lot of fun, but that's all I was.

TOMMY. I don't believe you.

BEN. It's off my chest. You can believe any damn thing you want.

TOMMY. You and Paul Muni, right down the line.

BEN. If you say so.

TOMMY. Don't die on me, Ben.

BEN. Who said anything about dying?

TOMMY. What are you laughing at?

BEN. You in that *Kumquats* show! Green stripes, feathers, one line and you tripped!

TOMMY. Hey, take it easy, Ben! You're not supposed to laugh.

BEN. Who says? Now beat it! I'll see you tomorrow. You and *Kumquats!* Hey, kid, walk in backwards and they'll think you're coming out! (*The lights fade down on Ben.*)

TOMMY. He died at 7:51 a.m. this morning. I wasn't there. Peacefully, they said, when I telephoned. He died peacefully. But I think they have orders to tell everyone that. I mean, did you ever call a hospital and they said the patient died violently?

NEDDA. Give him my love!

TOMMY. He's just fine! He sends you his love! And I'll get you out of there, too! I'll blow the place up if I have to, but I'll get you out!

NEDDA. I called my father.

TOMMY. Hunh?

NEDDA. He's flying in.

TOMMY. What did you do that for?

NEDDA. I want to get out of this place. I'm sorry!

TOMMY. Don't you trust me?

NEDDA. It's not like that!

TOMMY. What is it then? I thought we were in this together! (*Pause.*) Well say something! Nedda! Nedda!

NEDDA. Maybe you better take your things out for a while!

TOMMY. Yeah, sure.

NEDDA. I mean . . . !

TOMMY. Don't worry about it!

NEDDA. You know . . . !

TOMMY. Sure I know! (*More to himself.*) Fuck! (*Pause.*) Am I going to see you? Nedda! Nedda! (*The lights are fading on Nedda. Tommy gives up, goes to Arnold.*) What did she have to call her father for? You wouldn't do that on me, would you? Chin up, Arnold, I'll think of something. Shit! (*Lights down on Tommy.*)

TOMMY'S BIG BROTHER

TOMMY'S BROTHER. You've got the right idea, Tommy. Don't get married. Don't ever get married. Take it from your big

brother: he's been there and back. I wish to hell I had a telephone number for you. All I've got is a page of crazy "care of's."
I really need to talk to you. I'm putting Charlie into a military
academy. I feel like hell about it but I just don't have the time or
patience for him anymore and Rita is no help at all in that department. You remember Rita. She's my wife. We're married. It
might interfere with her golf lessons at the club. Or her sleeping
around. She does, Tommy. I know it. Jesus Christ, I've practically caught her in bed with some of the sons of bitches. The
dumbest move I ever made was not taking your advice about
heading north for awhile before settling down. Now I'm so settled I couldn't move if I wanted to. I guess I never really took
the time to find myself. I envy you up there, footloose, single, no
responsibilities, laying everything in sight if I know you. You've
got my number. Call collect, if that's the problem. I just want to
talk to you. I'm very down. I did something terrible to Rita last
night. She didn't want to make love. She lets me get on top of
her but she never wants to make love. Well last night I didn't
feel much like making love myself, so I just grabbed her by the
hair and got going at her like she was just some flesh. I wanted
to hurt her that way. You know. Then I made her take me in her
mouth. She would never do that for me. She said that was what
whores did and I said I know. Afterwards we just looked at each
other a long time. She didn't say anything. She knew. I love you
like hell, Tommy, but you're never around. No one is. (*The
lights come up on Tommy in a telephone booth.*)

OPERATOR'S VOICE. I have a collect call for anyone at this number.

TOMMY'S BROTHER'S VOICE. Where's the call from, operator?

OPERATOR'S VOICE. New York City.

TOMMY'S BROTHER'S VOICE. I don't know, Rita! Who's calling,
operator?

OPERATOR'S VOICE. Your party wishes to know who's calling, sir.

TOMMY. No one.

OPERATOR'S VOICE. I can't hear you, sir.

TOMMY. Tell him no one.

TOMMY'S BROTHER'S VOICE. Hey, Tommy! Tommy, is that you,
Tommy?

OPERATOR'S VOICE. Do you wish to accept charges, sir?

TOMMY'S BROTHER'S VOICE. You're damn right I do!

OPERATOR'S VOICE. Go ahead, New York.

TOMMY'S BROTHER'S VOICE. Hey, Tommy, old man! What's this "no one" business? I—! (*Tommy hangs up.*)

CALIFORNIA DREAMIN'

(*A young girl, 16, 17 years old tops, has entered and been watching Tommy. Her name is Bunny Barnum and she carries a map and a camera. Obviously Bunny Barnum is from out of town. Also, she is a knockout. Fantastic legs and tan.*)

BUNNY BARNUM. Hello. My name is Bunny Barnum from Tarzana, California, outside of Los Angeles? It's where Edgar Rice Burroughs is from, he wrote *Tarzan*, that's why it's called Tarzana and I'm here for five days with my high school civics class on our annual "Know America" trip, the Tarzana Kiwanis Club and American Legion post are sponsoring us, and everyone else is taking that Circle Line boat trip around the island right now except me; I snuck off, and I believe that people should really try to talk to one another and I'd like to talk to you. (*She's already taken Tommy's picture with her Instamatic camera.*) You're a hippie, aren't you?

TOMMY. (*Dazzled.*) Oh wow!

BUNNY. That's okay. We have hippies in Tarzana, too. Mildred Miller's taken LSD three whole times.

TOMMY. She has?

BUNNY. It made all her hair fall out. I bet you smoke marijuana, too.

TOMMY. I do, miss, I most surely do.

BUNNY. I don't. I think people who smoke marijuana should be electrocuted.

TOMMY. You do?

BUNNY. Oh yes. My parents started turning on—my daddy's a nuclear physicist, he was born in Mannheim, that's in Germany, but I was born in Tarzana and he's a naturalized Amercan now; my mother's a real Okie, ugh!—anyway, they were stoned half the time, real heads, the two of them, and they were growing their own stuff right in the backyard and so I turned them in. Citizen's arrest. Here. You look poor. How old are you?

TOMMY. Your parents were electrocuted for growing pot?

BUNNY. No! They were just busted! What's the matter? Wax in your ears? How old are you?

TOMMY. Thirty.

BUNNY. Thirty? You're thirty? Yikes!

TOMMY. (*Pleased.*) I know.

BUNNY. Drugs, hunh? You should see what Cubby Dodge looks like. A real wreck. I hate her. Do you mind if I say something? You're too pale. It's against the law practically to be that pale in California. Why don't you go to California? Too poor, hunh? I'd hate to be poor. I couldn't stand it. I'd probably have another nervous breakdown.

TOMMY. How many have you had?

BUNNY. (*Dismissing this.*) Just one! How many does it look like?

TOMMY. Oh, no more than that certainly.

BUNNY. I was Student Council recording secretary, head cheerleader and going steady with Rusty Winkler all in one semester! No wonder I flipped. Boy, I'd hate to live in New York City. Do you know how to surf?

TOMMY. Oh sure.

BUNNY. Randy Nelson is from Tarzana.

TOMMY. He is?

BUNNY. You don't know who Randy Nelson is? From what rock are you under? He's the world champion seventeen-year-old surfer. I'm supposed to be going with him. He's on the boat, looking for me probably. But I just had to ditch him today, you know? He's got fantastic knobs on both knees. He may even need surgery.

TOMMY. Knobs?

BUNNY. From surfing, dolt! We're reading Shakespeare on the bus and dolt's a very big word with everybody right now. Dolt, varlet, and bared bodkin. Have you ever taken a bus from California to New York? It's a drag. I told Mrs. Burmeinster, our chaperone, do you believe it? that if she didn't make them do something about the restroom I was going to call my father collect.

TOMMY. What would you like Mrs. Burmeister to do?

BUNNY. Bur*mein*ster. It's filthy in there. Please, can we change the subject? Thirty years old! I can't believe it. Yikes, that girl looks like Connie Nugent when she had both legs! Talk about resemblances! (*Calling off.*) Connie! Connie Nugent! (*Shrugs.*) You never know. Boy, I'd love some tacos and a chocolate milk shake right now. Mmmmmm! With french fries. I used to have pimples. Acne practically. I couldn't go anywhere. Ecch! What's the matter?

TOMMY. Connie Nugent when she had both legs.

BUNNY. Oh that! She was my brother Fritz's fiancee and they were driving home from somewhere, Disneyland, I think, and they had this terrible accident and they cut off Connie's leg. That girl looked just like her. Listen, stranger things have happened, right? Donna Barr lost the tip of her nose in a refrigerator door and they sewed it back on and all she has is a teen-tiny bump right there. Granted, it was a freak accident but *still*. Big Sur! They were coming back from group encounter in Big Sur.

TOMMY. Connie and Fritz?

BUNNY. Right. I almost lost my faith in God when that happened. But then I realized Fritz would have had to marry her and who wants a one-legged sister-in-law? I don't mean that cruelly, believe me, that is not a vicious remark. I'm just being realistic.

TOMMY. Then he didn't marry her?

BUNNY. Of course not! He was killed! That's why I almost lost my faith in God! It's true, people *don't* listen to one another.

TOMMY. I'm listening to you, all right, only I'm having trouble following you.

BUNNY. Drugs again, hunh? Boy, I'd love to see your chromosomes under a microscope! I bet they're really bent.

TOMMY. That's the most erotic thing anybody's ever said to me.

BUNNY. Erotic! Don't get me started on that!

TOMMY. On what?

BUNNY. Smut. I'll talk your ear off. There was a man in Tarzana we found out was making pornographic movies.

TOMMY. Let me guess: citizen's arrest.

BUNNY. We burned his house down.

TOMMY. We . . . ?

BUNNY. The Hi-Y's. This stupid girls' club my mother made me join. Coke parties, slumber parties, swimming parties, the whole schmear.

TOMMY. I don't suppose there's any chance we could continue this conversation somewhere else?

BUNNY. There's a very big one. I hope that's not your dog. I hate dogs. I'm allergic to them, as a matter of fact. If I'm fucking someone, pardon the expression, who's been ever near a dog in the past six months I break out in hives. Isn't that a crazy thing to be allergic to?

TOMMY. Dogs?

BUNNY. Yes, dogs. Of course, dogs. How could anyone be allergic to fucking? They'd have to be a freak or something. (*Breaks off, points.*) There's one! Will you look at that? One thing we *don't* have in Tarzana is queers. Unless you count Trevor Sloane, but he must be close to 90. He uses a cigarette holder and wears Capezio ballet slippers to work. I hate him. *Now* what's the matter?

TOMMY. I think you said the magic word.

BUNNY. You mean f-u-c-k? There's a reason. Notice I haven't used a single other bad word. I hate bad words, they sicken me, I actually vomit. But I also think the word *love* is the most over-worked word in the English language. You hippies have just ruined it. I love chocolate ice cream, you love bull fights, he loves abalone sandwiches, we love pedal pushers, they love Hawaii. Everything is love nowadays. I can't stand that. I'm sorry but that word is just too sacred to me to throw it around like that. F-u-c-k is something else. At least I can look a boy in the eye when I say it. I mean, just ask yourself, how could you and I make love? I don't even know you. But I can f-u-c-k you.

TOMMY. You have a point.

BUNNY. What time is it? We're giving a concert tonight in Collegiate Marble Church, wherever that is. If I miss that one, too, I'll really be in Dutch.

TOMMY. Who's giving the concert?

BUNNY. We are, my civics class. What did you think, it's all fun and games? Hah! We're also a chorus. The Tarzana Youth Tones present "Up, America, Up!." It's this sort of musical pageant we do in different churches. It's supposed to help pay for the trip or something. Not that any of us ever sees a penny from it. Oh well, it's for a good cause and I like the theme. I think people who don't like America should be electrocuted, too, don't you? (*Tommy dumbly nods, hypnotized by her bosom.*) Of course in California we only have gas chambers. When I was co-chairman of our Decent Teens club I got to go to Las Vegas. They shoot people in Nevada. I mean they have a real firing squad. Isn't that gruesome? What are you staring at? Oh that! Who wears a bra anymore? I'd have to be Doris Day or something. I hope you live around here. (*Tommy only nods.*) Now what?

TOMMY. You're a very desirable person, Bunny.

BUNNY. (*Shrugs.*) I guess.

TOMMY. Very desirable and very terrifying.

BUNNY. Terrifying? Me? Go on!

TOMMY. Terrifying. (*He takes her by the arm and they start moving off.*)

BUNNY. I'm glad that wasn't your dog.

TOMMY. Me, too; me, too.

BUNNY. (*Pointing.*) There's another one. This town is crawling with them. I'd hate that a whole lot. Hey, I don't even know your name!

TOMMY. It's Cohen, ma'am, Leonard Cohen. (*They are gone.*)

(*Stage lights fade except for pin spot on Arnold, left there on his leash.*)

ARNOLD'S SPEECH

ARNOLD. I didn't always have Tommy Flowers and I'm not at all sure I always will. I got him when I was given back to him by a friend of his who didn't want me after Tommy had given me to him in the first place. It's complicated, I know. This friend was a very lonely sort of person and Tommy decided that he should have a dog. Only he didn't want a dog. But when he saw me something inside of him must have snapped because his eyes kind of filled up like he was going to cry and he held me very close. I was this big then! And he didn't say anything and he walked a few feet away from everyone and stood with his back to them and just held me like a little baby. No one had to ask if he wanted me. You could just tell. I was so happy. But the next morning he didn't want me at all. There I was, just kind of slumped in my box, all droopy-eyed and warm-nosed and not looking at all too hot. Puppy chill is all it was. Tommy said they'd just take me to the vet but the friend didn't want a sick dog. He didn't want any dog. And you know what his reason was? They die on you. That's what he said. They die on you. We do, you know. Everything does. But is that a reason? How could anyone not want me? Oh, don't get any ideas. I'm not a talking dog. I'm a thinking one. There's a difference! (*Lights out on Arnold.*)

ANOTHER QUIET EVENING AT HOME

TOMMY. (*Appears with a towel—the American flag—around his waist.*) This is going to take a little longer than I thought. It must have been those banana splits she insisted on in Howard Johnson's because this is a highly irregular condition for me to be in. I've done it with real dogs, mercy fucks, and had less trouble.

BUNNY. (*Off.*) Mark!

TOMMY. And she is so gorgeous with all her clothes off, this Bunny Barnum creature is! Maybe that's it. Maybe I ought to put her in high stiletto heels and chase her around the bed a while.

BUNNY. (*Off.*) Mark!

TOMMY. Maybe I ought to put myself in high stiletto heels!

BUNNY. (*Off.*) Hey, Mark!

TOMMY. Mark? Oh shit, that's me! I switched it to Mark Rudd. She hasn't heard of him either. (*Calling off.*) What, Bunny?

BUNNY. (*Off.*) You want me to come in there? (*Tommy is rolling a joint.*)

TOMMY. No! Stay right where you are!

BUNNY. (*Off.*) Well hurry up!

TOMMY. I'm sorry but I couldn't do it out here with you people watching. Bunny could probably; hell, she'd love it, but not me. That's the way I am. But here, I want to show you something. It's—(*Sounds of someone trying to play a cello and badly, too.*) Bunny, please, don't touch that.

BUNNY. (*Off.*) It's so big!

TOMMY. It's a cello.

BUNNY. (*Off.*) It's still so big!

TOMMY. It's a Stradivarius! (*To us.*) Nedda's cello. She'd shit. (*Music has stopped.*) Thank you! Go back to bed! I'll be right in!

BUNNY. (*Off.*) You want to bet? What are you doing in there anyway?

TOMMY. Resting!

BUNNY. (*Off.*) From what?

TOMMY. (*Letting it pass, to us.*) Start that argument with a chick and you'll never get it up. But here, I was going to show you something. (*He is coming down into the audience.*) This business about people not being able to communicate, I just don't buy any. Everyone's got at least one true story in him if you're just willing to listen. You, sir, would you mind coming with me? I'm kind of busy right now and I could use a little help. Out here, wise guy, I could use a little help *out here!* Christ! Give one a spotlight and he turns into Lenny Bruce! I'm only kidding. Will you? Thanks. (*Tommy leads a man from the audience back up onto the stage.*) Buy someone a drink, it doesn't have to be real booze, a beer even, a total stranger, and see what you get for your sixty cents. People love to talk. What's your name? (*Man answers.*) The last time I was home, (*Name of man.*), I was hitching back East through our Great Southwest when I stopped off in this little roadhouse and saw this woman sitting alone at the bar. I dug her, not sexually, but dug her. She looked like she was waiting for someone to buy her a beer. She didn't look like a hooker. Oh no. She just looked like she wanted a beer. I bet she's still there. (*Lights coming up on Woman in Sunglasses sitting on a bar stool.*) I told her I'd buy her that beer if she'd tell me a true story. She didn't even hesitate.

WOMAN IN SUNGLASSES. Lou! Hey, Lou, make that another Falstaff!

TOMMY. What did she have to lose? We were total strangers. I'd never see her again. You'll never see her again either. (*Tommy has sat the man from the audience on a stool next to the Woman in Sunglasses.*) Hi. Remember me? (*Woman shakes her head.*) About six years ago? (*Woman shakes her head.*) Do you know my friend? (*Woman shakes her head.*) Tell him your true story and he'll buy you a beer.

WOMAN IN SUNGLASSES. Hey, Lou, make that *two* bottles. (*Bunny appears.*)

TOMMY. Hey!

BUNNY. Are you sure that wasn't your dog? I'm breaking out.

TOMMY. Those are goosebumps, Bunny, good old fashioned goosebumps. I'm covered with 'em myself!

BUNNY. What's that?

TOMMY. A therapeutic cigarette, doctor's orders.

BUNNY. I hope it works.

TOMMY. In there, Bunny, in there! (*To us, indicating the flag around his waist.*) Many a bum show has been saved by the flag. George M. Cohan, showman, 1919. (*Bunny squeals delightedly as Tommy takes her off. The lights come down except for necessary playing area for scene that follows.*)

(*We hear a jukebox playing. The Woman in Sunglasses has been served by now. She pours herself a glass of beer. The man from the audience will be sitting next to her. She begins to speak now.*)

A TRUE STORY

WOMAN IN SUNGLASSES. This is a true story. When I was a sophomore at Moodus King Senior High School in Crystal City, Oklahoma—it's about twenty-eight miles north of Norman, Oklahoma—there was a beer joint on the outskirts of town called the Javelina Club where they would sell five-point beer to minors. On weekends they had live music. I was going with this man then and we'd hit the Javelina Club nearly every weekend. He was a lot older than me and divorced but I wasn't exactly any Grace Kelly and my father had run off and we were real poor and my mother and me didn't get along and the garage apartment we lived in was real tiny and at least he got me out of there and was somebody to talk to and he must have thought I was a little pretty or why else would he take me out every weekend, 'cause I didn't let him go all the way with me for a long long time. Anyway, this story ain't about him. One weekend they were presenting a new young singer at the Javelina Club and his name was Elvis Presley. That's right, Elvis Presley, the same one, appearing at a little beer joint outside o' Crystal City, Oklahoma, but only he was real young then and just beginning. Lots of big name performers got their start in little beer joints like the Javelina Club I bet. I don't guess he was pulling down more than ten bucks a night and he only performed Friday and Saturday nights and what they called the Sunday afternoon matinee. Anyway, this story ain't about money either. Elvis was so beautiful then. I wish you could have seen him. Certainly he was one of the most tremendous talents I ever heard. He had this natural way of singing about things that was really special. I can't tell it too well but I do know I'd never heard anyone sing like that before Elvis and the things he would sing about were realer than other people, too. In some ways Elvis was better then, at the Javelina Club, than later on when he became so famous. There was a wildness then that made the audience wild, too, not like the Beatles and the way they made those little kids scream, we were older and I guess more mature, you know what I mean? and this wildness just kind of went from Elvis to the audience— just back and forth like that the whole time he was singing. That part of Elvis is kind of gone now it seems. Unless maybe it's just that he's older or I'm older or everybody's older. I don't know. (*Short pause.*) Now here's what this story's about: Some nights this man I was going with would get really drunk and then he'd turn real surly and violent-like and he'd just be looking for a fight. The night I first heard Elvis Presley was one of those nights and next thing you know he was accusing me of staring at Elvis, you know, like I was attracted to him, and I told him to just hush and I could look at anybody I wanted to in any way I wanted to and I wasn't staring at Elvis in any special way no how and so then this man he started making these real loud sarcastic comments about how Elvis was dressed and his long sideburns and ducktails and his suede shoes and pink suede belt and how punks who wore their hair and clothes like that were no better than greasers, you know, Mexicans, and that hoods like him just better high ass it out o' town if they just knew how generally unpopular they was. Now while he was saying all this the whole place was going wild over Elvis and nobody was paying this man any heed at all. Finally he got so mad and futile-feeling he got up from the table and tried to get near Elvis who was up on this little stage sort of thing and all the while he kept making these real loud ugly comments and then he took like a swing at Elvis only he was so drunk and Elvis was so high above him that he just spun around and fell right down. Everybody noticed him then and they all started laughing, and most of all ol' El himself who kept right on singing, too, so that the whole Javelina Club was rocking and laughing all at the same time. This man I was with got to his feet, came over and grabbed me out o' there by the arm so hard I said he was hurting me. Boy, was I mad at him! It wasn't even near closing time. I told him to go to hell and I never wanted to see him again. I guess he knew how mad I was, too, 'cause he didn't try anything with me all the way home. That Monday as soon as school let out I went to the record shop with my best friend, Roberta, and I asked if Elvis Presley had made any records yet and they looked him up in this big catalogue of every record ever made and he wasn't in there. I tried describing him to Roberta, how he sang and moved and how cute and sexy and handsome he was, only it wasn't like seeing him or hearing him for real and we both guessed we'd never hear Elvis Presley again unless he got famous and started making records 'cause there wasn't anybody in town who was about to take us to the Javelina Club that coming weekend. The next Saturday I was getting ready to go to the movies with Roberta when he pulls up, this man I was going with, just like nothing had happened and acts real surprised that I'm not ready to hit the Javelina Club, business as usual. So I called up Roberta and told her my mother was sick and changed into my best clothes. As soon as we got into the car he started sneering 'bout how he knew I couldn't resist another look at my new lover boy sensation and I just sneered right back that I didn't care if Minnie Pearl was appearing at the Javelina Club, I just wanted to go to the only place in the county where I could hear me some live music and get served some five-point beer. We was fighting about Elvis just like last week and we hadn't even got there yet! When we did, the place was packed like I'd never seen it. I guess word about how tremendous Elvis was had gotten out. It was like a football game the way everybody was pushing and shoving to get a table or a better view or closer to the stage or dancing room. I'd never been in a crowd just listening to rock and roll like that all in a group. It was strange 'cause even though it was the crowd that made being there so exciting, you also felt like you were the only person there—an audience of one, just you and Elvis and the music he was playing for you. It was like a dream but it was real, too, you know what I mean? I guess I vaguely remember this man I was with excusing himself for a while and going outside where the cars were. But I do remember that when he came back he was real sweet and didn't seem at all jealous of Elvis or anything like he was the week before. He even offered to buy Elvis a beer when he walked by our table after the first show. I didn't get to meet

Elvis then but he looked at me and kind of smiled and I felt real funny. Well sir, we stayed for the second and third shows, too, and this man I was with was on his very best behavior, hardly got drunk at all, and next thing you knew it was 2 a.m. closing time and they turned on these real bright lights to hustle everybody out of there and we were all outside in the parking lot and there was this crowd gathered around this 1954 chopped-back white Cadillac Coupe de Ville convertible with Tennessee plates. It was Elvis'. The windshield had been smashed in with a brick, the tires were all slashed, the canvas roof had been tore open, the hood was up and there was distributor wires hanging out all over the place, there was red paint all over the customized white leather seats and on the door on the driver's side somebody had painted Memphis Grease Ball. People were just standing around staring at it, like when there's been an accident. This man I was with said "Aw gee, who'd do a thing like that?" and from the way he said it I just knew he'd messed up Elvis' car when he went outside that time. Pretty soon Elvis himself came out and he saw this crowd and then he saw what somebody had done to his car and I guess he didn't have any real friends there 'cause none of the guys said anything to him and none of the girls could and pretty soon everybody just started drifting away to their own cars without nobody saying a word and Elvis was just staring at his tore-up white Caddy and I said to the man I was with couldn't we give him a ride and this man he sneered "Hell no" and I felt like yelling out "Hey Elvis, I know who messed up your car" only I was scared to 'cause this man could be violent to me and just then the owner of the Javelina Club came out and he was talking to Elvis and you could tell that he was going to give him a ride back to wherever Elvis was staying. On the way home I told this man that now I *really* never wanted to see him again, and that if I ever saw Elvis I would tell him what he'd done and then Elvis would tear him apart just like he'd done Elvis' car. He kept denying it but I wouldn't shut up and pretty soon he hit me and I slapped him right back and then he hit me again only really hard this time and now I was really scared and I didn't say anything to him the rest of the way home. I never saw that man again. The very next day I was downtown and I saw Elvis driving a Ford pickup that somebody must have loaned him until his own car got fixed. And then two days after that I was driving my mother to the hospital where she worked and there was Elvis hitchhiking and he had a suitcase so I knew he was leaving town and I wanted to stop for him but my mother said no, I couldn't pick up any hitchhiker and she would be late for her shift and besides, what was I, some kind of a whore? I practically started crying I wanted to be with him so bad. Well, sir, I dropped her off at the hospital and tore ass back to where I'd seen Elvis. He was still there! When I pulled over he looked kind of surprised that a girl had stopped for him but he asked how far I was going and I said quite a way and he said fine and he got in beside me and he was real polite and didn't act at all the way he looked which *was* hoody but in a handsome way and we drove a long time and he didn't say much and all the time I was hoping he'd touch me so bad I couldn't stand it anymore so finally I told him I knew who he was and that I'd seen him at the Javelina Club and how tremendous I thought he was and he told me he was on his way back to Memphis to cut two sides for a small company called Sun Records (these are the same records RCA Victor heard and immediately signed Elvis up to an exclusive contract and then he recorded "Heartbreak Hotel" for them and six weeks later he was nationally famous) and then I told him I knew who had tore up his Cadillac and he said he was gonna be so rich and famous some day he'd have twenty Cadillacs and he'd never have to play in a dead ass town like Crystal City, Oklahoma, again and that was why he was leaving this one there. He didn't talk for a while after saying all that but then I guess he realized how much I was hoping he would touch me 'cause he started asking why I'd stopped for him and where exactly and just how far was I going and I got confused and flustered and started blushing and he asked me if I wanted him to drive and I said yes and he took the wheel and without saying anything he just turned off the main road onto this little dirt road and we followed it a long while until finally we stopped in the shade of this mesquite tree and he kissed me and started feeling me all up and he had his hands everywhere and he was undressing me now and we were in the back seat of my mother's pink and white Ford Fairlane with the chrome dip in the door and I can tell you Elvis was the best person I've ever made love with and we did things I didn't know people *could* do and most people don't and since him it's never been like that with anyone and I never thought I would say this, I never thought I would think it even: his cock was beautiful. It was thick. I can still feel it inside me. I can still feel it inside my mouth. After we'd come, we were just kind of lying together there in the back seat when all of a sudden a pickup truck with this colored family in it was on top of us and the man and the woman could tell what we'd been doing and they both looked at us and just started laughing and then we started laughing back at them, too, and for a minute it was a very happy and human and innocent thing between the four of us with their two children just staring wide-eyed at us like we was all crazy. Then the truck and the colored people was gone and we was alone on this dirt road and we got dressed and drove on back to the main highway and Elvis said to let him off there, he was okay, and it was getting late and I'd better head back to Crystal City, Oklahoma, with my mother's Förd Fairlane car and he would send me a postcard from Memphis and a copy of his Sun Record when it came out. He never did but that's okay, too. I followed his career, of course, couldn't help *but* he got so famous, and for a while I kept a scrapbook on him that got yay big in no time there was so much being written about him and so many pictures everywhere and all, and I'd see his chopped-back white Cadillac Coupe de Ville convertible every so often being driven around by a Mexican boy with lots of pimples and really tacky clothes which made me real mad at first. About two years later Elvis was in Norman, Oklahoma, giving a one night concert at the downtown civic auditorium and I remember the ticket prices were way high. "Not like the old days at the Javelina Club" was the standard, boring comment. I sat up in the balcony with the boy I was engaged to. Later on, when I was home again and we'd been drinking beer all night, I tried to call Elvis but the hotel wanted to know who was calling or no calls were going through and "just say an old friend who wonders if he has twenty Cadillacs yet" wasn't good enough and they just pulled the plug on me and I felt so stupid. Six months later I married the boy I was at Elvis' concert with and then my mother died and we had two girls, Jeanette and Maurine, and after a while I didn't see Elvis' white

Cadillac or the Mexican boy around town anymore and then we got a divorce 'cause Billy started drinking and couldn't hold a job down anymore and everything got to be a mess and now the girls and me are living in the Chateau Normandie Apartments and I'm working part-time as a checker at the Food Fair over at the Hill N' Dale shopping centre and I'm gonna marry this carbonated beverages salesman from near Tulsa as soon as his divorce is final and then I won't have to work anymore he says. He don't like me working now as a matter of fact but it's better I told him. The last time one of Elvis' movies played in town I didn't even go see it. Jeanette, my eldest, she's thirteen, Jeanette did and she said Elvis looked fat in it. (*Pause.*) Well, that's my true story. Thanks for the beer. (*From offstage there is a shrill scream: it is Bunny Barnum.*) Lou. (*With a nod and a wave, the Woman in Sunglasses gets off the bar stool and exits, leaving the man from the audience sitting there. Again that shrill scream of Bunny Barnum's. Tommy runs on, the American flag still around his waist.*)

TOMMY. I gave her a joint. Just one little joint. I thought it would help. And bingo! Just like that, she went bonkers! It wasn't even good stuff.

BUNNY. (*Off.*) I hate you! I hate you!

TOMMY. This is terrible. Bunny, please, stop that!

BUNNY. (*Off.*) I'll kill you, Phil! I'll kill you!

TOMMY. Phil Ochs. (*To man from the audience.*) You'd better go back to your seat. Come on. I'm sorry about this.

BUNNY. (*Off.*) Let me in there! Let me in!

TOMMY. Look. She did that. With her nails. I don't know what came over her.

BUNNY. (*Off.*) I said let me in! (*Tommy is going into the audience as he takes the man back to his seat.*)

TOMMY. I'm on the john!

BUNNY. (*Off.*) I'm warning you, Phil, I really mean it this time!

TOMMY. Does anybody want to take a naked seventeen-year-old nut with a body like *you*-won't-believe-what-it's-like-either-who'll-think-you're-Bob Dylan-if-you-tell-her-you-are off my hands?

BUNNY. (*Off.*) Are you going to let me in there or not?

TOMMY. No!

BUNNY. (*Off.*) Why not?

TOMMY. I don't know!

BUNNY. (*Off.*) I hate you!

TOMMY. That's one good reason!

BUNNY. (*Off.*) I'll kill you!

TOMMY. That's two!

BUNNY. (*Off.*) So let me in there!

TOMMY. Why? Why do you want to kill me?

BUNNY. (*Off.*) You know what you did! You know what you did!

TOMMY. I didn't do anything! That's when the trouble started. It's all my fault, Bunny!

BUNNY. (*Off.*) You know what you did!

TOMMY. Please, just go away! I'm sorry about the whole thing!

BUNNY. (*Off.*) You know what you did!

TOMMY. Go back to your hotel!

BUNNY. (*Off.*) No!

TOMMY. Go give your concert! "Up, America, Up!," quick, Bunny, before it sinks!

BUNNY. (*Off.*) No!

TOMMY. Then go back to Tarzana! You think I give a shit?

BUNNY. (*Off.*) Faggot!

TOMMY. I was waiting for that.

BUNNY. (*Off.*) Queer!

TOMMY. It's not the first time. (*Sounds of a car driving by.*)

VARIOUS VOICES. (*Speeding by.*) Queer! Fairy! Fruit! Faggot!

TOMMY. (*Yelling after them.*) Fuck you, too, you goddamn rednecks!

BUNNY. (*Off.*) Cocksucker!

TOMMY. Got you, Bunny! That's a bad word. Now go ahead and vomit.

BUNNY. (*Off.*) I'll give you three!

TOMMY. Three what?

BUNNY. (*Off.*) One!

TOMMY. My name's not Phil Ochs!

BUNNY. (*Off.*) Two!

TOMMY. It's John Lennon!

BUNNY. (*Off.*) Three! (*Silence.*)

TOMMY. Bunny? Bunny? What's she doing in there? I'm not taking any chances. This scratch hurts like hell. (*Sounds of a car driving by: in the opposite direction this time.*)

VARIOUS VOICES. Fruit! Pansy! Faggot! Queer!

TOMMY. Up yours, you no-dicked mother-fuckers! (*The voices and the sound of the car have faded away.*) The only guy I ever went to bed with was my best friend, Gareth Linsley. I had a big crush on James Dean when I was in high school, who didn't then? but Gareth Linsley is the only guy I ever actually did it with. I mean as a grown-up. I'm not counting circle jerks, first-one-to-come everyone has to give a quarter. I mean Big League, both eyes wide open, the age of innocence is past homosexuality. I'm not ashamed I did. Things like that happen, you know? All the time. I think Gareth was already queer when I met him in college. I mean I didn't make him that way. Whenever we'd go to a whorehouse or sneak girls into the dorm I think he was screwing them just to keep me from knowing about him. Looking back, I can't imagine he ever really liked it. (*Sounds of the car driving by again.*)

VARIOUS VOICES. Queer! Fruit! Faggot! Fairy!

TOMMY. (*Yelling after them.*) Fuck you, you Nazi cocksuckers! (*Sounds of the car braking to a halt.*) We both came to New York and went our separate ways. I thought it was strange at first, your best friend not wanting to see you anymore, but after a while stories started trickling back and I knew the reason why. (*Sounds of car door slamming.*) But then one night we ran into each other and started drinking and talking and Gareth said why didn't I come over, his roommate was out of town, so we went there and drank some more and pretty soon Gareth was telling me what I'd already heard. He was a queer. (*Some men have entered.*) Hello. (*Continuing, to us.*) He told me the guy he was living with was his lover. I remember how he said the word. Lover. I'd never heard a man use that word about another man before.

ONE OF THE MEN. His what?

TOMMY. His lover. (*Continuing, to us.*) He said we couldn't pretend to be friends unless I knew that about him and I could leave now if he disgusted me but he was glad he'd told me no matter what happened between us. It was something he'd wanted to tell me for years.

ONE OF THE MEN. What was?

TOMMY. That he loved me, Gareth Linsley did. (*Continuing, to us.*) And how he'd loved me ever since he'd first met me and how really I was the only person he'd ever loved and how I'd always be his best friend even though we hardly saw each other and our lives were so different and that he had never, never tried to have sex with me because it would have ruined our relationship, which was true, and certainly he would never try it now that I knew about him and how he would still think of me when he masturbated and now that I knew everything could we please change the subject. And we did.

ONE OF THE MEN. What did he think of when he did that exactly? What part?

TOMMY. He didn't say. I didn't ask him. (*Continuing, to us.*) We didn't completely change the subject. Every so often I'd ask him if it were true if so-and-so or x,y,z were queer, like I'd heard, and he'd answer yes or no or just laugh, like I was some kind of hick for even asking, which, I guess, I was at the time. I mean everybody in New York knows about Benjamin Franklin, right?

ONE OF THE MEN. Right.

ONE OF THE MEN. What about that actor, you know, what's his name?

ONE OF THE MEN. And that politician! You know who I mean.

TOMMY. Their names didn't come up. (*Continuing, to us.*) And then I asked about one name too many and Gareth got mad at me, said I was insensitive and what did I think he was? Information Please? and told me to leave. (*The men have moved in quite close to Tommy now. There is a sinister, menacing circle closing in on him, in fact.*) I couldn't blame him. (*Continuing, to us.*) About four hours later, after I'd left him and gone to another bar and gotten really drunk, I went back to his place. To this day I still don't know why.

ONE OF THE MEN. (*Giving Tommy a shove.*) Sure you do, fruit!

TOMMY. (*Standing his ground.*) No, not really. (*Continuing, to us.*) Gareth let me in, he was half asleep, and I said could I stay there? and he mumbled yes and pointed to the sofa and staggered back to bed. I waited a little while in the dark living room and then I took all my clothes off and stood outside his bedroom door. I could hear him breathing. Gareth Linsley breathing. And after a while I went in and lay down beside him. He didn't wake up. I didn't move for a long time.

ONE OF THE MEN. (*Another shove.*) How long was that, faggot?

TOMMY. Ten, fifteen minutes, I don't know. It seemed like forever (*Continuing, to us.*) And then I put one arm around him. (*The first blow is struck. One of the men has pinioned Tommy's arms.*) And then another. I was hugging him now. (*Another blow.*) And then I touched his cock. (*Smack!*) It was soft but after a while it got hard and so did mine . . . (*Smack!*) . . . and then he was awake and turning to face me . . . (*Smack!*) . . . and I kissed him . . . (*Smack!*) . . . and then all at once we were making love . . . ! (*Smack! Tommy's voice is rising.*) . . . only I didn't know what to do . . . ! (*Smack!*) . . . I felt so clumsy and I wanted to please him . . . ! (*Smack!*) . . . and I took his cock . . . ! (*Smack!*) . . . and I guided it in me . . . ! (*Smack!*) . . . and it was hurting me . . . ! (*Smack!*) . . . and he was going at me! Like I was just flesh! I could have been anyone! Just going at me! Going at me! Going at me! (*Smack! smack! smack!*) And I hated him for that!! (*The men release Tommy. His face is a bloody pulp. Hideous.*) When it was all over he said didn't I want to come, too? and I said no and so we just lay there on the bed in the dark not touching now and I was thinking what I'd tell him when he asked me why I'd done that when he started snoring and I realized Gareth Linsley didn't love me at all.

ONE OF THE MEN. You didn't like it, faggot?

TOMMY. No. Too messy, you know? (*He smiles crookedly. Much blood but unafraid. One of the men knees him and he goes down.*)

ONE OF THE MEN. What did you say, queer?

TOMMY. I said, too messy, you know? (*The man kicks Tommy. This time he doesn't move.*)

ONE OF THE MEN. Now, *you* know, fruit! (*He kicks him again.*) Let's go. (*They start moving off.*)

ONE OF THE MEN. Is he dead?

ONE OF THE MEN. (*Taking Tommy's picture with a flash camera.*) Don't he wish! Don't you, scumbag, hunh, don't you? (*He gets his final kicks in.*) Hey, wait up!

ONE OF THE MEN. Where's Lino?

ONE OF THE MEN. Where do you think, asshole!

ONE OF THE MEN. Okay, Barry, okay. Just asking. (*They are gone.*

Sounds of car doors opening, then closing and the car driving off. Tommy raises his head.)

TOMMY. Fuck you, you slimey mother-fuckers! Fuck you once, fuck you twice, fuck you three whole times! We're gonna bury you! (*Then, resuming, to us, sitting up.*) And so I got dressed, went out and walked around until the sun came up, which wasn't very long, had bacon and eggs at Riker's on Sheridan Square and never saw Gareth Linsley again. (*He is speaking with some difficulty.*) About three years ago and at least five years after that night, Gareth stuck a German Luger in his mouth and pulled the trigger. Awful. I would never do that. Too messy, you know? (*A crooked, broken smile.*) But Gareth did. She lost her head, Miss Linsley did. I forget who said that. Some wag. I didn't feel any responsibility at all for Gareth's self-slaughter. Enormous and profound grief but no responsibility. When I heard they were flying his body to Dayton, Ohio, for the funeral it kind of bothered me. I'd always remembered him as being from Allentown, Pennsylvania. His family must have moved. I didn't attend. About a year later I saw the lover coming out of a gay bar, the one on West 10th Street, at least somebody told me it was him, and I almost said something to him. When someone you . . . *knew* . . . yes, when someone you knew does that to himself, you wonder a lot, ask yourself all sorts of questions. But I never felt responsible. (*Again, that crooked, broken smile.*) Too messy, you know? (*There is a timid knocking sound.*) What is it?

BUNNY. (*Off.*) Can I come in now?

TOMMY. Go away.

BUNNY. (*Off.*) I'm all right now.

TOMMY. No.

BUNNY. (*Off.*) Please, Phil.

TOMMY. My name isn't Phil.

BUNNY. (*Off.*) I don't care what your name is.

TOMMY. It's Tommy Flowers and I blow things up.

BUNNY. (*Off.*) That's okay. Please, Tommy! I promise I'm all right now.

TOMMY. It's open. (*Tommy starts toweling himself off, his back to Bunny who enters. She looks almost catatonic. There is a straight-edged razor in her hand.*)

BUNNY. (*Seemingly unaware of the razor in her hand.*) See how calm I am? I mean I feel really peaceful now.

TOMMY. (*Always with his back to her as he wipes and dabs at his face with the towel.*) That's nice.

BUNNY. (*Quiet exaltation.*) Wow!

TOMMY. Just go soon, hunh, Bunny, please? And I'm very sorry about the entire episode. It was all my fault: the lack of performance, the dope, everything. I don't want you thinking it was you. You're a regular knockout; I'm the dud.

BUNNY. That stuff you gave me, I don't know, it gave me a nightmare like terrible things were happening. That's why I started screaming.

TOMMY. Don't worry about it.

BUNNY. I don't hate you.

TOMMY. I'm very glad to know that.

BUNNY. And I don't want to kill you either.

TOMMY. You're making my day.

BUNNY. Wow!

TOMMY. Now why don't you start to think about leaving? I don't want to rush you. Just ponder it a little.

BUNNY. Okay.

TOMMY. Good girl.

BUNNY. They killed me.

TOMMY. You're not concentrating, Bunny.

BUNNY. They raped me, then they killed me.

TOMMY. Think about leaving.

BUNNY. All sorts of people. White and brown and yellow and red. Some were real big and some were real little.

TOMMY. And they were all leaving for somewhere, weren't they, Bunny?

BUNNY. They wanted to get at me and there was no place to be safe from them. I knew I was in New York City but at the same time I was in Tarzana, too, and there was no way to keep them out.

TOMMY. So you left. That's what you did, Bunny, you left.

BUNNY. (*As she speaks, she is standing behind Tommy and describing imaginary circles in his back with the straight-edged razor. He doesn't see this.*) I was in my pretty pink bedroom with my posters and pennants talking on my pink Princess telephone to Stephanie Lawrence. She's a cheerleader and was voted Most Likely To Succeed three years in a row. I like her. She's my best friend. And then all of a sudden the line went dead and I looked up and saw a whole bunch of them looking in the window at me.

TOMMY. (*Turning.*) I'm going to have to shower, Bunny.

BUNNY. (*Concealing the razor.*) They shouldn't have been there. No one should've been there. They were standing on our pretty bushes.

TOMMY. Sure they were.

BUNNY. I screamed and ran into our living room and there were all these people. (*Tommy has gone into the shower. Sounds of water running.*) White and brown and yellow and red strange people walking on our nice clean rugs, sitting in our pretty new chairs, watching our color television. Like pigs they were.

TOMMY. (*Off.*) Be sure you don't run any water while I'm in here. It's an old building and the pipes are shot, okay?

BUNNY. (*She's given up trying to reach Tommy now.*) And there was my father lying on the floor and his throat was all cut and my mother was all bloody and crying over him and my little brother, they were hurting him, too, and so I ran into our kitchen and there were more strange people making a terrible mess on our tables and sink tops and they were into our refrigerator, eating our food and frying things on our stove, cooking things and spilling grease and our maid Nana was in there and I told her to stop and she just laughed and slapped me in the face and told me that she was one of them and that they belonged there as much as I did and this was how things were going to be now and I didn't live there anymore and they were going to put me in a concentration camp and feed me pig slop and let the men do things to me for the rest of my life and then she slapped me again and I ran back into our living room and there were these men holding momma down on her avocado green rug now and her skirt was up and then one of them saw me and said: What about the girl? She's a finer piece than the old bitch mother! and they started chasing me and I ran into the garage and there were all these people sitting in our cars, running the engines and working the windshield wipers and the electric windows and honking the horns and playing the 8-track stereo tape decks and the noise and the smell in there was just terrible and the people in the cars started chasing me, too, and I ran out into our yard and there were people pulling up our pretty bushes and chopping down our lovely trees and then there were all these horrible little children in our filtered swimming pool and they were swimming and splashing and peeing in it too, and the only place left I could run to was Nana our maid's little cottage and I went in there and locked all the doors and the windows and turned off all the lights and waited and prayed to God and cried and then I found this knife. (*Sounds of water being turned off.*) But there was no way to keep them out. The doors and the windows and the walls and the roof just started coming in. Nothing broke. (*Tommy reappears, starts drying himself off.*) It was more like something was pressing in on them. Squeezing them closer and closer together until I would be trapped and crushed in there and all I had was this knife and they kept pressing in on me and then the walls and the ceilings and the windows and the roof got so squeezed in on me I couldn't move anymore and then I was dead.

TOMMY. Hey, Bunny, I'm getting dressed. Time to go now.

BUNNY. And then when I was dead, they raped me, all of them did, and they threw my body into our swimming pool, the horrible little children were still playing in it, just like nothing had happened, and as I sank to the bottom I saw my father and my mother and my little brother and our color television set and our furniture and our appliances and my mommy's mink stole she wears to the country club dances and my daddy's barbecue pit and my little brother's horse books and my pink Princess telephone, nearly everything we ever owned, in fact.

TOMMY. Let's go, Bunny, let's go!

BUNNY. And there we were, my entire family and all our earthly possessions at the bottom of the deep end of our nearly Olympic size swimming pool and our faces started rotting and our fingers, the skin on them was kind of flaking off and up at the top you could still see the little white and brown and yellow and red legs of the terrible little children just kicking and splashing away as happy as could be.

TOMMY. Come on, Bunny, get your clothes. I've got to split.

BUNNY. And then the sharks and the eels and the octopuses started coming and the sharks were tearing at my daddy's and my little brother's faces, taking big bites, and they started looking like skulls and this horrible octopus had my mother in his tentacles and was squeezing her right into his fat, pulpy head and the eels were all wrapped on my arms and legs and holding me down and I couldn't even get my knife to stab at them anymore.

TOMMY. Where did you leave them? Which room? Shit! (*He goes.*)

BUNNY. And everybody was dead except for the white and brown and yellow and red people swimming in our pool and living in our house.

TOMMY. (*Off.*) (*A furious sound.*) Hey! Hey!

BUNNY. Everybody in America dead except for the white and brown and yellow and red people anymore. (*Like a child fascinated with a new toy, she is slashing at her wrists with the razor.*)

TOMMY. (*Off.*) When did you do this?

BUNNY. Everybody dead.

TOMMY. (*Off.*) You goddamn little bitch! You vicious little bitch! You even smashed her cello for Christ's sake!

BUNNY. My daddy said the reason nothing works in America anymore is because all the inferior people are making them. In Germany that wouldn't be allowed to happen. High technological achievement goes hand in hand with high technological accomplishment in Germany, my daddy said.

TOMMY. (*Entering.*) What's the matter with you? Are you crazy? You destroyed her whole apartment, everything in it, you stupid little bitch!

BUNNY. They swam in our pool. Everybody dead now.

TOMMY. Answer me! (*Tommy goes for her. Bunny slashes at him with the razor and draws some blood.*) Give me that! (*Tommy grabs her wrist, takes the razor, sees the blood on her wrists, realizes what she's doing.*) Oh my God! . . . When? . . . Oh my God!

BUNNY. Don't spank me, don't spank me. I want my daddy! (*Bunny has slipped to the floor in a sitting position. Tommy runs to the window and calls down.*)

TOMMY. Hey, you, mister! Please! Get an ambulance up here! Don't keep walking! You hear me! Turn around and look at me! Don't walk away from this! You goddamn heartless bastard! May your soul rot in hell! Lady, please! An ambulance! The phone's out! (*Answering her.*) The phone's out. I didn't pay the bill. Please. Thank you. The fifth floor. God bless you. Hurry! (*He goes back to Bunny, speaks as he rips the flag in half and tries to stop the bleeding by bandaging each wrist.*) What are we doing to ourselves? Bunny, Bunny Barnum from Tarzana, California, you're not going to die on me, girl. Stay awake, look at me. You've got to keep your eyes open until they come. Can you do that, Bunny? Will you do that for me, girl?

BUNNY. I can't.

TOMMY. You've got to.

BUNNY. I'm sleepy.

TOMMY. Look at me then.

BUNNY. I want my daddy.

TOMMY. He's coming.

BUNNY. When?

TOMMY. Soon, very soon, Bunny. Keep your eyes open and he'll be here.

BUNNY. Tell me a story.

TOMMY. (*Hugging her fiercely.*) Okay, okay.

BUNNY. Everybody's dead.

TOMMY. No, Bunny, nobody's dead. That's what the story's about. Everybody's alive. That's the good news today. Everybody's alive. The sun is out so bright today you can hardly stand it. Blue skies and good air just like they used to be. Green grass and flowers, a day for going barefoot.

BUNNY. I'm barefoot.

TOMMY. You should see the park today. That's where we're going. Why it's just filled with wonderful happy people on a day like today. Everybody's alive today. Open your eyes, Bunny, and see the park all filled with people.

BUNNY. White and brown and yellow and red?

TOMMY. All sorts, all sizes.

BUNNY. No, everybody's dead now. I don't believe you.

TOMMY. They're in the park, Bunny, I can see them and they're all alive.

BUNNY. What are they doing?

TOMMY. Laughing and singing and playing games and riding bicycles and having picnics and dancing.

BUNNY. Dancing?

TOMMY. Sure they are!

BUNNY. There's music?

TOMMY. Wonderful music! Free music! One old man is doing a beautiful Greek folk dance all by himself. Maybe he was born there even, in Sparta or Crete, who knows? but there he is in our park now, Bunny, and he's dancing for us. Can you see him?

BUNNY. No.

TOMMY. I see him.

BUNNY. You do?

TOMMY. You have to want to see him!

BUNNY. I do.

TOMMY. All right, then there's a middle-aged couple dancing a tango under the copperwood trees. And right nearby two kids are dancing the Lindy. They're so young. Somebody must have taught them. Maybe it was the middle-aged couple. People do that.

BUNNY. The Lindy?

TOMMY. A very old dance.

BUNNY. I like the name. It's funny.

TOMMY. I like it, too.

BUNNY. Can you do it?

TOMMY. Unh-hunh.

BUNNY. How come?

TOMMY. Because I'm very old myself. I'll teach you.

BUNNY. That's nice.

TOMMY. I promise.

BUNNY. Tell me more story.

TOMMY. Okay, so everybody is alive, the park is full of very happy people, and you know what? They love one another, Bunny, all these people love one another, or anyway they're sure trying to love one another.

BUNNY. Love?

TOMMY. Sure there's love, I know there's love, I can feel there's love. See it, hear it, touch it, taste it. The love of those people in the park is so big it could swallow you up if you're not careful.

BUNNY. And nobody's dead then?

TOMMY. No, nobody. Everybody is alive and loving in that park and that's how the world is and how it's going to be or else no-body's going to want to be in it and most of all me.

BUNNY. That's not a story.

TOMMY. Then you weren't listening. It's the only story I had for you, the only one I know. Believe it, girl. I do.

BUNNY. I guess.

TOMMY. Bunny. Bunny look at me. (*There is a knock.*) In here! (*To Bunny.*) It was a true story, Bunny, you just didn't stick around long enough to find out how true it really is. (*Tommy kisses her very tenderly on the forehead and moves quickly away, like a fugitive, from that particular playing area. Lights down on Bunny as two ambulance attendants enter.*)

TOMMY'S WALK

(*During this sequence we will see and hear pictures and music indicative of the violence of the reality that is pressing in on Tommy. His actions, by contrast, are to ignore these sounds and images by literally blotting them out by everything he says or does. He seems determined to stay "loose" in the face of every-thing.*

Pictures on the screens: muggings, knifings, murders, riots, acci-dents, arson, and lots of hostile, angry faces. Among them and in contrast, we see an occasional face that will be familiar from earlier in the play: Greta Rapp, Ben, Nedda Lemon, Bunny Barnum, etc. The music we hear is hard, aggressive, driving rock. The Stones' "Street Fighting Man" would be perfect.

From now until the end of the play, all the actors will double, triple, quadruple if necessary as various Pedestrians on the streets of New York. Also, the tempo of the sequence will grow faster and more breathless as Tommy draws closer to his final destination: Greenwich Avenue outside the Women's House of Detention.)

TOMMY. (*Panhandling.*) You got any spare change? Thank you, sir, thank you very much. (*To another Pedestrian.*) Hello. (*Blocks their path, offers the money.*) Here.

PEDESTRIAN. No, thank you.

TOMMY. It's money.

PEDESTRIAN. I don't want it.

TOMMY. It's not mine. It's his. (*Pedestrian sidesteps him.*) He doesn't want your rotten money either! (*He throws the coin in the air and walks on. Two people scramble for it.*) Excuse me, sir, but I think you're a very handsome man and I just thought that you might like to know that's what I thought. (*Gives the man a big kiss on the cheek.*) Trick or treat, lady. No, I mean that! I need busfare. I'm desperate for busfare. I'll do anything for busfare except leave you alone. I'll follow you home, sit on your doorstep and you won't be able to go out for months. Thank *you!* (*Tommy is on a crowded bus.*) Excuse me, do you have the time?

PASSENGER. It's ten after four.

TOMMY. It's later than I thought. (*To another Passenger.*) Hello. Guess what? It's ten after four. It's later than you think. Pass it on. (*In a very loud voice.*) The new flic at the 8th Street Playhouse is a real stinker! Don't say nobody told you! Getting off! (*He jumps off the bus.*) Doesn't anybody want to take in a down-and-out anarchist and his lovable mutt for the night? I do dishes but I don't do no woodwork! (*Darting towards a woman.*) Miss Taylor! Miss Taylor! Could I have your autograph, Miss Taylor? You're not Elizabeth Taylor? Oh go on, you are, too! I'm terribly sorry. You look just like her. (*He dances wildly. People look at him.*) I love the world! I love the world! It's what you've done with it I can't stand! (*Dashing off.*) Mr. President! Wait for me, Mr. President!

LAST SCENE

(*The music grows gentler. On the screens we see pictures of Nedda and Arnold at each side and the Women's House of Detention in the center.*)

TOMMY. Arnold? Arnold! (*There is no sign of Arnold or his leash even around the parking meter.*) Hey, did you see a dog? A big scruffy dog? I left him tied up here just a little while ago. Arnold, Arnold! Did anybody see my dog? Here, boy, here! (*Sighs, stands hands on hips, looking up and down the avenue, then shrugs.*) He'll be back. (*Calling up to the Women's House of Detention now.*) Nedda! Nedda!!

VOICE. Fuck you!

TOMMY. No, you don't mean that!

VOICE. Fuck you, I don't mean that!

TOMMY. Tell her it's me, lady. Tommy, Tommy Flowers.

VOICE. Fuck you, too, Tommy Flowers!

TOMMY. Where is she? Where's Nedda?

VOICE. Fuck Nedda!

TOMMY. I've got to talk to her!

VOICE. Fuck talking to her!

TOMMY. I've got to tell her what happened!

VOICE. Fuck what happened!

TOMMY. Tell her I'm sorry!

VOICE. Fuck being sorry!

TOMMY. Tell her I think maybe I love her.

VOICE. Love!

TOMMY. Yes, love! That's what it's all about, lady!

VOICE. Fuck love! Fuck everything! Fuck you!

TOMMY. Nedda!!! (*Silence.*) Arnold!!! (*Silence. The streets are empty now.*) That's one thing about Arnold. He'll come back. He always comes back if you just wait for him. (*The stage lights come down very fast and suddenly it is night. There is a pin spot on Tommy who sits, waits and rummages in his red paper shopping bag. The rest of the stage is quite dark and deserted except for the pictures of Nedda, Arnold, and the Women's House of Detention on the screens above.*) I can wait. It doesn't end here. Tomorrow's another day. I'll meet another girl if I want to, get another dog if I have to. Sometimes they're the same thing. People like me, we just go on. Actually, I wouldn't mind calling home collect tonight and seeing how everybody is. (*Finds a magazine in the shopping bag.*) The June 1954 issue of *Photoplay*. A picture of Debra Paget on the cover. Anybody interested? (*He sails it into the audience.*) Travel light, brother. Read it in good health and then pass it right on. (*One other, and one only, light has begun to come up in the theatre. It is another pin spot. This time on a man seated in the middle of the audience. He is very elegantly dressed in theatre clothes, maybe even an opera cape and top hat. We should not be able to take our eyes off him or what he is doing: assembling a rifle in full view of the audience.*) All this talk about America being on the eve of some revolution, I don't understand it. The revolution is now. I mean it's already started. Do all of you know how to make your own bomb? It's easy. (*As he takes the necessary materials out of his red shopping bag.*) You start with something to put the bomb in. A cigar box will do. And then you need dynamite. And ordinary flashlight batteries. And some wire. And an alarm clock. That's all. Now watch how I do this. (*As he works on the bomb.*) It's a remarkably safe avocation. You'd be surprised. They don't have a clue who we are. Did you see the paper yesterday? That projected profile of a revolutionary? It was supposed to be me. A lot of psychological garbage about how screwed up my glorious childhood was and how rotten my parents were, them, those two sainted angels! And how I had feelings of inferiority that were now manifesting themselves in antisocial aggression, which is both untrue and rhetorically redundant. And my politics, it said, were probably influenced by a left-wing professor under whose tutelage my impressionable mind was easily swayed. Tutelage. That's a *New York Times* word if ever I heard one. Tutelage your own horn, Mr. Sulzberger. My politics! I have no politics. I am my politics. (*He waves at the man in the audience assembling the rifle.*) Hello. I said hello. (*No response. Tommy puts his new bomb in his shopping bag.*) One thing I was really looking forward to was going to a concert sometime and hearing Nedda play. I had it all planned how I would get a seat where she could see me and all during the concert I would try to get her to laugh. It wouldn't have been difficult. She's easy to make laugh. I could just tell her to look me in the eye, even when she was mad at me, and try to count to ten without breaking up. Ten? She couldn't even get to three! (*Suddenly and from the gut.*) Nedda! (*It is increasingly apparent that Tommy knows what is going to happen.*) And I had another great plan for her. Even better. Nedda hated birds. I mean she'd see a pigeon in the park and get hysterical. Well she was going to be playing with a group in Central Park this summer and I was going to throw birdseed on the stage. That way the birds would come. Lots of them. I guess I could still do it, only I don't guess she'd think it was funny now. (*Another cry from the gut.*) Arnold! (*To us.*) Well, like I said, there's more girls, more Arnolds. The only

reason that dog wouldn't come back to me would be if someone
had done something terrible to him. I've actually heard about
people who go around dog-napping. Can you imagine stealing
someone's dog? Even worse, there are people who walk around
feeding stray dogs poisoned meat. (*To the man in the audience
assembling the rifle.*) It's true! They caught one two weeks ago
on Avenue C. An old Armenian woman. And did you know it's
against the law for a waitress in a New York City restaurant to
serve you if she's not wearing a hair net? That's another plan on
my Free Eats Program. Well who wants somebody's hair in their
food? You see? You and me, maybe we're friends after all!
(*Tommy starts slapping on black face.*) I start my new job tonight. Another one night stand. (*He pats the shopping bag.*)
Louise T. Coxe. Yassuh, boss, yassuh, that's me, ol' Louise T. A
maid on the night shift at the General Motors Building. $1.10 an
hour and carfare. Yassuh! (*The man in the audience has finished
assembling the rifle and is beginning to take aim.*) You don't
have to do that. Hey, don't point that thing at me, man. I don't
have my magic bracelets on. (*Two wild cries.*) Nedda!!! Arnold!!! (*Suddenly out front, directly to us, as he begins his coin-
dropping tap dance.*) Has anybody here ever fainted on the
grand staircase at Radio City Music Hall with a box of popcorn
in their hand? That's something else I wanted to show you.
(*Coins fall.*) Thank you, sir, thank you! (*He keeps on dancing.*)
It's a terrific sensation. If you get enough momentum going,
you can start on the balcony level and make it all the way down
to the main floor. (*More coins.*) God bless you, madame! (*He
dances.*) And then when there's a big crowd around you, you
pretend to come to and say it was the movie and half of them
start looking for the manager to get their money back before
they've even seen the flic. (*More coins.*) Thank you! Thank you!
(*BANG! BANG! BANG! BANG! BANG! BANG! Six shots.
Tommy's body jerks with each of them in the dance of death.
The man in the audience with the rifle is on his way out of the
theatre.*) You didn't have to do that. No, sir, you didn't have to
do that at all. (*The man is walking up the aisle now.*) Don't
you even want to talk about it even? (*The man keeps right on
walking.*) Walk out backwards and they'll think you're coming
in! (*The man is gone. No trace of him.*) Hey, Nedda! (*Tommy's*

voice is very weak now. The picture of Nedda is extinguished.)
Come on, Arnold, come on, boy! (*The picture of Arnold is extinguished.*) Hey, no fair. I didn't have my magic bracelets on.
(*He slumps a final time.*)

VOICE. Fuck you! Fuck everybody! (*With a final gesture, Tommy gives back her finger and dies. And at once there is another explosion and the three screens above the stage are filled with a huge photograph of the American flag. Music. Peter, Paul, and Mary singing "Where Have All The Flowers Gone?" would be ideal. Pedestrians are crossing the stage. Back and forth, back and forth. A man in a raincoat takes pictures of Tommy with his flash camera. It starts to rain. People put up umbrellas. Arnold enters on the leash of a stranger. He licks Tommy's face until he is pulled away. Nedda walks on by and doesn't notice. So does Greta Rapp. Soon the stage is empty. It continues to rain. Thunder and lightning. The Showgirl enters in a raincoat and carrying an umbrella. She is obviously in a hurry.*)

SHOWGIRL. God forbid we should ever be twenty years without a rebellion. Thomas Jefferson, 1787. Thank you and good night. (*She exits rapidly through the audience.*)

ANNOUNCER'S VOICE. The management of this theatre has asked me to remind you that flowers for the artists will be accepted at the stage door only and must not be thrown onto the stage. Thank you.

VOICE. Marilyn? Marilyn, honey! (*The special light comes up but there is no Marilyn this time.*)

CUBAN ACCENT. She's beezy! She's very, very beezy!

MARILYN'S VOICE. Oh wow! I sure am! Later, honey, much, much later! (*We hear her giggle and the special light is gone. The Black Stagehand has entered and stands looking down at Tommy.*)

BLACK STAGEHAND. Where Has Tommy Flowers Gone? The end. (*He picks up the red shopping bag with the bomb in it and smiles hugely at us.*) Shee-it! (*He shuffles off. The bag and the bomb are his. The stage is bare. Special spot on Tommy. Three loud explosions. With each blast, a portion of the flag is extinguished. Smoke. Darkness. The play is over.*)

"...AND THINGS THAT GO BUMP IN THE NIGHT"

(1965)

From ghoulies and ghosties
Long leggitie beasties
And things that go bump in the night
Good Lord deliver us!
     —14th CENTURY SCOTTISH FOLK PRAYER

For my father and mother

"... AND THINGS THAT GO BUMP IN THE NIGHT" by Terrence Mc-Nally was performed on February 4, 5, 6, 7, 1964, at the Tyrone Guthrie Theatre, Minneapolis, under the auspices of the Office For Advanced Drama Research. It was directed by Lawrence Kornfeld. Set by Dahl Delu. Costumes by Sally-Ross Dinsmore. Lighting by Richard Borgen.

CAST OF CHARACTERS

FA	Alvah Stanley
GRANDFA	Ferdi Hoffman
SIGFRID	Robert Drivas
LAKME	Lois Unger
RUBY	Leueen MacGrath
CLARENCE	Joseph Chaikin

The Broadway production presented by Theodore Mann and Joseph E. Levine in association with Katzka-Berne Productions opened on April 26, 1965, at the Royale Theatre, New York City. It was directed by Michael Cacoyannis. Set by Ed Wittstein. Costumes by Noel Taylor. Lighting by Jules Fisher.

CAST OF CHARACTERS

FA	Clifton James
GRANDFA	Ferdi Hoffman
SIGFRID	Robert Drivas
LAKME	Susan Anspach
RUBY	Eileen Heckart
CLARENCE	Marco St. John

THE SETTING

A living room. Two doors. The one, Stage Left, leads to the bathroom. The other, Stage Right, leads to the various bedrooms. In the rear stage wall there are two openings: an archway with iron stairs leading to the rooms above and a windowed alcove. The tops of the steps are not visible, so that someone coming down the stairs is heard before he is seen. Through the windows of the alcove we see a photographed mural of the nighttime skyline of a large city. Facing this mural are two large chairs. Whoever sits in them is invisible to the audience.

There is an electric spinet piano against the Stage Left wall. Near it is a low table with an intercom system and a tape recorder.

The other furnishings in the room—various sofas, chairs, small tables, etc.—are stark and modern.

The lighting is white: a brilliant, blinding white which is of a uniform intensity throughout the room. There are no shadows or semitones.

The time is the present.

THE PLAYERS

FA: Short, overweight and almost bald. He is in his middle fifties.
RUBY: His wife. Somewhat older but a good deal more youthful looking. She is larger, too.
SIGFRID: Their son. Twenty-one years old. Blonde and good-looking.
LAKME: Their daughter. Thirteen years old. She is wiry and tough, rather like a rooster.
GRANDFA: Very, very old. But the eyes are quick and bright.
CLARENCE: Early twenties, thinnish, irregular features.

ACT ONE

At Rise: The stage is empty. Absolute silence. Pitch dark. After a moment the red light on top of the intercom goes on and we begin to hear the terrible grunting and groaning noises of a person just waking up from a long and deep sleep. The sounds must be amplified to an almost unendurable volume. The theatre should reverberate. The sounds continue. Then, after a yawn of agonizing dimensions, we hear:

RUBY'S VOICE. (*A pronouncement.*) I'm up. (*Another huge yawn.*) Well almost. What time is it? (*A sound of glass breaking.*) . . . goddamn bottles . . . (*A long groan.*) *Gran dio!* Well I'm awake but I may not get out of bed. I might just stay--here and read . . . or something. Mmm, I think I will. *Lakme, carina, il mio cafe . . . subito, subito . . . io moro.* (*A pause; the lights begin to come up—slowly, slowly, slowly.*) Is everyone out there? . . . the four of you? . . . my four . . . my four *what?* . . . are you? . . . that's nice . . . I like it when the four of you are out there . . . it comforts me . . . *yes!* (*A pause.*) The coffee, child. *Presto, pres—* (*She breaks into a cough, recovers herself, then continues in a more seductive voice.*)

Sigfrid, come in here and give Ruby a nice rub on the back . . . hmm? You can come, too, Lakme . . . when you bring the coffee . . . only please, *please* don't bounce on the mattress. (*A pause: lights coming up.*) What's it like out tonight, Sigfrid? . . . *il fait beau . . . aupres de ma blonde ou non?* . . . hmm? . . . *la lune* . . . that crazy old *lune* . . . what about her? . . . (*A pause.*) . . . *beaucoup d'etoiles?* . . . (*A pause.*) . . . the big dipper, Lakme! *Is* there a big dipper? . . . Your mummy's the big dipper! (*Her laughter fades into silence. A pause.*) I don't like this little game you're playing, children. I think we can stop now. I know you're out there. (*A pause; the lights are up to half.*)

Grandfa! The chocolate-covered maraschinos you so dote on. You may have one. No, two! For being such a nice Grandfa. They're in the credenza . . . a blue box . . . Grandfa? . . . you're working on your *novel* . . . aren't you, Grandfa? . . . your novel about *us* . . . your piece of *fiction* . . . yes! . . . sweet, sweet Grandfa . . . it's all *lies*, Grandfa, your book is all *lies*. (*A pause.*)

I'm not amused by this. I warn you . . . all of you . . . there will be retributions. I said I am *not* amused . . . Answer! (*A pause; lights coming up.*)

Ciao, Fa, Ciao! Come stai? That's Italian for "Hi, Fa, hi! How are you?" . . . Well? . . . I had a dream, Fa. Yes! And guess who I dreamed of? Us. Really! We were ice-skating and the ice was pink . . . a beautiful, beautiful pink. And you kept falling down . . . oh, I laughed! . . . your pills, Fa . . . after every meal, he said . . . you didn't forget to take them, did you? . . . Fa? . . . (*A pause.*) So don't take them! Have your goddam little heart attack! Fall on the floor dead! Go ahead! Die! Die laughing! . . . the four of you . . . you think it's so funny! Well I do, too! . . . miserable little . . . I know you're out there. So you can just stop pretending you're not. This doesn't frighten— If I ever thought you'd really left me alone in this terrible house I'd . . . I don't know what I'd do. Kill myself. I suppose you'd like that! (*A final pause; the lights are at full brilliance now; and then the terrified outburst.*) I WON'T BE ALONE IN THIS HOUSE! . . . SOMEONE . . . SOMEONE, COME IN HERE!! (*Footsteps are heard coming down the iron stairs.*)

Who's that? . . . on the stairs . . . who? . . . CHILDREN! . . . make them behave, Fa. Make them tell me who it is . . . FA! (*Fa appears on the stairs. We see only the top of his head, as he holds the paper he is reading in front of his nose. He continues down into the room.*) WHO'S OUT THERE! . . . PLEASE! . . . SOMEONE! . . . TELL ME! . . . WHO? . . . WHO? (*Without looking up from his newspaper, Fa has switched off the intercom. The room returns to an utter stillness. Fa goes to his chair in the alcove, the one with its back to the audience, and sits. Not once have we seen his face.*)

FA. (*After reading in silence for several beats.*) Tech, tech, tech! (*A pause.*) Mmm! (*A pause; he burps. Another pause; he sighs heavily. The silence again. Then a great banging sound from the top of the stairs. It is Grandfa's wheelchair bouncing down the stairs. It lands with a thud at the bottom. Fa does not look around; his nose remains buried in the paper.*) Now just hold your horses, Grandfa. I'll be done in a minute. (*He continues reading.*) . . . mmm . . . did you see this? Fifteen thousand dead in . . . Nitanganyabba? . . . wherever the hell that is. We tried to move those Africans out of those grass huts . . . told them to go underground . . . but do you think they'd listen to Uncle Sam? Not on your life! Fifteen thousand of 'em . . . just like that! (*More footsteps are heard at the top of the stairs.*) And another twelve in New Delhi. At least we know where *that* is. Always had a stable government . . . those Indians. Seems some riot got started during a protest march . . . communist agitators, the paper says, and I don't doubt it . . . students probably . . . young people! . . . all twelve thousand trampled each other to death. You know, you should take more of an interest in world affairs, Grandfa. It's fascinating what goes on these days. (*Grandfa, surly and scowling, is seen on the stairs.*) They'll probably throw all the bodies in that holy river they got over there . . . what's its name . . . the Grange! . . . and just let 'em float out to sea. Hell, it's cheaper than digging all those holes, isn't it? And you can't be much more underdeveloped than those Indians already are, can you now?

GRANDFA. (*Plopping himself down in the wheelchair.*) I found 'em. And guess where the little monster put 'em? Guess!

FA. (*Always reading.*) . . . mmm . . . this is interesting . . .

GRANDFA. The cookie jar!

FA. The government says it's moving west.

GRANDFA. (*Poking around in a large cloth bag he carries with him.*) The cookie jar, mind you! Not in the freezer again . . . not like last time . . . oh no, not her . . . but the cookie jar!

FA. Listen to this. "A definite westerly movement in its—" . . . and then inside a little parenthesis it says "the Dread, *sic*," The Dread! That's a good one for it . . . the Dread! . . . let's see now . . . ah, yes . . . " 'westerly movement in its motion is clearly discernible,' a high-ranking government spokesman who declined to reveal his identity told Washington reporters today. 'Alas,' the anonymous spokesman added."

GRANDFA. (*Who has produced a long strip of black knitting from inside the bag.*) My teeth in a goddam cookie jar!

FA. Alas, he added! How do you like that? . . . So it's headed west, is it?

GRANDFA. (*Knitting furiously.*) Oh, am I ever glad this is my last night in this house. You don't *know* how glad I am.

FA. They've outlawed female circumcision in the Gabon Republic . . . too risky.

GRANDFA. No one knows how glad I am!

FA. They uncovered a nest of nudists right outside of Bloomington . . . it was integrated.

GRANDFA. *I* don't even know how glad I am.

FA. The new Miss Universe is a Labrador girl . . . she edged out Miss Nigeria . . . it says Miss Nigeria put up quite a stink . . . that was ungracious of her . . . (*After a pause.*) . . . which way *is* west?

GRANDFA. We are.

FA. Are you sure?

GRANDFA. We *are* the west, much good that ever did us.

FA. (*Flat.*) Oh.

GRANDFA. (*He can't get over it.*) Eighty-five dollar teeth in a goddam cookie jar! (*An appeal to someone.*) Gods!

FA. (*Folding the paper, handing it to Grandfa.*) Well, at least the Chinese have forged ahead in the Olympics. That's some consolation. (*He lights a cigar; great clouds of smoke rise over the chair.*)

GRANDFA. If that were my child . . . my *children*, I should say . . . the two of 'em . . . I'd . . . (*A growl.*) . . . ooh!

FA. (*Pondering.*) . . . moving west, hunh?

GRANDFA. I wouldn't let that bother me. Not with this contraption. (*He indicates the room with a wave of his hand.*) Not with that fence out there. How many million volts is it?

FA. (*Speaking over a huge yawn.*) Three thousand, Grandfa, only three thousand. What time are they coming for you?

GRANDFA. Early. As soon the streets are open. This infernal curfew . . . I could've gone tonight.

FA. (*With another yawn.*) We'll miss you.

GRANDFA. I won't. Should've done this years ago. Only I thought *you* had to commit *me*. Didn't know I could do it myself. (*Slight pause.*) Well maybe you . . . a little bit . . . miss, I mean. Blood's blood. (*He looks up from his knitting.*) Dozing off on me, hunh?

FA. Just a little snooze, Grandfa. A little after-dinner snooze.

GRANDFA. Don't tell me about your little snoozes. Last all night. Days sometimes . . . weeks! . . . months! Don't see what dinner's got to do with it. Seems to me you're *always* snoozing. Certainly don't expect you up when I go in the morning . . . probably the last time we'll see each other for a while then . . . maybe never . . . guess this is goodbye . . . I don't suppose you want to kiss me. (*The first snore from Fa.*) SON!

FA. (*Immediately responding, but groggy.*) I'm listening, Grandfa.

GRANDFA. I said . . . (*An old gentleman's embarrassment.*) I said I didn't expect you wanted to kiss me.

FA. Now Grandfa!

GRANDFA. I didn't think so. (*A slight pause.*) It's been done before, you know.

FA. (*Sleep overtaking him again.*) Yes, Grandfa.

GRANDFA. It's a sign of affection . . . a kiss is. And stop calling me that! That's *their* name for me.

PA. (*Even sleepier.*) We'll drive up every Sunday that it's nice.

GRANDFA. Well don't!

FA. . . . every Sunday . . . just like Ruby said . . .

GRANDFA. You won't find me!

FA. . . . every Sunday that it's nice . . .

GRANDFA. I'll hide! I'll hide in a thicket!

FA. (*Going fast now.*) . . . we'll find you . . .

GRANDFA. You think . . . you think!

FA. (*Lapsing into sleep.*) . . . we'll find you . . . Grandfa . . . oh yes! . . . we'll . . . (*The snoring begins: an even, rhythmic drone. Grandfa sits a moment. He is sad. Then he goes slowly over to Fa and puts his hand on Fa's shoulder. He looks at Fa. He does not move. There is a stillness. Then:*)

GRANDFA. (*A gentle moan; a benediction, a forgiveness.*) Oh. (*Now he moves away from Fa. He clears his eyes with his fist . . . for there has been a tear or two. His eyes chance to fall on the paper in his lap. He reads a moment, almost against his will, then throws the paper from him with a little cry. He looks back once at Fa and then, with a sudden shudder.*) Oh these are terrible times to be old in! (*More noise at the top of the stairs. Voices, footsteps, and then Sigfrid bounds into the room. He wears a heavy-knit navy blue sweater wtih a large white "Y" on the front. He carries a football.*)

SIGFRID. (*Acting out the following with great enthusiasm.*) "Fifteen seconds to go and listen to that crowd roar! . . . will they do it? . . . there's the snap! . . . and it's Sigfrid . . . the all-American Sigfrid fading back . . . he spots his receiver . . . the fabulous Grandfa's in the clear . . . it's going to be a long throw, fans! . . . WILL HE DO IT??" (*Sigfrid throws the ball across the room. It hits Grandfa in the stomach with a thud. Sigfrid assumes an attitude of immense disappointment.*) Aaaaw. We could've had 'em, Grandfa. Some school try that was. Where's your oomph? You all out of oomph? (*Grandfa charges wildly at him with his chair.*)

SIGFRID. (*Easily eludes him.*) Atta boy! That's the spirit.

GRANDFA. (*More sad than angry.*) If I had a gun . . .

SIGFRID. . . . you'd shoot yourself! Okay, I'm sorry. Peace? (*No real truce is established. Grandfa only moves away.*)

(*Lakme is heard at the top of the stairs. Her entrance is announced by the sound of a small child bawling her head off.*).

SIGFRID. Enter one crocodile . . . tearful. (*Lakme appears: her face a study in childish misery. She sobs, howls and in general carries on like there is no tomorrow. It is almost convincing. Her dress is tomboyish and appropriate for a thirteen-year-old. She might wear her hair in pigtails. She carries an array of photographic equipment: cameras, cases, etc.*)

LAKME. (*Howling like a banshee, yet perfectly capable of stopping should it be to her advantage.*)

SIGFRID. (*With mock cheerfulness.*) Hello there, little one! What seems to be the trouble? You pick another fight with that German shepherd down the road? (*Lakme increases her howling.*) Poor little Lakme. All forsook and chewed on. Comfort her, Grandfa.

LAKME. (*In heaving breaths between sobs.*) Gran . . . Grandfa! . . . Grandfa, Sigfrid tackled me! . . . hard!

SIGFRID (*Mocking.*) Not true, not true.

LAKME. He *did!* Look! (*She hunts for and finds a tiny cut on her knee.*) See? . . . see? (*Grandfa snaps his teeth at her—three times. Lakme uses her normal voice; it is an ugly one.*) Where did you find those? . . . hunh? Sigfrid, did you—?

SIGFRID. (*Absolving himself with a gesture and then pointing to her injured knee.*) That was quite a recovery . . . even for you.

LAKME. (*Tough.*) Oh yeah? (*She begins howling again ... though not quite so effectively as before ... and limps her way over to Fa. Again the congested voice.*) Fa! . . . Sigfrid . . . Wake *up*!

FA. (*A moment of groggy consciousness.*) . . . moving west, hunh? . . . (*He is asleep again.*)

LAKME. (*Furiously shaking him.*) How are you going to have that heart attack if you sleep all the time? . . . Hunh? . . . LIAR!! (*Sigfrid has been enjoying this enormously. He bursts into laughter now; a full, open laugh. Lakme turns on him.*) Well it *hurt*!

SIGFRID. (*Explaining to Grandfa.*) It was nearly an hour ago. She said "ouch" . . . that's all. And not one whimper all the way home. Then the moment we walk through that door upstairs . . . this!

LAKME. (*The anger dissipated into a general sulkiness.*) Well you certainly don't expect me to waste my tears on *you*! A lot you care . . . stinky! (*She sits and examines the cut on her knee.*)

SIGFRID. (*So patiently.*) Grandfa, you haven't turned your hearing aid off again, have you? (*He checks the mechanism in Grandfa's vest pocket.*) Unh-hunh! We be a naughty Grandfa. (*Then, while fiddling with the mechanism, with a trace of baby-talk:*) We put this wire here . . . and that wire there . . . and we jiggle this little knobby-poo . . . and now we all well again . . . yes! . . . now we can *hear* . . . goodie! . . . now we can hear Sigfrid tell us not to do those bad-type things anymore . . . cause Ruby frets when we do our little no-goods . . . cause Sigfrid frets . . . and Lakme . . . cause *everybody* frets when Grandfa does his no-goods. (*He puts the hearing aid mechanism back in Grandfa's pocket.*) And now we be a nice Grandfa . . . now we be an obedient Grandfa . . . now we be a quiet Grandfa. And we sit in our nice little corners . . . (*Indeed, he has maneuvered Grandfa and his chair to a tight little corner, Stage Right.*) . . . and we knit quietly away at our nice little . . . (*He holds up Grandfa's knitting a moment.*) . . . shrouds? . . . and we write our nice little *novels* . . .

GRANDFA. *Chronicle!*

SIGFRID. . . . and no one even knows we're alive. Yes!

GRANDFA. (*Steely-eyed; making it a noun.*) Abominable!

SIGFRID. (*Not at all unpleasantly.*) Oh you foul-mouthed old Shakespearean you! Shame on you. Not even a decent iambic. (*Coming back over to Lakme.*) How now, scab?

LAKME. There *will* be one! And I have a dance recital coming up next week . . . two solos! It'll look terrible.

SIGFRID. Then you'd better tippy-tap-toe your way into Ruby's bedroom and let her kiss it. *That*'ll make it go away.

LAKME. (*Flaring.*) I don't tap dance! We do modern . . . acrobatic modern.

SIGFRID. All right, then acrobat-modern your way in there . . . *slither.*

LAKME. (*Rolling down her pants leg.*) You're such a cheat, Sigfrid. You say we're going to play touch football and then as soon as I get the ball you change it to tackle.

SIGFRID. And what about that stiff-arm? You practically gouged my eye out.

LAKME. That was different. That was a tactic. (*The little lady bit now.*) Besides, if I were a twenty-one-year-old . . . boy? hah! . . .

SIGFRID. (*He means this.*) Watch it, Baby Snooks!

LAKME. (*Continuing.*) . . . I'd certainly be embarrassed to be seen playing football in a public park with a thirteen-year-old child.

SIGFRID. Oh you would?

LAKME. Yes! And when the thirteen-year-old child just happens to be a thirteen-year-old *girl*! . . .

SIGFRID. A *what?*

LAKME. . . . his own little *sister*, in fact . . . well, that's just about the worst thing I ever heard of. And then hurling her to the turf like that . . . a vicious *tackle*!

SIGFRID. (*Suddenly on the defensive for the first time.*) Now look, you little dwarf, you *tripped*.

LAKME. (*Amazed that he could have taken her seriously.*) I know that, stupid. Of course I did. Honestly, Sigfrid, you can be so *dense* sometimes. You know what a little liar I am. (*Sigfrid sulks*). Wow! Aren't we getting touchy all of a sudden.

SIGFRID. (*Still put off.*) What time is it?

LAKME. (*Shrugging.*) Probably time to wake her. Gee, Sigfrid, I was only kidding. You've got about as much of a sense of humor as that thing in the park . . . what's-his-name. What a puss on that one! A lousy catch, too.

SIGFRID. (*He has turned on the intercom and now speaks into it.*) Ruby? . . . Wake-up time. (*Then to Lakme.*) There's some jokes I don't like.

LAKME. (*With great affection.*) You're such a dope. (*She gets up to join him at the intercom and makes a final reference to her injured knee.*) I don't mind getting 'em here so much . . . I mean the principle behind the thing . . . it's just the *ploys* you use. This really hurts. (*She joins him at the intercom and puts one arm affectionately around his waist.*)

SIGFRID (*Again into the intercom.*) Hey Ruby! . . . wake-up time! (*Then to Lakme.*) I can't help it. It's just my nature. I'm very . . .

LAKME. (*Anticipating him, so that they say the word together.*) . . . *ployful!* (*They laugh and jostle each other like the very best of friends . . . which, of course, they very often are.*)

RUBY'S VOICE. (*On the intercom; it is very small, very frightened.*) Sigfrid? . . . is it you, Sigfrid?

SIGFRID. No, Karl Marx and Trotsky! Who do you think?

LAKME. Batman and Robin!

RUBY'S VOICE. (*With some relief.*) Lakme!

SIGFRID. (*The little game over.*) Come on, Ruby, hustle it.

LAKME. Get up to "get up." Wait'll you see him, Ruby! The *game.*

RUBY'S VOICE. (*Firm now; the rage mounting.*) You miserable little . . . vipers! . . . pythons! . . . *asps!*

SIGFRID. (*Himself annoyed now.*) Hey, now can it, snake-woman, and just get up! Christ! You ask us to wake you and then—

RUBY'S VOICE. (*Hell hath no fury.*) I AM UP! . . . you bastards! . . . you utter, utter bastards! . . . you think you're pretty *funny,* don't you? . . .

SIGFRID. (*He and Lakme have been exchanging perplexed glances since the outburst.*) Ruby!

RUBY'S VOICE. . . . had our little kicks for the evening, didn't we? . . . hunh? . . . we showed *her* what kind of games we can play . . . we had ourselves one big fat *laugh!* HAH!

SIGFRID. (*Who has been trying to get a word in.*) Ruby, what—?

RUBY'S VOICE. (*Colder now, more under control.*) If you ever do that again I will take you upstairs and push you off the roof . . . the four of you!

LAKME. Do what? She's flipped, Sigfrid. She's finally flipped.

RUBY'S VOICE. (*Exploding again.*) HOW *DARE* YOU PRETEND YOU'RE NOT OUT THERE! . . . HOW *DARE* YOU!!

SIGFRID. We didn't. I mean we weren't.

RURY'S VOICE. (*Much, much calmer.*) . . . such bastardy . . . such unspeakable bastardy . . . (*A final groan of rage and despair.*) Ooooh!

LAKME. She must have had one of her dreams again. Were you down here, Grandfa? (*Grandfa, as usual, only glowers and goes on knitting.*)

SIGFRID. (*With his oh-so-weary, patient tone.*) I'll be right in there, Ruby.

RUBY'S VOICE. Don't. Besides, the door's locked . . . *and* bolted.

SIGFRID. Then will you just calm down and let me explain?

RUBY'S VOICE. Scorpion!

SIGFRID. Are you? . . . are you calm now?

RUBY'S VOICE. (*In complete control now; imperial tones; relishing every moment of the exchange. After all, she is being made up to.*) Considerably . . . and don't patronize.

SIGFRID. All right, now tell me what happened. Was it one of your dreams again?

RUBY'S VOICE. (*A deliberate sulk.*) No.

SIGFRID. You're sure . . . you're sure it wasn't one of your nightmares?

RUBY'S VOICE. (*Peevish.*) Yes I'm sure! and the word's *cauchemar*.

SIGFRID. Then you must have—

RUBY'S VOICE. (*Regal.*) Say it!

SIGFRID. (*Anything to accommodate.*) Cauchemar.

RUBY'S VOICE. (*Wincing at the pronunciation.*) Mon dieu! Lakme!

LAKME. (*With great care and love for every syllable.*) Cauchemar.

RUBY'S VOICE. (*After a slight pause for consideration.*) Bravo! Is Sigfrid blushing? I should hope so.

LAKME. (*So in love with herself.*) Cauchemar.

SIGFRID. (*His turn to explode now.*) Damn it, Ruby! If you're not interested in this—!

RUBY'S VOICE (*Curt.*) I am *extremely* interested.

LAKME. (*Delirious.*) Cauche— (*Sigfrid slugs her.*)

RUBY'S VOICE. (*After a slight pause.*) What happened?

LAKME. (*Not in a whine.*) Sigfrid hit me.

RUBY'S VOICE. (*Matter-of-fact.*) Hit him back. (*Lakme does so. Sigfrid doesn't respond. They are used to this ritual.*)

LAKME. I did.

RUBY'S VOICE. (*Continuing where she left off.*) I am extremely interested as to why . . . *why* with all the care, love and protection I have lavished on you . . . *why* with all the lovely and nice things I have given you . . . this house, to mention only one . . . *why* with your fabulous good looks, your locks so fine and golden, your firm, trim, *beautiful* body . . . which I alway encouraged you to nurture . . . *why* with so *much* . . . with so *many* goodies in your little hopper . . . *why* (*With an abrupt change of tone.*) . . . you turned out to be such a miserable son of a bitch. (*Short pause.*)

GRANDFA (*To his private world-at-large.*) I could answer that. (*But he doesn't.*)

SIGFRID. (*He's had it.*) Christ!

LAKME. (*Virtue triumphant.*) That puts your little light under a basket!

RUBY'S VOICE. (*Gently remonstrating.*) Bushel, dear, *bushel!*

LAKME. (*Discovering a delightful new word.*) Bushel-basket! (*Then making it an expletive to hurl at Sigfrid.*) Bushel-basket!

RUBY'S VOICE. (*Stopping Lakme cold.*) And that goes for you, too! (*Pause.*) You're *both* sons of bitches. (*Pause.*) You're all *four* sons of bitches. Can you imagine what those fifteen minutes were like for me? Can you possibly conceive the *terror* of them? Of thinking you're alone in this fearful, hideous house? Utterly, completely *alone?* And then hearing footsteps . . . on the stairs . . . and no answer . . . no answer at all? Can your pea-sized little hearts even *begin* to understand what an experience like that does to a person? . . . Can they? (*Pause.*) I *quivered!* . . . yes! . . . for fifteen minutes . . . I quivered like a fern! . . . not knowing *who* was out there . . . *what* was out there . . . it could have been *anything!* Fifteen minutes of unspeakable terror! . . . and you people . . . you smug, hurtful, hateful *monsters!* . . . making me think that I was alone . . . that it had finally *happened* even! Yes! I was that terrified . . . pretending you weren't there when I most needed you. Oh you must be very pleased with yourselves. (*Her emotions are spent; the recall of the terror has been a complete one; she is silent now.*)

SIGFRID. (*With a sad sigh.*) Ruby, Ruby, Ruby. You *will* jump to conclusions, won't you? and scare yourself half to death. If it's happened once, it's happened a hundred times. (*His tone is extremely gentle, as if he were talking to a child.*) What *really* happened? . . . you called and no one answered?

RUBY'S VOICE. (*A little girl nursing her wounds.*) Yes.

SIGFRID. So you *assumed* we were trying to frighten you? By pretending not to be here?

RUBY'S VOICE. You might have been.

SIGFRID. Oh, *Ruby!*

RUBY'S VOICE. We all play tricks on each other . . . don't we?

LAKME. But not like *that.* Never tricks like *that.*

SIGFRID. Did you really think we'd go that far? That we'd make *jokes* about it?

RUBY'S VOICE. (*A plea for understanding.*) I get so frightened when I'm alone . . .

SIGFRID (*Cutting in.*) But you weren't *alone!* (*A pause.*)

RUBY'S VOICE. (*A trifle disappointed.*) I wasn't?

SIGFRID. No! You woke up early, that's all. No one had come down yet.

LAKME. Sigfrid and I were here in plenty of time for wake-up. We all were.

SIGFRID. If you were upstairs maybe there'd be some *reason* . . . well *no*, not even then. Christ, Ruby, it's a good thirty minutes 'til curfew.

LAKME. Sigfrid and I were on the *streets* up until ten minutes ago, and we're not all gone to pieces. (*A pause; no response from Ruby.*)

SIGFRID. Ruby . . . ?

RUBY'S VOICE. The four of you are out there, you said. What about Grandfa? I don't hear Grandfa. Is he working on his novel?

SIGFRID. He's knitting.

LAKME. Say something to her, Grandfa.

GRANDFA. (*Obligingly, loud and clear.*) Harpy! And stop calling it that! It's a *chronicle*. I'm writing a *chronicle!*

RUBY'S VOICE. (*More cheerful by the moment; sing-song.*) Hello, Grandfa! It's a piece of fiction, Grandfa. You're writing a novel, Grandfa. And Fa! How's Fa? Is he . . . ?

LAKME. No. Just sleeping.

RUBY'S VOICE. I wasn't going to say that.

LAKME. Well he might just as well be.

SIGFRID. Ruby!

RUBY'S VOICE. I'm coming! Did you find someone?

SIGFRID. (*Weary, patient; but getting her out of there.*) Yes, Ruby.

RUBY'S VOICE. Male or female? and *do* say male.

LAKME. (*Sibilating.*) Oh, yes! V*ery* male. Very *definitely* male.

RUBY'S VOICE. Oh. It's going to be one of *those* nights.

SIGFRID. (*Endless patience.*) That's right, Ruby. One of *those* nights.

RUBY'S VOICE. I don't approve, of course, but *la vie n'est pas en rose.*

LAKME. We had a little trouble with him. He kept thinking better of it.

RUBY'S VOICE. But he's *coming*, Sigfrid? You're *sure* of it?

SIGFRID. Yes, Ruby, he'll be here.

LAKME. He'd *better* be. Can you imagine it alone down here? Just the four of us? Yikes!

RUBY'S VOICE. Oh it's going to be a lovely, lovely evening! I can feel it in my . . . what, Sigfrid?

SIGFRID. (*Still playing along with her.*) Fangs, Ruby, you can feel it in your fangs.

RUBY'S VOICE. Yes! Yes, I do.

SIGFRID. (*Finally impatient, but not unpleasant.*) It *might* be if you'd just get out here.

RUBY'S VOICE. (*In a tiny dither now.*) I'll *be* there! . . . don't fuss at me . . . I'm struggling with this damn peignoir . . . all these pearl buttons. If you're so impatient turn on the recorder. I taped another Message to the World this morning . . . probably my last . . . it's rather a summation.

LAKME. (*Rushing to the tape recorder: paroxysms of joy.*) Another Message to the World, Ruby?

RUBY'S VOICE. I'd call it definitive . . . the very last word. See what you think. *I* certainly can't imagine anything else to say on the matter. It's a closed book now, as far as I'm concerned.

SIGFRID. (*Good naturedly; joining Lakme by the tape recorder.*) You're such a pope, Ruby. You and your encyclicals. What's this one called?

RUBY'S VOICE. (*So grand.*) The Way We Live! (*The red light on the intercom goes off, as Lakme sets the tape reels to spinning.*)

RUBY'S RECORDED VOICE. (*A private voice, such as one uses when alone; yet with a full range of color and nuance.*) The Way We Live. Message to the World number 812. (*Short pause; Sigfrid and Lakme have settled themselves on the floor.*) The Way We Live . . . and perhaps this is regrettable . . . it would seem is open to some question. (*Short pause.*) *Some* question. Open to question, that is, if certain nameless people were to have their say . . . to *protest*, as it were. (*Sigfrid and Lakme glare suspiciously at Grandfa, who glares right back at them.*) And by that I mean you . . . yes, *you!* (*Now Sigfrid and Lakme glare at each other with suspicion.*) A fuller explication then has been demanded and shall be given. *Explication*, my unseen accusers, and I know you, not exculpation. (*Short pause.*) The way we live is compounded of *love* . . . love which neither nurtures the receiver nor lays fallow the sender but will suffice for each . . . of *hate* . . . and more of it than we can often cope with . . . yes! . . . and of a numbing, *crushing* indifference . . . an indifference which kills . . . slowly, finally, *totally!* and for which our cruelty (and pain now is our only reminder that we yet live) . . . for which the cruelty we do unto each other is but a temporary antidote . . . (*Short pause: then in a frightened, timid, funny little voice.*) C'est triste . . . n'est-ce pas? (*Another short pause and a change of tone.*) God . . . gods . . . some*one* . . . some*thing* . . . *whatever*: things done or not done and then called good or bad; the price of eggs even! . . . these *things* men speak of, attain to, do battle for . . . the way we live does not involve us with them. They are the concerns . . . no, *were!* . . . *were* the concerns of peoples, nations . . . yea individuals . . . who thought they were to prevail. We shall *not* prevail . . . so be it. We shall *not* endure . . . but who was ever meant to? And we shall *not* inherit the earth . . . it has already disinherited us. (*Ruby enters the room through the door Stage Right. Sigfrid and Lakme turn and are about to greet her when she motions them with her hand to keep silence. She goes towards them and, with one hand on each of their heads, she joins them as they listen.*) The way we live is a result . . . a response . . . an *oblivion* to ourselves, each other . . . and what is out there. If we are without faith, we find our way in the darkness . . . it is light enough. If we are without hope, we turn to our despair . . . it has its own consolations. And if we are without charity, we suckle the bitter root of its absence . . . wherefrom we shall draw the sustenance to destroy you. (*And this is the saddest part.*) Go . . . seek not to know us . . . to understand . . . the compassion of it will exhaust you and there is so little strength left us now . . . so little. (*Short pause; then, very quickly, in an everyday tone:*) Spoken by me this December morning. Unwitnessed, unheard, alone. (*A word now about Ruby's appearance. It is a spectacular disappointment. Oh, the peignoir she wears is fancy enough and there are many rings on her fingers and expensive slippers on her feet. But Ruby herself will disappoint you. Her face is without make-up and seems almost anonymous. The intense lighting in the room, you see, washes the "character" out of her face, so that it is impossible to tell very much about her except that she is no longer young. As for her hair, well she might as well be bald, for she wears one of those large elastic cloth bands women use to pull the hair back from their face before applying make-up. The appearance of her entire face, in fact, is best suggested by this word* bald. *Or* plucked clean. *Or* erased. *The gaudy rings only draw attention to the unvarnished fingernails, some of which are bitten to the quick. And the few toes which peep out through an opening in front of the slippers are not especially clean. So this, for the time being, is Ruby. Immediately after the conclusion of Ruby's long speech on the tape recorder, there is a good moment of silence. Then:*)

FA. (*Waking momentarily.*) Goodbye, Grandfa . . . Come and kiss me, Grandfa.

GRANDFA. (*Fa's had his chance.*) I'm knitting.

FA. . . . poor Miss Nigeria . . .

GRANDFA. Knitting and listening to this harridan spout balderdash. You never heard such— (*But Fa is already asleep again.*) Balderdash, Ruby! . . . pure balderdash! (*Neither Ruby, Lakme nor Sigfrid have moved since the conclusion of the tape. Now Ruby, making something of a moment of it, switches off the machine.*)

RUBY. (*Chanting almost.*) Ecco la testimonia d'una traviata . . . una testimonia nera.

LAKME (*Flopping over backwards on the floor; quite overcome by, though not really understanding, all she has just heard.*) Nero: *nerissimo! . . . wow!* (*Sigfrid has remained silent and brooding to one side.*)

GRANDFA. (*Continuing to grouse away in his corner.*) Message to the World, she calls it. That's no message . . . it's garbage, *that's* what it is . . . *pig* food!

LAKME. (*Trying to reconstruct a certain phrase.*) "And if we are without faith . . . we shall suckle . . . ?" . . . is that right, Rúby? . . . "suckle" . . . ?

GRANDFA. Yes, that's right. *Suckle!* Suckle your way like pigs!

LAKME. ". . . suckle our bitter root in the darkness . . . ?"

RUBY. (*Completing it.*) . . . it has its own absence."

LAKME. Absence?

RUBY. (*Getting it right now, a little irritable.*) Consolations. It has its own *consolations.*

LAKME. Which has? Our bitter root or our darkness?

RUBY. Well *something* like that! How should I know?

LAKME. You *said* it!

RUBY. That was this morning . . . hours ago . . . *centuries.*

LAKME. (*A little mollified.*) That part about destroying you. That's the part I liked best.

RUBY. You would. (*Then, pressing her hands to her temples.*) Suddenly I have a headache. Ruby's evening vapors.

LAKME. (*They all love these little word games.*) You mean vespers. Ruby's evening *vespers.*

GRANDFA. (*He does, too.*) No, *vipers!* She means *vipers!* Evening *vipers!* The three of them.

RUBY. I mean *vapors!* (*Sinking into one of the armchairs.*) Presto, cara, presto.

LAKME. Wait'll you see this fink we got coming over here tonight! One of those demonstrators!

RUBY. *Va! Fuggi!*

LAKME. (*Running on.*) Finks! They're all finks. They're not going to change anything. Not with signs!

RUBY. *Fuggi,* damn it, *fuggi!*

LAKME. (*Stopped cold.*) *Fuggi?*

RUBY. From *fuggire:* to make haste . . . to pick up our little feet and vanish . . . to *scram!*

LAKME. (*Still puzzling.*) *Fuggi—?* (*Now she's got it.*) Oh.

RUBY. Yeah, *oh!* Piccola nitwit.

LAKME. (*Nice and prissy.*) I'm sorry, Ruby, but we can't *all* of us be such opera queens. I mean some of us are *normal.* Some of us speak *English* when we want something. Some of us—

RUBY. (*Stern, but a little amused in spite of it.*) Will you get in there and get that coffee?

LAKME. (*On her way out, but wanting to prolong it, so she sings.*) "Mi chiamano Lakme, ma il perche, non so."

RUBY. (*Very strong.*) Va!

LAKME. (*In a charming little voice.*) Vo. (*She fairly twinkles through the door, Stage Right, and is gone.*)

RUBY. (*After thinking it over a moment.*) I am *not* an opera queen. Sigfrid, you don't think I'm an opera queen, do you? (*Sigfrid turns away from her.*) God knows I'm *some* sort of a queen, but not *that.* (*Then, feeling a little chill.*) Where's that draft coming from? Sigfrid, you didn't leave the door open? (*She turns to him, really turns to him for the first time since her entrance, and immediately bursts into a wild gale of laughter.*) Sigfrid! . . . look at you! . . . that outfit! . . . that *costume!* . . . I *never!* . . . Where on *earth!* . . . You're *outlandish* in that sweater! (*Then, singing hilariously.*) "Boola boola, boola boola, bool—" (*Sigfrid, furious, hurls a cushion to the floor, then moves away to another part of the room. Ruby pauses, then mockingly.*) Oh, a little more than kin and less than kind, are we this evening, I see.

GRANDFA. (*Moving forward, ready to do battle.*) Leave Shakespeare out of this! Abuse the language in your own words, woman . . . and my God how you abuse it! . . . but not in his . . . not in Shakespeare's.

RUBY. (*Acknowledging this.*) Grandfa! Sweetest old thing on two wheels! How old? Will you never tell us? Two hundred? . . . three hundred? . . . four?

GRANDFA. It's criminal how you abuse the gift of speech, woman, *criminal!*

RUBY. (*Effusive.*) Each day could be . . . *should* be . . . your very last . . . but it never is. Keeping us in such suspense! Sly, sly Grandfa.

GRANDFA. (*Determined to be heard.*) CREATURES LIKE YOU SHOULD HAVE THE VERY *TONGUES* CUT OUT OF THEIR HEADS!

RUBY. (*Stopping her ears.*) Grandfa! Don't shout at us like that. We're not the deaf ones; *you* are.

GRANDFA. Well you *should.* Right out of your heads with a big rusty knife.

RUBY. (*Saccharine.*) Yes, dear. We all heard you. Grandfa thinks I abuse the gift of speech, Sigfrid. He thinks I should have the very tongue cut out of my head with a big rusty knife. He thinks I'm a creature.

GRANDFA. (*Rumbling on.*) Message to the World! I never *heard* such contamination.

RUBY. We can't *all* be your beloved Shakespeare, Grandfa.

GRANDFA. I'll say!

RUBY. (*A little less playful here.*) I meant it when I said it.

GRANDFA. So did he!

RUBY. Forsooth!

GRANDFA. And it didn't come out garbage! It was poetry. It *sang!*

RUBY. With a hey-nonny-nonny and a ho!

GRANDFA. Shakespeare *respected* words! And you know why? Because Shakespeare respected *people!* . . . human beings . . . *men!* But *you* . . . this family! . . .

RUBY. How you prate, nuncle, how you will prate!

GRANDFA. Message to the World! It would've turned my stomach if that meal I had to cook for myself hadn't already turned it.

RUBY. And how nice for you that it was your last one.

GRANDFA. Last what? Meal? You're damn right it was . . . nice for me.

RUBY. And *won't* you be happy up there on that little farm? All you old retired actors . . . all you old Shakespeareans . . . lolling around all day . . . in wheelchairs . . . being *pushed!* . . . just lolling around and mewling sonnets at each other all day long? Mewling sonnets over social tea biscuits and a drop of sherry? Won't that be *fun?* And doing real live theatricals for the Sunday visitors? Grandfa as Lear! Grandfa as Macbeth! Grandfa as *Lady* Macbeth! Well why not? They did it in *his* time. They did it in *god's* time. And won't *that* be fun! Grandfa in a skirt with candle . . . enters deranged . . . *uno sonnambulo!* . . . and tears the house down. Oh, you'll be *very* happy up on that farm. I just *know* you will.

GRANDFA. (*A little sad now, his prospects are none too cheerful, but with a simple dignity.*) I have friends up there . . . *some* . . . old thespians like myself . . . there's a few of us still left . . . they say the food's not too bad . . . the care . . . I'll . . . *manage.* (*A pause. Ruby, restless as ever, moves away from Grandfa, who remains Center Stage, brooding. Silence.*)

FA. (*Muttering in his sleep.*) Moving west, hunh? . . . so it's moving west? . . .

RUBY. (*With a somewhat forced gaiety.*) *What* is? What's moving west? What is Fa mumbling about? (*No one answers. Long silence. A tension is building.*) It can get so *silent* down here! . . . so *dead!* I ask you: are we the only people in the world or are we not? Hmm? Sometimes I think we are. I really do. (*Another pause. More silence. More tension.*) When is this person coming, Sigfrid? Not soon? . . . now *now?* I mean just look at us. We haven't even begun to get ready . . . any of us! (*He does not answer; pause, silence, tension.*) Sulky boy. (*The silence is deafening.*) Lakme! (*Short pause.*) If somebody doesn't say something, if somebody doesn't say something *soon* . . . (*Suddenly she stops short. What has happened is that Grandfa has made a funny sound. It might have been merely a sigh. But then again, it may have been the signal for a seizure. Anyway, Grandfa has not moved since he last spoke. He makes the funny sound again. Ruby rushes to his side. Her voice and movements now indicate apprehension, yes, but also a certain amount of relief. After all, her energies are engaged.*) Grandfa! . . . What's the matter, Grandfa! (*Grandfa doesn't respond.*) It's Grandfa, Sigfrid, it's Grand—!

GRANDFA. (*Cutting her off, suddenly alert.*) What are you howling about, woman?

RUBY. Oh!

GRANDFA. What are you howling about now?

RUBY. I thought you were—

GRANDFA. (*Warding off her attentions.*) Keep your distance! Don't need you fiddling at me. Thought I was . . . *I* know! Didn't you? Well I *wasn't!*

RUBY. (*A little icy now.*) I *thought* you were. It alarmed me.

GRANDFA. *Hoped!* you mean, don't you? Hoped!

RÚBY. All right, Grandfa, all right.

GRANDFA. You want to know what I *was* doing?

RUBY. Not especially.

GRANDFA. I was *thinking!*

RUBY. How nice for you, Grandfa, how very nice for you. Grandfa was only *thinking*, Sigfrid!

GRANDFA. That's right, *thinking!*

RUBY. I *said* how very nice for you.

GRANDFA. Thinking it over. *Everything!* . . . you . . . me . . . us . . . *everything! That* ought to put the fear of God in you, woman, not that you ever believed in Him!

RUBY. (*A little sorry she got into this.*) You just put everything you're thinking about in that little book you're writing, Grandfa. Scribble it in your little novel.

GRANDFA. (*She has touched a sore point.*) *Chronicle!* It's not a novel. It's a *chronicle.*

RUBY. Chronicles record the *truth*, Grandfa. Your book is full of *lies.* Therefore, your book is a *novel.*

GRANDFA. "Time Was: A *Chronicle.*" A book of *facts* . . . *historical facts!*

RUBY. Not *facts*, Grandfa. *Lies!* Unhistorical non-facts! Nonsense!

GRANDFA. (*Never relinquishing the offensive.*) Facts about *you* . . . the *truth!*

RUBY. (*Her last defensive.*) That's *wonderful*, Grandfa. You go right *on* with your little novel. You go right on deluding yourself. Don't waste a *minute!* There's so little *time* left!

GRANDFA. (*Not to be stopped.*) I *will!* Old people *remember*, you know. They remember *everything!* That's their function . . . to *remember!*

RUBY. (*Retreating now.*) Lakme! . . . Where *is* that child?

GRANDFA. (*Pursuing.*) Only younger people don't *like* that! . . . they don't *like* to remember . . . they're *afraid!* . . . afraid of the *truth* . . . facts *frighten* them . . . *memory* frightens them . . . *old people* frighten them!!

RUBY. (*With more than a little desperation.*) Isn't it wonderful, Sigfrid? . . . at his age . . . so *spry!*

SIGFRID. (*Turning on her with a rage that has been building inside him ever since the tape recorder episode.*) LEAVE HIM ALONE, RUBY! JUST ONCE, LEAVE PEOPLE ALONE!! (*Ruby is quite taken aback and for the moment absolutely speechless.*)

GRANDFA. Don't you stand up for me! I don't need your help!

SIGFRID. CHRIST, RUBY, CHRIST! (*Sigfrid's explosion has produced a tense, angry silence. Even Granfa is willing to withdraw for the moment and he goes back to his corner. From inside his knitting bag he will soon produce a small book, his chronicle. From time to time during the following he will write in it. But only after much deliberation. Sigfrid has moved away from Ruby who stands watching him, her own anger mounting. Then, after a long pause:*)

RUBY. (*With a repressed and terrible fury.*) That wasn't called for, Sigfrid. That wasn't called for at *all*. (*Sigfrid doesn't answer.*) And I *told* you to take off that ridiculous sweater. You're *home* now. The camouflage is no longer necessary!

LAKME'S VOICE. (*A sudden intrusion on the intercom.*) Hey, opera queen! Black?

RUBY. What?

LAKME'S VOICE. Your coffee. How do you want it? Black?

RUBY. No, *blue!*

LAKME'S VOICE. Well *sometimes* you take a little brandy in it.

RUBY. (*Always glowering at Sigfrid, her eyes never off him.*) Brandy never changed the color of anything . . . except maybe my teeth. (*Then, directly to him.*) That was disloyal, Sigfrid. That was a *betrayal*.

LAKME'S VOICE. So that's how you want it?

RUBY. *Yes*, that's how I want it! (*Then, again to Sigfrid.*) I don't *like* betrayals. I don't *need* betrayals. I *won't have* betrayals!

LAKME'S VOICE. (*More confused than ever.*) With *brandy?* You want it with *brandy?*

RUBY. YES, I WANT IT WITH BRANDY!

LAKME'S VOICE. (*The little snot.*) I'm sorry, Ruby, but we haven't studied "Tanking up Mommy" yet. That's a *high school* course. Elementary school children aren't supposed to *know* about things like that.

RUBY. (*The rage always directed at Sigfrid.*) Well they *should!*

LAKME'S VOICE. Take it up with the PTA. Parent Termites Association, if they let you in.

RUBY. (*Directly to Sigfrid again.*) *Some* people we don't humiliate each other in front of. Those are the *rules* . . . the way things are *done!* . . . and I think you'd just better *stick* to them.

LAKME'S VOICE. (*Another sally.*) Parent Tarantulas! (*Ruby snaps off the intercom. The room is silent. She paces again: tense, irritable. Then:*)

RUBY. There *is* a draft. *Did* someone leave that door open or didn't they? (*Again no one answers; then, going to Sigfrid and taking his lowered face in her hands, utterly without guile or a trace of anger.*) Hey, I love you, prince. (*She kisses him on the forehead.*) No matter what I say . . . although I meant it . . . I do love you.

SIGFRID. (*Anguished, trying to explain to her.*) You went too far this time, Ruby. Your Message went too far.

RUBY. (*A vocal caress; stroking his brow.*) "Love which neither nurtures the receiver nor lays fallow the sender but will suffice for each."

SIGFRID. You *said* it, Ruby. This time you *said* it.

RUBY. (*Always soothing him.*) What, Sigfrid, what did Ruby say?

SIGFRID. How it is! You *acknowledged* it . . . the way we live. You can't do that, Ruby. You'll wreck it . . . the set-up . . . *everything*. It all falls apart then.

RUBY. (*Oblivious to the real cause of Sigfrid's anguish, she continues to stroke and soothe him.*) Sshh, *caro*, sshh!

SIGFRID. (*Deliberately, wanting her to understand this.*) There is a line, Ruby . . . I thought you knew about it, but I guess not . . . a *line* . . . a line about *that* thin between making a go of it anymore or not. And it's not easy, Ruby. *God* no! A line that holds everything together for us down here in this stinking basement. And that's what it is: a stinking hole in the ground . . . a goddamn *prison!* . . . no matter *how* much we'd like to pretend that it isn't. A *line* . . . and that's *all* it is but it's the only thing left us between . . . what? . . . *that thing out there . . . each other?* It's our *life*line, Ruby . . . what we hold on to. *Paper-thin*, I know that . . . *transparent*, you just saw right through it . . . but it's *there* and, oh *Christ*, how very much we need it. So *please*, please Ruby, don't ever play hopscotch with it like that again . . . don't cross over it and think you'll land safely on the other side . . . don't . . . you *won't*, Ruby . . . you *can't* . . . don't.

RUBY. (*Almost a murmur.*) How beautiful he is . . .

SIGFRID (*He has tried to reach her.*) Ruby!

RUBY. . . . how very beautiful.

SIGFRID. (*Defeated, an edge creeping into his voice now.*) Don't you *understand*, Ruby? Don't you understand *anything?*

RUBY. A prince! My son is a *prince!*

SIGFRID. Or maybe you just don't *listen*. Maybe you don't listen so you won't have to trouble yourself. So you can *prattle!*

RUBY. (*Making light.*) Oh, Sigfrid!

SIGFRID. You *do*, Ruby. You've started to *prattle! Listen* to yourself. Listen to *someone* for a change.

RUBY. (*Attempting to defend herself now.*) Grandfa and I were only—

SIGFRID. Grandfa has nothing to do with it! Are you *deaf?* Didn't you *hear* what I just said? Don't you listen to *anyone?*

RUBY. Sigfrid, when you get like this—

SIGFRID. And *you!* How do *you* get? You rattle off a goddam Message like that and then come sailing in here like the Queen of Sheba!

RUBY. (*Desperately trying to take control of the situation.*) That's who I am. The Queen of Sheba!

SIGFRID. (*Not letting her: grabbing her wrist maybe; hard, in her ear.*) The *Message!* You went over the *line* with your goddam Message!

RUBY. (*Writhing.*) It was . . . I didn't *mean* to, Sigfrid!

SIGFRID. (*Merciless.*) It won't *work* for us down here that way, Ruby! It *can't!* It's not *strong* enough! *We're* not strong enough! And you *accepted* it. You gave *in* to it! THAT *IS* HOW WE LIVE!

RUBY. (*Breaking.*) I was alone, Sigfrid! . . . *alone!* . . . the *strain* sometimes . . . the *strain!*

SIGFRID. Don't tell me about the—! (*He breaks off as Lakme enters with the coffee.*)

LAKME. (*Brightly.*) Eccomi!

RUBY. (*Low, to Sigfrid.*) The *strain!*

LAKME. (*Taking a look over Grandfa's shoulder as she passes him.*) "Message to the—?" Hey, now Grandfa's started one! That ought to be something. (*She gives the coffee to Ruby, who has come back to her chair.*) Here, slurp. (*Then, suddenly flinging her arms around Ruby's neck and kissing her on the cheek.*) Oh how much I love my Ruby! Nobody loves their Ruby as much as I love mine.

RUBY. (*Responding warmly, almost desperately.*) And my Lakme!
How I love my little Lakme! (*Then, hugging Lakme close to her
bosom, but with her eyes directly on Sigfrid.*) Both my children
. . . such beautiful children . . . so *strong* . . . so . . . *right.*

LAKME. (*Seeking and finding a little girl's comfort in Ruby's
arms.*) That was a sad Message to the World, wasn't it? The
saddest one you ever made. They're not usually so . . . sad.

RUBY. (*Holding Lakme close, but really an appeal to Sigfrid.*)
But not to frighten you . . . no! . . . never that.

LAKME. But I *do* get so frightened sometimes, Ruby . . . when I
wake up and I haven't left a light on and my room is dark . . . I
get so frightened!

RUBY. (*In a soft voice, almost to herself.*) We all do, Lakme. We
all do.

LAKME. I imagine things . . . terrible things! . . . and I hear them,
too! . . . noises . . . noises I don't know about . . . and I see them
sometimes! . . . forms! . . . shadows! . . . everything buzzing! . . .
swirling!

RUBY. Yes, Lakme . . . yes.

LAKME. Is that why, Ruby? Is that why you made the Message?

RUBY. (*Not a direct answer because it is Sigfrid she is trying to
reach.*) In the morning . . . early . . . when you're sleeping . . .
the four of you . . . and I'm alone . . . sitting here . . . thinking
. . . waiting for it to end . . . the night . . . another night and it
has not yet happened . . . *then* . . . when it's quiet . . . no sounds
. . . no sounds at all . . . I try to . . . *understand* . . . understand
what has happened to us . . . why . . . and sometimes I have pre-
monitions . . . tremors . . . not heart tremors . . . nothing like that
. . . but *soul* tremors . . . tremors of the *soul* . . . when the very
earth seems to rise up . . . hover a moment, suspended . . . somehow suspended . . . and then fall back. (*And this directly to
him.*) Sigfrid knows these moments, too.

LAKME. (*In answer to this.*) Yes! When I was little and the wind
blew and there was thunder.

RUBY. (*With a soft smile.*) Yes, when you were little and the wind
blew and there was thunder. And Sigfrid! Especially Sigfrid.
How he howled when the shutters banged and the thunder
clapped!

LAKME. But it's not that way now . . . not anymore . . . not when we're together.

RUBY. Remember, Sigfrid? Remember those nights? The howling, the hiding under the bed, the— (*Sigfrid bolts to his feet and goes out the door Stage Right, banging it behind him.*) It was the *strain*, Sigfrid!

LAKME. What's the matter with *him?* Everybody's so moody in this family.

RUBY. (*Getting up, moving away from Lakme and with a note of irritation in her voice.*) That door *is* open.

LAKME. (*Exasperated.*) Oh *no*, Ruby! Not you, too, now.

RUBY. Go upstairs and close it.

LAKME. Just because Sigfrid's in a lousy mood, *you* don't have to—

RUBY. (*Making herself understood.*) Someone's left that door open!

LAKME. (*Relieved, she thought Ruby was in a bad mood.*) Oh *that.* Well of course it is.

RUBY. Then go upstairs and close it.

LAKME. (*Peevish; it's a ridiculous request.*) But *why?* It's not even time yet. Wait 'til curfew.

RUBY. I don't care what time it is. I don't like that door left open.

LAKME. Ruby!

RUBY. *Anytime!*

LAKME. (*A quarrel is building.*) Well it *is.* It's open *lots.* We just don't bother to tell you. You can get so hysterical over *nothing*, Ruby.

RUBY. This isn't nothing!

LAKME. Usually it's open right up until the last minute. You only *think* it's closed.

RUBY. Thank you. I hadn't known that. I'll take care of it *myself* from now on.

LAKME. *That'll* be the day.

RUBY. (*Lakme has scored a point.*) I'm asking you to go up there and close it.

LAKME. It's not *time*, yet, Ruby! How are we ever going to get any fresh air down here if we keep that door closed all the time? Answer *that!* We'd all suffocate if we left it up to you.

RUBY. (*As her desire becomes more insistent, her tone of voice becomes more desperate.*) I don't want that door left open.

LAKME. (*The voice getting meaner; victory is sweet.*) People need *air*, Ruby. They have to *breathe*. *Some* people, that is. *Normal* people. I don't *know* about opera queens. I don't know what they use for oxygen. Arias, probably. Love duets!

RUBY. *Please!*

LAKME. (*Giving no respite.*) Of course we could cut little gills in our necks and then flood this place and live like fish. I suppose *then* you'd be happy. All of us turned into a bunch of *fishes!* (*A pause; then:*)

RUBY. (*Evenly.*) It's simply that I feel safer when I know that door is closed . . . that's all I meant . . . that I would feel *safer*.

LAKME. But it can't *happen* until after curfew!

RUBY. They *think*.

LAKME. Well it can't.

RUBY. They only *think!*

LAKME. (*Stubborn, but on less firm ground.*) They're almost *certain*. It's never happened yet. With all the millions of people killed *after* curfew, you'd think one . . . just one, after all these years . . . would've gotten it *before* if it was *ever* going to happen then. (*Short pause.*) Besides, even when it *does* happ— . . . I mean, *if* it ever happens . . . how do we know it won't come right through that door and down those stairs? Right *through!* How do we *know?*

RUBY. Because the government—

LAKME. (*Furious at herself, the situation, and the tears welling up within her.*) The government! What do *they* know? What does anyone *know*? (*Short pause; then, in a sudden outburst of rage:*) What about last week, Ruby? Remember *that* little incident? You turned the fence on at noon! At *noon!* If that dog hadn't put his leg up against it to *pee*, Sigfrid and I would've *both* gotten it! You were afraid, so you turned the fence on at *noon* and nearly *killed* us! You've gotten so afraid, Ruby, you'll *make* it happen! You'll *kill* us, you're so frightened!

RUBY. (*Who has regained her composure, but with some effort.*) Are you going to go upstairs and close that door or not?

LAKME. (*Wild defiance.*) NO!

RUBY. I see.

LAKME. Why don't you go up there and do it yourself, Ruby? Or are you too *scared* to go back up once you've come down?

RUBY. (*An indefinite threat.*) *All* right, Miss Lakme, *all* right!

LAKME. (*Moving in for the kill now.*) You *are* too scared, aren't you? Hunh? *Aren't* you?

RUBY. I think you're going to regret this little interview.

LAKME. Oh *am* I now?

RUBY. Yes, *are* you now!

LAKME. Do tell! Do tell!

RUBY. I *tell!* I *tell!*

LAKME. You don't say!

RUBY. I *say!* I *say* all right—! (*Disgusted, she cuts herself off when she realizes she has allowed the argument to degenerate into childish bitchiness. Then, turning in her chair, she addresses Grandfa, her only escape.*) What time are they coming for you, Grandfa?

LAKME. (*At once, realizing she has lost the advantage and determined to pursue the argument to the finish.*) How? How am I going to regret it? You going to have Fa *spank* me? Then first you'll have to *wake* him and I doubt even *you* could wake Fa up.

RUBY. (*Flaring briefly.*) I've *tried.* You know how I've tried!

LAKME. (*Unrelenting.*) Or are you going to cut my allowance off? Go ahead! Buy your own booze for a change. Get *Sigfrid* to buy all those stupid movie magazines.

RUBY. (*Losing this round, too.*) They . . . they *help* me!

LAKME. (*Like machine gun fire.*) How *else?* How *else* am I going to regret it? Go ahead. Tell me. Because I don't think I'm going to regret it at *all.* You're too scared to make *anyone* regret *anything.* You're even scared of *us,* I bet. *Aren't* you, Ruby, *aren't* you?

RUBY. (*Blurting an ugly, painful truth.*) Yes, if that makes you any happier, *yes!*

LAKME. (*Still not satisfied with the blood she has drawn.*) You never *do* anything, you never *go* anywhere, you haven't been out of this house in . . . *years,* practically! All you do anymore is sleep in there in the daytime and then come out here and sit up all night.

RUBY. (*The anger mounting now: the confession of fear should have mollified Lakme.*) That will do, Lakme.

LAKME. And look at yourself! Have you done that lately . . . *looked* at yourself? You used to be beautiful. You *were* a queen . . . a *real* queen. But *now!* And your mind! *That's* going, too. You used to *talk*, Ruby . . . make *sense* . . . really *talk*. And people would *listen* to you . . . *could* listen to you. But that was *before*. Before the booze. Before the movie magazines and junk. Before all day in bed with a bottle and a copy of *Screen Stars*. Why don't you get a *real* screen star in there with you for a change? *Someone!* You haven't even had *Fa* in bed with you since . . . since *me* probably!

RUBY. (*Out of control.*) I SAID THAT WILL DO!

LAKME. (*Quite matter-of-factly.*) You've gone to pot, mother. That's what— (*A buzzer sounds, loud, drowning Lakme out. It is a harsh, ugly, rasping noise. Ruby chokes back a scream. Her knuckles whiten, she is holding the arms of her chair so tight. Lakme only marks time, ready to resume speaking the moment the buzzer is silent. Five seconds of this terrible sound. And then utter stillness.*)

LAKME. (*At once.*) That's what I think. You've gone to pot. (*Then, getting up:*) Come on. Fifteen minutes. He'll be here. We'd better start getting ready. (*Ruby sits trembling, whimpering almost.*) That was just the warning buzzer, Ruby! It's fifteen minutes 'til curfew! That's exactly what I was talking about! (*She goes to Ruby, embraces her and continues with enormous tenderness.*) Look, Ruby, I'll close the door. I'll turn the fence on. We'll be all safe and sound again. But *after*. After curfew. Honest I will. Even *Grandfa* wants the door closed then and he's so old he might as *well* be . . . dead! But he still wants that door closed. Don't you, Grandfa? (*Grandfa looks up from his journal, growls at her, and then resumes writing.*) You just can't be nice to that man. (*Then, to Ruby, with a little laugh.*) Besides, goose, if we closed that door now our little guest might not think we were down here and trot right back where he came from. Or what if he ran into the fence while it was on? He'd end up like that dog . . . *sizzled!* That would be great . . . just great! An evening without someone! Just the five of us! You know what happened the last time we tried *that*.

RUBY. (*Very low, toneless, a private memory.*) We nearly killed each other.

LAKME. You're telling me! And we certainly don't want *that* to happen again. Now, kiss-and-make-up, Ruby.

RUBY. (*The same.*) Sigfrid actually had his hands around your throat. I almost let him.

LAKME. (*Demanding.*) *Ruby!* Kiss-and-make-up! Kiss-and-make—! (*Ruby slaps her sharply across the cheek.*)

RUBY. Kiss-and-make-up, Lakme. Kiss-and-make-up. (*Long pause. No one moves. Then, breaking the silence, Sigfrid's voice on the intercom.*)

SIGFRID'S VOICE. Ruby? . . . Ruby?

RUBY. (*In a strange, almost monotone voice which will seem all the more sinister because of its deadly calm. And all the while she talks to Sigfrid, she never once takes her eyes from Lakme.*) Yes, Sigfrid, Ruby's here.

SIGFRID'S VOICE. I'm all right now, Ruby.

RUBY. Yes, *caro*, yes.

LAKME. (*Low, her eyes locked with Ruby's.*) I knew you'd do that.

SIGFRID'S VOICE. Are *you*, Ruby? All right?

RUBY. Oh yes . . . yes. (*And with slow, deliberate movements . . . almost like a priest performing some sacred rite . . . she loosens the hairband. Masses of hair tumble to her shoulders. This is the beginning of* Ruby's transformation.)

LAKME. (*Low again.*) Sooner or later . . . I knew you would.

SIGFRID'S VOICE. I'm sorry I blew up like that. But sometimes . . .

RUBY. Yes . . . I know . . .

SIGFRID'S VOICE. What you said . . . about the strain . . .

RUBY. (*Combing her hair out with long, slow strokes.*) There *is* no strain . . . not now . . . in fifteen minutes there will be no strain.

SIGFRID'S VOICE. His name is Clarence.

RUBY. Clarence.

LAKME. Clarence. (*A pause.*)

RUBY. We are strong, children. In some ways we are strong.

SIGFRID'S VOICE. Clarence.

LAKME. Our guest.

RUBY. It's only *before* that we are not so strong.

LAKME. Clarence.

SIGFRID'S VOICE. Our game.

RUBY. But soon . . . in fifteen minutes . . . *then* . . . then we are strong.

SIGFRID'S VOICE. Clarence . . . our guest.

LAKME. Clarence . . . our game.

RUBY. Fifteen minutes and we will be strong again. (*A pause.*)

SIGFRID'S VOICE. Lakme! You'd better get ready.

LAKME. (*Getting to her feet.*) Coming. You need any help, Ruby?

RUBY. (*Always in that strange voice, as if she were talking to her-self.*) And if we are without charity, we suckle the bitter root of its absence . . .

LAKME. Hey! That's it.

RUBY. . . . wherefrom we shall draw the sustenance to destroy you. (*Short pause.*) Clarence.

LAKME. You *do* remember it.

RUBY. There's only one trouble, Sigfrid . . . just one. They always *stay* the night. They never leave. They always *stay*.

SIGFRID'S VOICE. I know.

RUBY. They never . . . go *out* there.

LAKME. (*On her way out.*) I think I know what you're talking about.

RUBY. *Why*, Sigfrid, why do we let them *stay* the night?

SIGFRID'S VOICE. You always said . . .

LAKME. (*At the door.*) I *think* I do. (*She is gone.*)

SIGFRID'S VOICE. . . . . not to go too far.

RUBY. I did?

SIGFRID'S VOICE. We agreed on it. The three of us.

RUBY. I see. (*A pause.*)

SIGFRID'S VOICE. Ruby?

RUBY. Yes.

SIGFRID'S VOICE. What are you thinking?

RUBY. That we might.

SIGFRID'S VOICE. Try?

RUBY. Yes.

SIGFRID'S VOICE. I don't know.

RUBY. It's a possibility.

SIGFRID'S VOICE. Yes.

RUBY. That way we would know . . . for once and for all we would know.

SIGFRID'S VOICE. Yes.

RUBY. It would serve some . . . *purpose*.

SIGFRID'S VOICE. Yes.

RUBY. Clarence. (*A pause.*)

SIGFRID'S VOICE. We'll see, Ruby. All right? We'll *see*. (*Sounds of a slight scuffle are heard over the intercom.*) Dammit, Lakme!

LAKME'S VOICE. Well it's *mine!*

SIGFRID'S VOICE. Give it to me!

LAKME'S VOICE. Oh piss on you! (*The intercom snaps off. Ruby sits combing out her hair. A moment of silence. Then Grandfa begins to move in on her, slowly at first but then picking up speed.*)

GRANDFA. (*Circling her chair, needling like a mosquito.*) Who's it going to be, Ruby? Who's the victim for tonight? I know what goes on in here after I go to bed. I *know.* Thank God I never had to *watch.* Thank God for *that.* I thought I'd seen plenty in my time, but *this . . .* what you people do.

RUBY. (*Lipsticking her mouth a brilliant red.*) There are things, Grandfa, things which you do not understand.

GRANDFA. I understand corruption . . . decay! I understand *that!*

RUBY. (*With studied disinterest as she continues making up.*) Do you?

GRANDFA. I can *smell* it, woman! Smell it! There's a stench in this house. A stench of putrefying *rot.* Human *rot! . . . people! . . . flesh!*

RUBY. Things which you do not understand.

GRANDFA. (*Not pausing.*) And it's all here! Written down! The truth! Everything!

RUBY. Your *novel,* Grandfa? Are you referring to your novel?

GRANDFA. It's not a novel! It's a chronicle! How it was! I wrote it down. I remembered it. The truth. "Time Was: A Chronicle."

RUBY. But your book is full of lies, Grandfa. We don't know those people. They're fictitious . . . fabrications. They never existed. Chronicles are meant to tell the *truth.* No, dear, you've written a *novel . . .* a book of *lies.*

GRANDFA. (*Finding himself on the defensive.*) You've *made* it that way. There was a time—

RUBY. (*With great force; she has no intention of continuing this conversation.*) WAS! (*Short pause.*) There *was* a time, Grandfa . . . *was.* (*Another pause; Ruby puts the final touches to her make-up. The Transformation is nearly complete.*)

GRANDFA. (*After a while; very sadly.*) It wasn't meant to be this way.

RUBY. (*Rather distantly.*) Perhaps Grandfa . . . just *perhaps.*

GRANDFA. (*His voice growing fainter.*) Things weren't meant to be this way.

RUBY. But they *are, caro* . . . they *are*.

GRANDFA. (*Fainter still.*) People weren't meant to be this way.

RUBY. (*With a sad mockery in her voice.*) How, Grandfa, how were people *meant* to be? (*Grandfa scarcely tries to answer her question. Ruby takes out a large and fantastic wig and settles it on her head. Facing Grandfa fully she repeats her question with a bitterness turned more against herself than him.*) Tell us, Grandfa. Tell us how people were *meant* to be. For we should dearly like to know. (*The wig is in place. The Transformation is complete now. The Ruby before us is utterly different from the "anonymous" woman of her entrance. What we see now is garish, hard, almost obscene. There is a pause. The silence is broken by Fa crying out in his sleep.*)

FA. (*In great terror; he is having a nightmare.*) WEST! . . . IT'S MOVING WEST!

GRANDFA. (*Trying to answer Ruby now.*) Not like . . . not like you.

FA. RUN! . . . RUN FOR YOUR LIVES!

GRANDFA. Like . . . like here . . . (*He holds up his Chronicle.*) . . . as you were . . .

RUBY. (*With the same sad mockery.*) Imperfect? . . . weak? . . . afraid?

GRANDFA. (*Low, but spitting it out.*) Human, woman . . . *human*.

RUBY. (*The beginning of a wild laugh.*) As you *portrayed* us, Grandfa, in your funny, funny book? Your *novel*? You want us to behave like *that*? (*POW! A rubber-tipped toy dart has been fired through the Stage Right door hitting Grandfa squarely in the back of the head. The Chronicle falls from his hand. He does not turn to see who fired the dart. He knows. Lakme bursts into the room. She is in the highest spirits, dressed in her Green Hornet costume and ready for Clarence.*)

LAKME. *Sic semper tyrannis!* (*Then, rushing towards Grandfa, doing a little dance around him.*) The Green Hornet! Bzzzzzzz! Bzzzzzzzz! (*Grandfa turns away from her and moves slowly towards the Stage Right door.*)

RUBY. (*Calling after him, at the end of a laughing jag.*) Why is it, Grandfa, why is it that you can be so quiet at times . . . like a mouse . . . a knitting mouse . . . and at other times so noisy? Why is that?

LAKME. Hey, Grandfa! Aren't you going to chase me? Come on, try to run me down! (*Then, to Ruby, truly perplexed.*) What's the matter with *him*?

RUBY. Your Grandfa is suffering from an acute attack of how-it-was.

LAKME. Oh, he's off on *that* tack again! (*Then, stooping and retrieving the Chronicle.*) Hey, Bede! You dropped your Chronicle, Bede! (*Then, again to Ruby.*) The Venerable Bede. I know about him from school. He wrote chronicles, too.

RUBY. But your Grandfa is a novelist. The oldest first novelist in captivity.

LAKME. (*Annoyed: she wants to finish this.*) Please, Ruby, *please.* And you know why he was venerable? Because he was old . . . just like Grandfa. That's the only reason he was venerable.

RUBY. That's a very good reason.

LAKME. (*Bitchy.*) Well of course I wouldn't know about that . . . *age.* Besides, what's so venerable about being old? Just a lot of blue veins on your legs and gums. That's all old is. Hell, that's no accomplishment.

RUBY. Lakme!

LAKME. (*Mincing.*) *Cripes,* that's no accomplishment. (*Short pause.*) Ruby, are you venerable?

RUBY. *Taci, fanciulla, taci!*

LAKME. (*Clapping both hands over her mouth.*) Umph! (*It might be remembered at this point that everyone, including Sigfrid, who now enters through the Stage Right door, is in the sunniest of dispositions. Joy, for the moment, is abounding.*)

SIGFRID. (*He is dressed entirely in black; he calls over his shoulder to Grandfa who has already exited through the same door.*) Cheer up, Grandfa. It's your last night here. (*Then, to the others.*) I spied a tear on Grandfa's cheeklet. One large, goopy tear. Right here.

RUBY. Who would have thought the old man to have so much salt in him? (*Sigfrid has joined Ruby while Lakme, to one side, begins to thumb through Grandfa's Chronicle.*)

LAKME. (*Reading from the Chronicle.*) "Message to the World." That's all he wrote: "Message to the World." And then it's blank.

SIGFRID. How do I look?

RUBY. Like hell. Look how you stick out there. You used to have such a firm stomach, Sigfrid. I'd never seen such firmness. Whatever happened to it? You're all soft around there now.

SIGFRID. (*Glumly regarding his waistline; maybe there is a hint, just a hint, of flabbiness.*) Well . . . your bazooms have dropped.

RUBY. Well of course they have! There's no one I especially want to keep them *up* for. And that's the only thing that keeps them up there: will-power! . . . sheer concentration. So naturally they're drooping from the lack of it. They're probably piqued. Well wouldn't you feel neglected? (*She addresses her bosom.*) Isn't that what you're doing down there . . . sulking? . . . isn't it? (*Sigfrid, still concerned with the real or imaginary bulk at his waistline, has begun a set of strenuous sit-ups. Lakme continues with the Chronicle.*)

LAKME. (*It doesn't make any sense to her.*) "There is a *line*, Ruby . . . a line about *that* thin." What is this stuff? (*She turns to another place in the Chronicle.*)

RUBY. What about *me*? How do I look? Apart from my fallen grapes, that is.

SIGFRID. (*Always exercising.*) You look . . .

RUBY. *Attention!*

SIGFRID. . . . Rubyesque. Why don't you go put your costume on?

RUBY. I thought you told me it was going to be one of *those* nights.

SIGFRID. It is.

RUBY. Considering how *long* it's going to be before you need me . . . considering the hour *wait* while you two play Boy Scouts . . . considering what's going to *happen* as soon as he gets here . . . considering all *that*, I don't see what the rush is.

SIGFRID. Well while you're *waiting*, sweetheart—

RUBY. (*Perfectly aware she is interrupting.*) Sigfrid, it just occurred to me! Whenever it's a girl, you introduce her to me before you go in there, and when it's a boy you don't want him to meet me until *after*. Why is that?

SIGFRID. It's the way things are *done*, Ruby.

RUBY. Oh?

SIGFRID. It's a heterosexual society we live in.

RUBY. Preposterous!

SIGFRID. I'm sorry, Ruby, but it *is*.

RUBY. Well . . . then I don't see the connection between before and after. (*Short pause.*) Oh yes I do. Oh *yes* I do!

SIGFRID. As I was saying, *madre* . . . while you're in your little boudoir *getting-up* . . . while you're in there *considering* the agonizing *wait* . . . why don't you consider slipping into that *walkure* outfit. You know, the one with the cast iron boobies and the winged helmet.

RUBY. (*Correcting.*) Wingèd. And thank you all the same.

SIGFRID. Ruby! You look so feminine in steel.

RUBY. No! It *chafes.*

SIGFRID. (*The last sit-up.*) Suit yourself.

RUBY. Oh! I *will!* I *always* do. (*Sigfrid gets up, paces a moment.*)

LAKME. (*Looking up from the Chronicle.*) Hey, Sigfrid! This part's all about you. He even wrote down some of those poems you used to write. (*She delves into the Chronicle again with renewed interest.*)

RUBY. I don't think he's coming, Sigfrid. I think our little guest has stood you-know-who up.

SIGFRID. He'll *be* here, Ruby.

RUBY. You're *sure?*

SIGFRID. I *know.*

LAKME. "Sigfrid is a sickly child, prone to respiratory ailments. Sometimes his face and little hands turn an alarming blue. Ruby is heart-sick." Did you used to be *blue,* Sigfrid? I didn't know that. (*No one responds; she continues reading.*)

RUBY. But *when?* According to *my* watch—

SIGFRID. (*Checking his own.*) Christ! Why didn't you tell me it was so late?

RUBY. The warning buzzer, Sigfrid . . . nearly fifteen minutes ago . . . I can't imagine you didn't hear it.

SIGFRID. (*Getting into a foul mood; maybe Clarence isn't coming.*) Dammit, Clarence.

RUBY. (*Her resignation is calculated to annoy him.*) Well . . . I think you'd just better run upstairs and lock up for the night. Turn the fence on. It's obvious he's not coming.

SIGFRID. I said he'll *be* here and he *will!*

RUBY. Two minutes, Sigfrid, two minutes 'til curfew. (*A pause; Sigfrid paces, the inner tension rising. Ruby watches with some amusement.*)

LAKME. (*Again a voice in the silence.*) "We read Shakespeare together in the late afternoon. Sigfrid's enthusiasm is boundless. He has the makings of a poet. A poet's soul." *You*, Sigfrid, a *soul*? Hah!

RUBY. (*Deliberately provoking.*) Who is this person, Sigfrid? Who is this person who isn't coming?

SIGFRID. His name is Clarence.

RUBY. I *know* what his name is. What I'm asking you is something *about* him. Some nights there is a *link*. Is there a *link* with Clarence?

SIGFRID. (*Impatient, always looking at his watch.*) The incident about the slide.

RUBY. *That* Clarence?

SIGFRID. *That* Clarence.

RUBY. (*Smiling strangely.*) Well . . . in that case . . . what we said . . . what we said about letting them *stay* the night . . . assuming they ever *come* . . .

SIGFRID. (*Curt.*) No.

RUBY. (*Starting to laugh.*) . . . instead of going *out* there? . . .

SIGFRID. No I said.

RUBY. (*Her laughter mounting.*) Why, Sigfrid . . . murder? . . . would it be murder?

SIGFRID. (*Moving away from her, about to explode, literally counting the seconds till curfew.*) Come on, Clarence, come *on!*

LAKME. (*Approaching to show him something in the Chronicle.*) Sigfrid—

SIGFRID. (*Pushing her away from him.*) Shut up, Lakme!

LAKME. (*Indignant.*) What did I do?

SIGFRID. Jesus, Clarence, *Jesus!*

LAKME. (*Loud and mean; fixing Sigfrid's wagon.*) You want to hear some poetry everybody? You want to hear some of Sigfrid's *poetry?*

SIGFRID. (*Immediately aware of what she is up to.*) Cut it, Lakme!

LAKME. (*Fearless.*) We'd forgotten, Sigfrid. We'd forgotten what a poetic *genius* you were!

SIGFRID. I said *cut* it!

LAKME. (*Reading.*) "A sky, a blue sky, the eagle soars."

SIGFRID. (*Going after her.*) Give that to me.

LAKME. (*Dodging him.*) "High soars, high soars the eagle." What kind of sores, Shakespeare? Big pussy ones?

SIGFRID. GIVE ME THAT BOOK!

LAKME. "Can I soar? Can I soar, too?" Suits us, Shelley. Take a big flying-leap right off the roof!

SIGFRID. You goddam little bitch!

LAKME. You were some poet, Sigfrid. Some poet! I mean this stuff is a real eye-sore. A real "I soar." You were a *Shelley!* You *are* a—! (*His hands are on her throat. Sharp silence.*)

RUBY. (*She has been in a private reverie during the quarrel and is coming out of it now. There is still a smile on her lips.*) Murder, Sigfrid? Would it be—? (*She turns, aware of the silence; then, at once:*) Sigfrid! (*Short silence, no one moves, the doorbell sounds.*) Allons, mes enfants, il faut commencer. (*Short silence, again no one moves, again the doorbell sounds.*) Il faut commencer! (*Sigfrid slowly takes his hands from Lakme's throat. An ugly moment of silence between them.*)

SIGFRID. (*Terrifying.*) Don't you ever . . . ever . . . EVER! do that again.

LAKME. (*A threat.*) That *hurt*, Sigfrid, that really *hurt.* (*The doorbell again, insistent this time.*)

RUBY. (*Cutting them apart with her voice.*) The door, Sigfrid! The game is at the *door!*

SIGFRID. Get the camera ready.

LAKME. I'll *kill* him!

SIGFRID. (*About to go upstairs.*) And Ruby, do it *right* this time.

RUBY. (*Again with the same strange, cruel mockery.*) Murder, Sigfrid? Would it be murder? (*Sigfrid has disappeared up the stairs. Ruby and Lakme are on their way out. The curfew buzzer sounds again; this time louder than before. Ruby and Lakme freeze. Ruby covers her ears wtih her hands. Five seconds of this terrible noise. Then the silence. Ruby moves quickly towards the Stage Right door.*)

LAKME. (*Following.*) I'll *kill* him! (*Ruby is out.*) Ruby? What's the matter, Ruby? (*Now Lakme is gone, too. The stage is empty. No sounds, nothing moves. Then, from upstairs, the sound of an enomous iron door slamming shut. Reverberations. Then silence again. Footsteps are heard and a moment later Clarence is seen*) *coming down the stairs. He carries a large placard, the type that pickets carry, which reads: "There Is Something Out There."*

CLARENCE. (*With a nervous laugh.*) Whew! That was close. The bus . . . (*His voice trails off as he realizes he is alone on the stairs. Then, turning, he calls back up.*) Sigfrid? . . . (*As he turns, we can read the other side of his placard: "We shall prevail." The curtain is beginning to fall.*) Gee, it's nice down here . . . very nice. (*Clarence is into the room. Sigfrid is heard on the stairs. And now the curtain is down.*)

ACT TWO

At Rise: The room is the same. As before, the lighting is white and brilliant. Clarence's placard, the "There Is Something Out There" side facing us, rests against the wall near the Stage Left door.

Clarence is alone in the room. He wears a woman's dress, stockings (fallen to the ankles) and shoes. But there is no mistaking him. We are perfectly aware it is a male in the wrong attire. We only wonder how he got there. His uneasiness in this strange and empty room is immediately apparent. His movements are tense and fidgety. He wanders.

A long silence. And then a loud snortle from Fa in his chair. Clarence stiffens, retreats a little, pauses. Another snortle.

Clarence is edging towards the chair. He is there. He looks down at Fa, hesitates, bites his lip and then throws caution to the winds.

CLARENCE. I'm Clarence. (*No response.*) My name is Clarence.

FA. (*Giggling foolishly.*) Hello, Miss Nigeria! . . . hello there!

CLARENCE. No, *Clarence.*

FA. Bye-bye, Grandfa! . . . come and kiss me, Grandfa!

CLARENCE. Sir?

FA. (*Almost a mumble.*) West . . . moving west . . . unh . . . (*Fa lapses into a deep sleep. Snoring sounds.*)

CLARENCE. (*After a while; thoroughly miserable.*) Oh this is dreadful . . . Sigfrid! (*And at once Grandfa comes through the Stage Right door. He has a suitcase.*)

GRANDFA. (*A parody of senility.*) Well well well. Looky here.

CLARENCE. Good evening.

GRANDFA. Fa! Wake up! Fa! We got company. Something of Sigfrid's. Something Sigfrid dragged home.

CLARENCE. I'm Clarence. My name is Clarence.

GRANDFA. Who?

CLARENCE. Clarence.

GRANDFA. You sure?

CLARENCE. Sir?

GRANDFA. Nice name.

CLARENCE. Thank you. (*Pause.*) It's English.

GRANDFA. What's that? You're English.

CLARENCE. No, my *name*. *Clarence* is English.

GRANDFA. And you? What are you? Or shouldn't I ask that question? (*He laughs wildly. Clarence manages a weak smile.*) You're the guest.

CLARENCE. Sir?

GRANDFA. The guest. You.

CLARENCE. Well I'm *a* guest. I don't know if I'm *the* guest.

GRANDFA. You are.

CLARENCE. I'm a friend. A friend of Sigfrid's.

GRANDFA. Ah yes, Sigfrid. Fine lad, fine lad.

CLARENCE. Yes, isn't he?

GRANDFA. Lakme, too.

CLARENCE. Lakme?

GRANDFA. His sister. Fine lad, fine lad.

CLARENCE. Fine *lad?*

GRANDFA. And let's not forget Ruby. Fine lad, fine lad.

CLARENCE. Ruby?

GRANDFA. Their mother. Fine lads, all of 'em. You, too. Fine, fine, lads and laddies.

CLARENCE. (*Taking the suitcase and setting it down.*) Here, let me take that for you.

GRANDFA. Thank you, thank you kindly.

CLARENCE. You're taking a trip?

GRANDFA. Off to the looney-bin, first thing in the morning.

CLARENCE. The *where?*

GRANDFA. The looney-bin. Bin for loons. I'm a loon.

CLARENCE. You're joking, of course.

GRANDFA. I don't know. I suppose that's why I'm a loon. (*He laughs his wild laugh again. Clarence moves away from him, ever so slightly.*)

CLARENCE. Gee, it's nice down here.

GRANDFA. We like it. It's nice and homey.

CLARENCE. That's what's so wonderful about it. It doesn't look at all like a basement. It's so . . . so cheerful.

GRANDFA. Well, we've tried to brighten it up some. A little blood, a little spleen.

CLARENCE. (*Trying for firmer ground.*) I guess you're Sigfrid's grandfather.

GRANDFA. (*Enormously funny.*) Who'd you think I was? His grandmother?

CLARENCE. (*Laughing, too.*) Well not *really!*

GRANDFA. Oh, you're a droll one, you are.

CLARENCE. (*Reckless.*) Of course you might've been his *aunt!* (*The laughter is raucous, slightly hysterical.*)

GRANDFA. Or his auntie! (*Then, quickly, straight-faced.*) Nice dress you got there.

SIGFRID. (*Snapping to.*) Sir?

GRANDFA. Eh? Sorry, I don't hear too well.

CLARENCE. I suppose you're wondering why I have this dress on.

GRANDFA. (*Breezy.*) Oh no! No no!

CLARENCE. Well you see—

GRANDFA. Happens all the time around here. It's a regular little Junior League Sweden. If you're not one thing, you're the t'other.

CLARENCE. Sir?

GRANDFA. You don't hear so well yourself. (*Short pause.*) Florence.

CLARENCE. Sir? (*Then, correcting himself.*) I beg your pardon?

GRANDFA. Florence.

CLARENCE. No, Clarence.

GRANDFA. Funny name for a young man.

CLARENCE. Clarence?

GRANDFA. No, *Florence. Florence* is a funny name for a young man.

CLARENCE. Yes! . . . Yes it is. (*A pause.*) I'm *Clarence. My* name is—

GRANDFA. (*Crabbed.*) I *know* what your name is. I was *saying* that *Florence* is a funny name for a young man. If your name were *Florence*, it would be funny.

CLARENCE. Yes . . . I suppose it would . . . Florence . . . *my!*

GRANDFA. (*Sweetly.*) Nice frock, Clarence.

CLARENCE. Sir?

GRANDFA. (*Thundering.*) I SAID: NICE FROCK, CLARENCE!

CLARENCE. Oh.

GRANDFA. I haven't *seen* such a nice *frock* in a *long* time.

CLARENCE. Thank you.

GRANDFA. (*The goading becoming more obvious.*) Sort of a . . .
Florentine design.

CLARENCE. Yes. (*Then, aghast.*) Oh, but it's not *mine*.

GRANDFA. Finally!

CLARENCE. Sir?

GRANDFA. Nothing!

CLARENCE. I can't find mine.

GRANDFA. You lost it?

CLARENCE. Just vanished.

GRANDFA. You actually lost it?

CLARENCE. Poof!

GRANDFA. You actually managed to lose your *frock?*

CLARENCE. No, my *clothes*.

GRANDFA. (*Dead-pan.*) Oh.

CLARENCE. I lost my *clothes*.

GRANDFA. (*Daylight dawning.*) Ah! You lost your *clothes*.

CLARENCE. This is all I could find.

GRANDFA. Now I understand.

CLARENCE. I don't wear a frock . . . *dress!*

GRANDFA. Unless, of course, you've lost your *clothes. Then* you
wear a frock.

CLARENCE. Well I certainly hope you don't think I came *over* here
like this. A boy in a *dress!* That would be a sight!

GRANDFA. Oh yes! indeed it would . . . *is*, in fact.

CLARENCE. It's the craziest thing. Everything I had on when I got
here . . . gone! . . . just like that. I can't understand it. I've
looked everywhere.

GRANDFA. It's a careless generation, the younger one.

CLARENCE. My socks even.

GRANDFA. Well, you know the old saying: sooner or later we all end
up in our rightful clothes.

CLARENCE. No, I never heard that one.

GRANDFA. Well you trust in it. When all else fails, boy, trust in the
old sayings and they'll never let you down.

CLARENCE. (*With a smile and a shrug.*) Well you certainly can't
say I'm not a good sport about it. Most men would . . . (*His
voice trails off; he moves across the room.*)

GRANDFA. (*With a sadness now.*) Yes . . . they would . . . most men. (*Grandfa seems about to leave the room. Clarence with his back to him, continues:*)

CLARENCE. (*With a relaxed genuiness we have not seen yet.*) Talk about giving the Movement a bad name! We've got a major demonstration in the morning. I'm a squadron secretary; I'll be leading an entire platoon. That's all we need at a time like this: a squadron secretary in a dress! There's enough opposition to us as it is. (*Grandfa is listening to Clarence.*) Why people should be against anyone trying to make this a better world, I'll never know. But they *are*. We've actually been *hooted*. Physically attacked sometimes. It's awful when that happens.

GRANDFA. (*A sad realization. Softly. Almost to himself.*) You don't know what's going to happen, do you?

CLARENCE. (*Without pause.*) But *someone's* got to care about it ... the world ... and I'm willing to be one of them. Especially *now!* Sure it's out there and sure it gets a little closer every day and sure it's probably going to win out in the end ... but so what? We've *still* got to oppose it. And so what if we fail? We've got to *try*. That's the only justification for being alive any more ... *trying*.

GRANDFA. (*Ibid.*) Why they brought you here and you don't even know?

CLARENCE. You may think this is crazy ... and lots of people do ... but I don't believe in despair. No matter what happens ... and a lot has ... I can't, I won't, *don't* believe in despair. It's not something you can believe *in* ... despair. It's a dead-end. It'll choke you to death.

GRANDFA. Poor baby, poor baby.

CLARENCE. But I don't believe in ... what? ... joy? ... happiness? ... I don't believe in them either. I can't. I just can't. It's the *struggle* I believe in ... the endeavor ... the struggle from one to the other. People trying to be better than they really are. No, I don't mean that ... People trying to *change* things. Yes! People trying to change things. I hate not being able to change things. It's like man's perfectability ... who cares about that? It's his *im*perfectability that matters. I suppose that's why I don't think about God very often. He's not very interesting. (*Short pause; then, turning to Grandfa with a smile.*) Am I making any sense to you? Probably not.

GRANDFA. (*Just looking at Clarence.*) You poor, poor baby.

CLARENCE. And I probably shouldn't get so up in arms about it . . . the Movement.

GRANDFA. (*Directly to him.*) You weren't talking about the movement, Clarence.

CLARENCE. Oh I was! I probably talk too much about it. It's just that it's sort of a passion with me. Sometimes I wonder what I'd do without it. Stop boring people half to death, I suppose! (*He laughs, wanders a little, checking his watch.*)

GRANDFA. You're the movement, Clarence. You. You are.

CLARENCE. (*Again ignoring a remark he'd rather not deal with.*) Gee, I wish Sigfrid would come back. He went to get his mother. What did you say her name was? Ruby? I hate introductions.

GRANDFA. (*A weary sigh.*) Go home, missy . . . please . . . go home.

CLARENCE. (*Awkward.*) It was such a coincidence . . . running into each other like that this afternoon. We hadn't seen each other since the sixth grade. That's . . . (*He is counting the years up on his fingers.*)

GRANDFA. While there's time . . . pick up your skirts and run along home.

CLARENCE. (*Unable to prolong it.*) I beg your pardon?

GRANDFA. You heard me . . . maybe you didn't want to . . . but you did.

CLARENCE. I . . . no, no I didn't . . . something about home?

GRANDFA. (*Flat.*) That's right. Something about home.

CLARENCE. Well? Well *what?*

GRANDFA. You *like* bringing out the worst in them? Is that it?

CLARENCE. Well if you don't speak up, if I can't even *hear* you, I don't see how I'm supposed to *converse* with you.

GRANDFA. Do you know *why* you were brought here?

CLARENCE. Sigfrid and I—

GRANDFA. *Sigfrid! Sigfrid* is why you were brought here. And Sigfrid is why you came.

CLARENCE. Well of course he is! We're old friends.

GRANDFA. Sigfrid doesn't have any friends. He has victims . . . *mice.* Mice for the cats to play with. They'll rip your guts out. The imperfectability of man! That's their food. They'll devour you. Run, boy, I say run for your life. Get up those stairs and run.

CLARENCE. (*A little peevish.*) I honestly don't know what you're talking about.

GRANDFA. I'm talking about what will happen to you if you stay here. He's already put you in a dress. And God knows what happened in the other room. I'm sure it wasn't very pretty. But that was only a beginning. It's your *soul* they're after now and they won't sleep tonight until they've had at it. Had at it *good*! Your *soul*. And that hurt doesn't heal so easy. I know. I live here.

CLARENCE. (*Edgy.*) I don't know what you're talking about.

GRANDFA. (*Full voice.*) I'm talking about *you*. Who you are! I *know* who you are. *What*! So do they. AND THEY WILL REVILE YOU FOR IT. That is their *function*. They'll make you *belong* in that dress. They'll make you what you already *are*. They'll make you want to *die*.

CLARENCE. (*Ugly.*) I DON'T KNOW WHAT YOU'RE TALK-ING ABOUT!!! (*A silence.*)

GRANDFA. (*Gently.*) God help you, Clarence, God help you. (*The quiet is shattered by the horn fanfare announcing Norma's entrance from Bellini's opera. There is no specific source for the music. It is very loud. It will continue.*)

CLARENCE. (*Distracted.*) What? . . . music . . . the music . . . where? . . . why? . . . Sir! (*Grandfa is headed for the door: slowly, slowly.*) Wait! Where is everyone? . . . what's going to happen? . . . this music . . . I didn't know what you were talking about . . . I didn't *know* . . . please, *stay*! (*Grandfa is gone.*) I didn't . . . know . . . (*He is alone. The music builds. At the first beat of the orchestral verse of the chorus, Lakme comes skipping into the room. She wears her Green Hornet dress and cape. As she skips about the room in time to the music, she scatters rose petals from a tiny basket. Clarence watches, stupefied, unable to speak at first. Then:*) Who . . . ?

LAKME. (*At once, always skipping.*) Lakme . . . the Bell Song one . . . Delibes. Ruby used to sing it. You didn't know our mother was an opera queen? An *ex*-opera queen? Sigfrid didn't tell you? (*Clarence looks with jaw agape.*) A *real* old friend.

CLARENCE. (*Strangled.*) What?

LAKME. (*A cheerful explanation.*) The intercom. You and Grandfa. And isn't *he* the old pro? Pro for *prober*.

CLARENCE. What's happening?

LAKME. Ruby. It's her entrance. (*Then, quickly, as an after-thought.*) Oh! and you knew. You knew what he was talking about. Grandfa. (*And before Clarence can get out even a muffled reply to this, the volume of the music goes up several decibels and a chorus begins singing the second verse of Norma's entrance music. Lakme, always dancing, joins in at once.*)

VOCAL CHORUS.

Norma viene: le cinge la chioma
La verbena ai misteri sacrata;
In sua man come luna falcata
L'aurea falce diffonde splendor.
Ella viene; e la stella di Roma
Sbigottita si copre di un velo;
Irminsul corre i campi del cielo
Qual cometa foriera d'orror.

(*And, just as Lakme entered on the first beat of the orchestral verse, Sigfrid has entered on the first beat of the vocal selection. He still wears his black shirt and slacks. But now he carries an enormous sabre. He holds it out in front of him with great reverence, as if it were a sacred object. His expression and movements are solemn, trancelike. He walks a slow circle around the room, taking no notice of Clarence who, as soon as he entered, has been questioning him.*)

CLARENCE. Where have you been? Sigfrid. Where? And will you please tell me what's going on? You tell someone to wait for you and then ... this. Sigfrid?

SIGFRID. (*With a terrible, controlled fury.*) Ruby! Her entrance!

CLARENCE. (*After he has recovered from this.*) I . . . I don't understand.

LAKME. (*Helpful.*) You'd better sing. She won't like it if you don't.

CLARENCE. I . . .

SIGFRID. (*The same voice.*) Sing! (*Clarence, rather foolishly, tries to join in. The music is coming to another climax.*) Down. (*Sigfrid and Lakme kneel, facing the Stage Right door.*) Down! (*Clarence kneels, too. The horn fanfare sounds again and Ruby makes her long-awaited entrance. It and she are spectacular. She is wearing an elaborate, flowing white dress, rather suggestive of a nineteenth-century wedding dress. There is a splash of blood*) *across the bodice and part of the skirt. She moves majestically to a spot Center Stage and stands there, motionless, until the music ends. Clarence, Sigfrid and Lakme are almost prone on the floor, their heads bowed, they are not looking at her.*)

RUBY. (*After a pause, with an imperial gesture, Norma's opening recitative:*) "Sedizioso vo—" (*She stops singing on the vowel "O" and yawns hugely, not bothering to cover her mouth. Then she stretches, very slowly and yawns again. Ruby acts affectedly, and she knows it.*) *La Ruby non canterá stanotte.*

SIGFRID and LAKME. (*Together, exaggerated cadences.*) *Che peccato!*

RUBY. *È troppo stanca.*

SIGFRID and LAKME. *Maledetto.*

RUBY. *È troppo vecchia.*

SIGFRID and LAKME. *Poverina.*

RUBY. (*Sitting.*) *Buona sera a tutti!*

SIGFRID. (*Low, to Clarence.*) Isn't she terrific? Didn't I tell you?

RUBY. *Mi sento male. Mi sento noiosa. Mi sento* many things. But most of all *mi sento* blue.

SIGFRID. (*Ibid.*) One in a million.

LAKME. One in *ten* million.

RUBY. (*Arms outstretched.*) *Abbraciami, tesori, abbraciami.*

SIGFRID. (*Excusing himself to Clarence.*) She wants to embrace us.

LAKME. No, she wants *us* to embrace *her.* There's a difference.

RUBY. (*Taking Lakme and Sigfrid into her arms.*) *Ah, mes enfants. Mes veritables enfants. Comme je suis heureuse. Et comme je ne suis pas heureuse. Mais ce soir . . . peut-etre . . . je—* (*"Seeing" Clarence, she breaks off.*) Who is that, please?

LAKME. That? Oh that's Maria Malibran.

RUBY. Maria Malibran, you little dwarf, *the* Maria Malibran . . . the very *great* Maria Malibran . . . is neither a snippit nor a waif. That one *is.* Furthermore, she is quite dead and has been for some time now. Sigfrid, who is this?

SIGFRID. *Qui?*

RUBY. (*Pointing.*) That. That person.

SIGFRID. (*Terse whisper.*) *L'invité.*

RUBY. Ah! Our guest! (*To Clarence.*) *Nous vous avons attendé, cheri.*

CLARENCE. (*From across the room.*) Hello. I'm—

RUBY. (*Brightly.*) We'll be with you in a moment, dear.

LAKME. *Il s'appelle Clarence.*

RUBY. Hmm, I thought as much. Where did you find this one?

LAKME. *À la demonstration. Clarence porte des affiches.*

RUBY. (*Amused.*) *Davvero*, Sigfrid?

LAKME. They're old friends. They went to school together. Up to the sixth grade.

SIGFRID. (*Low, not for Clarence's ear.*) The slide. The incident on the slide.

RUBY. (*Scrutinizing Clarence.*) *Piccolo naso* . . .

LAKME. (*Translating for Clarence.*) She says you've got a small nose.

RUBY. . . . *mento debole* . . .

SIGFRID. Weak chin.

RUBY. . . . *orecchi grandi* . . .

LAKME. Big ears.

RUBY. . . . *pallido* . . . *troppo pallido* . . .

SIGFRID. And you're pale. Much too pale.

RUBY. *Ma la vestita è carina* . . . *molto carina.*

LAKME. (*To Ruby.*) It should be. It's yours. (*To Clarence.*) But your dress is sweet. Very sweet.

RUBY. And what a perfectly atrocious body!

LAKME. Sigfrid knows that, Ruby.

RUBY. I wouldn't have thought he was your type at all. Never in my life.

SIGFRID. It was the best I could do.

RUBY. It's the bottom of the barrel, Sigfrid. The veritable bottom of the barrel. This is hardly worth the effort.

SIGFRID. You try it next time, you think it's so easy. You try finding someone.

RUBY. To think your standards have fallen so low. I'm deeply shocked. It mustn't have been very pleasant for you.

LAKME. As he said, it was the best he could do.

RUBY. (*With a sigh of finality.*) *Ebbene, comminciamo la commedia.*

LAKME. (*Yelling to Clarence.*) Hey! You!

RUBY. Not that way, Lakme. Properly, very properly. Sigfrid, he's your friend.

SIGFRID. Just . . .

RUBY. Yes, darling? (*He only looks at her. She smiles up at him. Then Sigfrid goes over to Clarence, takes him by the arm and leads him back to Ruby. There should be a suggestion of royalty granting an interview during the next scene.*)

SIGFRID. Clarence, I'd like you to meet my mother. Ruby, this is Clarence.

RUBY. *Enchantée.*

CLARENCE. *Enchanté.*

RUBY. I beg your pardon?

CLARENCE. (*Who doesn't speak French or Italian or anything.*) *Enchanté?* (*Ruby shifts in her chair.*) Please don't get up!

RUBY. (*Settling back.*) Oh I won't. I wasn't, in fact. But you sit down. Here . . . on the hassock. (*Clarence sits at her feet.*) You've met our little Lakme? Our own *piccola cosa nostra?* Why yes, of course you have.

CLARENCE. No, I don't think so.

LAKME. Yes he did. In the park this afternoon. He played football with us. *Attempted* to play football with us. He's pretty stinky at it.

CLARENCE. Was that you?

RUBY. Lakme's twelve. Aren't you, sweetheart?

LAKME. (*Peeved.*) Thirteen, Ruby.

RUBY. Well how am I supposed to know?

LAKME. (*Beginning a long one.*) Thirteen years old and total monster.

RUBY. *That* we know.

LAKME. Will you let me finish this? Will you let me do it right this time?

RUBY. You haven't said hello to Clarence. You're not being polite.

LAKME. (*Brusque.*) Hello, Clarence. Now may I?

RUBY. *Avanti, avanti.*

LAKME. (*Finding her place.*) . . . years old and total monster. Have been for some time. I'm bright . . . extremely bright. Close to genius, in fact. I know everything a thirteen-year-old girl isn't supposed to know. Even ninety-three-year-old girls aren't supposed to know what I know. I know so much they don't know what to do with me. "They" meaning everyone. Everyone outside this house. Ruby and Sigfrid are different. At least they hate me. (*Appropriate comments from Ruby and Sigfrid.*) I have talents. I must have. Only I don't know what they are yet. So I play the piano. Bach, mostly, but sometimes Mozart. My favorite thing in the world is the Green Hornet. He makes people tell the truth and goes "Bzzz, bzzz" at them until they do. I do love the Green Hornet. My unfavorite thing is . . . well, lots of things . . . finks being in the vanguard. Fink! My favorite color is white . . . because it's blank. Time of day: night . . . blanker. Time of year: winter . . . blanker blanker. Fink! Millions of tiny sprouts of golden hair on my legs and arms. In the sun they glisten. Breasts moving along nicely. Not much bigger than a scoop in a nickle cone right now. Eyes and teeth: sharp and healthy. Fink! Other favorites: book, *The Iliad*; poem: "The Rubaiyat" . . . yeah, "The Rubaiyat"; movie: none; ocean: the Dead Sea; tree: tulip; flower: pansy . . . the flower variety; dress: the one with strawberries I wear on Fridays; painter: none . . . well maybe Leonardo; color: black; person: me. Fink! (*She finishes with a flourish; Sigfrid and Ruby express their approval.*)

RUBY. *Brava, Lakme, brava!*

SIGFRID. Hey, you've made a few changes in it.

LAKME. (*So pleased with herself.*) Unh-hunh! (*Then, to Clarence.*) Yeah?

CLARENCE. I thought you were a . . . a boy. The way you were dressed. Sigfrid's little brother or something.

LAKME. I *could* say something about appearances being deceiving, but I won't. *If* you know what I mean.

SIGFRID. Clarence had quite a little tête-à-tête with Grandfa, Ruby.

RUBY. Yes, I heard them.

CLARENCE. . . . heard? . . .

RUBY. The intercom. Poor Grandfa. Look, children, over there. His little bag's all packed. We're putting him in an asylum tomorrow.

CLARENCE. Yes, so he told me.

SIGFRID. Grandfa is insane.

CLARENCE. Yes, he told me that, too.

RUBY. He's written a novel.

CLARENCE. Oh. (*Pause.*) Is that what makes him insane? (*Ruby nods her head.*) Oh. (*Pause.*) How does that make him insane?

LAKME. He thinks it's the truth.

CLARENCE. Oh. (*Pause.*) Well, lots of famous writers cracked up right towards the end. (*A joke.*) Sometimes before!

LAKME. (*Tight-lipped.*) Grandfa isn't famous.

SIGFRID. (*Ibid.*) Grandfa isn't a writer.

RUBY. (*Ibid.*) Grandfa is insane.

CLARENCE. Oh. (*Pause.*) Still, it's sad putting old people away. I don't believe in it unless it's absolutely necessary. My grand—

RUBY. It was, Clarence, in this case it was. Nevertheless, that's a lovely sentiment. Extremely lovely. You have our support. (*An extremely loud snortle from Fa.*) Oh, Fa! I do wish he'd go somewhere else to make those dreadful noises. He can be such a water buffalo about it.

CLARENCE. Is that . . . ?

RUBY. That's our Fa. Rip Van Winkle with a bad heart. Fa won't be with us much longer, we're afraid.

LAKME. (*Skeptical.*) Afraid? Hah!

RUBY. It's imminent. We've been expecting the worst for quite some time now.

CLARENCE. That's awful.

RUBY. Yes, I suppose it is. But you see, Clarence, Fa has not been affectionate with us. He's slept, while we have . . . how shall I say it? . . . not slept. It's been a hard row to hoe without our *babbino*, but we've managed.

SIGFRID. *Triumphed*, Ruby. *Triumphed* is a better word.

RUBY. (*Arms outspread to Lakme and Sigfrid again.*) *Abbraciami ancora, tesori, abbraciami!* (*She holds them close.*) Aren't they wonderful, Clarence? Aren't my babies wonderful?

CLARENCE. They're . . . very nice.

RUBY. You use words so judiciously, Clarence. So judiciously. (*Then, in another tone.*) Halloween?

CLARENCE. (*Not catching the implication.*) Please?

SIGFRID. (*Moving away from Ruby, the efficient host bit.*) Drinks! I completely forgot. Ruby? What are you having?

RUBY. Cognac, a little cognac, darling. (*Then, directly to Clarence.*) *Je ne pouvais pas exister sans le cognac.*

CLARENCE. Yes.

SIGFRID. Lakme?

LAKME. A martini, stupid, what do you think? (*Then, to Clarence.*)

You should have seen your face when I first came in here. Stupefication!

SIGFRID. Clarence? (*And before Clarence can answer.*) You're not uncomfortable? Sitting on the floor?

CLARENCE. No, I'm fine, just fine.

SIGFRID. Let's see, does that get everyone? All-righty. And a pernod for me. (*He works at the bar.*)

LAKME. (*Who has been considering all this.*) Stupefaction. I can *say* stupefaction. I *prefer* stupefication. It's more stupefacient than stupefaction . . . stupefication, is. Stupid!

RUBY. That will do, Lakme. I should think that will do for quite a while now.

LAKME. I'm being *nice*. Aren't I? Aren't I being nice?

CLARENCE (*To Ruby.*) My little sister—

RUBY. (*Beaming.*) It's such a relief to see Sigfrid bring someone nice home for a change. We've had some of the most awful people here. Right where you're sitting. Riffraff! And if there's one thing I won't have in my basement, it's riffraff. Trash is all right . . . and Sigfrid's brought home enough of it . . . but I draw the line at riffraff . . . Well, do you blame me?

CLARENCE. It's not very pleasant.

RUBY. I wish you could have seen the girl he brought home with him last week. A belly dancer. An Arab belly dancer.

SIGFRID. She was amazing.

RUBY. I'm glad you thought so. The hair, Clarence. Horrible black hair. Everywhere. And the skin. Oily, oily.

SIGFRID. Olive, Ruby, an Arab's skin is olive.

RUBY. I call it *oily*. Now if that had been a *real* stone in her navel . . .

SIGFRID. Well Clarence isn't riffraff, Ruby.

RUBY. (*To Clarence, sharing an enormous joke.*) Just *trash?* (*Everyone laughs; Clarence manages a smile.*) You don't say much, do you?

SIGFRID. (*Coming forward with the drinks, passing them around.*) Clarence is shy, Ruby. Clarence has a father who used to beat him as a child. Clarence has a mother—

CLARENCE. Sigfrid!

SIGFRID. Relax, sweetheart. It's no skin off *your* nose. You told me and now I'm telling them.

CLARENCE. That was . . . different.

SIGFRID. Not really. (*Continuing.*) . . . a mother who smothered him with affection. She still does, in truth. And Clarence works in the public library. It is not difficult, therefore, to *explain* why Clarence is shy. It is not difficult to explain *Clarence*. There are reasons for him. (*Toasting.*) *Skol*, Clarence.

RUBY. *Skol*, Clarence.

LAKME. *Skol*, Clarence.

CLARENCE. (*Instinctively raising his hand to drink.*) *Skol*. (*They drink to him.*)

RUBY. (*Reflectively.*) There's something about you, Clarence . . . I can't quite put my finger on it . . . something about you that makes me think it's Halloween.

SIGFRID. It's the dress, Ruby.

RUBY. Mmm, I suppose it is.

SIGFRID. Clarence can't find his clothes. He asked if there wasn't something of yours he might put on.

CLARENCE. No!

RUBY. Well it *is* a bit damp down here this evening. You were afraid he might catch cold. I don't mind, do I?

CLARENCE. That's not true.

RUBY. (*Running on.*) Mind? Of course I don't mind. One thing life has taught me . . . and perhaps this is *all* it has taught me . . . is never to mind anything. Since I stopped minding, which was not so many years ago, I have . . . on occasion . . . been amused. And I suppose being amused is the closest thing left us to grace. (*Then, directly to Clarence, with all her charm.*) Don't you think so, Clarence?

CLARENCE. Mrs. . . .

RUBY. Ruby. The name is Ruby.

CLARENCE. That's not true about . . . I didn't ask to . . .

RUBY. To *what*, dear?

CLARENCE. This . . . this dress.

RUBY. (*Placating.*) Sigfrid's only joking . . . *maybe* he's only joking . . . either way, I know that. Besides . . . hmm? (*Lakme is whispering into Ruby's ear. Ruby laughs and nods her head affirmatively several times. Meanwhile, Sigfrid joins Clarence on the hassock, putting one arm affectionately around his shoulder.*)

SIGFRID. Ruby's a good sport. We all are. So you be one, too. Just . . . relax.

CLARENCE. (*A whisper.*) That was a lie.

SIGFRID. (*Good-natured.*) Oh, grump, grump, grump.

CLARENCE. Well it *was*. It was embarrassing.

SIGFRID. (*Logically.*) How can it be a lie when it's not true in the first place? . . . hunh?

RUBY. (*Back to Clarence and Sigfrid.*) I'm sorry. You were saying . . . ?

SIGFRID. (*Sweetly.*) Clarence was just accusing me of telling a lie and I was explaining to him that it's not a lie unless it's true.

RUBY. Why of course! *Tout le monde* knows *that*. There's no point to a lie if it's not true. (*As before.*) Don't you think so, Clarence? (*Lakme is at the rear of the room.*)

SIGFRID. What's she up to?

RUBY. Lakme thought our little guest might enjoy a little music. Little guest, little music. One of the records, dear.

CLARENCE. Mrs. . . . Ruby. It's just not true.

SIGFRID. Sshh. You're going to like this.

RUBY. (*Rising to the occasion. A command performance.*) I had a career in grand opera, you know. I was a diva . . . a prima donna . . . quite one of the best. "La Regina dell'Opera": me! The Queen of Opera. Or as the children so idiomatically put it: I was an opera queen. That's idiomatic *and* literal both! . . . Well, to press on: I was beautiful then and there was music in my voice . . . beautiful, beautiful music. I could sing anything . . . and I often did. There was no role too high, too low, or too in-between. And on stage . . . ah! on stage . . . and you must believe this, I was beautiful . . . so very, very beautiful.

SIGFRID. (*Whispered.*) That's Ruby's Lucy Lammermoor Mad Scene Dress. See the blood? She's just killed her husband.

RUBY. Lucy Lammermoor, Beatrice di Tenda, Elvira in Puritani, Amina . . . ah! such very good friends we were! How I loved them! How I was loved *as* them!

SIGFRID. (*Whispered.*) Ruby specialized in mad scenes. "La Luna dell'Opera."

RUBY. And now they are both gone: the beauty and the music . . . dearly departed ornaments of my being. They are but shadows now . . . happy or unhappy shades I do not know. The one, frozen for a single terrifying instant snatched from eternity, my eternity, in a red Moroccan leather album of yellowing photographs . . . hundreds upon hundreds of them. The other, my voice . . . my beautiful voice . . . echoed endlessly on the eroded grooves of a spinning black disk . . . just this one. *Ascolta*. (*The music starts now. Instantly her mood lightens and her speech tempo becomes faster. The recording played should be that of an incredibly awful soprano singing an elaborate coloratura aria. Florence Foster Jenkin's recording of the Queen of the Night aria is suggested. The actress should "play" with the music at all times during the following speech: mouthing certain phrases of music, pausing in her speech to listen to certain passages, conducting a little. Sigfrid and Lakme alternate between rapt attention and trying to keep a straight face. Clarence is flabbergasted.*) Aaaah! Wolfgang Amadeus! *Bravo, mei figli bravi* . . . the unhappy mother, the enraged Queen of the Night, swears vengeance and vows to deliver Pamina from her captor's hands . . . Vengeance! . . . This phrase: lovely, lovely . . . I sang this once in Moscow . . . at the Bolshoi . . . in Russian, no less . . . those dreadful thick vowels . . .

CLARENCE. (*In a whisper.*) Who's—? (*Sigfrid fiercely motions him to be silent.*)

RUBY. After the performance I was delivered to my hotel in a troika drawn by several thousand delirious students who then proceeded to serenade me with folk songs from the streets beneath my windows . . . I sat alone on my balcony . . . it was a warm evening, warm for Moscow . . . alone and weeping . . . weeping and toasting them with vodka . . . they sang until dawn . . . when the Kremlin's domes first were flecked with the morning sun's gold. . . . Here! The cadenza! Marvelous! . . . Once in Milano . . . after my debut at the Scala in a revival of "Gianna D'Arco" . . . revived for *me, ca va sans dire* . . . the manager, the manager of Scala said to me: "Ruby, *tu hai la voce delle anime di Purgatorio*" . . . which means, roughly translated: "Ruby, you sing with the voice of the souls in Purgatory" . . . well, *something* like that. You see, he'd heard the *pain* in my voice . . . and not only the joy. It was the exquisite mingling of the two that so enthralled him . . . This part, now. I would rush about the stage brandishing this enormous dagger. One

critic said it was an awesome moment . . . Oh, the memory of
those nights! . . . those days . . . the continental tours with
Brunnhilde, my pekingese, and my three male secretaries . . .
the steamer trunks stickered ten times over with those magic
names: Paris, Rome, Vienna, London, Bayreuth, Peiping, Ma-
nila, Camden, New Jersey . . . yes, Camden, New Jersey . . .
Athens, Napoli, Palermo . . . Palermo where I first met Fa, after
a Delilah at the Teatro Massimo. He'd come there to export the
olives. . . . Here! The portamento! . . . Oh the glory! the glory!
(*Her voice trails off and she is lost in revery, listening to the
music with closed eyes, her head back. The music ends. There is
a pause. Then Ruby opens her eyes and leans forward towards
Clarence.*) Well?

LAKME. Well?

SIGFRID. Well?

CLARENCE. I . . . unh . . . I . . .

SIGFRID. Tell Ruby what you thought, Clarence. Go on.

CLARENCE. I . . . I don't know very much about music. I really
shouldn't venture to make a judgment.

SIGFRID. Oh, go ahead, venture!

LAKME. (*Sing-song.*) Nothing ventured, nothing gained.

CLARENCE. Especially opera. I don't know anything about opera.
(*A weak joke.*) Wagner wrote Puccini as far as I know. (*They
are not amused.*) Really . . . I'm not qualified.

RUBY. (*Edgy.*) The quality of the *voice*, dear. We're interested in
what you think of *that*.

CLARENCE. Oh . . . *that* . . . it was wonderful, Mrs. . . .

LAKME. Ruby. Her name is Ruby.

CLARENCE. . . . just wonderful.

RUBY. Yes?

CLARENCE. What else can I . . . ? It reminded me of . . . of a bird.
A lark maybe. I don't know. But it certainly was wonderful.
You're very talented. (*The three of them explode with laughter.*) What? . . . What's so funny? . . . Did I say something
wrong?

RUBY. (*Rocking with laughter.*) He's so pathetically polite.

SIGFRID. (*The same.*) You're very talented, Ruby!

RUBY. And so patronizing.

LAKME. A bird. You reminded him of a bird.

CLARENCE. (*The light slowly dawning.*) Oh . . . I see . . . that wasn't you!

LAKME. Do tell!

CLARENCE. (*Joining in the laughter himself.*) No wonder! . . . well I'm glad it wasn't . . . ha ha . . . that was the worst thing I ever heard in my life . . . ha ha ha . . . it was awful . . . where did you find that record . . . who was she? (*Abruptly, the laughter ceases and they stare fiercely at Clarence.*)

RUBY. (*Sharp.*) A very dear friend.

CLARENCE. (*Caught in mid-laugh.*) Oh.

RUBY. A seventy-two-year-old lady.

LAKME. A seventy-two-year-old Negro lady.

SIGFRID. A seventy-two-year-old Negro *servant* from the deep Deep South.

RUBY. Seventy-two-year-old Negro lady servants from the deep Deep South who sing Mozart arias are *not* to be ridiculed. *Ever!*

LAKME. Racist! Dirty Nazi racist!

CLARENCE. (*Thoroughly chastened.*) I . . . I didn't know.

RUBY. You may laugh *with* us, Clarence, at yourself . . . but not at sweet old Aunt Jemima from the deep Deep South. (*Again they explode with laughter. Clarence sits dumbly, not knowing what to do or say or think. Ruby leans forward to pat his cheek.*) Clarence! Where's that smile! That famous smile of yours? (*Clarence doesn't react.*) Now! Together! Sing! (*She leads them in a rousing chorus of "For He's a Jolly Good Fellow." Suddenly the lights dim to half and hold there. The singing falters. Ruby is determined to finish the song, but for a moment she is the only one singing. Then Sigfrid joins in, rather limply at first, but soon belting it out with his full voice. Lakme has stopped singing altogether and moves away from the others. Even though her back is to us, we can tell from her heaving shoulders that she is fighting to hold back enormous sobs. The lights come swiftly back up to full, as Ruby and Sigfrid finish the song boisterously.*)

CLARENCE. I don't know what to think of you people. One minute you're friendly, the next you're making fun of me.

SIGFRID. (*Poo-pooing.*) Oh! Don't mind us. That's our way.

CLARENCE. Fun at my expense!

RUBY. (*Looking across the room at Lakme.*) Lakme!

SIGFRID. And whose fault is that? *You* admired the singing. A cat in heat, a God-knows-what, and you admired the *singing*.

CLARENCE. Because I thought it was . . . I was only trying to be polite.

RUBY. Stop that, Lakme.

SIGFRID. So you made a fool of yourself? Oh baby, learn to laugh at yourself. Learn it quick. It's the only thing that makes sense anymore.

CLARENCE. I'm sorry, but I don't have a sense of humor.

SIGFRID. (*Flip.*) Neither do we. Think about that.

RUBY. Lakme, I asked you to *stop*.

SIGFRID. What's the matter with her?

RUBY. The fence. Go to your room, Lakme.

SIGFRID. (*Going to Lakme, not unkindly.*) Come on, little one, calm down now.

LAKME. (*Pulling away from him.*) Keep away from me!

SIGFRID. We're here. We're all together. Don't—

LAKME. KEEP AWAY!

SIGFRID. (*Getting angry.*) Now look, Lakme!

RUBY. Make her go to her room, Sigfrid.

LAKME. I said keep *away!*

RUBY. (*Delighted sarcasm.*) Brave little Lakme. Fearless little Lakme. Our own little St. Joan of the Underground. "Leave the door open, Ruby. It's fifteen minutes 'til—"

LAKME. Shut up, Ruby, just shut up!

RUBY. (*Delighted wtih herself.*) Coraggio, Lakme, coraggio!

LAKME. JUST DO WHAT YOU SAID YOU WOULD. MAKE HIM GO OUT THERE. BUT GET IT OVER WITH AND LEAVE US ALONE. JUST DO IT. (*She leaves quickly through the Stage Right door.*)

SIGFRID. (*Following.*) Lakme!

RUBY. Sigfrid! Not yet.

SIGFRID. But she'll—

RUBY. Be all right.

SIGFRID. But she won't—

RUBY. She will. Sit.

SIGFRID. But—

RUBY. SIT! (*He obeys.*) The line, Sigfrid, you said something about the line? (*He doesn't answer.*)

CLARENCE. (*A voice in the void.*) Is there anything the matter? (*A long pause.*) Is there?

RUBY. (*Abruptly.*) Tell us about the way you live, Clarence.

CLARENCE. Sir? I mean . . . (*He laughs.*) Excuse me.

RUBY. (*Not amused.*) The way you live. I want you to tell us about it.

CLARENCE. I don't understand. The way I live? Me?

SIGFRID. (*Reasonably.*) What you believe in, Clarence. A statement of principles . . . life principles.

CLARENCE. Like my philosophy? Is that what you mean? My philosophy of life?

RUBY. (*An edge in her voice.*) It's called the way you live.

CLARENCE. (*Amused.*) But why? I'm not even sure if I have one.

RUBY. You're alive, aren't you?

CLARENCE. Well, yes.

RUBY. Then you have one.

CLARENCE. Well, I suppose I do . . . I must . . . only I hadn't really thought about it.

RUBY. You gave Grandfa an earful.

CLARENCE. Please?

SIGFRID. (*Always more conciliatory than Ruby.*) Now's your opportunity, Clarence.

CLARENCE. What do you want with it? My philosophy of life?

RUBY. (*Insistent.*) It's called the way you live.

SIGFRID. We'd like to tape it.

CLARENCE. Tape it? You mean on a—? (*Sigfrid nods.*) But why would anyone want to do a thing like that? Tape someone's phi— . . . way he lives?

SIGFRID. Ruby collects them. All our guests do it. She's looking for the answer.

RUBY. I *have* the answer. I'm looking for corroboration. I find it consoling. Usually.

CLARENCE. (*A little intrigued with the idea.*) You mean we'll probably end up saying the very same thing? Or just about?

RUBY. Or just about. (*Sigfrid has been setting up the recorder.*)

RUBY'S RECORDED VOICE. (*Very loud.*) ". . . wherefrom we shall draw the sustenance to destroy you. . . ."

RUBY. On *"record,"* dear, not on *"playback."* (*Sigfrid has already turned the machine off and now sets a microphone in front of Clarence.*)

CLARENCE. (*To Ruby.*) That was *you*. Was that from *your* . . . ? (*Noticing the microphone.*) Is this what I talk into? I feel like I'm on the radio. Gee, I bet I make a mess out of this. (*Sigfrid motions for silence and points to the spinning reels.*) You mean I'm on already? Heavens! I'm really not prepared, you know. (*A pause.*) Unh . . . unh . . . the way I live . . . no, let me start again . . . unh . . . (*He takes a deep breath.*) The way I live . . . The way I live is . . . the best I can do. I try. I mean I really try. And I think I am improving. I think I am becoming a better human being day by day. I really do . . . Anyway, I'm trying. (*Then, turning to Ruby and Sigfrid.*) This is awful. I told you— (*They motion him to continue.*) I believe in . . . well, lots of things. (*From this point he begins to warm to his subject.*)

It's hard to express them. They're like abstractions. *They're* not abstractions, but what there is about them that makes me believe in them is . . . an abstraction . . . sort of. People . . . trees . . . the sunshine . . . snow . . . a clear cold day in November . . . things like that. Beauty. Something . . . beautiful. (*Short pause.*) And I think it's sad that we can't enjoy these things the way we were meant to. Because of . . . the circumstances. No, these were not the best of times to have been born in. I should have preferred the Renaissance, when it was easier to . . . live, I suppose. And that's the important thing. To live. That's why we're alive. Otherwise, there's no point to it . . . life. (*Shorter pause.*) I love life. I suppose that's a corny statement, but I do. I know it's fashionable to be morose these days, but I frankly can't see anything to be morose *about!* . . . well, *some* things, but certainly not enough to talk about killing yourself or not giving a damn anymore or anything like that. Just about the last thing I'd ever do is kill myself. There aren't enough reasons to. There are just too many good things in the world not to want to be alive. Just think of all the beautiful things men have made. Music, art, literature . . . Shakespeare alone is a reason to be alive. How could anyone not want to be alive after there's been a Shakespeare on this earth? I can't imagine it. And even if I've never seen it real . . . and maybe I never will . . . how could anyone

not want to be alive when there is a city in Italy named Florence? How could they? Just *knowing* about Florence! . . . what it *means* to us that it's there. That there *was* a Florence, is and will be. It . . . it makes the rest of this planet tolerable. Florence is *why* we're alive. It's what we're *about*. (*A pause*.)
And the things you can do! The simple things. What about them? Just to take a walk even. It can be wonderful. Or to be by the sea and feel that air on your face and see what the horizon means. You can actually *see* the curve of the earth. Just what they taught you in school and it's true. That's a wonderful thing to see for yourself. Or just to sit in a park . . . with the sun spilling all over you . . . watching the people. The other people. They're not you, and that's what's so beautiful about them. They're someone else. Sit and wonder who they are. What they ate for breakfast, what paper they're reading, where they live, what they do . . . who they love. And that's another reason. Everybody loves somebody . . . or they will . . . sometime in their life. (*A pause*.)
Anything that makes you want to live so bad you'd . . . you'd die for it . . . Shakespeare, Florence . . . someone in the park. That's what I believe in. That's all. That's the way I live. (*A silence. Sigfrid turns off the recorder*.)

RUBY. Shakespeare, Florence, and someone in the park. That was nicely spoken, Clarence.

CLARENCE. Was it all right? I sort of enjoyed it once I got into it. What happens now? With the tape, I mean.

SIGFRID. We put it aside . . . save it . . . keep it for reference.

CLARENCE. Were they very similar? Yours and mine?

RUBY. Not quite, Clarence, not quite.

CLARENCE. (*Completely at home now*). And another nice thing . . . I should've taped it . . . sometimes you run into old friends. People you haven't seen for over ten years. It's very nice when that happens. (*To Ruby*.) Only he doesn't remember anyone from that school. All the friends he had and he can't remember a single one. He didn't remember *me* until I—

SIGFRID. Just one.

CLARENCE. Who is that? Billy . . . unh . . . Billy . . .

SIGFRID. The kid on the slide.

CLARENCE. Oh . . . him.

SIGFRID. The one who fell off the slide and broke his arm . . . and then said he was pushed. Remember him?

CLARENCE. Only the incident. But remember Mrs. Chapin? . . . the fifth grade? . . . the one with the long neck? Old rubberneck? We used to draw her picture on the blackboard with miles and miles of neck snaking all over the place. Don't you remember her? You were her favorite. It got her. About two years ago. She must have been out after curfew. They found her in the park.

SIGFRID. Well, those bachelor ladies who prowl the parks after dark usually come to a bad end.

CLARENCE. I thought you liked Mrs. Chapin. And even if you didn't . . .

SIGFRID. Yes?

CLARENCE. That's not a very nice thing to say. After all, the woman's *dead*.

RUBY. (*A sudden exclamation.*) Now I know who you're talking about . . . this boy on the slide. Not the boy who *fell* off the slide, Sigfrid, the boy you *pushed*. *Then* he fell, after you'd pushed him. Yes, of course, he fell and broke his leg.

CLARENCE. Arm.

RUBY. Arm was it?

CLARENCE. I . . . I think it was.

RUBY. Funny, you seemed so certain a moment ago.

SIGFRID. (*Rather amused.*) I pushed him, Ruby? He didn't fall and *then* say I pushed him? I really did push him in the first place?

RUBY. Yes, *caro*, yes. And so they expelled you.

SIGFRID. Well, what do you know about that? Clarence?

CLARENCE. I'd always heard he . . . fell.

RUBY. And little Sigfrid was expelled. That wasn't the only reason, of course. There had been previous incidents. But all the same, you *did* own up to it. Well, after a fashion you owned up to it. In your own sweet time, you might say . . . after they'd *tricked* you into it. (*To Clarence directly.*) Were you at that assembly?

CLARENCE. Yes.

RUBY. Police state methods! That's what it was. Putting that injured boy up on the stage with his leg in a cast . . . arm, you said? Well, whatever it was . . . putting him up there and making the other students stand up one at a time until he could say "*Him.* He's the one who did it." Well of course Sigfrid owned up to it! Who wouldn't? With some brat's finger, accusing you, stuck in your face and that man, that principal with all the moles, shouting at you? Naturally Sigfrid said he did it. (*Short pause.*) And he *had*! (*Shorter pause.*) So they expelled him. (*Longer pause; she moves away from them.*)

CLARENCE. (*Breaking an awkward silence.*) What happened then, Sigfrid? After the sixth grade?

SIGFRID. (*Curt.*) Nothing.

CLARENCE. Nothing?

SIGFRID. Nothing.

CLARENCE. Well *something*—

SIGFRID. NOTHING.

LAKME'S VOICE. (*Suddenly, on the intercom.*) "A sky, a blue sky, the eagle soars." That's what happened, Shelley, that's what happened after the sixth grade. You wrote poetry.

SIGFRID. You goddamn little—

LAKME'S VOICE. (*Joshing.*) Oh come on, eagle, I can't find the projector.

SIGFRID. Just lay off me, dwarf girl, hunh?

LAKME'S VOICE. You can be such a poop sometimes, Sigfrid. Now will you get in here and help? I'm in the darkroom. (*The red light on the intercom goes off.*)

SIGFRID. (*Getting up.*) Ruby?

CLARENCE. (*Getting up, too.*) Can I—?

SIGFRID. No.

CLARENCE. Where are you going?

SIGFRID. You'll see.

CLARENCE. Is something going to happen?

SIGFRID. You might say that. (*He is gone.*)

CLARENCE. I hate surprises. (*Then, to Ruby.*) Is that what happened? Sigfrid wrote poetry? (*No response.*) I wrote a poem once. For my mother. On her birthday. When I was little. "God bless the Lord. God bless my mother. She has good things in her oven." She's always saved it. (*Long pause.*) It was unfortunate.

RUBY. (*Irritable, facing Clarence for the first time since she last spoke.*) What was?

CLARENCE. That they expelled him. Sigfrid was very popular at that—

RUBY. Lots of things are *unfortunate*. Sitting here in this goddamn

basement night after night is *unfortunate.* That thing out there
is *unfortunate.* Life is *unfortunate.*

CLARENCE. The Situation. You mean the Situation.

RUBY. (*Flat.*) That's right . . . the Situation.

CLARENCE. (*In solemn agreement.*) It's been this way so long now
. . . all my lifetime.

RUBY. (*Bitter.*) Twenty years, isn't it? Isn't that what the *text-
books* say?

CLARENCE. You know, I've never seen a sunset . . . and the moon
only in the daytime when it's not really the moon . . . the way
it should be the moon.

RUBY. Twenty years . . . two hundred . . . two thousand.

CLARENCE. Before the curfew, when you could go out nights, did
you ever see an eclipse of the moon? I think I'd rather see an
eclipse of the moon than the moon itself. From what I've read—

RUBY. Once.

CLARENCE. What was it like?

RUBY. Dark, very dark.

CLARENCE. (*Disappointed.*) Oh.

RUBY. It was in Florence.

CLARENCE. Florence! You've been in Florence!

RUBY. It was lovely . . . very dark and very lovely.

CLARENCE. Everything is *was* now.

RUBY. Shakespeare, Florence, and someone in the park.

CLARENCE. That's scarcely what I'd call a deathless sentiment. (*The
lights suddenly dim to half.*) The lights again! Something's happening to— (*The lights come back to full.*) See how jittery I
am? Something happens, a little thing like the lights, and I start
. . . shaking, almost. Anything goes wrong and I think it's started
to happen . . . that it's finally out there. If we only knew *when*
. . . or if it's *ever* going to happen. It's this waiting that's so terrible . . . the not-knowing.

RUBY. We know it's out there. That's enough.

CLARENCE. But we don't even know what it *is* . . . specifically what
it is. Oh, I read books, newspapers accounts, but . . . well I wish
I could *see* it. So I could know what it is we're so afraid of. Not
up close. I know you can't come face to face with it . . . what
happens then. But from a distance: that's what I'd like. If I
could be on the top of a very high mountain and look down

into a valley where it was happening. I'd have a telescope and I'd scrunch down in the foliage and spy on it. Just so I could get some idea of what it was like . . . some inkling . . . even from far off. But they say all the safe hiding places are gone now. Sure you can see it . . . millions of people have . . . and they're all dead.

RUBY. Here it's safe. No one dies down here.

CLARENCE. All you can do is try to imagine it . . . what it's like. Do you do that? I see this cat . . . a big cat, but more like a monster, sitting outside a mousehole. It's out there . . . all the time . . . waiting to pounce. It's got long claws and teeth . . . big teeth. Except it doesn't eat you . . . just takes you away to someplace alone . . . someplace dark and cold . . . with no sounds. And it won't ever go away unless . . . unless . . . I don't know what will make it go away. But if we stay here, where it's light and warm, just a little bit even, it can't get at us. It can't take us away with it to that place. But if you go out there. . . . (*Pause.*) What do you think it is?

RUBY. I don't know.

CLARENCE. Don't you have any idea what it's like?

RUBY. Not really. I would only suggest . . . *suggest* . . . that it has something to do with the unbearable difference between the way things are . . . us, for example . . . and the way they should be . . . us, for example.

CLARENCE. Oh.

RUBY. Does that disappoint you?

CLARENCE. (*It does, of course.*) No. It's just that I'm so frightened of it and your idea sounds so . . . so intellectual. *Aren't* you frightened of it?

RUBY. If it gives you any pleasure to know this, Clarence, I am terrified beyond belief and, occasionally, out of my mind. (*The lights dim again, hold a moment and then come back to full strength.*)

CLARENCE. What's happening? The fuses keep—

RUBY. It's not the fuses. It's those dumb stray animals wandering into the fence.

CLARENCE. You mean it's . . . electrified?

RUBY. We have to keep people out somehow. There are signs posted at regular intervals. Of course if Darwin were right the animals should have learned to read by now. You don't approve, I suppose?

CLARENCE. No . . . it's just that . . . well how often does it happen?

RUBY. Four or five a night. Dogs . . . cats . . . an occasional parakeet. The city picks them up the next morning along with the garbage.

CLARENCE. (*Sickened.*) That's awful . . . it shouldn't be like this . . . fences, basements, curfews . . . no . . . it shouldn't be this way.

RUBY. Well it is.

CLARENCE. That's exactly why I'm so concerned! Because it *is* this way and it must *not* be.

RUBY. That's right! You're concerned. I'd nearly forgotten.

CLARENCE. Of course I'm concerned. One *has* to care . . . passionately!

RUBY. (*"Finding" a sock under one of the sofa cushions and holding it up rather conspicuously.*) Passion . . . ah yes, one must have passion . . . where would we be without passion? (*She has found another sock.*) Passion for Shakespeare . . . passion for Florence . . . passion for someone in the park.

CLARENCE. (*A little nervous; those are* his *socks.*) Don't you care? . . . about . . . ? (*He gestures vaguely towards the outside.*)

RUBY. The only issue of *passionate* concern in this family . . . the only one any of us really care about . . . is who's going to get who: where, when and how.

CLARENCE. (*The smugness beginning to creep into his voice.*) I was talking about something else. Those are social relations . . . personal problems . . . neuroses. I was talking about more universal themes . . . the ones that really count.

RUBY. (*Idly, examining a pair of undershorts she has found under another sofa cushion.*) Oh . . . and what are they?

CLARENCE. Life . . . survival . . . that thing out there . . . I don't know.

RUBY. (*Helpful.*) The big things?

CLARENCE. Yes.

RUBY. The major issues of our times?

CLARENCE. That's right.

RUBY. And not personal . . . how shall I put it? . . . unpleasantness?

CLARENCE. Especially not that.

RUBY. (*"Convinced."*) I see. Well in that case perhaps we *should* concern ourselves . . . so much being at stake. Universal themes at our back door and we're worried about ourselves! Heavens!

CLARENCE. (*Confidentially, to an ally.*) People think too much about themselves these days. They encourage their neuroses. They coddle them, if you ask me.

RUBY. Well we'll certainly put a stop to *that.*

CLARENCE. I hope I'm not sounding smug or anything.

RUBY. You? Smug? Clarence!

CLARENCE. I have that tendency.

RUBY. But how exactly does one go about it? Being concerned, I mean. What does one *do,* for example?

CLARENCE. It's more a question of being than doing actually.

RUBY. You must do *something.*

CLARENCE. Well, I *read* . . . I've been in a few demonstrations . . . I wrote a letter to—

RUBY. I asked you what you were *doing.*

CLARENCE. Well . . . don't you see . . . it's more a question of allowing myself to become involved . . . recognizing my responsibilities to the issues at large. Commitment! That's the important thing: to be committed.

RUBY. I don't understand. Committed to what? An asylum, like Grandfa?

CLARENCE. No! Something large.

RUBY. Elephants are large. Are you committed to elephants?

CLARENCE. You know what I'm talking about. Something larger than myself . . . something . . . I don't know . . . *purer!* . . . a cause, an ideal . . . something outside of me . . . away from the littleness inside . . . nowadays people are all hunched over their navels when they have the stars to reach for!

RUBY. Had.

CLARENCE. I beg your pardon?

RUBY. *Had* the stars to reach for.

CLARENCE. (*Sadly.*) Yes, *had.*

RUBY. "Everything is *was* now." Those are your words. (*Short pause.*) Well, if that's all you're doing I suppose it's better than nothing. I suppose it's better than us.

CLARENCE. Maybe I'm not as aggressive as I'd like to be . . . outgoing . . . I'm more introspective.

RUBY. But committed.

CLARENCE. I try to be.

RUBY. Dedicated . . . no distractions.

CLARENCE. Well sure. You can't worry about these things twenty-four hours a day.

RUBY. (*The coup de grâce.*) I shouldn't think so. I mean there you were: marching around town all afternoon in this nippy weather . . . waving your little sign . . . the wind trying to pull it out of your hands. Marching and waving that sign and being committed and all. That's what I call a big day. You need a distraction after an afternoon like that. No wonder you toddled over to the curb when you saw that good-looking son of mine giving your little sign the once-over. No matter how committed you are, you certainly don't pass up a good-looking distraction like Sigfrid without at least inquiring. After all, he might be committed, too! No harm in asking. "Hello there. I'm looking for something larger than myself. What about you?" asks the commitment. . . . I know this scene well . . . The distraction smiles but does not answer. They never do. "Oh dear," fidgets the commitment, "I *do* wish he wouldn't stare at my little sign like that." The other marchers, with whom the commitment had begun the parade, marchers of a somewhat different commitment, perhaps, are moving along now. Soon they will be out of sight. "Are you a commitment or a distraction?" pleads the boy with sign. "Are you one of us or not? I must know." The distraction only smiles, beckons with his head and begins to move away. "But I'm committed! I can't go with you!" he cries after the departing form. What to do? What to do? And as he stands there, soon to be alone . . . his feet numb with cold . . . watching the commitments march up the street one way and the distraction walk slowly down it the other . . . he remembers those immortal words of Clarentius, the saddest commitment of them all: "You can't worry about these things twenty-four hours a day." Hey! Distraction! Wait for me! (*She whistles with two fingers in her mouth, then breaks into laughter and prods Clarence in the ribs.*) Wasn't it that way, Clarence? Wasn't it?

CLARENCE. (*Turning away.*) I don't know what you're talking about.

RUBY. That boy of mine may be a lousy commitment but he's one hell of a distraction!

CLARENCE. I'm sure I wouldn't know.

RUBY. Oh you wouldn't, would you?

CLARENCE. No I wouldn't!

RUBY. (*Fast and tough.*) Look, sweetheart, you check the guilt baggage at the front door when you come into this house. It's not like outside down here. We don't play games . . . well, that's not true exactly . . . but we don't play *those* kinds of games. We deal with what's *left* us . . . not what we'd like to *add* to the mythology. It's a subtraction process and if the answer is zero that's okay, too. Now you just be a sweet little distraction and simmer down.

CLARENCE. I'm not a distraction!

RUBY. You're just someone who happened in off the street, all committed up for Halloween? Is that it?

CLARENCE. NO!

RUBY. (*Making him look on her face.*) "And someone in the park!" That's your commitment, Clarence. Not Shakespeare, not Florence, not what's out there, but someone in the park! And that someone happened to be Sigfrid!

CLARENCE. (*Broken now.*) I . . . I didn't come here for that.

RUBY. But Sigfrid wanted it that way. So you let him.

CLARENCE. I didn't want him to.

RUBY. But you let him. Oh Clarence . . . Clarence, Clarence, Clarence.

CLARENCE'S RECORDED VOICE. (*A mocking echo.*) Oh Sigfrid . . . Sigfrid, Sigfrid, Sigfrid.

RUBY. I beg your pardon? (*He neither answers nor looks at her. Sigfrid and Lakme enter through the Stage Right door. He carries a slide projector; she, a movie screen.*)

LAKME. Here we are. Ready to go.

SIGFRID. Did you two have a nice talk while we were gone? Did Clarence try to convert you to the cause, Ruby?

RUBY. Sshh! The Clarence is temporarily out of commitment.

SIGFRID. Aaaaaw!

CLARENCE. I'd like to go home, please.

SIGFRID. But love-blessing! Lakme's produced an entertainment . . . a sight and sound entertainment . . . especially for you.

CLARENCE. I'd like to go home.

RUBY. *Pounce!* Remember, Clarence? . . . that mean old pussycat?

SIGFRID. What old pussycat?

RUBY. You're an old pussycat.

SIGFRID. (*He and Lakme are busy setting up.*) Do you know what Clarence did, Ruby? He told his father I was a girl. Me. Can you imagine it? And he told his mother he was coming over to see a boy. Such double-think!

RUBY. Oh I see! His daddy lets him sleep with girls and his mummy lets him sleep with boys. They're a very conventional pair, your parents.

CLARENCE. (*Strong, for him.*) Stop it!

RUBY. That's right, Clarence. Tell us off.

CLARENCE (*Standing.*) I'd like my clothes, please. My *own* clothes.

SIGFRID. But, buttercup, you're in them.

CLARENCE. WHERE ARE THEY?

SIGFRID. (*Mocking.*) Hoo hoo! Hoo hoo!

LAKME. (*Simultaneously.*) Arabella's in a huff. She's *huffled!*

SIGFRID. We're getting waspish! Oh oh oh oh!

LAKME. (*A little dance.*) Bzz . . . bzz . . . bzz!

CLARENCE. I don't have to stay here.

LAKME. Oh yes you do. (*Mock horror.*) There is something out there! Grrr!

CLARENCE. Not if I can find my clothes I don't.

LAKME. Poor lady, poor lady Godiva.

CLARENCE. Do you know where they are?

SIGFRID. Pout, pout, pout. Pretty Alice Pout.

CLARENCE. Stop that! I'm not pouting. I'm getting mad. And my name's not Alice.

SIGFRID. Sorry, Joan.

CLARENCE. (*The explosion.*) WHERE ARE MY CLOTHES!

SIGFRID. (*Ugly, ugly, ugly.*) WHERE'S YOUR SENSE OF HUMOR YOU MEAN!

LAKME. THAT'S WHAT YOU'RE LOOKING FOR!

SIGFRID. YOU CAN'T LIVE WITHOUT A SENSE OF HUMOR! NOT ANY MORE! NOT NOW!

LAKME. DOPE!

SIGFRID. SO WHERE IS IT! HUNH!

LAKME. HUNH! (*Long pause.*)

SIGFRID. (*Quietly, and with a hideous calm.*) You've also got a lousy body.

LAKME. Skin and bones.

SIGFRID. (*He means it.*) Shut up, Lakme.

CLARENCE. (*Pathetic.*) I didn't say you *hid* them.

SIGFRID. We did, of course.

CLARENCE. I didn't accuse you.

SIGFRID. Maybe you should've.

CLARENCE. . . . (*A sickened, moaning sound.*) . . .

SIGFRID. (*Almost gentle.*) You're rather a toad, aren't you?

CLARENCE. I'm . . . I'm just not strong. But I think things!

SIGFRID. Yes, I suppose you do.

RUBY. (*Not breaking this mood.*) Shakespeare, Florence, and some-one in the park. Two are names and one's a person. Right, Clarence? . . . right?

CLARENCE. (*Sitting, numbed.*) Right. (*A pause. Lakme, Sigfrid, and Ruby are ready now and return to a lighter mood.*)

RUBY. Lakme, what's the name of your production?

LAKME. "The Way You Live."

RUBY. The way who lives, dear?

LAKME. Him!

RUBY. Clarence! It's about you. Lakme's entertainment is about you.

LAKME. (*Finishing the arrangements.*) Okay. You ready, Sigfrid?

SIGFRID. All set.

RUBY. (*Clapping her hands.*) It's beginning, it's beginning! *Nous commençons, Clarence. Nous commençons!* Can you see all right from there? (*Sigfrid sits where he can control both the slide projector and the tape recorder. Lakme sits at the piano.*)

LAKME. "The Way You Live. Clarence Fink: This is Your Life." Lights! (*All the lights in the room go off except for a dim spot on Clarence, who sits with his back to the movie screen. Not once will he look at it. Throughout the scene that follows our concentration is on Clarence live on the hassock and Clarence on the screen. The voices of Sigfrid, Lakme, and Ruby are but sounds in the dark.*)

LAKME. (*Narrating over musical commentary.*) Lakme Productions bring you "The Way You Live" . . . an entertainment conceived, produced, and directed by Lakme Herself. Visuals and audio by Sigfrid Simp. With occasional shrieks, howls, and whoopings by Ruby Rat. Clarence Fink! This is your life! (*The picture on the screen comes sharply into focus now. We see Clarence marching along with his poster.*) There you stand, Clarence Fink. A young man of bold convictions and forthright ideals. Admired . . . loved . . . respected even by all who know you. As you march boldly into the future, wagging your sign behind you, do you remember . . . beneath that facade of confidence and hope . . . do you remember, Clarence Fink, do you remember this? Ruby! (*The slide changes to a wretched grass hut.*)

RUBY. It was a miserable beginning. The palace had seen better days. The windows all were broken and the great marble floors were cracked and stained. Your mother, good queen Nefertiti, was reduced to taking in dirty linen and your pa, Old King Cole, was putting on airs. (*We see a very old, very toothless Chinese couple working in a rice paddy.*) Yet you loved them all the same. And *you* . . . why you were the favorite child . . . their pride and joy. At feeding time they always made certain you had a dab more food in your bowl than the others. Sigfrid! (*Hundreds of starving children holding up empty bowls.*)

SIGFRID. You were a bright child: walking at five years, talking at ten, committing nasties behind the barn . . . I mean hut . . . at fifteen. Oh, you were a precocious one. Pretty soon it was time to move on. Your horizons were unlimited. And after all, look at what happened to your brothers and sisters . . . all two hundred of them. (*A cemetery with hundreds of identical markers.*) The fearful chee-chee fly was rampant!

LAKME. First you said goodbye to your pa. He'd given up putting on airs and found a more spiritual occupation. (*A colored nun playing baseball.*) It was a difficult parting.

CLARENCE'S RECORDED VOICE. "Are you sure it's all right in here, Sigfrid? I mean no one else will come in?" (*Clarence barely responds to the sound of his own voice. His head, shoulders only sag even more.*)

LAKME. See, Ruby? Sight *and* sound.

SIGFRID. Your mother was more reluctant to see you go. You were the only child left . . . and the firstborn, too . . . and she had plans for you: Hollywood plans. (*A Shirley Temple pin-up.*) But she relented.

RUBY. That last time you saw her! Who can forget it? Misty-eyed you stood at the rear of the train, waving a lavender hanky-pank at the receding figure you had loved so well. (*A rather whorey nude with enormous breasts.*) That's *her*, Sigfrid! That Arab girl you had here last week!

SIGFRID. Olive-skinned. What did I tell you?

RUBY. Will you look at those . . . ?

LAKME. Knockers.

RUBY. Lakme!

LAKME. Sorry.

CLARENCE'S RECORDED VOICE. "I think it's their fault. I really do. Ask any psychiatrist. Parents make their children . . . well, you know."

SIGFRID. What, Clarence? Make their children what?

CLARENCE'S RECORDED VOICE. . . . (*An absurd giggle.*) . . .

SIGFRID. Oh, *that*.

LAKME. You came to the big city. It was cold and you were lonely. You drifted, spent hours at the movies, took odd jobs. (*The Radio City Rockettes.*) But nothing seemed to last.

SIGFRID. You did strange things. There was no rhythm to your life . . . no internal logic. You took to roller-skating, mumblety-peg, anacrostics . . . You were beginning to let people push you off slides . . . Oh, various and sundry vices . . . you embraced them all. (*A small boy urinating against a wall.*) In short, you were a mess.

CLARENCE'S RERORDED VOICE. "Not very often . . . you see, I . . . well I'm almost a virgin."

LAKME. Categorically untrue!

CLARENCE'S RECORDED VOICE. "Really! Cross my heart and hope to die."

LAKME. Not after tonight you're not. Sigfrid took care of that. Clarence didn't even get to have his own organism, Ruby.

RUBY. Sshh! Sigfrid, where were we?

SIGFRID. In short, you were a mess.

RUBY. Ah! But salvation was just around the corner . . . well at the curb, actually . . . and you went right over to it. (*Sigfrid dressed in the collegiate sweater he wore at his first act entrance.*)

RUBY. SNAP! And the poor little fishy gobbled up the big bad worm.

SIGFRID. Now that's what I call commitment.

CLARENCE'S RECORDED VOICE. "I'll probably lose my rank for leaving the parade like that. They're very strict. I'm a squadron secretary."

SIGFRID. You can be our squadron secretary, Clarence.

CLARENCE'S RECORDED VOICE. "Oh well, I'll tell them I got sick. I doubt if they'll check up on me." (*Sigfrid and Clarence talking on the street.*)

LAKME. (*More agitated.*) Now this is where it gets exciting. Your heart starts to beat faster. It's the moment supreme! What you've been waiting for. Talk to him, Clarence! Pour your heart out. Tell him in your very own words!

CLARENCE'S RECORDED VOICE. "Is there a hanger? . . . This is my best pair of slacks."

SIGFRID. Is that all you said to me? At a time like that! Clarence.

CLARENCE'S RECORDED VOICE. "Oooooooo, these sheets are cold! Brrrrr!"

RUBY. That's better. Go on, go on. (*Clarence and Sigfrid outside a house.*) Fa! We simply must have the hedges trimmed. Look at them.

SIGFRID. That's a rotten picture of me, Lakme.

CLARENCE'S RECORDED VOICE. "I always leave my socks on . . . well, if it's going to bother you."

LAKME. Clarence wanted to wear his socks to bed.

RUBY. I can hear that, dear. Sshh.

SIGFRID. I think it's uncouth to wear one's socks to bed.

RUBY. Well *you!* (*Clarence by a bed, unbuttoning his shirt.*)

LAKME. This is the beginning of the sexy part. I used an F15 lens. (*From this point the slides are shown more rapidly. The "slide" directions that follow are merely an indication of where we generally are in the sequence.*)

CLARENCE'S RECORDED VOICE. "Gee, I'm glad we ran into each other. It's been a long time . . . six years after grade school . . . then college . . . it's been over ten years . . . and I still recognized you the instant I saw you . . ." (*Clarence with his shirt off.*)

RUBY. (*Awed by the sight.*) Oooooooo!

SIGFRID. Aren't those pectorals something, Ruby? Pret-ty snazzy.

RUBY. These are wonderful pictures, Lakme, just wonderful.

LAKME. Thanks.

CLARENCE'S RECORDED VOICE. "Sigfrid, do you ever get lonely? I mean for someone more than just a friend ..."

RUBY. You mean someone in the park, dear.

SIGFRID. He means me.

CLARENCE'S RECORDED VOICE. "Someone you can really be with ... I do ..." (*Clarence taking off his pants.*) "Sometimes ... you may think this is silly ... but sometimes ... at night ... I cry about being lonely ... at night ... when I can't sleep ... and that thing is out there ... I get frightened ... and I cry ... (*Clarence in his undershorts. Each slide is met with increasing hilarity.*) I get frightened ... and I'm lonesome ... and I cry ... (*Sigfrid has set the tape recorder at a faster speed. Clarence's recorded voice takes on a ridiculous tone.*) Maybe I talk too much but ... I don't feel safe most places ... I'm nervous ... I feel cold sort of ... but not here ... oh, no, not here ... I feel safe here ... it's warm ... very, very warm. (*Sigfrid and Clarence in bed.*) Oh, Sigfrid ... Sigfrid, Sigfrid, Sigfrid."

LAKME, RUBY, and SIGFRID. (*Mimicking in unison.*) Oh, Sigfrid ... Sigfrid, Sigfrid, Sigfrid. (*At this moment, which has been building up inside him ever since this sequence began, Clarence stands with an incredible look of pain and terror on his face. At the same instant, his face appears on the screen in close-up with exactly the same expression on it. The two faces should seem to overlap.*)

CLARENCE. .... (*An animal howl from the guts.*) ... (*A brief silence and suddenly Clarence has bolted across the room and we hear his footsteps running up the stairs. A moment later and we hear the iron door opening. A long silence in the dark room. The only light comes from the slide of Clarence's face.*)

SIGFRID. (*After a pause, tentative.*) Ruby?

RUBY. (*Calm.*) He'll be back, Sigfrid. Clarence will be back.

SIGFRID. But maybe he—

RUBY. (*Strong.*) Clarence will be back.

CLARENCE'S RECORDED VOICE. "I don't want to ever go home. I could stay heeerrre foooorrevv—" (*The tape drags to a halt; the lamp in the projector goes out. Absolute darkness now.*)

SIGFRID. (*After another pause.*) Ruby?

RUBY. It's one of the animals, Sigfrid.

SIGFRID. (*A decision.*) Lakme, get the flashlight.

RUBY. The light will come back, Sigfrid. It always does.

SIGFRID. I'm going up there.

RUBY. It was one of the animals, Sigfrid!

SIGFRID. We don't know, Ruby. WE DON'T KNOW! (*He runs up the stairs, Lakme right behind him.*)

RUBY. Sigfrid! Lakme! Come back here! Don't leave me alone down here! SIGFRID! LAKME! PLEASE! (*Silence, darkness.*) You miserable . . . you goddam miserable . . . (*She has found a flashlight, turns it on and is somewhat comforted.*) I WON'T BE LEFT ALONE DOWN HERE! (*She is standing over Fa's chair.*) Fa? . . . Fa? . . . Fa! . . . you son of a bitch . . . you did it . . . you went ahead and did it . . . when? . . . when? . . . (*A hysterical laughing jag is building.*) . . . you son of a bitch . . . you really did it . . . without even telling us . . . the goddam son of a bitch went ahead and did it . . . children! . . . children! (*The laughter builds and builds. Sigfrid appears at the top of the stairs, carrying Clarence's body. Ruby shines her flashlight on them.*) He did it . . . your son of a bitch Fa went ahead and did it . . . do you hear me? . . . Fa's dead . . . Fa's finally dead. (*The laughter, completely out of control and hysterical, continues. Sigfrid is coming slowly down the stairs with Clarence in his arms.*

Tableau.

The lamp in the slide projector comes back on and once again we see Clarence's face. The tape recorder starts playing.)

CLARENCE'S RECORDED VOICE. ". . . ever and forever and forever. I don't want to ever go home . . ." (*Fast Curtain.*)

ACT THREE

At Rise: The room is again the same. But now the slide of Clarence's face dominates the stage. The picture is enormous, filling the entire rear wall. A person will seem very small standing next to it.

Candlelight. Black crepe . . . maybe.

Fa is still in his chair, the top of his head or perhaps one arm barely visible to the audience. Ruby, Sigfrid, Lakme, and Grandfa are seated facing away from each other and each one at the greatest possible distance from the other three. It is a formal grouping. After all, the final grimmest ritual is being played out now.

There is a stillness in the room we have not heard before.

CLARENCE'S RECORDED VOICE. ". . . and that's another reason. Everybody loves somebody . . . or they will . . . sometime in their life. (*A pause.*) Anything that makes you want to live so bad you'd . . . you'd die for it. That's what I believe in. That's all. That's the way I live." (*And then, with a foolish giggle in his voice.*) Was it all right? (*A long pause; no one moves.*)

RUBY. (*Dispassionate.*) The strong have survived . . . the weak have not . . . and what is there more to say? Those who remain . . . and those who do not . . . it is that simple. The survival of the strong. There is strength and there is weakness and there is only they. But oh! such a din there is when they collide. Am I not right, Clarence? There is trembling . . . there is clamor . . . there is a spasm of the earth. There is *struggle*. And then . . . there is this . . . how it ends . . . the silence. (*Somewhere, in the nethermost region of the theatre, there sounds a faint, dull thump.*) This is how the world is. This. And so be it. (*A pause.*)

GRANDFA. (*Very sad, very low, and very far away.*) No.

RUBY. Lakme.

LAKME. (*Controlled, yet with some difficulty.*) The strong have survived . . . the weak have not . . . and what is there more to say? (*Tiny pause.*) . . . the way his eyes were open . . . just like the dogs' are . . .

RUBY. Those who remain . . .

LAKME. (*At once.*) . . . and those who do not . . . it is that . . . (*Change of voice.*) I never saw dead before. *People* dead.

RUBY. Simple, Lakme. It is that simple.

LAKME. Yes! It is that simple. There is strength and there is weakness and there is only they. But oh . . . (*Faltering.*) . . . but oh! . . .

SIGFRID. (*With a terrifying suddenness.*) BUT OH! SUCH A DIN THERE IS WHEN THEY COLLIDE!

LAKME. . . . when they collide. (*Pause.*) I don't remember.

RUBY. (*Gently coaxing.*) There is trembling . . . there is clamor . . . there is a spasm of the earth.

LAKME. There is struggle.

RUBY. And, then, there is this . . . how it ends . . . the silence.

LAKME. Yes. (*And again, the thump.*)

LAKME and RUBY. (*Low, in unison.*) This is how the world is. This. And so be it.

GRANDFA. (*Despairing with all the force an old man can summon.*) NOOOOOOOOO! (*A sharp silence. Nothing stirs.*)

LAKME. (*A faint, distant voice.*) Just like the dogs' are.

RUBY. Sigfrid. (*No response.*) *Parle, mon beau prince, parle.*

SIGFRID. (*Low.*) I can't do it, Ruby.

RUBY. The strong have survived . . . the weak—

SIGFRID. I SAID I CAN'T DO IT! (*Sharp silence again. Ruby laughs softly.*)

LAKME. (*After a while.*) What about Fa? Why doesn't anyone say anything about Fa? (*A pause and again the thump, ever so slightly louder.*) He's dead, too.

SIGFRID. (*It is a mixture of sadness and contempt; for Clarence, himself . . . everything.*) You were so . . . simple for us, Clarence. So simple.

RUBY. (*At once, trying to steer him back on the right track.*) The strong have survived . . . the weak—

SIGFRID. (*Drowning out the sound of her voice.*) You were so simple!

RUBY. (*If she must relent.*) Be careful, Sigfrid. Be very careful then.

SIGFRID. (*Never looking at or listening to her; this is actually a monologue that follows.*) You let us trample you. You made us. It was too simple. There was so much at stake and you didn't fight back.

RUBY. The line, Sigfrid . . . that was *your* speech . . . don't cross over the line.

SIGFRID. So much at stake . . . *you* . . . and you didn't fight back. Why, Clarence? Just tell us *why*.

LAKME. (*To herself, but seemingly in answer to Sigfrid*.) There is strength and there is weakness and there is only they.

RUBY. (*In direct answer*.) It *is* that simple, Sigfrid.

GRANDFA. (*Numbed now*.) No.

RUBY. We are the victors, Sigfrid. Remember that. Remember who we are. We are the victors.

GRANDFA. (*His voice always the most remote and distant sounding*.) "I'll never care what wickedness I do if this man come to good."

LAKME. (*An observation beginning a revery that will end in an outburst, but the beginning is low*.) Just like the dogs' are. I don't like dead.

SIGFRID. It was pointless, Clarence, what you did was pointless. We knew the fence was out there . . . that it could kill. We already knew that. You could have told us something else. You could have told us what was out there. What is finally out there. There might have been some point to it . . . some point to going out there . . . that we might have *known* . . . but *this* . . .

RUBY. (*Seizing on Sigfrid's "this."*) This . . . how it ends . . . the silence, Sigfrid . . . the silence.

SIGFRID. YOU WERE POINTLESS, CLARENCE!

RUBY. Gently, Sigfrid . . . *speak* gently . . . use gentle words. It is their *requiem* . . . the requiem for the weak.

SIGFRID. (*Obeying involuntarily*.) So pointless.

GRANDFA. (*Again and always as from afar*.) "If they live long and in the end meet the old course of death, mankind will all turn monsters." (*A pause; the thump*.)

LAKME. I don't *like* them to be dead.

RUBY. How pathetic to believe the world is anything but the way it is. What was your word for it, Clarence?

LAKME. I don't *want* them to be dead.

RUBY. (*Finding it*.) Unfortunate. Yes! Unfortunate. (*With a smile of remembrance*.) So judiciously.

LAKME. I don't want anyone to be dead . . . *ever!*

RUBY. To believe in anything but strength. To believe in weakness. How *unfortunate*. How unfortunate for *you*, Clarence.

LAKME. (*Beginning to climax.*) Dead is bad . . . I never saw dead . . . you didn't tell us, Ruby . . . you didn't tell us how bad dead was.

RUBY. (*Opening her arms to Lakme whose back is still to her.*) I couldn't . . . not until now . . . now, this night.

LAKME. I DON'T LIKE IT . . . DEATH! I DON'T LIKE IT AT ALL.

RUBY. (*As if Lakme were in her arms.*) Hush . . . hush now . . . yes! . . . shhh . . .

LAKME. (*Wildly, turning on Ruby, the first time in the scene that anyone has confronted anyone else.*) WHY DIDN'T YOU TELL US HOW BAD DEAD WAS?

SIGFRID. (*Very low.*) Answer her, Ruby . . . answer *us*.

LAKME. (*With a sharp cry, rushing at last into Ruby's open arms.*) JUST TELL US WHY!

RUBY. (*Comforting her.*) Some things can't be told, Lakme . . . best not . . . (*Then, for Sigfrid.*) . . . or answered. (*Again to Lakme.*) They just . . . happen.

LAKME. (*Her head buried in Ruby's arms.*) Death? You mean death?

RUBY. (*Her eyes on Sigfrid.*) The silence. (*A pause; the thump.*)

LAKME. (*Much, much calmer.*) But Clarence . . . that thing out there . . .

RUBY. (*At once.*) People like Clarence don't need something out there to come to a bad end.

LAKME. But we *made* him—

RUBY. (*She must make this point.*) People like Clarence don't even need *us*. They find it on their very own . . . even in broadest daylight . . . under the bluest skies. They sniff it out . . . hunt and scratch for it under every stump and log until they finally dig it up like some rotten truffle. It is their propensity. They are as attracted to a shabby, dismal, *futile* end as surely as . . .

SIGFRID. (*Alone and far away.*) We are.

RUBY. Are *not*. As surely as we are *not*. (*A pause; the thump.*) Consider the Clarences of this world . . . and they are out there . . . just as he was . . . millions upon millions of them . . . no different—not really—from this one . . . consider these Clarences . . . consider them *objectively* . . . with neither tears nor laughter . . . *objectively* . . . and you will know this: that no good will come to them.

SIGFRID. (*With a sad smile . . . perhaps.*) Objectively. The most important emotion . . . objectivity. The teaching emotion, Ruby? Isn't that what you told us? . . . *taught* us.

RUBY. They . . . just as he . . . do not understand what we have understood and we *have* . . . *will* . . . are *determined* to survive them. Understood that there *is* no . . .

SIGFRID. Shakespeare . . . Florence . . . someone in the park.

RUBY. (*With finality.*) Anything. Just . . . us. (*A pause; the thump, a tiny bit louder.*) The litany, Sigfrid. I think we can begin now. (*He still does not, will not turn to her. Lakme, however, unburrows her head from Ruby's arms and, kneeling at her feet, looks up at her. Ruby has taken a deep breath and now begins a kind of chant.*) Fear is not strong.

LAKME. (*With the same cadences.*) Fear is not strong.

RUBY. Fear sickens.

LAKME. Fear . . . Come on, Sigfrid, do it!

RUBY. Fear corrupts.

LAKME. Fear corrupts.

RUBY. We were not strong . . .

LAKME. We were not strong . . . Sigfrid!

SIGFRID. (*Finally turning on and to Ruby directly; taking part, if he must, in the "litany."*) Are not. Are not strong.

RUBY. (*In deadly combat.*) . . . once!

LAKME. . . . once!

SIGFRID. Now! . . . still! . . . ALWAYS!

RUBY. (*Always a little louder, more forceful than Sigfrid.*) But we have dealt with fear . . .

LAKME. But we have dealt with fear . . .

SIGFRID. No! It has dealt with *us*. Warped . . . maimed . . . MUTILATED!

RUBY. (*Relentless.*) . . . not succumbed to it.

LAKME. . . . not succumbed to it.

SIGFRID. We *have* succumbed. We're suffocating with fear.

RUBY. But dealt with it.

LAKME. Dealt.

SIGFRID. (*Trying to reach Lakme.*) Don't listen to her.

RUBY. (*Stronger in his moment of weakening.*) Because we had to.

LAKME. (*Breaking out of the cadence of the litany, a simple concern for her brother now.*) We had to, Sigfrid.

SIGFRID. I've heard these words. All my life I've heard them.

RUBY. (*Never breaking the cadence of the litany, forcing it, in fact.*) Because demands were made on us . . .

LAKME. We agreed, Sigfrid. The three of us. We *agreed* to do it this way. The way we live . . . remember?

SIGFRID. (*Close to the breaking point.*) WE ARE NOT LIVING AND WE HAVE MURDERED FOR IT. WHY, RUBY, WHY!!

RUBY. Because we could no longer cope with . . .

SIGFRID. (*Now.*) OURSELVES!!!!!

LAKME. (*Shrinking.*) I'm frightened, Ruby, I'm frightened.

RUBY. (*Tremendous.*) . . . IT!!! BECAUSE WE COULD NO LONGER COPE WITH IT!!!!

SIGFRID. (*A prayer, a desperate prayer.*) Please . . . someone . . . make it *stop*.

LAKME. Ruby!

SIGFRID. *Let* it stop.

RUBY. (*Ice.*) What stop, Sigfrid? Let "what" stop?

SIGFRID. Us. . . . everything. . . . the suffocation. . . .

RUBY. What else is there, Sigfrid?

SIGFRID. I don't know . . . *something* . . .

RUBY. (*Caustic.*) Bridge? . . . anacrostics, maybe? . . . or tiddley-winks?

SIGFRID. I SAID I DON'T KNOW . . . SOMETHING . . . SOMETHING ELSE. THIS ISN'T ENOUGH, RUBY.

RUBY. (*Rapping it out.*) It will suffice!

SIGFRID. It's a mechanism, the way we live. That's all it is . . . a machine. It runs *us*. Sitting here . . . night after night . . . pretending—

RUBY. No, Sigfrid, no pretending.

SIGFRID. PRETENDING! Pretending not to feel . . . to live. Rituals . . . requiems . . . litanies . . . guests . . . devices! Excuses for living. LOOK AT HIM! LOOK AT CLARENCE! That is the way we live . . . the result of it. WE DON'T LIVE. WE . . .

RUBY. Yes? Sigfrid. Go on.

SIGFRID. (*With a terrible anguish.*) WE DO! WE ARE NOT ALIVE ... WE ARE! (*A silence, the thump.*)

GRANDFA. (*Still from his remote position at the beginning of the act.*) Now, Sigrid, yes ... *now!*

RUBY. (*Not looking at him.*) You won't win him, Grandfa. I won't let you.

GRANDFA. Now ... this night ... *yes!*

SIGFRID. (*A quiet, careful beginning. The moment and what he will say are important. He knows this.*) The fact of us. There is the *fact* of us. That we *are!* What we are, who we are, where. (*Short pause.*) And *why.* Why we are. That, too. All these are the fact of us.

LAKME. (*Still cuddled in Ruby's arms.*) What's Sigfrid doing?

RUBY. Sshh, *cara*, sshh.

GRANDFA. Go on, Sigfrid, go *on.*

SIGFRID. I have no Message to the World ... only a question. No, *questions!* I have questions to the world. Answer one ... any *one* of them ... and maybe, *maybe* we can start all over again.

LAKME. Is something bad happening? (*And again the thump.*)

GRANDFA. Yes! Oh thank God yes!

RUBY. He's only beginning, Grandfa. The questions are easy. But the answers, wait till the answers.

SIGFRID. This room ... the fact of this stifling, wretched room. And yet there is a reason for it. Windows, none ... the air, stale ... the door, there, that door, locked. I would repudiate this place ... I would *like* to ... but I cannot. We each have bred the other and finally, yes, *deserve!* This room ... we are safe in this room. This room ... I AM SUFFOCATING IN THIS ROOM.

LAKME. It *is* something bad! (*Ruby comforts her, though never taking her eyes from Sigfrid.*)

SIGFRID. Which is the way out of this room I cannot leave? Up there? Is it up there?

GRANDFA. Yes, Sigfrid, up!

SIGFRID. Or further down? Further down than we already are?

RUBY. Down. Our way is down, Sigfrid.

SIGFRID. I don't care anymore. The "fact" is that we are here. (*Sudden.*) WELL, WHO HAS THE KEYS TO IT? THE KEYS TO LET US OUT? THERE MUST BE KEYS! (*Vicious, to the picture.*) YOU, CLARENCE, YOU?

GRANDFA. You!

RUBY. No one. (*A silence; the thump.*) The fact of us, Grandfa. This is the fact of us.

SIGFRID. This house . . . there is the fact of this rotting, stinking house. Yes, there is an upstairs . . . with rooms . . . other rooms . . . darkened, empty daylight rooms. Rooms for when it's safe. Rooms we don't know how to live in. Rooms we've *forgotten* how to live in. There is a room up there with a bed in it. My room. A bed I can remember sleeping in. My bed. My bed before . . . *this*. Before we descended. Before we *had* to descend. It was a soft bed . . . a warm bed . . . a deep bed. I had a quilt on that bed . . . a quilt with calico patches. Every night . . . even the very coldest . . . I would sleep with the windows open. They were that warm . . . my bed and my quilt with the calico patches. And I would dream . . . real dreams. Not nightmares. Not like now. I would dream of Persia and flying carpets and every far-off place I'd ever read of. I *could* dream of them under my quilt with the calico patches, all snuggled deep in my soft, warm bed. (*Slight pause.*) But so what?

GRANDFA. (*Gently.*) Sigfrid.

SIGFRID. (*Ugly.*) SO WHAT? What does the memory of a warm bed have to do with anything? How does that *change* anything? How does a memory change *now*? I ASK YOU, CLARENCE, SO WHAT?

GRANDFA. So *everything*. Can't you see that, Sigfrid? Understand it. *Try*.

LAKME. Did I have a bed upstairs, Ruby, and a quilt with calico patches?

RUBY. No, child.

LAKME. Why?

RUBY. Sshh. (*A silence, the thump.*)

SIGFRID. This person . . . this residue of a possibility . . . this me. There is the fact of me. Yes, I am a monster and, yes, I have done damage . . . irreparable damage . . . to myself most of all, but others, too. (*An explanation.*) Because. *Because* this room, *because* this house, *because* this person. BECAUSE!

GRANDFA. But not always, Sigfrid. There was a time . . . "A sky, a blue sky."

SIGFRID. Monstrous! Now I am monstrous. I have *become* that. And who wants to make something out of it? *Why* doesn't someone want to make something out of it? Or am I to be allowed to happen?

RUBY. (*Mocking.*) Grandfa?

SIGFRID. ARE THERE NO MORE COCKED FISTS, CLARENCE?

GRANDFA. *Your* fist. Cock *your* fist, Sigfrid.

RUBY. Good *questions*, Sigfrid. Now try to *answer* them. (*A silence, the thump.*)

SIGFRID. That thing out there . . . the reason for this room, this house, this . . . maybe for this person. That thing out there. (*Long pause; no one moves. And again the thump: a good deal louder than before but it might be possible not to hear it distinctly yet.*) WHAT IS THAT THING OUT THERE? . . . DID YOU SEE IT, CLARENCE? THEN TELL US . . . SOMEONE TELL US WHAT IT IS. IT HAS MADE US NECESSARY! AND WE MUST KNOW WHAT IT *IS*. (*A very, very long pause and again the thump.*)

LAKME. (*Low, scarcely breaking the quiet.*) Ruby, I want a bed like Sigfrid had and a quilt with calico patches.

SIGFRID. (*Husky.*) What?

RUBY. I've won him, Grandfa. With that one question I have won him.

SIGFRID. (*With that same mingling of sadness and contempt, turning directly to her for the first time since he began this long section.*) Have you, Ruby?

RUBY. (*Her eyes locked with Sigfrid's.*) What did I tell you, Grandfa?

SIGFRID. Not yet . . . not quite. (*Ruby laughs softly: that cruel, insinuating sound.*)

GRANDFA. Save yourself, Sigfrid . . . oh, sweet God, save yourself.

SIGFRID. (*A distinct, new beat; with a brighter vocal tone probably.*) The way we live . . . finally that. The way we do not live . . . and at long last the fact of that. Us. (*Then, making the suitable acknowledgments.*) My Ruby, my Lakme, my . . . (*He remembers.*) . . . and me. We are perfect people. We are especially perfect . . . people. Consider us.

RUBY. (*What's he up to?*) Is this necessary Sigfrid?

SIGFRID. *We . . . we* are necessary. And perfect. I don't know about "this."

RUBY. (*Unwilling to explore this new territory; it is a resumption of the litany.*) "With hands . . ."

SIGFRID. (*Pow!*) LISTEN TO ME. (*He is obeyed.*) Consider first, consider my Ruby. *Che bella, eh?* The matriarch triumphant. The madonna entombed . . . excuse me, I meant enthroned. Medusa rampant on a field of . . . Medusa rampant. Call her any name but mother. It hurts her ears.

RUBY. (*Not amused.*) What is this all about, Sigfrid?

SIGFRID. We understand each other, my Ruby and I. That is *one* substitute for love. We also happen to be on to each other, which is *not*.

RUBY. I'm on to what you're doing and I'm asking you to stop.

SIGFRID. "Asking me?" Hoo hoo!

RUBY. *Telling* you!

SIGFRID. (*Charging ahead, delighted.*) What I most like about my Ruby are her teeth. She has always snapped them at anyone come to frighten me and hugged me close. At anyone come to take me away from here . . . our little nesty . . . which frightens *her*. My Ruby is a lion in that respect. A lady lion. A lioness. Tonight she snapped her teeth at Clarence . . . who didn't frighten anyone.

RUBY. (*Steel.*) If you are not like Clarence . . .

SIGFRID. (*Quick.*) I'm like Sigfrid?

RUBY. . . . if you are *not* like him . . . *if* . . . it is because of me. Because I wouldn't *let* you be like that. Because I insisted that you be stronger.

SIGFRID. You did do that. And I am! Clarence felt my muscles. He was impressed. I'm only sorry he didn't get a look at your biceps.

RUBY. He had a good look!

SIGFRID. Oh, you've taught us well to cope with a Clarence. Good Ruby, good mommy, good.

RUBY. Without me . . .

SIGFRID. (*At once.*) I might be free of all this.

RUBY. (*Continuing.*) . . . that would have been *you* in that dress.

SIGFRID. I'M IN A STRAIGHT JACKET.

RUBY. (*After a moment.*) There are the stairs, Sigfrid. Go on. Go out for a little stroll. And then when you come back you can tell us what your little friend didn't. You can report to us what's out there. Take a breath of air. I hate to see you stifling. (*A pause. The thump. Sigfrid looks up at the door. Ruby looks at him. Then, almost with a jerk, he turns to Lakme.*)

SIGFRID. And Lakme. Little, little Lakme.

RUBY. (*A challenge.*) Admit your fear of what's through that door.

SIGFRID. Child of her time. Ruby's masterpiece. This century's.

RUBY. ADMIT!

SIGFRID. (*Moving in on Lakme.*) Too young to remember anything but this. And you have been forgiven much because of it. Because of your youth.

LAKME. (*Standing her ground.*) Don't start in on me, Sigfrid.

SIGFRID. No! Because of your non-youth. Thirteen years in this goddam basement has made you five thousand years old.

LAKME. (*Not understanding, but sensing attack.*) I know plenty of bad things about you, too!

SIGFRID. You know everything and understand nothing. And you never will. You can't. Not down here. Nothing *happens* down here. Except us.

LAKME. I know how to get you mad. I know that. (*Throwing it in his face.*) "Sky, a blue sky!"

SIGFRID. (*Immediately turning away from her.*) You don't have to, Lakme. Please . . . don't do that.

LAKME. (*In pursuit.*) "The eagle soars!"

SIGFRID. (*He hasn't said this in a long, long time. It hurts.*) I WANTED TO. I WANTED TO DEAL WITH WORDS. DO SOMETHING WITH THEM. AND I *TRIED.*

LAKME. (*Unappeased.*) "High soars, high soars the eagle."

SIGFRID. (*Bursting with it.*) IT WAS NOT GIVEN TO ME. I WAS DENIED THAT GIFT.

LAKME. (*Hard, in his ear.*) "Can I soar? Can I soar, too?"

SIGFRID. (*Burst.*) I COULD NOT DO IT. (*A pause.*)

LAKME. (*Low, almost toneless now.*) "For my longing is as great." (*Another pause; Ruby's laugh.*) Sigfrid?

RUBY. (*Serene.*) Shall we resume now, Sigfrid?

LAKME. I'm sorry, Sigfrid. Honest I am.

RUBY. (*Taking up the litany where she left off.*) "With hands . . ."

SIGFRID. (*Instantly getting hold of himself, yet more and more des-*

perate with every word and gesture.) You're not going to win tonight, Ruby. I am. I'm going to finish myself off this time! (*He has moved near Fa.*) I had a father who meant nothing to me. Nothing nothing nothing nothing nothing. Wake up, Fa, just once wake up and take a gander. See what's become of us. See what's become of your poor innocent bobbies. There is something out there and see how we've dealt with it. *YOU MEANT NOTHING!*

GRANDFA. Sigfrid!

SIGFRID. (*And with almost a skip he is over to him.*) Grandfa! Scribe and scrivener. How now, old wart!

GRANDFA. It's too *easy* this way, Sigfrid.

SIGFRID. How's your book coming along, Grandfa? How progresses that novel you're writing?

GRANDFA. It doesn't mean anything to give in to it like this.

SIGFRID. You're so old. You're so damnably old. Why do you continue? On what *grounds?* Why do you even bother to wake up in the morning?

GRANDFA. I will not despair! There was a time—

SIGFRID. I don't understand, Grandfa. I don't understand what keeps you from doing what we did years ago. You're so *old!* What keeps you from death?

GRANDFA. (*The most important point he can make.*) IT'S OUT THERE FOR ALL OF US. (*A pause; he has been heard.*) It's out there for all of us.

SIGFRID. Then what's the point of going on with it?

GRANDFA. (*Low, this is to Sigfrid.*) To stand *up* to it.

SIGFRID. From a wheelchair? (*A pause.*)

GRANDFA. (*Slow, with difficulty.*) Does there have to be a point to anything? Is that what men insist upon these days?

SIGFRID. (*In spite of himself.*) I suppose not, Grandfa. I suppose not . . . if you're nine thousand years old and you're standing up to it sitting down in a wheelchair. *Then* I suppose there doesn't have to be a point to it. (*A pause; the thump.*)

RUBY. (*Consoling, from across the room. She can afford to. Sigfrid is nearly done now.*) Soon, Grandfa. They'll be here for you soon. It won't be much longer now.

SIGFRID. (*Brightly again, moving all about the room during this speech.*) You're a Clarence, Grandfa. That's who you are. Clarence thought he could change things. Clarence even thought he could change us. Wasn't that sweet of him, Grandfa? And wasn't that sad. Sweet Clarence, sweet Grandfa. Sad Clarence, sad Grandfa. He couldn't do it, Grandfa. And neither can you. Things are the way they are. We are the way we are. Look what it took Clarence to find out he couldn't change anything . . . most of all himself. He stomped all over town . . . stomp, stomp, stomp . . . bells ringing . . . banners waving . . . his own little children's crusade . . . ta ta ta ta ta! Wanting to *change* things. And all he accomplished was this. Why he didn't even accomplish me. (*The viciousness, the hysteria are mounting now.*) I buggered him, Grandfa, I buggered him good. WE CAN'T HAVE BUGGERED SAINTS NOW CAN WE, GRANDFA? (*Turning to the picture and addressing it.*) We're sorry, Clarence, but your bid for martyrdom is rejected. It was a real good try, baby, but you just didn't have the stuff. This is the court of last resort down here and you and your ideals . . . your buggered ideals . . . have been found lacking. They lack the substance, they lack the granite, they lack the simple facts of life. The facts of *you!* (*And now, facing full front, his fists clenched against an imaginary antagonist.*) Yes, we're horrible. But *who*, who is there to make something of it? Stand up and be counted. This house is horrible. But do you know how to build a better one? The way we live is horrible. Then teach us *your* way. But don't send us this for an answer, world, don't send us a Clarence. It simply won't do. And tell us first . . . before you send us another Clarence . . . AND THERE WILL BE MORE OF THEM . . . tell us *why*. Why this horribleness. *Why* this room without windows. *Why* Clarence who does not move. *Why* Fa who meant nothing. *Why* that thing out there without a name. Why us. WHY! (*Then, turning to Ruby, but without breaking the tempo and emotion of the moment.*) All right, Ruby. We may resume now. (*He has begun the litany.*) With hands!

RUBY. (*Sinking back into her chair.*) Ah!

SIGFRID. . . . with mind! . . .

GRANDFA. (*Low, his head bowed.*) No, Sigfrid.

SIGFRID. . . . with *passion!* . . . we have managed an existence.

RUBY and LAKME. (*Picking it up.*) An existence!

SIGFRID. . . . an arrangement . . .

RUBY and LAKME. . . . an arrangement . . .

SIGFRID. . . . an arrangement that works . . .

RUBY and LAKME. Yes!

SIGFRID. . . . something for *us!*

RUBY and LAKME. Us!

SIGFRID, RUBY, and LAKME. We have done that . . .

SIGFRID. . . . done that! . . .

SIGFRID, RUBY, and LAKME. AND WE HAVE SURVIVED YOU!
(*These last words were very loud: shouted almost. Now there is
a sharp silence. No one moves. There should be the suggestion
of a tableau. Sigfrid and Lakme are next to Ruby, their heads
lower than hers. Grandfa is apart from them. We hear the
thump. The moment looks and feels like the end of the play.
Then Sigfrid, abruptly breaking this mood, crosses the stage and
turns on the overhead lights. After so much darkness, the room
should seem unbearably, unnecessarily bright.*)

RUBY. (*At once, and as she leisurely begins to remove her wig and
costume ornaments.*) Your *viola de gamba* lesson, Lakme. Is it
tomorrow or the day after? I can never remember which.

LAKME. (*Listless, removing her Green Hornet costume.*) Tomorrow. The day after. I don't know.

SIGFRID. I'm sorry, Grandfa. I tried. You know, I really tried this
time. (*Grandfa turns away from him.*) All right, then, where's
your Message to the World? Your little bundle of tidings and
joy? (*He snatches the Chronicle from Grandfa's lap.*) I didn't
think you had one! (*He throws down the Chronicle and moves
away. The thump.*)

RUBY. Put something on the phonograph, Lakme. Something exhil-
arating. *La Grande Messe des Morts* should do very nicely.
(*Lakme goes over to the phonograph.*) I understand the Libyans
are agitating for land reforms. Or isn't that what they're saying?
It's so difficult to keep up these days . . . nearly impossible. Tur-
moil under every bushel. (*No response. The thump: a little
louder than before.*) I am an admirer of the works of Miss Jane
Austen. In re-reading *Pride and Prejudice* . . . it was only last
night . . . I was struck by the similarity of her writing to the music of Mozart. Each so precise, so balanced . . . so *controlled,*
that's the word! Don't you think so? (*No response. The thump.
Then, irritably:*) What are you doing, Lakme?

LAKME. It's broken.

RUBY. Don't be ridiculous.

LAKME. ALL RIGHT IT'S NOT BROKEN!

RUBY. Well! I can see that certain little girls get cranky when they're allowed to stay up after bedtime. You were wrong about your sister, Sigfrid. I'm afraid she's every inch a *twelve*. (*Sigfrid has removed his black shirt and is seen to be wearing a white one underneath.*) *Soit une ange, caro,* and snuff out the candles. It's so wasteful with the lights on. (*Sigfrid obeys, almost mechanically. A silence. The thump. Then, clapping her hands together, joyfully:*) Children! I just figured it out . . . finally! The reason your Ruby looks so young and glamorous. It's because she so seldom laughs. (*Then, this irritable aside:*) *Lakme! Ne cueillez pas ton nez!* (*She waits for Lakme's usual reply.*) "I'll pick it if I want to." You're not going to say that? So don't. (*And back to the joyful mood.*) Laugh! Go ahead, laugh. Or smile very broadly. (*She demonstrates.*) See the wrinkling it causes? Millions of horrible little crinkles. (*Sigfrid and Lakme remain stony-faced.*) Well, don't worry about it! Either of you. And turn off the projector. I'm sick of looking at him. (*Again Sigfrid obeys. A silence. The thump.*) Grandfa! Will you favor us with one of your dramatic recitations? And may I suggest the Richard II deposition scene. It should have particular significance for you this evening. No? An old trouper like you passing up an opportunity for a gala farewell performance? *Ein kleine schwanengesang?* Grandfa! (*A short silence. The thump. Then, turning to Sigfrid, wth irritation, the projector is still on.*) I thought I asked you to—

SIGFRID. (*Curt.*) It's jammed.

RUBY. How long is *this* little sulk going to last?

SIGFRID. Try it yourself then!

RUBY. (*On her feet, going to the projector.*) Just tell me *when*. (*She fiddles with the projector.*) Oh . . . it is. And the phonograph. It really won't . . . ? (*The thump. Then, with a nervous laugh:*) Retribution! Well what else could it be? Divine retribution! (*A taut silence. The thump.*) What shall we do now? No music, Grandfa won't recite, *les enfants sont* sulking . . . look at Clarence the rest of the night? (*The thump; it is becoming increasingly difficult not to acknowledge it.*)

LAKME. I'm going to bed. (*She is on her way.*)

RUBY. Lakme! (*Lakme returns and gives Ruby a perfunctory kiss. The thump.*)

LAKME. (*Perhaps she has heard it.*) I wish . . .

RUBY. For a deep, warm bed and a quilt with calico patches. I know.

LAKME. (*She means this.*) I wish we hadn't done this tonight.

RUBY. (*Ignoring this, yet comforting her.*) Now say goodbye to Grandfa. He won't be here in the morning. (*The thump. Lakme crosses to Grandfa.*)

LAKME. (*Simply.*) Grandfa. (*He only looks at her.*) We'll all miss you. And I hope you'll be very happy wherever it is you're going. I hope— (*He lunges at her with the chair.*) I HOPE YOU DIE ON THAT FARM! I HOPE WE ALL DIE! (*She runs across the stage, on her way out, and as she passes in front of the picture of Clarence:*) FINK! (*She is gone. Brief silence. The thump.*)

RUBY. Sigfrid? (*He looks at her.*) Nothing.

SIGFRID. What, Ruby?

RUBY. Nothing. (*Sigfrid is moving towards the door now.*) That is the most extraordinary photograph. Sigfrid! (*He turns.*) Please. Not just yet.

SIGFRID. It's late.

RUBY. (*With that forced gaiety.*) I'm not asking you to stay up all night with me! Just a little while longer. Besides, we don't have anything planned for tomorrow.

SIGFRID. Oh but we do.

RUBY. What on earth are you talking about?

SIGFRID. Another Clarence, Ruby. We have another Clarence planned for tomorrow.

RUBY. (*Always trying to keep him with her.*) Not if you don't want to, Sigfrid! *I'm* perfectly willing to . . . be here with you.

SIGFRID. (*Moving towards Grandfa.*) And all the poems, Grandfa, think of all the poems I must write tomorrow. Eagle poems. Little Sigfrid can't write his wondrous eagle poems with fuzz in his noggin, can he now, Grandfa?

GRANDFA. (*Vibrant.*) He never *tried.*

SIGFRID. Is that what the facts say, Grandfa? The facts of your fiction?

GRANDFA. (*His last chance with Sigfrid; he knows this.*) It's not fiction. You know it's not— (*A terrifically loud thump. Each of them, in his fashion, starts perceptibly. A loud silence.*)

SIGFRID. Ruby? (*She looks at him.*) Nothing.

RUBY. What, Sigfrid?

SIGFRID. Nothing. (*He is on his way out.*)

RUBY. Sigfrid! (*He stops but does not turn to her.*) Five minutes? (*He starts to go again.*) SIGFRID! (*Again he stops and again does not turn to her.*) What will become of us?

SIGFRID. (*After a moment.*) Nothing.

RUBY. No?

SIGFRID. We will continue. (*The thump.*)

RUBY. Yes?

SIGFRID. Ask Clarence. (*He is going.*) We will continue. (*He is gone. The thump. Ruby and Grandfa are alone.*)

RUBY. We will continue. Did you hear that, Grandfa? Sigfrid said we will continue. (*A pause; the thump. Grandfa has begun and will continue to very slowly tear the pages, one by one, from the Chronicle.*) And that nothing will happen to us. Ask Clarence, he said. (*A pause; the thump. Each time a little louder now.*) But Clarence doesn't have anything to say. Clarence is dead. (*A pause; the thump.*) Then what did Sigfrid mean by that? (*A pause; the thump. Then, like lightning:*) I AM NOT A STUPID PERSON. WHAT OTHER ALTERNATIVES WERE THERE? (*A pause; the thump.*) We are eagles, Grandfa, we are. We have, you see, some stature. We are not little people. We are not pathetic people. There is something heroic about us. (*A pause; the thump.*) WE ARE SAFE. DOWN HERE WE ARE SAFE. (*A pause; the thump.*) Ask Clarence? I have nothing to *ask* Clarence. I'll *tell* him. Tell him something he should have known. For all his talk about commitment, we were, after all, as it turned out, the committed ones. We were. (*A pause; the thump.*) IT WILL PASS. THIS THING WILL PASS US BY. (*A pause; the thump.*) You see, Clarence, we, too, have taken a stand against these things, only we have *acted* on it. We have acted *accordingly*. We are no longer life-size. We are larger than you. We have transcended— (*An enormous THUMP. She falters. Then, forcing herself to continue:*) We have survived everything and we shall survive now this night. We shall do that. We are *prepared* for now this night. Our lives were meant for it. It is our meaning. We are vindicated . . . now this night . . . finally . . . totally . . . we are vindicated now this night! (*The thud: terrifying, overwhelming, crushing. Like a hard punch in the stomach. No reverberations. A dull, hard, crunching thud.*) SIGFRID SAID WE WILL CONTINUE! . . . WE . . . WILL . . . (*And again that devastating sound. And now silence, a very long one. Ruby and Grandfa like statues.*)

RUBY. (*Without moving, numbed and toneless.*) Grandfa? (*THUMP.*) Sigfrid? (*THUMP.*) Lakme? (*THUMP.*) Fa? (*THUMP.*) No one? . . . No one! . . . NO ONE! (*THUMP. THUMP, THUMP.*)

GRANDFA. (*Tearing the last pages from the Chronicle.*) And then there is this . . . how it ends . . . the silence. (*And, indeed, there is one now. A very, very long silence. Sigfrid and Lakme come slowly into the room. They stop at the door and look at Ruby. No one moves. Silence.*) This is how the world is. This. And so be it. (*There is one last page left in the Chronicle. He writes on it with a large, decisive stroke.*) No. (*THUMP. Silence. Ruby has moved almost somnambulistically to the tape recorder. The wheels are spinning.*)

RUBY'S RECORDED VOICE. ". . . who thought they were to prevail. We shall *not* prevail . . . so be it. (*Thump.*) We shall *not* endure . . . (*Thump.*) . . . but who was ever meant to? (*Ruby is walking slowly back to her place in the center of the room.*) And we shall *not* inherit the earth . . . it has already disinherited *us.* (*THUMP. THUMP. Ruby sits. Staring straight ahead and not looking at them, she extends one hand each to Sigfrid and Lakme who come forward and sit one to each side of her. They do not move.*) If we are without faith, we find our way in the darkness . . . it is light enough. (*Thump.*) If we are without hope, we turn to our despair . . . (*Thump.*) . . . it has its own consolations. (*Grandfa has gotten out of his chair.*) And if we are without charity, we suckle the bitter root of its absence . . . wherefrom we shall draw the sustenance to destroy you. (*THUMP. Grandfa has begun to climb the stairs: slowly, slowly.*) Go . . . seek not to know us . . . to understand . . . the compassion of it will exhaust you and there is so little strength left us now . . . so little. (*Grandfa is nearly there. Ruby, Sigfrid, and Lakme never move.*

Even their eyes do not move. They stare straight ahead and nothing more. The lights are beginning to fade.) Spoken by me this December morning. Unwitnessed, unheard, alone." (*The Thump. Silence. Grandfa is out. No one moves. The Thump. Silence. The Thump. Silence. The* thump. *And silence. The stage is completely dark.* THE THUMP.)

WHISKEY

(1973)

For Leonard Melfi
Like the song says,
a good man is hard to find.

WHISKEY was first performed on April 19, 1973, at Theatre at Saint Clement's in New York City. It was directed by Kevin O'Connor. Sets by Kert Lundell. Lighting by Charles Cosler. Costumes by Lorie Watson. Sound by Lewis Rosen. Production assistants were Suzanne Gedance and Hall Powell. The production stage manager was Jimmy Cuomo.

THE CAST
(in order of appearance)

ANNOUNCER	Kelly Fitzpatrick
I. W. HARPER	Tom Rosqui
TIA MARIA	Charlotte Rae
JOHNNY WALKER	Beeson Carroll
SOUTHERN COMFORT	Susan Browning
JACK DANIELS	Michael Sacks

THE PLAYERS

THE LUSH THRUSHES:

I. W. HARPER: Middle-aged, slightly balding and a little plump. His is an extremely affable nature, but when sufficiently aroused he can crack a mean bullwhip. Certainly at first glance he is extremely likable.

TIA MARIA: Middle-aged and a little plump herself. She's basically a warm and sentimental dame but occasionally the facade of brassiness obscures that fact. She is either extremely down or extremely up: laughing too hard . . . or crying. Above all, there is something very nice and maternal about her.

JOHNNY WALKER: Middle thirties, dark eyes and hair. *He* thinks he's handsome. He also thinks of himself as a mean bastard which means that he *acts* like a mean bastard. Well, most of the time.

SOUTHERN COMFORT: Early twenties, red hair and built. She's wild and sexy and arrogant and flaunts her sexuality and drinks a lot and gets like a cat in heat and just generally behaves like a bundle of dynamite.

JACK DANIELS: Early twenties, blue eyes and blonde. He has an engaging grin which isn't engaging enough to conceal the fact that he is a very dumb bunny indeed. If you told him this to his face, he wouldn't be too upset. In fact, he'd probably grin and bear it. You see, he rather enjoys playing the buffoon.

WHISKEY: A mean-tempered, extremely musical horse who occupies that very special place in the heart of America left empty when the first and original Lassie retired from the screen. WHISKEY's millions of fans, of course, have no idea how mean he is. Believe me, this horse is a killer.

Also appearing in the play (*but never seen*) are:
ANNOUNCER'S VOICE: Smooth, unctuous and Texas as all git out.
URGENT VOICE: A total hysteric.

THE SETTING:
   The Houston Astrodome and then a large suite in a very swanky
   hotel in downtown Houston.

THE TIME:
   Now.

Darkness. We hear the expectant, excited murmurings of a huge crowd. Then there is a long drum roll followed by a crash of cymbals.

ANNOUNCER'S VOICE. Mr. President, honored astronauts, ladies and gentlemen, and all you other y'alls, Houston's unique, one-of-a-kind, internationally world-famous and fully air conditioned Astrodome brings you live and in the flesh for the first time anywhere outside of your home color TV screen, the stars of America's longest running TV series . . . ! (*He's said all this in one breath. Now he pauses, takes one, before trumpeting the name.*) THE LUSH THRUSHES AND WHISKEY! ! ! (*A neon light across the top of the proscenium is illuminated to read: "The Lush Thrushes and Whiskey." While the orchestra vamps under each introduction.*) He's made you laugh an' he's made you cry. A quick man with the bullwhip but even quicker to right social injustice and grievances. Like the song says, a good man is hard to find. Who am I talking about? (*Pause.*) WHY I. W. HARPER, THAT'S WHO! ! ! (*A light comes up revealing I. W. Harper standing inside a cut-out of a huge bottle of I. W. Harper's. I.W. is wearing a fawn-colored Stetson, a buckskin fringed shirt, expensive cowboy pants and black boots with rattlesnakes on the sides. The crowd roars its approval. I.W. looks terrified.*)

I. W. HARPER. (*When the crowd will let him speak.*) Howdy. After all those years you've been watching us on your TV screens, it sure is nice to see you for a change. And I'll tell you something. I've done a lot of living, a lot of loving and a lot of elbow-bending. And drunk or sober, I never met a man I didn't like. Yahoo! (*He tries, rather unsuccessfully, to crack his bullwhip. The Announcer's Voice and the orchestra come quickly to his rescue.*)

ANNOUNCER'S VOICE. Behind every great man there's a little woman an' I. W. Harper's no exception. What Sophia Loren is to Italy, what Joan of Arc was to France, is this little lady to our great and golden Southwest. That bowl of peaches and cream with just a wee dab bit of vinegar to make the sweet part taste even sweeter . . . ! (*Pause.*) TIA MARIA! ! ! (*A light comes up revealing Tia Maria standing inside a cut-out of a huge bottle of Tia Maria. She is wearing a white Stetson but it is hanging down her back from the drawstring around her throat. She wears a blouse, a suede vest, a cowskin skirt and high red boots. Again the crowd roars its approval. Tia Maria looks terrified, too.*)

TIA MARIA. *I* never met a man *I* didn't like. (*She pauses, and this is her legendary comic timing. You can almost feel the crowd counting the beats with her.*) Until I married I.W.! (*The crowd laughs. Tia Maria is in! She visibly relaxes and improvises a yodelled rondelay around the orchestra's vamping.*)

ANNOUNCER'S VOICE. He's mean, he's tough, he packs a big swift side iron. He don't say much but when he does you better listen. He'd as soon shoot you as spit on you. Your favorite badman and mine . . . (*Pause.*) JOHNNY WALKER! ! ! (*A light comes up revealing Johnny Walker standing inside a cut-out of a huge bottle of Johnny Walker Black Label Scotch. Johnny is wearing a cowboy outfit entirely of black leather: hat, shirt, pants, boots, everything. Since he's squinting and trying to look real mean at the same time, he looks less nervous than I. W. Harper and Tia Maria. But he isn't.*)

JOHNNY WALKER. (*After waiting for the entire Astrodome to get as quiet as a mouse; it's a long wait, too.*) I'll tell you something, cowpoke. (*You could drive a Mack truck through his drawl.*) I'd as soon shoot you as shit on you. Spit on you! I mean spit on you! (*General consternation. Johnny Walker draws both pistols and fires, the orchestra plays loudly, anything to cover up. Johnny Walker's facade has visibly wilted.*)

ANNOUNCER'S VOICE. Now all right, you young tads, and some of you not so young ones, too! This next little gal's a real little lady and I wouldn't want her leaving Houston thinking the men here were just a pack o' prairie wolves. (*Appropriate and appreciative yells and whistles from the men in the audience.*) Aw shucks! she was born and raised in Houston, so she already *knows!* (*There is a burst of flame and a shrill scream from the shadows.*) Why she's just burning to get out there and entertain y'all . . . SOUTHERN COMFORT! ! ! (*A light comes up revealing Southern Comfort standing inside a cut-out of a huge bottle of Southern Comfort. She is wearing what could only be described as a very mini and*

*a very mod version of a cowgirl's outfit. Lots of thigh and breast
but her accessories are pretty groovy, too. At the moment, she
isn't at all ready. Someone put too much kerosene on her baton
ends and they are flaming dangerously. She holds them at arms
length, clearly terrified and not at all ready to do anything with
them but hold them as far away from her as she possibly can.
Realizing she must do something, she turns and faces the audience, a flaming baton in each hand, and forces a kind of frozen
smile.)*

SOUTHERN COMFORT. Tableau, ladies and gentlemen! I call this my
flaming tableau!

ANNOUNCER'S VOICE. *(To the rescue.)* And a mighty pretty one it is,
honey. Ain't that a pretty sight, folks? Hunh? Ain't it? Well, let's
show the little lady how pretty we think it is! *(He leads the
audience in reluctant applause.)* Hey, now just a second y'all,
settle down and see if you can help an ol' cowpoke out. I know
there's *five* Thrush Lushes and Whiskey but I'll be dollgarned if
I can only think of *four* o' them! Who's the one I'm missing?
(An inaudible voice from the crowd.) Who? *(More voices calling out the name.)* You'll have to speak up a whole plumb lot
louder than that. *(More and more voices.)* How do you 'spect
me to hear you when you're all talking at once? Now I want to
hear that name loud and I want to hear it clear. One! two! three!
(We hear the audience loud and clear.)

AUDIENCE. JACK DANIELS! ! !

ANNOUNCER'S VOICE. Who? Captain Samuels?

AUDIENCE. JACK DANIELS! ! !

ANNOUNCER'S VOICE. Dan Janiels?

AUDIENCE. JACK DANIELS! ! !

ANNOUNCER'S VOICE. Oh! You mean that one and only rib-tickler,
that court jester to the great and golden Southwest, that cowboy
with a bale of hay where his head should be . . . *(Pause.)* JACK
DANIELS! ! ! *(A light comes up revealing Jack Daniels standing
inside a cut-out of a huge bottle of Jack Daniels. He is hatless
and wearing a gingham shirt under denim coveralls. He is barefoot, too. He grins foolishly and the audience goes wild. He tries
the simplest of rope tricks, makes a botch of it and his pants
fall down. Clearly an audience favorite, Jack Daniels is.)*

JACK DANIELS. You know what the Texan said after he opened a bottle of Lone Star Beer with his front teeth? "Do I swallow this here little dohickey or chew?" And you know what the Yankee said who tried the same thing? "Phphphphphphph." (*He lisps through imaginary broken front teeth. The crowd laughs. The orchestra has broken into a rousing cowboy song. The five Lush Thrushes, each standing inside the appropriately marked cut-out bottle, are singing along and urging the audience to join them, especially for the hand claps. While the Lush Thrushes sing, each of them does his or her own thing: I. W. Harper cracking his bullwhip; Tia Maria improvising yodels; Johnny Walker shooting his gun; Southern Comfort trying to twirl her massively flaming batons; and Jack Daniels attempting rope tricks. All in all, it is a very colorful stage picture. One panel of the Lush Thrushes and Whiskey tableau, however, is still dark.*)

ANNOUNCER'S VOICE. (*Over the music.*) And now, with all respects to this glittering array of multimillion dollar talent and very pretty feminine pulchritude . . . the word's in Webster and it's *not* dirty! . . . the star of our show. That Paderewzski on the hoof, that equine Frank Sinatra, America's favorite horse and I'm tempted to say person! . . . the one, the only, the what-other-word-but-inimitable! . . . (*Pause.*) . . . WHISKEY! ! ! (*A light comes up on the cut-out silhouette of a horse. The only trouble is there's no real horse inside it when there very clearly should be. The Lush Thrushes sing another chorus of their song and wait at the end of each line for Whiskey to tap a response with his hoof or appear . . . or anything. Consternation among the Lush Thrushes. The song continues. Tia Maria goes behind the show curtain, the other four continue singing. But even above the music we can hear Whiskey's loud whinnying and crashing hooves and Tia Maria's even louder yells. Tia Maria reappears looking disheveled, angry and holding her arm. I. W. Harper goes behind the show curtain and again we hear Whiskey whinnying and crashing his hooves. We even catch a glimpse of I. W. Harper struggling unsuccessfully with a rope that is clearly attached to Whiskey's bridle. The crowd has recovered itself sufficiently and begun to react. First there were just a few catcalls but now the general laughter is unmistakable and growing.*)

I. W. HARPER. Whiskey'll be right out, ladies and gentlemen. He's just feeling a little . . . well, frisky this evening!

JACK DANIELS. You show me a horse who won't take center stage spotlight when it's offered him and I'll show you a Mexican burro who's trying to pass for a horse!

ANNOUNCER'S VOICE. Ladies and gentlemen, please. Whiskey'll be right out here to entertain you. Just a simple case of stable fright! Opening night nerves! In the meantime, I suggest we all join the Thrush Lushes in a good old-fashioned Texas sing out! (*Pandemonium reigns. The Lush Thrushes valiantly struggle to keep the song going but they have clearly lost their audience. Whiskey must be completely out of control by now from the look of I. W. Harper's struggles with the rope. Several times he has been thrown to the ground. And no matter how loud the crowd's laughter and the music, Whiskey's whinnying is louder than all. Suddenly, an excited hush falls over the crowd. From the looks on the Lush Thrushes' faces we can clearly see that something dreadful has happened. They barely continue to sing, just kind of mouthing the song as they watch this dreadful thing happening. Hardly anyone in the orchestra is bothering to play anymore. Above this ominous almost-silence, Whiskey's whinnying will seem very loud indeed.*)

I. W. HARPER. He's leaving!

TIA MARIA. The President's leaving.

JOHNNY WALKER. He's walking out!

JACK DANIELS. He's not coming back! (*What has happened and what the Lush Thrushes have seen and followed with their very own and astonished-and-humiliated eyes is this: the President of the United States has walked out on them! I. W. Harper, Tia Maria, Johnny Walker and Jack Daniels are studies in abject humiliation. Southern Comfort, however, is seething with anger. She's not about to be humiliated like this, not in her old hometown, even if he is the President.*)

SOUTHERN COMFORT. (*Running to the footlights and nailing him with her voice, it's a strong one.*) Mr. President! Hey, jowly boy, that's right, I'm talking to you! (*This time you could hear a pin drop in the Astrodome. The President has clearly turned and is listening to Southern Comfort.*) You ought to try slipping into one o' these for size! (*And with that she flips her skirt up over her head, does a neat backbend and stays there. And now total consternation. The crowd roars, the band plays loudly, the other Lush Thrushes hustle Southern Comfort offstage and the Announcer is reduced to babbling in his microphone. Above the pandemonium . . . louder than it, in fact . . . we hear Whiskey whinnying and crashing his hooves: a sound that will continue while the light and sound of this scene fade and during the short blackout which follows while the following legend is flashed on the curtain* MUCH LATER THAT NIGHT. THE NEXT MORNING, IN FACT. *Whiskey's whinnying subsides to a peaceful and occasional snortle. His crashing hooves become an occasional shift of weight. A silence. And in the darkness we hear Jack Daniels singing "The Streets of Laredo" in a very sweet and very true voice. We are in a hotel suite. There are no lights on but enough is spilling in from the window to give us some idea of where we are. By the window, on a window seat, in fact, is where Jack Daniels is sitting and singing his song. It looks like there's been a very big party in the room not too long ago. Empty glasses and liquor bottles, overflowing ashtrays, several rolling tables sent up by room service, etc. We hear assorted snores, grunts and other sleeping noises from somewhere in the room but it is too dark to tell who is making them or from where. All this while Jack Daniels sings "The Streets of Laredo," which is a very beautiful and very sad song. Oh yes, from his singing it should be quite clear that Jack Daniels is totally, thoroughly, blissfully and roaringly drunk. Stinking. Blotto. Wiped out. Suddenly there is a loud and urgent knocking on the door outside the suite and we hear an urgent voice.*)

URGENT VOICE: Fire! Fire! The hotel's on fire! Everybody out and into the street! (*The voice by now is a shriek of hysteria.*) The main thing is stay calm! Don't anybody lose their head! (*Jack Daniels continues his song, clearly not hearing or comprehending this message of impending disaster from outside the suite. Next we hear the sound of many people in the corridor as they flee their rooms and head for the elevator and stairs. From the occasional yells, shouts and screams it should sound like a stampede is going on right outside the suite. Jack Daniels continues his song. The sounds of the stampede have faded away. Silence and*

Jack Daniels singing. A small bedside lamp is switched on and in the tiny shaft of light it spills we see I. W. Harper. He is wearing pajamas but they have been custom-made to look very much like the cowboy outfit he was wearing at the Astrodome: the buckskin fringed shirt, for example, is really only a stencilled pattern on a simple cotton pajama shirt but it looks pretty convincing for a moment. I.W. rolls out of bed and heads for the bathroom. From his somnambulistic movements we can tell that he is not really awake and from his swaying walk we can see that he, too, is stinking drunk. There is just enough light spilling into the bathroom to see I.W. enter and seat himself on the toilet. Jack Daniels continues his song, as unaware of I. W. Harper as I. W. Harper is unaware of him. Another bedside lamp (on the other side of the same bed, in fact) is switched on and we see Tia Maria. She is wearing a lady's nightgown version of I. W. Harper's cowboy pajamas. When she rolls out of bed and heads for the same bathroom, we can see that she, too, is only half awake and stinking drunk. With the two bedside lamps burning, the bathroom is even brighter and this is what we see: I. W. Harper sitting on the toilet and Tia Maria heading towards him. They are clearly on a collision course. I.W.'s jaw hangs open, he looks like he's seeing a ghost. He cannot move, he dares not speak. Tia Maria is almost on top of him when she turns and sits directly on his lap. What Tia Maria then does is this: produce the loudest, longest and most bloodcurdling scream in the history of the theatre.)

TIA MARIA. AAAAAAEEEEEIIIIIIOOOOOOOUUUUUUUU!!!!

I. W. HARPER. Honey?

TIA MARIA. AAAAAAAEEEEEEEEEIIIIIIIIIOOOOOQOUUUUUU UU!!!!

I. W. HARPER. Is that you, honey?

TIA MARIA. AAAAAEEEEEEEEOOOOOOOOUUUUUU!!!!

I. W. HARPER. You scared me.

TIA MARIA. Oh! Oh! Oh!

I. W. HARPER. That's not funny. (*Tia Maria has fainted dead away. I.W. is still sitting on the toilet.*) Wow! Wow, my heart is pounding. Listen to that ol' ticker o' mine pump! First I didn't see you. Then I wasn't sure if it *was* you. And then I got afraid that if I said something I'd scare whoever it was more than they was scaring *me*. I mean I could *see* what was gonna happen but at the same time I just couldn't believe it really *would*. People don't sit on other people when they go to the toilet. I mean they just don't do that. Same goes for the people already *on* the toilet. Other people just plain don't sit on *them*. I sat in a lady's lap once but that was in a movie theatre and it was a real bright day out, my eyes hadn't adjusted yet, and I just didn't see her. Scared the bejeezes out o' me. Sure *felt* funny, too. (*Pause.*) Come on now, honey, get up. You know I can't go with you in here.

TIA MARIA. (*Stirring.*) What happened?

I. W. HARPER. You passed out.

TIA MARIA. Feel like I fainted.

I. W. HARPER. You been hitting that stuff pretty hard tonight.

TIA MARIA. I know what passing out feels like and this is different. It's . . . it's . . . headier.

I. W. HARPER. Headier?

TIA MARIA. More in the head. Passing out's more in the gut. I need a pill. (*She struggles to her feet.*) I'm turning on the light.

I. W. HARPER. I don't have my shades on.

TIA MARIA. Close your eyes then.

I. W. HARPER. It'll hurt, honey.

TIA MARIA. It's gonna hurt like hell. (*She turns on the bathroom lights, they both wince at the brightness.*) Oh! Wow! Oh wow!

I. W. HARPER. You okay?

TIA MARIA. I had the worse nightmare, I.W.!

I. W. HARPER. Baby! Why didn't you wake me?

TIA MARIA. It was a major one.

I. W. HARPER. Those damn stingers. They'll do it every time.

TIA MARIA. I was walking along, you know? . . . just walking, nothing chasing me or anything like that . . . I was in a woods! . . . and I heard this stream . . . no, it was more like a waterfall . . . and I got real tired and I just had to rest. So far everything was real peaceful and I was feeling real good. But when I went to sit down . . . and this is the horrible part . . . I felt— (*Tia Maria has sat on the edge of the bathtub. From behind the drawn shower curtains there is a terrific whinnying and crashing of hooves. Tia Maria leaps to her feet, the shower curtains sway menacingly.*) AAAAAEEEEEIIIIIIOOOOOUUUUUU!!!

I. W. HARPER. Whiskey!

TIA MARIA. AAAAEEEEIIIIUUUU!!!!

I. W. HARPER. Now hush up in there, you hear me? Now hush!

TIA MARIA. He's trying to kill me, don't tell me he's not!

I. W. HARPER. Thattaboy, Whiskey, steady now there. Momma
didn't mean to frighten you.

TIA MARIA. Frighten *him?*

I. W. HARPER. You know he doesn't like it when you do that, Tia.

TIA MARIA. I'm sorry, but I keep forgetting that he's in there!

I. W. HARPER. Thattaboy, back to sleep now, momma's sorry . . .

TIA MARIA. Like hell she is!

I. W. HARPER. Sshh!

TIA MARIA. Goddamn that horse anyway!

I. W. HARPER. Tia!

TIA MARIA. I mean doggurn, only it comes out goddamn!

I. W. HARPER. Look at you, you're all het up. (*Whiskey is quiet now
and the shower curtain stops swaying.*)

TIA MARIA. I'll say I'm het up! He tried to kill me again. That's
grounds for hetting! (*She sobs.*) What did I ever do to him?
That's what I'd like to know. Why does it have to be *me* he
wants to get at?

I. W. HARPER. (*Getting her onto the toilet seat.*) Honey!

TIA MARIA. Well it hurts! (*And now for the first time perhaps we
can see very clearly that her left arm is in a cast.*)

I. W. HARPER. Now don't wave it around like that.

TIA MARIA. Wave it? Thanks to that blasted horse tonight I may
never even be able to move it again!

I. W. HARPER. It's a simple fracture, honey.

TIA MARIA. I'd like to know what's so simple about it.

I. W. HARPER. You heard the doctor.

TIA MARIA. A doggurn horse rears up and kicks my arms with his
doggurn hard hooves and breaks my goddamn *tibia majore—*

I. W. HARPER. *Tibia menore.*

TIA MARIA. I don't call that simple.

I. W. HARPER. Doctors do.

TIA MARIA. That little quack.

I. W. HARPER. It happens all the time.

TIA MARIA. To little kids falling out o' apple trees! Not to 48-year-old women with lung and liver conditions still recovering from a hysterectomy.

I. W. HARPER. That was two years ago.

TIA MARIA. My liver n' lungs are now. Bones don't heal at my age. Remember Aunt Edna? She started out breaking her little finger. Then it was her hand, then it was her wrist, then it was her arm, then it was her hip and next thing you know she was dead.

I. W. HARPER. (*Giving her a pill and a glass of water.*) Take this.

TIA MARIA. (*Not even looking at it.*) It's called the "Brittle Bones Syndrome." I know all about it. *Time Magazine* had a whole long piece on it.

I. W. HARPER. Aunt Edna was in her eighties.

TIA MARIA. So! (*She gulps the pill down.*)

I. W. HARPER. Your bones aren't brittle. They're soft and warm and cuddly and plump.

TIA MARIA. (*A new fit of misery.*) That's my outsides you're talking about!

I. W. HARPER. Well I love 'em! Inside or out, honey, I love you all over.

TIA MARIA. I hate the way I look. I'm going on a diet.

I. W. HARPER. I like you just the way you are.

TIA MARIA. What do you know? While they were cutting out my ovaries I should have had 'em cut all the fat off while they was at it. I bet they could do it, too.

I. W. HARPER. Honey!

TIA MARIA. Well why not? They can cut everything else out o' you, so why not fat? If they can have heart transplant operations, they sure as shooting must have fat ones, too! Hunh, I.W., don't you think?

I. W. HARPER. Sure thing, honey.

TIA MARIA. I bet that doctor right here in Houston does 'em!

I. W. HARPER. If anyone does, honey, I reckon it's him.

TIA MARIA. Will you call him?

I. W. HARPER. First thing in the morning.

TIA MARIA. Can I have one?

I. W. HARPER. You bet.

TIA MARIA. You won't mind?

I. W. HARPER. Not if you don't.

TIA MARIA. Thank you, I.W. You're a good man. Like the song says.

I. W. HARPER. All better now?

TIA MARIA. (*Dissolving again.*) No!!!

I. W. HARPER. You want another drink?

TIA MARIA. I hate this hotel room. I hate Houston. I hate Texas. I hate Texans. My arm hurts. I'm fat. I miss Beverly Hills. Yes, I want another drink!

I. W. HARPER. Don't cry.

TIA MARIA. We made fools of ourselves.

I. W. HARPER. I hate it when you cry.

TIA MARIA. It was bad enough them laughing, but then *him* walking out right in the middle and *her* pulling that stunt . . . !

I. W. HARPER. Honey, I told you, first thing in the morning I'm gonna fire that agent.

TIA MARIA. You said you was gonna call that doctor!

I. W. HARPER. I'll call 'em both.

TIA MARIA. Can't we fire him now?

I. W. HARPER. It's after three.

TIA MARIA. Well, let's wake him, that little ten-percent runt. We're sure not getting any sleep tonight.

I. W. HARPER. Honey, let's just hope he hasn't fired *us*.

TIA MARIA. I'd like to see him try! It's all his fault.

I. W. HARPER. Of course it is.

TIA MARIA. Well isn't it?

I. W. HARPER. Sure it is, honey. He never should've booked us. We're not a live act.

TIA MARIA. Even if we were, that Astrodome's too big for people. Barbra Streisand wouldn't work in that place if she tried to. And the acoustics! Just what about them? I couldn't even hear my cues they were . . . (*She bursts into new tears.*) . . . laughing so loud!

I. W. HARPER. (*It's hopeless.*) Now you just sit right there. I'm going in there and fix us two o' the stiffest drinks anybody ever tasted. Something that'll put a little hair on your chest.

TIA MARIA. (*New wails.*) I got hair on my chest! Two black ones. I do! I do! It's those goddamn hormone shots. That goddamn doctor, I'm gonna sue that little quack. He's turning me into a goddamn gorilla! (*I. W. Harper leaves Tia Maria sitting on the toilet alone in the bathroom. He comes into the main room where Jack Daniels is still sitting staring out the window and kind of humming and strumming his song.)*

I. W. HARPER. Who's that?

JACK DANIELS. It's jes' lil' ol' Jack Daniels, I.W.

I. W. HARPER. What are you doing in here?

JACK DANIELS. Nothing.

I. W. HARPER. Well go in your own room and do it.

JACK DANIELS. I can't, I lost my key.

I. W. HARPER. How'd you get in here?

JACK DANIELS. I never left.

I. W. HARPER. That's chutzpa for you.

JACK DANIELS. What is, I.W.?

I. W. HARPER. You! Most people would have the decency and common sense to go to their own room after the other people had gone to bed, especially other people whose free liquor and room service they'd been sponging on all night!

JACK DANIELS. Boy, that chutzpa sure means a heck of a whole lot for such a tiny little word. I reckon it must be one o' them Jewish show business words.

I. W. HARPER. I reckon it is!

JACK DANIELS. Southern Comfort's been teaching 'em to me. She says Tia Maria's a yenta, you and Johnny Walker are . . . let's see . . . schmucks? . . . and I'm a mensch! I'm just trying to figure out what *she* is after what she done tonight.

I. W. HARPER. Are you figuring on sitting there all night watching me and my wife sleep? ·

JACK DANIELS. I ain't been watching y'all sleep. I jes' been sitting here looking out the window, strumming my Gibson and sipping rye. Hell, I.W., what do you take me for? I ain't one of your perverts, like Johnny Walker. Leas' that's what Southern Comfort says he is, only she must be pretty perverted herself, doing a thing like that in front o' the President of the United States and those astronaut fellows. Some o' them are real fine men, I read. And some of them had their wives there, too. Boy, she sure set me to thinking 'bout what this country's coming to. My pa had a word for girls like Southern Comfort. He called 'em confused. And I reckon that's what Southern Comfort is. Just plain confused. Anyway, after I undressed y'all and put y'all to bed—

I. W. HARPER. You undressed us?

JACK DANIELS. I sure did! Stripped them costumes plumb off o' you and put you in your p-j's. Hell, I.W., I had to. You were both passed out dead drunk on the floor.

I. W. HARPER. You undressed my wife?

JACK DANIELS. Yep.

I. W. HARPER. Cut that cowboy crap! I'm trying to get a straight answer.

JACK DANIELS. Yep's 'bout as straight an answer as I can think o'.

I. W. HARPER. You actually undressed her?

JACK DANIELS. Both of you, I.W.

I. W. HARPER. That ain't chutzpa, brother, those are good old-fashioned American balls.

JACK DANIELS. What are, I.W.?

I. W. HARPER. Never mind! Just sit there and shut up. I don't even remember what I came in here for.

JACK DANIELS. You know why?

I. W. HARPER. 'Cause I'm drunk!

JACK DANIELS. That's why. Now you jes' sit there real still, I.W., and it'll come back to you. Or you'll pass out dead drunk again.

I. W. HARPER. Jesus, what a stomach!

JACK DANIELS. You ever try a raw turkey egg with kaopectate for one of those?

I. W. HARPER. No!

JACK DANIELS. Me neither. My pa swore by 'em. 'Nother time my big brother came home so drunk on moonshine and rot-gut he was like to die. Pa fixed him up real quick with a cod liver oil enema.

I. W. HARPER. I said knock it off!

JACK DANIELS. Sorry, I.W. (*Pause.*) You fixin' to throw up?

I. W. HARPER. What does it look like?

JACK DANIELS. I'll be real still then. (*Pause.*) Can I play my gittar? (*I. W. Harper nods his head.*) Can I sing?

I. W. HARPER. Anything, just don't talk. (*Jack Daniels plays and sings "The Streets of Laredo" again.*)

JACK DANIELS. I'm sure crazy 'bout this song. Sorry, I.W. (*He plays and sings a while.*) I.W.?

I. W. HARPER. What?

JACK DANIELS. Can I say jes' one thing?

I. W. HARPER. What?

JACK DANIELS. You know something?

I. W. HARPER. What!?

JACK DANIELS. Your wife's got hair on her titties. (*Before I. W. Harper can explode, Tia Maria does it for him from the bathroom with another of her bloodcurdling screams. What has happened is this: the toilet on which she has been sitting holding her head and commiserating with herself has suddenly, noisily and of its own accord flushed!*)

TIA MARIA. (*Bolting from the toilet seat.*) AAAEEEEEEIIIIII-OOOOOUUUUUUU!!!! (*Her yell has roused Whiskey, who responds with another deafening series of whinnies and a beating of hooves. Again the shower curtains sway violently. All this, of course, causes Tia Maria to scream again.*) AAAAAEEEEEE-IIIIIIIIIOOOOOOOUUUUUU!!!! (*She runs to the door, yanks at the doorhandle and it comes off in her hand. I. W. Harper in the meantime has run to one of the windows, leaned his head out and is busily being sick.*)

JACK DANIELS. She's screaming again, I.W. (*But I. W. Harper is in no condition or position to reply.*)

TIA MARIA. AAAAAEEEEEEIIIIIIIOOOOOOOOUUUUUUU!!!!
(*Jack Daniels goes to the bathroom door and from his side politely knocks.*)

JACK DANIELS. Ma'am?

TIA MARIA. Get me out of here!

JACK DANIELS. Anything wrong, ma'am?

TIA MARIA. I'm locked in the goddamn bathroom with a goddamn horse who's trying to kill me!

JACK DANIELS. What happened?

TIA MARIA. The goddamn toilet flushed! Now get me out of here!
(*Jack Daniels pulls on the door handle. It comes off in his hand.*)

JACK DANIELS. Ma'am?

TIA MARIA. What? Help! Help!

JACK DANIELS. You better try from your side.

TIA MARIA. I can't. The handle's come off.

JACK DANIELS. Well, ma'am, then I guess you're up shit creek 'cause mine has, too. (*This announcement proves too much for Tia Maria, who promptly faints again.*) I 'spose I could call room service. (*Jack Daniels crosses to a light switch and turns on the overhead lights. For the first time we get a clear look at the room and it is even messier than we had imagined. Clearly a tornado has passed through the premises. But the most startling sight of all is the figure of Johnny Walker. He is passed out dead drunk over a card table. In front of him is a deck of cards laid out in a solitaire pattern. He is wearing his gun and holster, his undershorts and his boots. Clearly he has been sitting there all along, passed out over the cards like this, only we couldn't see him in the dark. He raises his head groggily when Jack Daniels turns on the lights. Johnny Walker is in a very, very surly mood.)*

JOHNNY WALKER. What did you call me? *(Jack Daniels is having difficulty locating the telephone because of the mess in the room, so he is having to follow along the wire from the socket in the wall.)*

JACK DANIELS. You sho' was on a losing streak 'fore you passed out there, Johnny Walker.

JOHNNY WALKER. What did you call me?

JACK DANIELS. I heard o' strip poker, I played me some, too, but that strip solitaire's a new one on me.

JOHNNY WALKER. What did you call me, cowboy?

JACK DANIELS. Don't look too easy; don't look like much fun neither.

JOHNNY WALKER. Hey, hayseed, I'm talking to you! *(He takes clumsy aim with his pistol, fires, misses.)*

JACK DANIELS. *(On the telephone now.)* Hush up there now, will you? I'm trying to get room service.

JOHNNY WALKER. *(Turning his attention elsewhere.)* Hey you, fat ass, the one with his can in the air! *(He aims, fires, misses. I. W. Harper has turned back into the room. He slumps weakly on the window seat.)*

I. W. HARPER. Not tonight, Johnny, I'm too sick.

JOHNNY WALKER. What did you call me, cowpoke?

I. W. HARPER. Go in your room if you're gonna do that.

JOHNNY WALKER. Somebody called me a goddamn lousy, no 'count, shit-eating faggot! *(He fires the pistol several times.)*

I. W. HARPER. Over there, Johnny, they're over there.

JOHNNY WALKER. *(Turning.)* Where?

I. W. HARPER. You see 'em, Johnny. They're the ones, they're the ones who called you.

JOHNNY WALKER. (*Squinting, grinning.*) I see 'em, I see 'em all right. I see you red-necked, fat-assed, no-pricked bastards. I jes' hope you can see me all right 'cause you is looking at one mean drunk, pissed-off cowboy. Now which one o' you bastards said that? I want to know which one o' you called me that name. Goddamnit, I'm gonna blow somebody's goddamn lousy, no count, shit-eating head off 'fore I get through! (*Again he fires the pistol several times. A thoroughly non-plussed Jack Daniels waits patiently for room service to answer the telephone while a relieved I. W. Harper sits quietly trying to get his head and his stomach into some kind of shape.*) Jes' 'cause I wear a little pancake makeup and eye shadow don't make me no faggot. Goddamn it, I'm in show business and I have to! So I dye my hair! So do a lot o' other TV show business personalities. You calling Ed Sullivan a fruit? And yeah, I've been in a beauty parlor or two and had me a wash and a set. Show business ain't easy. Hell, I got a goddamn fully professional hair dryer . . . the kind with its own chair attached you can sit under and read magazines . . . right in my bedroom. That don't prove nothing. All right, so I look at myself in the mirror a lot. Women look in the mirror a lot and no one calls them faggots. And when I look in the mirror, cowboy, I got something to see. Those are arms, those are shoulders, that's a stomach, those are thighs, that's a cock. Goddamnit, someone calls me a faggot again and I'm gonna shoot this whole fucking town up!

JACK DANIELS. Boy, room service sure takes a long time to answer in this hotel!

I. W. HARPER. Jesus, have I got a head on me!

JOHNNY WALKER. What did you say? What did you say just then? The fucking CIA's bugging me, man, so don't start crowding me. This country's turning into a goddamn police state and they're hot after my ass. I can't go to Mexico without 'em searching me all over and taking off my hubcaps. They're bugging my phone, they got people at every fucking airport in this whole goddamn country watching and double watching me. Don't you call me no faggot, you goddamn CIA Jew!

JACK DANIELS. It's done rung forty-five rings so far!

I. W. HARPER. No one called you nothing, Johnny Walker.

JOHNNY WALKER. Goddamnit, I'm gonna pull this trigger if I hear that word again. Faggot? Faggot? I grew up in Waco and I was punching girls 'fore my daddy let me have my learner's permit to drive our pickup. I had their panties off and I was *in* there, and I don't mean with my finger, 'fore most guys' balls had even dropped! Shit, the only faggots in Waco was punched-up, beat-up and stomped-on faggots. And me and my boys did the punching and the beating and the stomping. Goddamnit, I went to Texas A&M! That's a military school. Did you ever hear of a faggot from Texas A&M? From *any* military school for that matter? Hell, a place like that's so goddamned screened you can't get near the place if your big toe looks a little queer to 'em. Boy, my blood is boiling. Boy, you're getting my goat. I know the CIA is listening to every goddamn word I'm saying. Jesus H. Christ, I was a goddamn football star. We beat Texas three years running when I was on varsity. We was conference champs. I was quarterback. Did you ever hear of a gay quarterback? A cheerleader maybe, but I'll give you $500 for every gay quarterback you can name. All right, I know gay's one of them "in" words. I know it don't mean happy. But goddamn it to hell anyway! I'm in show business. I meet people. I hear how they talk. I admit it. There are certain people of the homosexual persuasion in my profession.

JACK DANIELS. Sixty-nine!

JOHNNY WALKER. What? What did I hear?

I. W. HARPER. Johnny, please, my head.

JOHNNY WALKER. Goddamn it, I am sick of those filthy words. All right, I'll admit this, too, only it's the first and last time I'm ever gonna say it clear out. There was a pansy at Texas A&M. Just one. But he wasn't in the corps. He was in animal husbandry. Now I didn't know him personally but I heard he was a damn nice guy from Tyler. 'Course when we found out he was a pansy we stomped the shit out o' him. My four years at Texas A&M were the happiest and proudest of my life. And if you don't think I fucked every weekend, then you're way off base. Hell, those College Townies drop their drawers and flop over backwards at the first sight o' field boots. A&M cadets could get laid in a goddamn convent, that's the kind of studs they are. And me being voted the Most Valuable Player of the Southwest Conference three years in a row didn't exactly hurt none either. I got laid so much at A&M I landed up in the infirmary every spring semester with sexual hyperthesia.

JACK DANIELS. Should I keep trying, I.W.?

I. W. HARPER. I'm going to be sick again.

JOHNNY WALKER. What's that about Rick?

I. W. HARPER. Not Rick, Johnny. *Sick!*

JOHNNY WALKER. Now goddamnit, leave him out o' this! Rick's my buddy. A word agin' him is a word agin' me. That boy is the finest, most pure and masculine roommate a guy ever had. I know the talk agin' him, I know the CIA's behind it all, and my finger jes' gets mighty itchy when I hear that kind o' talk. So what we got a Yak rug in the living room and some o' them Gobelin tapestries on the walls? Rick likes nice things. He can't help it he's sensitive. The hours we spend lifting weights in our private gym are some o' the most intellectually stimulating o' my life. Rick-boy don't just work out. Hell no, he talks about philosophy and music and modern art and how much he gets laid. You didn't know that, cowpoke, did you? No, the papers are all full o' Yak rugs and yellow curtains but you don't read one thing 'bout how much we get laid. Well you ask any starlet in Hollywood . . . any starlet with big titties . . . and she'd tell you what it's like round Rick's and my's place every weekend. We fuck on the beds, we fuck in the pool, hell, we even fuck on that Yak rug. I know what you're thinking, mister, so take that grin off o' your face. Rick weren't doing nothing at that pajama party. He swore to me on a stack o' Bibles he didn't know what it was gonna turn into and his word's good enough for me. Let me tell you he was one plumb mad cowboy after he found out he was consortin' with fruits. Why when the police came and took all those pictures . . . spread all o'er tarnation thanks to the CIA and the *National Enquirer* . . . Ricky was so depressed and heartsick he took to his bed for a long, long time. And then when they had that goddamn trial, CIA again, that's when he got really sick and had to withdraw from his TV series. It ain't true he was fired. He was too sick, too sad and plain too disgusted to work. And you saw what happened: "Mr. George" went clear off the air six weeks after Rick-boy left it. Shit, I told him, a situation comedy 'bout a goddamn hairdresser ain't no good for a cowpoke's image anyhow. Anybody calling Ricky Rivers a goddamn faggot is calling Johnny Walker one, too!

JACK DANIELS. I'd hang up, I.W., only it says right here "24-hour room service."

I.W. HARPER. Beer. That's what I need.

JOHNNY WALKER. What did you call me?

I. W. HARPER. Beer. I said I could use a beer.

JOHNNY WALKER. I warned you, cowboy! (*Johnny Walker draws his pistols and fires wildly all around the room. It is a noisy and serious barrage of gun fire. I. W. Harper and Jack Daniels dive for cover. When it is over, the room will seem very quiet, except for Whiskey raising a new fuss in the bathroom. Johnny Walker stands, pistols smoking and a mean grin on his face.*) Now what did you call me?

I. W. HARPER. Nothing, Johnny Walker.

JACK DANIELS. Not one durn thing, Johnny.

JOHNNY WALKER. That's better. (*One of Johnny Walker's bullets has hit the bathroom door, which is slowly and creakily swinging open. Whiskey is still whinnying and beating his hooves. What they see, however, is Tia Maria passed out on the floor.*)

I. W. HARPER. Honey!

JOHNNY WALKER. Oh my God!

JACK DANIELS. You do that, Johnny Walker? (*I. W. Harper and Johnny Walker rush to the bathroom and bend over Tia Maria. Jack Daniels looks in from the door.*)

I. W. HARPER. Tia? Tia honey?

JOHNNY WALKER. I was jes' fooling.

JACK DANIELS. Sure don't look like you was, Johnny.

I. W. HARPER. She's still breathing.

JOHNNY WALKER. I swear to God, I.W., I didn't know she was in there.

JACK DANIELS. Somebody ought to call a doctor.

I. W. HARPER. We'll get her on the bed.

JOHNNY WALKER. I wouldn't hurt a fly, you know that.

I. W. HARPER. Take her feet. (*I. W. Harper and Johnny Walker carry Tia Maria into the main room and put her on the bed.*)

JACK DANIELS. Hush up now, Whiskey. We got a real sick lady on our hands. (*Jack Daniels closes the bathroom door. In a little while Whiskey will be quiet again.*)

JOHNNY WALKER. How bad is she?

I. W. HARPER. I can't tell.

JOHNNY WALKER. Where'd I get her?

I. W. HARPER. I can't tell that neither. I don't see any blood.

JACK DANIELS. That poor lady. We got booed in the Astrodome, the President of the United States got showed Southern Comfort's thing, we all got passed-out drunk and now Johnny Walker's shot her.

I. W. HARPER. (*Over his shoulder to Jack Daniels.*) Don't just stand there. Call a doctor.

JACK DANIELS. That's what I was saying, I.W. Somebody ought to call a doctor.

I. W. HARPER. You!

JACK DANIELS. Okay, I.W., if I can ever raise that operator. I think she must've gone to sleep. (*Jack Daniels goes to phone again, lifts receiver, waits patiently.*)

I. W. HARPER. Honey? Can you hear me, honey?

JOHNNY WALKER. It's me, Tia. Johnny. It's your old friend, Johnny.

I. W. HARPER. You're going to be all right, honey, everything's going to be all right now. Just tell me where it hurts. (*Tia Maria is beginning to come around.*) Don't try to talk. You'll tire yourself. Just lie back real still and wait for the doctor.

JOHNNY WALKER. Open the other eye, Tia. See if you can open the other one, too.

I. W. HARPER. Don't crowd her like that! Give her some air!

JOHNNY WALKER. Just stay calm, we're all here, nothing's going to happen.

I. W. HARPER. Can I get you something, honey?

JOHNNY WALKER. The main thing is to rest.

I. W. HARPER. How 'bout a shot?

JOHNNY WALKER. You're not running any fever.

I. W. HARPER. More pillows, honey?

JOHNNY WALKER. (*Offering his cigarette.*) Drag on this, it'll soothe you.

I. W. HARPER. I said quit crowding her!

JOHNNY WALKER. Who's crowding?

I. W. HARPER. You are!

JOHNNY WALKER. You're right on top o' her yourself!

I. W. HARPER. She's my wife!

JOHNNY WALKER. I shot her!

JACK DANIELS. Try spitting on her. Pa always used to spit on us and we all healed. He claimed spit was a natural healer. He made a fine honey-and-cobweb poultice, too.

I. W. HARPER. Are you getting that doctor?

JACK DANIELS. I'm trying to, I.W.

TIA MARIA. (*Sitting up.*) What happened?

I. W. HARPER. How do you feel, honey?

TIA MARIA. I'm not sure.

JOHNNY WALKER. Don't try to talk.

I. W. HARPER. Will you stop crowding my wife? Give her some room to breathe in!

TIA MARIA. What happened?

I. W. HARPER. Just lie back, honey, save your strength.

JOHNNY WALKER. I'm trying to see where she's wounded!

I. W. HARPER. What do you think I'm doing?

TIA MARIA. I remember this terrible nightmare . . . it must have been the stingers, I've never had one this bad before . . . I remember sitting in something . . . ! (*She shudders at the memory.*)

I. W. HARPER. Me.

TIA MARIA. Hunh?

I. W. HARPER. That was me you sat in.

TIA MARIA. That's not funny, I.W., I'm trying to get my thoughts straight.

JOHNNY WALKER. I don't see anything!

TIA MARIA. And then I came to in this antiseptic tile room . . . like a hospital only it was more like a restroom and you were there, I.W., and I said I was thirsty and you said you were going to fix me something with hair in it . . .

JACK DANIELS. That's called a hair o' the dog, ma'am.

TIA MARIA. No, you said a gorilla. You were going to fix me a gorilla. Next thing I was sitting, waiting for you to come back . . . it seems I was on a . . . you know, a sanitary convenience . . .

JACK DANIELS. You mean a toilet, ma'am?

TIA MARIA. And all of a sudden it flushed! I was just sitting there and it flushed!

JACK DANIELS. Boy, I bet that scared the shit out o' you! (*Jack Daniels has a yuk! yuk! yuk! kind of laugh when he tells and laughs at his own jokes.*)

JOHNNY WALKER. It's a new hotel, Tia. They don't have all the bugs ironed out yet. That's all it was.

TIA MARIA. And then . . . oh, my head is spinning! . . . and then . . .

I. W. HARPER. It's not important.

TIA MARIA. Don't I get a drink?

I. W. HARPER. Sure you do, honey. Johnny!

JOHNNY WALKER. She's your wife.

I. W. HARPER. You shot her.

TIA MARIA. Now I remember! He tried to kill me, I.W.!

JOHNNY WALKER. I didn't mean to, Tia, honest I didn't!

TIA MARIA. That damn horse tried to kill me again! It was horrible!

I. W. HARPER. (*Comforting her in his arms.*) Honey!

TIA MARIA. He hates me, I.W. Whiskey hates me.

I. W. HARPER. You're just imagining things. Like you said, you had a little nightmare.

TIA MARIA. It sure seemed real.

JOHNNY WALKER. You don't remember any shooting?

TIA MARIA. No!

JOHNNY WALKER. You're sure?

TIA MARIA. What's wrong with you? I sat in something terrible, the toilet flushed on me, a horse tried to kill me and now you want somebody shooting at me, too! Give me that! (*Tia Maria takes the drink from Johnny Walker and downs it in one gulp.*)

JOHNNY WALKER. I knew it! Hell, I don't think I even grazed her. She passed out dead drunk, that's all. She can sleep it off. And thanks for scaring me half to death.

TIA MARIA. What's he talking about?

JACK DANIELS. If'n I ever get that operator, I.W., should I tell her we don't need no doctor now? Or should I hang up? It's done rung fifty-four rings this time.

TIA MARIA. What's going on here?

I. W. HARPER. Now don't upset yourself, honey.

TIA MARIA. And what's all this fussing over me for? All o' them doing in our room?

JACK DANIELS. Lost my key, ma'am. Fifty-*seven*, I.W.

I. W. HARPER. Yes, hang up!

TIA MARIA. What's he calling a doctor for anyway?

I. W. WALKER. It's nothing, Tia. Never mind.

TIA MARIA. Not for me I hope.

JACK DANIELS. Yes, ma'am. I.W. was afraid you were a real sick little lady. We all were, 'specially Johnny Walker.

TIA MARIA. Why I feel fit as a fiddle and rarin' to go!

JOHNNY WALKER. Sure you do!

TIA MARIA. Why thank you, Johnny.

JOHNNY WALKER. You're stinking drunk.

TIA MARIA. What did you say?

JOHNNY WALKER. But hell, that's nothing unusual.

TIA MARIA. Who's calling who drunk?

JOHNNY WALKER. Oh, come off it, Tia, you're potted.

TIA MARIA. From the look o' you three, I'd say you were pretty stinko yourselves.

JACK DANIELS. That's right, ma'am, we are.

I. W. HARPER. Now don't move around too much, honey.

TIA MARIA. I can drink you three skunks under any table.

JOHNNY WALKER. We've seen you.

TIA MARIA. Any night o' any week.

I. W. HARPER. Don't rile her, Johnny, she'll start that damn screaming.

TIA MARIA. Who's getting riled? Look, look how steady I am. You see that hand shaking? Don't tell me I got the D.T.'s, you pickled fruit. And what are you grinning at, you little wino?

JACK DANIELS. Nothing, ma'am.

I. W. HARPER. Tia, honey, please.

TIA MARIA. Leave go o' me, you old rummy.

I. W. HARPER. (*To Johnny Walker.*) See what you started?

TIA MARIA. If there's one thing I can't stand it's being treated like a drunk.

I. W. HARPER. Nobody's treating you like anything, Tia.

TIA MARIA. Can you do that?

JOHNNY WALKER. What?

TIA MARIA. You're so drunk you can't even see straight.

JACK DANIELS. What'd she do, I.W.?

TIA MARIA. I crossed my eyes.

I. W. HARPER. You're not drunk, Tia.

TIA MARIA. 'Course I'm not.

I. W. HARPER. Nobody said you were.

JACK DANIELS. My pa could cross his eyes. All the time. My pa was cross-eyed. (*He laughs his yuk! yuk! yuk! laugh.*)

TIA MARIA. I had a nightmare and passed out. All this carrying on and calling up doctors, you'd think somebody *had* shot me. (*Tia Maria starts to laugh. It gets bigger and bigger. I. W. Harper and Johnny Walker start laughing, too.*) I wouldn't put it past you!

I. W. HARPER. Honey!

TIA MARIA. Or that one!

JOHNNY WALKER. Tia!

TIA MARIA. 'Course it sounds like something Southern Comfort would do!

I. W. HARPER. *Anything* sounds like something Southern Comfort would do!

JOHNNY WALKER. She'd flaming baton you to death, if she could ever get one lit!

TIA MARIA. Where is that little pill-popping, dope-smoking, alcoholic floozy anyway?

I. W. HARPER. God only knows, Tia!

JOHNNY WALKER. She's off entertaining the troops!

TIA MARIA. The war's over!

JOHNNY WALKER. Not hers!

TIA MARIA. Southern! Southern Comfort!

I. W. HARPER. Honey, ain't we got enough people in here?

TIA MARIA. Hell, no, this is a party. A shooting party. Gimme that gun, Johnny.

I. W. HARPER. Tia!

TIA MARIA. I'm going in there and shoot that goddamn horse.

JOHNNY WALKER. You shoot that horse, Tia, and I'll help you bury him!

TIA MARIA. That's one way to break up an act!

I. W. HARPER. Or cancel a too-goddamn-long running TV series!

JOHNNY WALKER. Get a few close-ups of us for a change!

TIA MARIA. Don't think I haven't thought of it! You have, too. And you!

I. W. HARPER. Who'd shoot Whiskey?

TIA MARIA. Who'd shoot anybody?

JOHNNY WALKER. Who'd shoot you?

TIA MARIA. Hoo hoo hoo!

I. W. HARPER. Ha ha ha!

JOHNNY WALKER. Hee hee hee! (*The laughter fades to silence.*)

JACK DANIELS. Johnny Walker shot you, ma'am. He thought some-body called him that name again, shot a whole round off to prove it and you ended up on the bathroom floor. (*Now Jack Daniels starts to laugh. It too gets bigger and bigger.*)

TIA MARIA. What'd he say?

I. W. HARPER. Nothing.

JOHNNY WALKER. Shut up, you durn fool.

JACK DANIELS. (*Still laughing.*) I cannot tell a lie.

TIA MARIA. He said *something*, I.W.

I. W. HARPER. Drunk talk, crazy stuff.

JOHNNY WALKER. Now keep your trap closed.

JACK DANIELS. (*Laughing.*) My pa said any man who tells a lie is a liar.

JOHNNY WALKER. Your pa also said any man who rocks the boat when the boat don't need rocking is gonna get a fist in his face.

I. W. HARPER. Two fists.

JACK DANIELS. (*Stops laughing.*) He did?

JOHNNY WALKER. You're goddamn right he did!

JACK DANIELS. You two knew my pa?

I. W. HARPER. A terrific old bastard.

JOHNNY WALKER. I loved that old fart.

JACK DANIELS. Boy, it sure is a small world.

I. W. HARPER. See, honey, nobody shot nobody.

JACK DANIELS. Anyway, Johnny Walker shot you, ma'am. (*Jack Daniels explodes in a new fit of laughter.*)

TIA MARIA. You what?

JOHNNY WALKER. I was jes' fooling around, Tia, honest, I didn't mean to.

TIA MARIA. Oh my God, I've been shot, I.W.!

I. W. HARPER. We just thought you'd been shot.

TIA MARIA. AAAAEEEEEIIIIIIOOOOOUUUUUUU!!!!

I. W. HARPER. But you weren't. See, there's no blood.

TIA MARIA. AAAAEEEEEEIIIIIIIOOOOOOUUUUUUU!!!!

I. W. HARPER. Come on now, honey, they'll think we're murdering someone up here.

TIA MARIA. AAAAAEEEEEEEEIIIIIIIOOOOOOOOOUUUUUU!!!!
(*And she faints again.*)

I. W. HARPER. I give up.

JOHNNY WALKER. How does she do it?

JACK DANIELS. She sure yells a lot, I.W. Hurts my ears.

JOHNNY WALKER. You didn't have to tell her what happened! We had her all calmed down.

JACK DANIELS. I'm sorry, Johnny, I wasn't thinking.

I. W. HARPER. Tia? Tia honey?

JOHNNY WALKER. Leave her alone. Out cold's the best thing for her.

JACK DANIELS. You want another doctor for her, I.W.?

I. W. HARPER. No!

JACK DANIELS. I jes' asked.

I. W. HARPER. My poor honey, my poor drunk honey. I was drunk when I met you, you was drunk when we married and we've been drunk together ever since. I'm going to make it up to you, honey, I swear to God I am.

JOHNNY WALKER. Hey, now come on, I.W.!

I. W. HARPER. This gal was an angel when I met her, a goddamn angel. She was so thin I could get my hands around her waist. Her hair was so gold in the sun it made you squint to look at her. And skin so cool and smooth and white it made you think of cream. A goddamn angel. She had nice titties, too.

JACK DANIELS. I don't think we should be hearing this, Johnny.

JOHNNY WALKER. It's okay, I.W., everything's gonna be okay.

I. W. HARPER. And now look at her. I did that to her. I did! I did!

JOHNNY WALKER. Don't, I.W., you're only tormenting yourself.

I. W. HARPER. I know.

JOHNNY WALKER. Well don't.

I. W. HARPER. I want to. Look what I did to her. I did! I did!

JOHNNY WALKER. No, you didn't.

I. W. HARPER. Yes I did.

JOHNNY WALKER. No you didn't.

I. W. HARPER. Yes I did.

JOHNNY WALKER. No you didn't.

I. W. HARPER. Yes I did!

JACK DANIELS. Seems he ought to know what he did to his own wife, Johnny.

I. W. HARPER. Just look at her and tell me I didn't do that. Go on, tell me! (*Tia Maria belches loudly in her sleep.*)

JACK DANIELS. What *did* he do to her, Johnny?

I. W. HARPER. (*Throwing himself on Tia Maria.*) My honey, my poor drunk honey. I'm going to make it up to you, honey, I swear to God I am.

JACK DANIELS. Don't cry, I.W.

JOHNNY WALKER. Leave him be. It's good for him.

I. W. HARPER. Did I ever tell you the story about the first time I met Tia Maria?

JACK DANIELS. Lots o' times.

I. W. HARPER. It was at Cotton's, this little beer n' bar-b-q joint outside o' Robstown.

JACK DANIELS. You told us, I.W.

I. W. HARPER. She was in the ladies' room being sick and I was so drunk I walked in there thinking it was the men's.

JACK DANIELS. That's how it happened.

I. W. HARPER. Did I tell you about our wedding night when we rolled off that balcony?

JACK DANIELS. Down in Mexico. That's a real good one!

I. W. HARPER. Our first real break in show business?

JACK DANIELS. You was on the radio, coast to coast, and that time somebody else got sick.

I. W. HARPER. How we broke into TV?

JACK DANIELS. Yep, that one, too.

I. W. HARPER. About our series and why it's been running so long?

JACK DANIELS. I'm on the series with you, I.W.!

I. W. HARPER. Don't anybody want to know what I did to my poor drunk honey? Don't anybody care?

JOHNNY WALKER. We all *care*, I.W. Trouble is, we all *know*.

I. W. HARPER. Nobody knows! Nobody cares! I'm going to make it up to you, honey, I swear to God I am. (*He throws himself onto her for a final time.*)

JOHNNY WALKER. It's okay now, I.W., everything's okay.

JACK DANIELS. Boy, he sure loves that little lady.

JOHNNY WALKER. Jes' let it all out now.

JACK DANIELS. I wonder if my pa loved my ma like that. I wish I hadn't been half an orphan all my life. And now I'm a whole one. (*And now Jack Daniels cries a little, too. Johnny Walker gets up and pours himself another drink.*)

I. W. HARPER. (*Sitting up.*) Why don't you clear out now? I *know!* You lost your key. Sleep in his room, sleep in the hall, I don't care.

JOHNNY WALKER. Les' have a nightcap, I.W. Jes' one.

I. W. HARPER. It's late.

JOHNNY WALKER. It's early.

I. W. HARPER. It's late!

JOHNNY WALKER. Speaking frankly, I.W., I don't think you're in any shape to be left alone right now.

I. W. HARPER. Sure I am.

JOHNNY WALKER. I don't think so, I.W.

I. W. HARPER. I am, too.

JOHNNY WALKER. No, you're not.

I. W. HARPER. I am, too!

JACK DANIELS. There y'all go again.

I. W. HARPER. Suit yourself, only don't tell me what kind o' shape I'm in. (*He pours himself a drink.*)

JOHNNY WALKER. Thanks, I.W. You see, I don't think I'm in much shape for loning it tonight, neither. That's one damn solitary hotel room I got waiting for me over there. Nothing but me and four walls. I jes' feel like being with someone tonight.

JACK DANIELS. Can I stay, too, I.W.?

I. W. HARPER. If you keep that dumb mouth closed.

JACK DANIELS. Like before?

I. W. HARPER. That's right.

JACK DANIELS. You fixing to be sick again?

I. W. HARPER. No!

JACK DANIELS. That's good. (*Jack Daniels pours himself a drink, sits on the windowseat and strums "The Streets of Laredo" on his guitar. I. W. Harper is leaning against the headboard of the bed with Tia Maria sleeping it off by his side. Johnny Walker is sitting on the floor.*)

JOHNNY WALKER. You really thinking o' cancelling the tour, I.W.?

I. W. HARPER. I sure as hell ain't thinking o' extending it!

JOHNNY WALKER. It's a lot o' money.

I. W. HARPER. That was a lot o' booing tonight, too.

JOHNNY WALKER. Damn that horse anyway. He's gonna come out on cue tomorrow night if I have to kill him.

I. W. HARPER. If there *is* a tomorrow night.

JOHNNY WALKER. They were pretty mad, the management, I guess, hunh?

I. W. HARPER. Hell no! Why they just loved refunding all that money!

JOHNNY WALKER. That damn agent promised us Whiskey wouldn't act up like that.

I. W. HARPER. That same damn agent promised me you'd be able to get your first line out.

JOHNNY WALKER. I'm sorry, I.W.

I. W. HARPER. I know you are, Johnny, and I'm sorry I said it.

JOHNNY WALKER. I'd as soon shoot you as spit on you. I'd as soon shoot you as spit on you. See? Now I can do it.

I. W. HARPER. Only right here and now ain't out there and then.

JOHNNY WALKER. Now I know why they call it stage fright.

I. W. WALKER. Now you know why they call it show business.

JOHNNY WALKER. Well Southern Comfort didn't exactly help things none either!

I. W. HARPER. And now I know what they call a show *stopper!*

JOHNNY WALKER. Well I blame her *and* the horse.

I. W. HARPER. We *all* stank, if you want to know the truth.

JOHNNY WALKER. Tonight was our first time live. We'll get better.

I. W. HARPER. Like hell we will. There's not enough talent in this room to piss on.

JOHNNY WALKER. I resent that, I.W.

I. W. HARPER. So resent it. You're young, you're dumb, you'll find out. Either that or you'll make it big like we did.

JOHNNY WALKER. I couldn't stand it if I felt like you.

I. W. HARPER. You heard that crowd tonight.

JOHNNY WALKER. A live audience is different.

I. W. HARPER. I know. They can get at you.

JOHNNY WALKER. You're forgetting one thing, I.W. People like us.

I. W. HARPER. They tolerate us.

JOHNNY WALKER. Our show's the longest running series on television.

I. W. HARPER. Drunk cowboys are still a novelty. Next year, ten years, it'll be drunk Indians.

JOHNNY WALKER. We're gonna last, I.W. Hell, everybody loves a drunk!

I. W. HARPER. Everybody loves Whiskey.

JOHNNY WALKER. That's what I'm saying.

I. W. HARPER. Everybody loves that horse! He's the whole show. The last ten episodes we haven't been on the screen more'n five minutes. He's bigger than Lassie. He's bigger than Flipper. He's bigger than Black Beauty. And you can just thank your lucky stars we're all a part of one big fat William Morris Agency package. Without him, Tia and I'd be back on Dust Bowl radio shows plugging Geritol and calling square dances, you'd be back driving that truck, that one would be back where we found him, standing out on the same farm road selling the same mangy vegetables off o' the same mangy truck bed, and Southern Comfort'd be off somewhere undergoing psychiatric treatment.

JOHNNY WALKER. I wasn't driving a truck when you met me. I was a football star.

I. W. HARPER. You was a former and faded football star, Johnny Walker, and you was driving something.

JOHNNY WALKER. It was only a temporary position. I was between things.

I. W. HARPER. Temporary positions like that have a funny way of turning into full-time ones. What you was between was sixty-five dollars and being flat on your ass.

JOHNNY WALKER. I had offers. Sports announcing, public relations, lots o' things.

I. W. HARPER. If you say so.

JOHNNY WALKER. It's true. You just never knew me in my prime.

I. W. HARPER. Well you sure caught me and Tia in ours! (*There is a pause. I.W. stretches out on the bed, ready to sleep.*)

JOHNNY WALKER. I.W.? It's been my prime, too. All o' ours prime. Don't cancel.

.I. W. HARPER. It may not be up to me, Johnny.

JOHNNY WALKER. Just don't you do it. The Lush Thrushes and Whiskey is all I got.

I. W. HARPER. Us, too, Johnny.

JACK DANIELS. I.W.?

I. W. HARPER. What?

JACK DANIELS. You and Johnny Walker are talking.

I. W. HARPER. I know!

JACK DANIELS. Well that don't seem rightly fair. I'm one of the Lush Thrushes, too.

I. W. HARPER. I said shut up.

JACK DANIELS. Okay, I.W.

I. W. HARPER. Now everybody shut up. Just sit there and drink. Nobody say nothing.

JOHNNY WALKER. I'll drink to that. (*At this point we begin to hear, though very faintly at first, a girl's voice singing "Hare Krishna" and the delicate ting! ting! of finger cymbals. Tia Maria belches loudly in her sleep. Jack Daniels stops strumming.*)

JACK DANIELS. I.W.?

I. W. HARPER. What?

JACK DANIELS. Can I say jes' one last thing?

I. W. HARPER. Yes.

JACK DANIELS. I hear music.

I. W. HARPER. Good.

JACK DANIELS. Somebody singing and little bells tinkling.

I. W. HARPER. That's nice.

JACK DANIELS. You hear something, Johnny Walker?

JOHNNY WALKER. Somebody singing.

JACK DANIELS. Me, too.

JOHNNY WALKER. More like chanting though. And a ringing sound, like little bells.

JACK DANIELS. I.W.?

I. W. HARPER. What?

JACK DANIELS. Johnny Walker hears somebody singing and little bells tinkling, too.

I. W. HARPER. He's right.

JACK DANIELS. Just thought I'd mention it. (*Jack Daniels strums his guitar again. Smoke is starting to billow out of one of the closet doors. Jack Daniels sniffs something, stops strumming again.*) I.W.?

I. W. HARPER. What?

JACK DANIELS. Now I smell smoke.

I. W. HARPER. That's nice.

JACK DANIELS. You smell anything, Johnny Walker?

JOHNNY WALKER. Smoke.

JACK DANIELS. That's what I said.

JOHNNY WALKER. But it's a sweet smoke.

JACK DANIELS. I thought there was something funny about it.

JOHNNY WALKER. More like incense.

JACK DANIELS. I.W.?

I. W. HARPER. What?

JACK DANIELS. Johnny Walker smells smoke, too.

I. W. HARPER. Good for Johnny Walker.

JACK DANIELS. But it's a sweet smoke.

I. W. HARPER. I'm glad.

JACK DANIELS. More like incense.

I. W. HARPER. If you keep this up, Jack Daniels, I am going to have a nervous breakdown.

JACK DANIELS. You are?

I. W. HARPER. Yes. I am very calm and very relaxed and very drunk but you are still giving me a nervous breakdown.

JACK DANIELS. I'm sorry, I.W. I'll try and be real still then. (*There is a long pause while Jack Daniels strums his guitar and Johnny Walker and I. W. Harper drift further and further away. Tia Maria stirs in the bed and finally sits up.*)

TIA MARIA. Oh!

JACK DANIELS. (*Whispered.*) How you feeling, ma'am? ..

TIA MARIA. What happened?

JACK DANIELS. You screamed and passed out dead drunk again.

TIA MARIA. Oooo, my poor head is ringing. I hear music.

JACK DANIELS. We all do.

TIA MARIA. Somebody singing and little chimes tingling.

JACK DANIELS. It's nice, ain't it, ma'am? (*Tia Maria pours herself another drink, leans back on the headboard next to I. W. Harper.*)

TIA MARIA. Something's burning.

JACK DANIELS. We know.

TIA MARIA. Where's it coming from?

JACK DANIELS. The closet.

TIA MARIA. It's pretty.

JACK DANIELS. The closet, ma'am?

TIA MARIA. The smoke. (*Tia Maria closes her eyes and enjoys the smoke. Jack Daniels strums his guitar.*)

JACK DANIELS. My pa always said where there's smoke there's fire.

TIA MARIA. (*Trying to focus.*) Fire?

JACK DANIELS. Yes, ma'am, that's what he said.

TIA MARIA. Fire?

JACK DANIELS. Where there's smoke there must be fire.

TIA MARIA. AAAAEEEEEIIIIIIOOOOOOOUUUUUU!!!!

I. W. HARPER. (*Stirring.*) Aw come on, honey, knock it off!

TIA MARIA. AAAAAAEEEEEIIIIIIIOOOOOOOOUUUUUU!!!!

JOHNNY WALKER. Damnit, Tia, we're trying to sleep!

TIA MARIA. AAAAAAEEEEEIIIIIIIIOOOOOOOUUUUUUU! (*She faints again.*)

JACK DANIELS. Boy, she sure does that a lot! And loudly, too! (*Jack Daniels sits and strums his guitar. Tia Maria is out cold. I. W. Harper and Johnny Walker have rolled back over and are trying to sleep. At the same time the closet door is opened from inside to reveal Southern Comfort. She is sitting on the floor in a lotus position. Several sticks of incense are burning in front of her. She's wearing a headband and finger cymbals and bra and panties.*)

SOUTHERN COMFORT. Goddamnit, anyway, will you make her stop!? I'm trying to meditate in here. And if I can't meditate I can't concentrate. And if I can't concentrate how the hell am I ever gonna levitate? Get my goddamn ass in the air? It ain't all that goddamn easy! So tell her to cool it, hunh? What's her goddamn problem anyway? (*Southern Comfort slams the closet door shut just as abruptly as she opened it. Jack Daniels has stopped strumming, of course, and from the doubletake he does you'd think he's never seen a half-naked girl before . . . which, quite possibly, he hasn't. Now he gets up, goes over to the closet door and politely knocks.*)

JACK DANIELS. Southern Comfort?

SOUTHERN COMFORT. Leave me alone.

JACK DANIELS. What are you doing in there?

SOUTHERN COMFORT. What the fuck does it look like I'm doing?

JACK DANIELS. I'm not rightly sure. Maybe if I could have one more look at you I could tell you that more clearly.

SOUTHERN COMFORT. I can't talk now.

JACK DANIELS. You don't have to talk, ma'am. Jes' come out here and kind o' stand around some.

SOUTHERN COMFORT. I said buzz off. I can't levitate with you yakking at me. (*Southern Comfort resumes singing "Hare Krishna" and playing the finger cymbals. Jack Daniels runs over to I. W. Harper stretched out on the bed.*)

JACK DANIELS. (*Trying to rouse him.*) I.W.! Hey, I.W., wake up now, quick! (*I.W. mumbles incoherently in his drunken sleep.*)

Southern Comfort's sitting in the closet, and she says she's fixing to levitate! (*I. W. Harper mumbles some more and rolls over onto his stomach. Jack Daniels now tries to rouse Johnny Walker.*) Johnny, wake up, Johnny! (*Johnny Walker mumbles incoherently.*) Southern Comfort's going to levitate!

JOHNNY WALKER. That's nice.

JACK DANIELS. Don't you want to see?

JOHNNY WALKER. Wake me when it's time. (*Johnny Walker rolls over and snores happily. Jack Daniels goes back over to the closet again.*)

JACK DANIELS. Southern Comfort?

SOUTHERN COMFORT. What?

JACK DANIELS. I've been wondering. 'Spose I came in there and levitated with you?

SOUTHERN COMFORT. Hah! I knew you'd ask me that!

JACK DANIELS. Hunh?

SOUTHERN COMFORT. I said I can't talk now. (*Southern Comfort resumes singing "Hare Krishna."*)

JACK DANIELS. Now how am I gonna get her out o' there or me in? (*He stands there thinking until he gets his one and only idea of this entire play. First he turns off the overhead lights so that the room is just light enough to see in. Next he picks up his guitar and starts strumming and singing "Hare Krishna" in his true and clear voice along with Southern Comfort in the closet. Their duet grows and grows, both more loudly and more exuberantly.*)

SOUTHERN COMFORT. Is that you, Jack Daniels?

JACK DANIELS. Yes, ma'am, that's who it is.

SOUTHERN COMFORT. You're sure grooving with that mantra.

JACK DANIELS. I know, ma'am. That's what I'm doing with it.

SOUTHERN COMFORT. Are you cool, man?

JACK DANIELS. Ma'am?

SOUTHERN COMFORT. Are you cool, man?

JACK DANIELS. Oh yes, ma'am, I'm real cool.

SOUTHERN COMFORT. Don't call me ma'am, man.

JACK DANIELS. I was jes' fixing to ask you the very same thing!

SOUTHERN COMFORT. Now keep grooving with that mantra. I'm coming out dancing.

JACK DANIELS. You bet, Southern Comfort! (*Jack Daniels attacks the song with fresh enthusiasm. The closet door slowly opens and*

*Southern Comfort comes out dancing and working her finger
cymbals. At the first sight of her, Jack Daniels's fingers fall right
off his guitar. But he recovers.*)

SOUTHERN COMFORT. Hey, man.

JACK DANIELS. (*Dazzled.*) Hey!

SOUTHERN COMFORT. I didn't know you were hip.

JACK DANIELS. You didn't?

SOUTHERN COMFORT. I thought you were as straight as they come.

JACK DANIELS. Me?

SOUTHERN COMFORT. It's nice to know we're soul brothers.

JACK DANIELS. It sure is.

SOUTHERN COMFORT. I like you, Jack Daniels.

JACK DANIELS. I like you, Southern Comfort.

SOUTHERN COMFORT. I can talk to you.

JACK DANIELS. Go ahead, shoot.

SOUTHERN COMFORT. How stoned are you?

JACK DANIELS. (*Uncertainly, he doesn't know this expression.*) Not
too stoned. Maybe fair to middling.

SOUTHERN COMFORT. Oh, that's too bad. I thought maybe you was
way up where I was.

JACK DANIELS. I'm pretty stoned, though. For me. But I could get
stonier.

SOUTHERN COMFORT. Stonier! I like that word, stonier. It was
groovy of you to use it.

JACK DANIELS. And if I get much stonier, I'll be a rock! No, a
boulder! (*Jack Daniels laughs his yuk! yuk! yuk! laugh.*)

SOUTHERN COMFORT. Don't be a drag, man. Like this dance is starting to be a drag. (*She stops.*) Like your guitar is starting to be a
drag. (*He stops playing.*) Things get to be a drag for me. I freak
out. That concert tonight was a drag.

JACK DANIELS. And you sure as shooting freaked out, Southern.

SOUTHERN COMFORT. I guess I showed him.

JACK DANIELS. You sure did. You showed eighty-one thousand other
people, too.

SOUTHERN COMFORT. If he don't know now how I feel about sexist
racism in this country, I don't guess he ever will.

JACK DANIELS. How *do* you feel?

SOUTHERN COMFORT. Like I'm getting ready to flip out again. (*She
sits.*) That trying to levitate gets to be a drag, too.

JACK DANIELS. Did it work?

SOUTHERN COMFORT. Only about yay high.

JACK DANIELS. Is that all?

SOUTHERN COMFORT. Well hell, I was only in there five or six hours. That swami said it could take all the way up to twelve. But who the hell's got that kind of time?

JACK DANIELS. What swami?

SOUTHERN COMFORT. (*Pouring herself a drink.*) Some creep who was trying to make me in the dressing room before we went on. At least he said he was a swami. He looked like a Mexican with a beard and a turban. Swami Sanchez he called himself. He couldn't keep his hands off me.

JACK DANIELS. Well I'm real glad you came out o' that closet, Southern Comfort. Ain't no fit place for a pretty girl like you.

SOUTHERN COMFORT. You say that like every other hung up, strung out, uptight cat I meet.

JACK DANIELS. How's that?

SOUTHERN COMFORT. Like the only reason you're glad I'm out of there is cause I'm not wearing any clothes.

JACK DANIELS. I'm not glad, Southern. I mean, I *am!* You know what I'm trying to say.

SOUTHERN COMFORT. Clothes are symbols, that's all they are.

JACK DANIELS. Damn right they are.

SOUTHERN COMFORT. Symbols of repression and I want to be free!

JACK DANIELS. I don't blame you, Southern.

SOUTHERN COMFORT. I'm never gonna wear any again.

JACK DANIELS. That's a damn good idea, Southern Comfort.

SOUTHERN COMFORT. It'll blow their minds.

JACK DANIELS. Yeeeeeeeoooooooooow!

SOUTHERN COMFORT. That's exactly what I mean.

JACK DANIELS. (*Realizing he's gone too far.*) I was jes' agreeing how good an idea it was for you not to wear anymore clothes ever again.

SOUTHERN COMFORT. Nobody's making me ashamed of my body. Are you?

JACK DANIELS. No, ma'am, I think you got a real fine one.

SOUTHERN COMFORT. Not my body, who cares about that? Yours.

JACK DANIELS. (*Looks down at his body, he's never thought about this before, then.*) How could I be ashamed of it? It's the only one I got.

SOUTHERN COMFORT. Beautiful.

JACK DANIELS. I wouldn't exactly call it that.

SOUTHERN COMFORT. Your mind's beautiful, your head. "How can I be ashamed of it? It's the only one I got." Can I write that in my journal if I can remember it?

JACK DANIELS. Sure.

SOUTHERN COMFORT. Everything in life is beautiful. What is, is. And what is, is beautiful. That's my philosophy.

JACK DANIELS. It's a damn pretty one, too.

SOUTHERN COMFORT. I know.

JACK DANIELS. It's just about the prettiest philosophy I ever heard. Boy, am I glad I got you out o' that closet so we could set and talk like this.

SOUTHERN COMFORT. There it is again.

JACK DANIELS. (*Startled, looking over his shoulder.*) What?

SOUTHERN COMFORT. That tone in your voice.

JACK DANIELS. Ain't no tone, Southern.

SOUTHERN COMFORT. Sexual hangups.

JACK DANIELS. I swear to God, Southern Comfort, the tone of sexual hangups is the last thing in the world you hear in my voice.

SOUTHERN COMFORT. You don't want me that way?

JACK DANIELS. No, ma'am, I most emphatically do not!

SOUTHERN COMFORT. That's okay, too, Jack Daniels. Love between two cats can be a beautiful and groovy thing.

JACK DANIELS. It's sure noisier'n hell.

SOUTHERN COMFORT. Or two chicks. It doesn't matter.

JACK DANIELS. (*While visions of chickens copulating dance in his head.*) It don't?

SOUTHERN COMFORT. But it's best between a cat and a chick.

JACK DANIELS. (*Choking on this one.*) It is?!

SOUTHERN COMFORT. (*Getting ready to sneeeze.*) Sure . . . ah! ah! ah! . . . what do you think? . . . ah! ah! ah! . . . you never tried it? . . . atchoo!

JACK DANIELS. You're catching cold.

SOUTHERN COMFORT. (*Shaking her head.*) It's my allergy.

JACK DANIELS. Can I get you anything?

SOUTHERN COMFORT. (*Lighting up a joint.*) This is the only thing that helps. (*Jack Daniels watches her smoke, his eyes widening in astonishment.*)

JACK DANIELS. Boy, you sure take deep drags. That's smoking like it's going out o' style. I guess it *must* help your allergy. (*Jack Daniels's eyes have been feasting all over Southern Comfort's body.*)

SOUTHERN COMFORT. What are you staring at?

JACK DANIELS. I thought I saw something on you. A bug.

SOUTHERN COMFORT. It's a mole.

JACK DANIELS. From here it looked jes' like a little bug.

SOUTHERN COMFORT. The mole's here. You were looking there.

JACK DANIELS. Maybe it moved. (*He hangs his head.*)

SOUTHERN COMFORT. Don't apologize, you don't ever have to apologize for anything. I'm turning you on, Jack. That's good, that's groovy. Go with it.

JACK DANIELS. I will, ma'am, I promise I will.

SOUTHERN COMFORT. If it had been a bug, Jack Daniels, just supposing it had been, what would you have done?

JACK DANIELS. Well, ma'am, first I would have plucked it off you and then I would have squashed it to death.

SOUTHERN COMFORT. That turns me off, Jack, that turns me off a whole lot, that answer does.

JACK DANIELS. I'm sorry, Southern Comfort.

SOUTHERN COMFORT. I'm beginning to think you were just pretending to be hip. Anybody who kills bugs, who doesn't respect all life, is no soul brother of mine. You're a plastic hippie, Jack Daniels. I'm going back in the closet.

JACK DANIELS. Don't do that! There's a reason I said I'd kill the bug.

SOUTHERN COMFORT. It would have to be an awfully good one to keep me out here. Boy, that answer turned me right off you, man.

JACK DANIELS. (*Stalling for time.*) It is, it is a good one.

SOUTHERN COMFORT. I'm listening.

JACK DANIELS. I saw a bug that looked jes' like your mole on my ma's shoulder once. I didn't kill it. And you know what happened? It killed her.

SOUTHERN COMFORT. Oh man, what a bad scene that must have been for you!

JACK DANIELS. Real bad, only worse for my ma. Ever since, whenever I see a bug like that I kill it. Ordinarily I wouldn't hurt a
fly. Hell, I even love black widow spiders and scorpions. It's jes'
that one bug I'm down on.

SOUTHERN COMFORT. What month were you born? November!

JACK DANIELS. (*Her changes of subject are too fast for him.*) What
month?

SOUTHERN COMFORT. You must be a Scorpio. I groove with Scorpios.

JACK DANIELS. Are we still talking about bugs?

SOUTHERN COMFORT. I groove on astrology. I'm Cancer.

JACK DANIELS. I was born in February.

SOUTHERN COMFORT. Pisces. That's okay, too. My first spade lover
was a Pisces.

JACK DANIELS. You had a spayed lover?

SOUTHERN COMFORT. Who hasn't nowadays?

JACK DANIELS. How'd he get spayed?

SOUTHERN COMFORT. He was born spade, silly.

JACK DANIELS. How'd you ever meet someone like *that*?

SOUTHERN COMFORT. I picked him up. I just walked right up to him
on Sheridan Square in that Greenwich Village . . . I was visiting
in New York when all this happened . . . and said to him "Hey,
man, you dig white chicks?"

JACK DANIELS. What'd he say?

SOUTHERN COMFORT. Nothing. He just grabbed my arm and dragged
me down in that subway stop they got there and raped the hell
out of me.

JACK DANIELS. That black bastard.

SOUTHERN COMFORT. Don't say that, I deserved it.

JACK DANIELS. I don't follow.

SOUTHERN COMFORT. (*Getting ready to sneeze again.*) Well
wouldn't you . . . ah! ah! ah! . . . rape me . . . ah! ah! ah! if
you were a spade? . . . ah! ah! ah! . . . and everything I'd done
to you? . . . atchoo!

JACK DANIELS. What exactly is it you're allergic to, Southern?

SOUTHERN COMFORT. (*Another sneeze coming on.*) Hair.

JACK DANIELS. You mean like fur rugs and things?

SOUTHERN COMFORT. My own hair. Atchoo!

JACK DANIELS. That must be hard.

SOUTHERN COMFORT. It's a goddamn drag! Atchoo! (*Southern Comfort lights another joint.*)

JACK DANIELS. You're lucky you got a good supply o' them cigarettes. What do you do when you run out? (*Southern Comfort shakes her head indicating she can't talk.*) Sorry, Southern. You keep that smoke in. My pa was allergic to yellow onions. He had to rub Crisco oil all o'er himself when he broke out.

SOUTHERN COMFORT. Oh wow!

JACK DANIELS. It's good, hunh? You're lucky. Most people hate anything that's good for 'em. (*Southern Comfort passes the joint to him.*) No, thank you.

SOUTHERN COMFORT. It's good stuff.

JACK DANIELS. In the first place, I don't have no allergies and in the second, I don't smoke.

SOUTHERN COMFORT. It'll loosen you up.

JACK DANIELS. I am loose. Hell, I'm so loose I jangle.

SOUTHERN COMFORT. I mean sexually.

JACK DANIELS. Oh. Well I guess I better try me some. Give me that butt, woman. (*Jack Daniels takes the deepest drag he can and holds it.*)

SOUTHERN COMFORT. I'm more than a vagina, Jack Daniels. (*Jack Daniels chokes on the joint.*) I am a human being.

JACK DANIELS. Yes, ma'am, I know that. That's jes' what I was thinking.

SOUTHERN COMFORT. That's what they all say. You don't know the real me. The real me's right here, staring you in the face, only nobody ever sees her.

JACK DANIELS. I see you, Southern.

SOUTHERN COMFORT. I know what you see when you look at me.

JACK DANIELS. Well, seeing's how you're not wearing any clothes . . . ! (*Jack Daniels laughs his yuk! yuk! yuk! laugh but this time it's to conceal his embarrassment.*)

SOUTHERN COMFORT. You're that terrified of any real commitment? I feel sorry for you, Johnny.

JACK DANIELS. I'm Jack. Sorry for me?

SOUTHERN COMFORT. Do you want to make love to me or not?

JACK DANIELS. Yes, ma'am, I surely do, but why sorry for me?

SOUTHERN COMFORT. Make love to me, Johnny. Here and now and hard and beautiful.

JACK DANIELS. (*Indicating with his head that they are not alone.*)
Don't you think maybe we ought to go in another room?

SOUTHERN COMFORT. I wouldn't give them that satisfaction.

JACK DANIELS. I'm talking 'bout our satisfaction.

SOUTHERN COMFORT. You want me, Johnny, don't you?

JACK DANIELS. Yes, I want you, I want you a whole lot but . . . ! 'N
my name's Jack.

SOUTHERN COMFORT. It's that important to you?

JACK DANIELS. No, but . . .

SOUTHERN COMFORT. I'm freaking out, Johnny, I'm really freaking
out. I feel bad vibrations coming from that ledge out there and
I don't want to have to do that again.

JACK DANIELS. Do what?

SOUTHERN COMFORT. Jump. Do I turn you on, Johnny? Tell me that
I turn you on.

JACK DANIELS. Yes, you turn me on.

SOUTHERN COMFORT. Oh God! Oh wow! Oh groovy!

JACK DANIELS. And you'd turn me on even more if you'd jes' call
me Jack.

SOUTHERN COMFORT. I hate Jack, I can't call you Jack. Jack was a
bass player with the Grateful Dead before they made it big and
it was a really bad scene with him. Don't ask me to call you
Jack, Johnny, please don't make me do that!

JACK DANIELS. Okay, Southern, okay!

SOUTHERN COMFORT. I'm freaking out, Johnny, I'm really freaking
out tonight.

JACK DANIELS. I think I can see that, ma'am.

SOUTHERN COMFORT. You have nice fingernails.

JACK DANIELS. What?

SOUTHERN COMFORT. You have nice fingernails. Tommy Tyler has
terrible fingernails. All bitten and ugly.

JACK DANIELS. Who's Tommy Tyler?

SOUTHERN COMFORT. A drummer I lived with for six months in
Hollywood. He gave me the clap. Let's not talk about him. It
was another bad scene. Hurry up, Johnny, please! (*Southern
Comfort rips open his shirt.*)

JACK DANIELS. Hey!

SOUTHERN COMFORT. Oh God, freedom!

JACK DANIELS. This is my good shirt. (*Then.*) What's the matter?

SOUTHERN COMFORT. You don't have hair on your chest.

JACK DANIELS. I know.

SOUTHERN COMFORT. You said you had hair on your chest. No! I'm confusing you with Stevie Mencken. It doesn't matter.

JACK DANIELS. Who's Stevie Mencken?

SOUTHERN COMFORT. Some sideman I met in Tiajuana. He's not important. He beat the shit out of me. I don't want to talk about him. You just reminded me of him for a minute. Only he had hair on his chest. Make love to me, Johnny, what's the matter, don't I turn you on?

JACK DANIELS. How many times do I have to say yes?

SOUTHERN COMFORT. Prove it then, Johnny, prove it. Don't be afraid of me. I'll be good with you. I won't laugh. I promise not to laugh.

JACK DANIELS. If you'd jes' set still for a minute maybe I could! (*Jack Daniels manages to kiss her. A good long kiss which gets more and more serious. Finally Southern Comfort breaks loose and holds him off.*)

SOUTHERN COMFORT. No!

JACK DANIELS. What's the matter?

SOUTHERN COMFORT. It's not fair to you like this.

JACK DANIELS. What ain't?

SOUTHERN COMFORT. There's something about me you don't know.

JACK DANIELS. Can't it wait?

SOUTHERN COMFORT. It's too important.

JACK DANIELS. Go ahead then.

SOUTHERN COMFORT. I'm frigid, Johnny.

JACK DANIELS. I don't mind.

SOUTHERN COMFORT. I can't have a climax. I can lie there and go through the motions but I can't have a climax.

JACK DANIELS. That's okay, too.

SOUTHERN COMFORT. It's not a very pretty story. I grew up right here in Houston. I was pretty, I was the national champion baton twirler and I only dated football players. Sound familiar? The typical American girl. The first boy I went all the way with was Bobby Barton. Bobby was the state champion high school quarterback and since I was a champion, too, only a national one, it was pretty natural that we should get together. It was in the back seat of his daddy's Ford Fairlane on our eleventh date. Re-

member them? They were two-toned with a chrome trim that
made kind of a dip along the door. Anyway, I really enjoyed it
and Bobby did, too. I started going all the way with him on every
date we had. Gee, it was swell. Then one day after school during
football practice somebody tackled Bobby and he just didn't get
up. I mean he was dead. So then I started dating Bobby's best
friend, Terry Walsh, who played right guard and who'd been the
one who'd accidentally killed Bobby when he tackled him during practice that time. I went all the way with him on the fourth
date. He had a sports car, a reptile-green MG, so we had to
spread blankets on the ground first. Terry got killed during the
game with Lubbock for the state quarter finals down in Austin.
Spontaneous concussion. My senior year at Sunset I started dating and going all the way with Tiny Walker, who played left end
and who used to be Terry and Bobby's real good friend. He drove
a blood-red, chopped down Plymouth Fury with dual carbure-
tors and two front seats that you could make go flat down like in
a dentist's chair. Tiny was small but powerful and he'd been
tackled lots of times by bruisers a whole lot bigger than that line-
backer from Sweetwater. But when Tiny died like that I stopped
dating football players. I felt like a jinx on 'em, you know what
I mean? and I knew people were starting to say things about me
behind my back. I stopped twirling, started drinking, got to hate
Houston so much I couldn't stand it here any longer, ran away
from home and got into show business. Now I sleep around a lot,
but only with musicians; they don't die on you like football
players. (*A pause.*) I told you it wasn't a very pretty story.

JACK DANIELS. Dog sad's what I'd call it.

SOUTHERN COMFORT. Dog what?

JACK DANIELS. Dog sad, ma'am. Sad like a dog.

SOUTHERN COMFORT. I see what you mean. I guess it is. I never
really thought about it like that. Dog sad.

JACK DANIELS. My pa thought it up. Never ever heard anybody say
it but him.

SOUTHERN COMFORT. You still want me, Johnny?

JACK DANIELS. Yes, ma'am, I think so.

SOUTHERN COMFORT. You're worried I'll be bad for you.

JACK DANIELS. Hell no, I never played football in my life.

SOUTHERN COMFORT. What then?

JACK DANIELS. There's something maybe you ought to know about me. I'm kind o' drunk, Southern. I may not be able to . . . you know.

SOUTHERN COMFORT. That's okay.

JACK DANIELS. It ain't like I don't want to, you understand. I want to real bad.

SOUTHERN COMFORT. Sometimes it's nice just holding someone real still and nobody talking even.

JACK DANIELS. Maybe so, but that don't mean I ain't gonna try first. (*Tia Maria is starting to stir on the bed.*) Jes' not in here, Southern, okay?

SOUTHERN COMFORT. Where's your room?

JACK DANIELS. We can't in there. I lost my key.

SOUTHERN COMFORT. Mine's out too. Hansel and the Toad People are crashing in there.

JACK DANIELS. Hansel and the Toad People?

SOUTHERN COMFORT. This rock trio I picked up at the Continental Trailways bus terminal. They're so freaked out and sex mad they'd be all over us. Orgies aren't my scene. Those creeps from the Brass Pussycat had me all over the place. Please, Johnny, I don't want to talk about them.

JACK DANIELS. What were you doing at a bus terminal?

SOUTHERN COMFORT. Meeting people, what else? Come on, and bring a bottle.

JACK DANIELS. Where we going?

SOUTHERN COMFORT. The closet, and bring your guitar, too.

JACK DANIELS. Ain't it awful small in there?

SOUTHERN COMFORT. What are you figuring on? A rodeo?

JACK DANIELS. I 'spose we could always levitate. (*Jack Daniels laughs his yuk! yuk! yuk! laugh as he follows Southern Comfort into the closet and closes the door behind them. Tia Maria sits up in bed.*)

TIA MARIA. I.W.? I.W.? The two kids went into the closet together and I don't think it was to hang up any clothes. (*I. W. Harper mutters in his sleep and snuggles up closer to Tia Maria, who fumbles for a cigarette and match, lights up and pours herself a drink.*) Boy, am I gonna have a head on me tomorrow morning. I don't want to think about it. I don't even want to wake up. I feel like that time we got drunk in Denver during that windstorm and I woke up in the middle of the night and told you I was gonna be sick only the toilet didn't work and you yelled "Over here" and when I ran to the window the damn thing blew open and my head went right through it. Eighteen stitches they took in my scalp. Boy, I was mad at you the next day. It wasn't your fault but I had to be mad at someone. You're a good sport, I.W. (*Tia Maria laughs and strokes I. W. Harper's head while he just snuggles closer.*) I know I'm just a fat 'n foolish, middle-aged lady drunk who screams a lot and eats too much candy and I don't know why you put up with me half the time but I do love you, I.W., and ain't that the main thing, loving somebody? And I guess you love me a little bit, too. Hell, honey, you'd have to! Look at poor Johnny Walker asleep on the floor there. He ain't got no one. Hey, Johnny! Johnny Walker! You want to get up here into bed with I.W. and me? We'll let you. (*Johnny Walker groans drunkenly in his sleep.*) He don't want to come, I.W. That's okay, too. I still love you, Johnny. Even sleeping it off on the floor like some drunk dog who ain't got no dignity, I still love you. And if those kids would quit a-hugging 'n a-kissing in that closet and come out here I'd tell them I loved them, too. I love all those kids like they was my own. I know I ain't their ma but I feel like their ma and I like that feeling. There ain't no harm in that. Is there, anybody? Me and I.W. wanted kids, didn't we, honey? We just couldn't have any and some nights that gets me really down and blue. But not tonight. Tonight we're just one big happy family. I like that feeling a whole lot, too. (*Whiskey whinnies softly from the bathroom.*) Sometimes I think that horse is trying to tell us something, warn us even, like maybe he knows something we don't know. 'Course most of the time I think he just hates us and is trying to kill me and I wish he was dead and stuffed and put on rollers. That would be a good kind of horse to have, I.W.! (*I. W. snores and snuggles closer.*) If they cancel the tour, I.W., we're gonna go right back to Santa Monica and work up a better act. I already got two new good ideas. One is you cracking a cigar out of Southern Comfort's mouth with your bullwhip while she's twirling her flaming batons. A cigarette would be too dangerous. Maybe it ain't so hot. The other is for me to dress a whole lot more lady-like, like Barbara Stanwyck, and sashay more. I don't think I'm doing nearly enough sashaying now. I'd look real nice in white, I.W., I think you'd be proud of me in the kind of white dress I'm envisioning. (*I. W. Harper snores and snuggles closer.*) But you know something, I.W.? Even if we don't ever appear in public again, even if they cancelled our series after what happened tonight, I'd still be the happiest, luckiest lady I know. I got you, I.W. I think having you next to me, hearing you snore is the nicest sound I know, even if you are drunker than a coot. Sleep now, baby, sleep away and dream of big blue skies and red earth and all them happy things. (*Tia Maria begins to hum very softly and very lovingly to I. W. Harper, who is nestled in her arms. With one hand she strokes his head, with the other she holds her cigarette and drink. Whiskey will be heard from time to time whinnying more and more restlessly in the bathroom.*) Yes, sir, I think you'd be real proud of me in the kind of white dress I'm envisioning! (*While Tia Maria hums now, she will be slowly drifting off to sleep. The lights in the room are coming down. We hear a gentle thud as the glass falls from her hand onto the carpet. She still holds the cigarette, however, and we see it spiraling smoke above Tia Maria and I. W. Harper asleep on the bed. Whiskey is whinnying more and he has started beating his hooves again. The lights in the room are nearly gone now but one stays a moment longer on that burning cigarette in Tia Maria's hand. Whiskey is making quite a bit of noise now and in the blackout that follows the sound will grow louder and louder and more terrifying, too. What we also hear are the terrible sounds and noises of a hotel fire! There are fire engines, their sirens wailing, the yells and screams of people calling for help, the hiss of high pressure hoses quenching flames and making steam. The terrible sounds build until they reach an ear-shattering, terrifying crescendo only to be abruptly cut off. What we then hear and at once is the mournful sound of a Hammond organ. When the lights come back up we are in the Houston Astrodome once again. What we see is the Lush Thrushes and Whiskey show curtain. All the cutouts where I. W. Harper, Tia Maria, Johnny Walker, Southern Comfort and Jack Daniels once stood are empty now, of course. Someone has draped them in black crepe. Whiskey's cutout is filled, however, by none other than Whiskey himself. He is an old, spindly, rather repulsive critter. As horses go, Whiskey is way down low on the totem pole. Right now he is contentedly standing in his very own spotlight noisily chewing his oats. He's been decorated with some kind of Red Cross badge but it's difficult to tell whether such awards mean very much to him. Certainly he's oblivious to the lugubrious accents of the Announcer's Voice as he drones the eulogy.)*

ANNOUNCER'S VOICE. *(Over the organ music.)* . . . indeed, the entire nation will not soon recover from this stunning and tragic loss to the entertainment industry. How Whiskey alone escaped the raging holocaust that turned their multimillion dollar, fully air-conditioned hostelry into a raging inferno is Whiskey's secret and his alone. There is one happy note, fans, if happy is not too inappropriate a word to utter on this sad occasion. I have just spoken on the telephone long distance to Whiskey's agent, a certain Howard Rosenstone of the William Morris Agency in New York City, who assured me only moments ago that Whiskey will return next season as the star of his own series. I believe package was the word he used, folks, some kind of William Morris package. And now, may I ask that we all rise and stand for a moment of silent tribute to the memory of these five so-well-loved, intimately unique and already sorely missed artistes? *(The Hammond organ continues to mourn but over it we hear the sound of Jack Daniels singing and playing "The Streets of Laredo." When he does appear he is dressed exactly like he was before—overalls, shirt, barefeet, etc.—only this time everything is a beautiful, gleaming white. Also, he has sprouted the biggest pair of snow-white angel wings anybody ever saw.)*

JACK DANIELS. I'm in heaven, Whiskey. I'm one o' God's little angels now. Ain't that nice? 'Cause judging from the crowds I seen, it looks like everybody comes to heaven and gets to be one o' God's little angels. Ain't hardly no distinction at all. It's jes' like earth, too. Some people singing, some people drinking, some people fighting. Sure are a lot o' black 'n brown 'n yellow people, though! I never seen so many skin tones. It's pretty. And God's jes' like I.W. I was telling Him 'bout the time my little brother got his big right toe caught in an International Harvester tractor tread and pa had to use bear grease to get him out and He told me to keep my dumb mouth shut. He said I could play my guitar and sing though. You miss us, Whiskey? You sure don't look like it. (*Johnny Walker appears. He, too, is dressed like before only now everything is a shiny white leather. And the new pair of wings he sports are just as white, if not quite as large, as Jack Daniels's. He's carrying a newspaper and he's fit to be tied.*)

JOHNNY WALKER. What did they call me?!

JACK DANIELS. Uh oh, Whiskey, Johnny Walker and he's all het up.

JOHNNY WALKER. Just guess what they called me?!

JACK DANIELS. I wouldn't rightly know, Johnny.

JOHNNY WALKER. Well guess!

JACK DANIELS. A fruit?

JOHNNY WALKER. What did you call me?

JACK DANIELS. I knew I shouldn't have answered when you're all worked up like this.

JOHNNY WALKER. Shut up, you dumb hick. I'll say I'm worked up. Listen to this! (*Johnny Walker is so angry he can hardly find the place he's looking for in the newspaper.*)

JACK DANIELS. Johnny Walker's gonna read us what they called him, Whiskey.

JOHNNY WALKER. "The entire cast of television's longest running series was killed last night when a fire swept through their hotel in downtown Houston."

JACK DANIELS. Is that what happened? Last thing I remember I was in that closet with Southern Comfort and next thing I knew I was here.

JOHNNY WALKER. "Miraculously, their horse and co-star escaped the flames."

JACK DANIELS. Good for you, Whiskey.

JOHNNY WALKER. "The 1,876 other guests in the hotel were evacuated without incident."

JACK DANIELS. Boy, for such a big hotel it sure had mighty poor room service.

JOHNNY WALKER. "Why only the five actors failed to leave their rooms has not yet been determined."

JACK DANIELS. Shoot, that's easy. We was drunk.

JOHNNY WALKER. Here it is, this is the part! "Authorities have ventured that one possible cause of the fire were the Lady Schick portable hair dryer and Carmencita hair curler set found in the room of the series' so-called he-man, Johnny Walker."

JACK DANIELS. They called you a so-called he-man, Johnny.

JOHNNY WALKER. Not between the lines, they didn't! I know what they meant! I know! CIA stuff, you hear me, CIA!!! (*Johnny Walker fires his pistol wildly in a violent rage. From offstage we hear a very loud OOOOOOOWW!*)

JACK DANIELS. This time you really hit someone.

JOHNNY WALKER. Oh no! (*Southern Comfort storms in. She is wearing an enormous pair of white wings and a white bikini.*)

SOUTHERN COMFORT. You grazed my butt!

JOHNNY WALKER. I'm sorry, Southern. .

SOUTHERN COMFORT. You grazed my butt, you dumb fairy!

JOHNNY WALKER. I didn't see you, honest I didn't.

SOUTHERN COMFORT. That big pouff grazed my pink touchas!

JACK DANIELS. It's only a crease, Southern.

SOUTHERN COMFORT. Well it hurt!

JOHNNY WALKER. I said I was sorry. I read something like this and I just go crazy.

SOUTHERN COMFORT. Do it again and I'll have a real cowboy work you over. (*Calling off.*) It's okay, Billy! He said he was sorry!

JACK DANIELS. Who you talking to, Southern?

SOUTHERN COMFORT. Billy the Kid.

JOHNNY WALKER. He's up here?

SOUTHERN COMFORT. This place is crawling with cowboys.

JACK DANIELS. I don't see him. Where?

SOUTHERN COMFORT. Over there, see? Talking to Calamity Jane.

JOHNNY WALKER. That's him all right.

SOUTHERN COMFORT. Who'd you think it was? Fat Gene Autry?

JOHNNY WALKER. Gene Autry ain't dead.

SOUTHERN COMFORT. Well you are, Johnny Walker.

JOHNNY WALKER. I know. (*Johnny Walker moves apart from Southern Comfort and Jack Daniels.*)

SOUTHERN COMFORT. What are you doing?

JACK DANIELS. Winking at that Calamity Jane. She winked at me so I thought I'd better wink right back at her.

SOUTHERN COMFORT. (*Greeting another new friend.*) Hi, Jesse, how y'all making it!

JACK DANIELS. Look, Johnny, Jesse James! It sure is crawling with 'em.

SOUTHERN COMFORT. Oh man, this place is a complete turn on!

JACK DANIELS. Have you seen Him yet?

SOUTHERN COMFORT. He flipped me out. Groovy as they come. I blew His mind, too. I walked right up to Him and said since I wasn't gonna wear any clothes down there I sure as hell wasn't gonna wear any up here either! He freaked right out.

JOHNNY WALKER. Look who's there.

JACK DANIELS. Who is it, Johnny?

JOHNNY WALKER. The President of the United States standing with his head bowed. He came back for the memorial service.

JACK DANIELS. Boy, he really must have liked us.

SOUTHERN COMFORT. (*Confronting an old adversary.*) Hey, Mr. President!

JACK DANIELS. He can't hear you, Southern. You're one o' God's little angels now.

SOUTHERN COMFORT. I know. Oh gee! Oh wow! We all are. (*Johnny Walker, Jack Daniels and Southern Comfort stand quietly looking down as they listen to their own memorial service. I. W. Harper and Tia Maria appear now. I.W. is wearing a very handsome white rancher's suit with boots. Tia is wearing her white Barbara Stanwyck-type dress, and she really looks quite lovely in it. Both are sporting a handsome pair of white wings. They enter arm in arm, almost gliding, like a very smooth promenade.*)

I. W. HARPER. Why look at you strut, honey.

TIA MARIA. This ain't no strut, I.W., this is a real North Texas sashay.

I. W. HARPER. You're sure swinging them hips, ma'am.

TIA MARIA. Them that has, does. Them that don't, can't help it.

I. W. HARPER. What does that mean?

TIA MARIA. I don't know. It was just fun saying it!

I. W. HARPER. Why I got a regular little filly prancing 'longside me here.

TIA MARIA. That ain't no filly, I.W., that's your wife.

I. W. HARPER. You sure look mighty pretty in that dress, Tia.

TIA MARIA. I told you I would.

I. W. HARPER. Mighty pretty!

TIA MARIA. And you're just about the handsomest-looking man I ever saw. Now come on, I.W., sashay!

I. W. HARPER. You're happy up here?

TIA MARIA. Happy? Why I'm jes' gonna yodel 'round God's heaven all day, I.W.! (*Tia Maria obliges with a dazzling cadenza of improvised yodels. They have come up next to Whiskey now.*) Look at that horse. He sure looks like he knows something we don't know.

I. W. HARPER. Hello, Whiskey. Just basking away in that spotlight, aren't you, feller?

TIA MARIA. Got it all to himself now.

I. W. HARPER. Tia!

TIA MARIA. I'm not saying he started that fire but he sure didn't break any legs trying to save anybody's life. I'd just like to know how he got out o' there. You gonna tell us, Whiskey?

I. W. HARPER. Leave be, honey, that's something ain't none of us ever gonna know. (*I. W. Harper and Tia Maria join Johnny Walker, Southern Comfort and Jack Daniels.*)

JOHNNY WALKER. We sure got a big crowd down there tonight.

I. W. HARPER. See that, Tia? Folks really did love us.

TIA MARIA. I kind o' always loved them, too, I.W.

SOUTHERN COMFORT. I guess I've twirled my last flaming baton.

JACK DANIELS. And I done twirled my last lariat.

JOHNNY WALKER. Goodbye, world.

TIA MARIA. Amen. (*A moment of silence and they break and begin to move apart.*)

JOHNNY WALKER. Anybody seen Wyatt Earp? I've always wanted to shake his hand.

I. W. HARPER. Wyatt's over yonder, having a shootout with Annie Oakley.

JOHNNY WALKER. Annie Oakley? She must be older than God! No wonder they call this place Heaven! (*Johnny Walker strides off.*)

SOUTHERN COMFORT. Jes' keep away from the James Boys, you latent faggot! I'm meeting them at the corral!

TIA MARIA. You look kind o' rumpled, Southern.

SOUTHERN COMFORT. You think I look rumpled? You ought to see the James Boys. Oh man, they flipped me right out! (*Southern Comfort runs off.*)

TIA MARIA. You mean she can still . . . you know . . . up here?

I. W. HARPER. Would you want her *not* to, Tia?

TIA MARIA. No, I guess not, I.W.

JACK DANIELS. I saw my pa, ma'am.

TIA MARIA. What'd he say?

JACK DANIELS. Nothing. He jes' cuffed me one real hard and said that's what I got for hanging around drunks. I'm gonna see if I can find my ma now. Then I won't be an orphan at all anymore. (*Jack Daniels goes off, playing his guitar and singing his song.*)

I. W. HARPER. He didn't mean that like it sounded, Tia.

TIA MARIA. Is that all we were, I.W.? Drunks?

I. W. HARPER. We liked our liquor, honey, there's no getting around that.

TIA MARIA. But drunks. I hate that word. Hell, it was cigarettes that killed us.

I. W. HARPER. (*Consoling her.*) We weren't just drunks, Tia. We were cowboys first off. Just poor ol' lonesome cowboys. Why, even Southern Comfort's got cowboy stamped all over her, only she don't know it yet. They could book us in the Astrodome, they could package us on TV, they could've moved us to New York City but they ain't never could've changed us. We knew who we were, Tia, and not many people do.

TIA MARIA. What were we, I.W.?

I. W. HARPER. *Cowboy* drunks.

TIA MARIA. (*Drying her eyes.*) Well, that's good enough for me. I jes' couldn't have stood being a drunk drunk, I.W.

I. W. HARPER. That's my girl.

TIA MARIA. Look at Whiskey now. He's grinning at us, I.W.

I. W. HARPER. That is kind of a smile, Tia.

TIA MARIA. You know, just looking at him being there like that, breathing and eating and grinning, and I wouldn't mind being alive again.

I. W. HARPER. You got me, Tia.

TIA MARIA. I know, I.W.

I. W. HARPER. And we got this. (*He produces a bottle of whiskey.*)

TIA MARIA. Like the song says, a good sour mash is hard to find.

I. W. HARPER. Like the song says. (*Tia Maria and I. W. Harper kiss very tenderly.*) Come on, let's get started on this. (*They start moving off, arm in arm, promenading again.*) So long there, Whiskey, don't let 'em stuff you like Trigger!

TIA MARIA. Look, I.W., look! Belle Starr driving a rig n' surrey!

I. W. HARPER. Well I'll be goddamned! (*Tia Maria and I. W. Harper are gone. The organ music fades up.*)

ANNOUNCER'S VOICE. (*Reciting the words dolorously.*) The eyes of Texas were upon them . . . all the livelong day. The eyes of Texas were upon them . . . they could not get away. Do not think you can escape them . . . rise up so early in the morn. The eyes of Texas are upon you, too, my friends, till Gabriel blows his horn. Goodnight, Whiskey. Goodnight, folks. (*The lights begin to fade. The organ tremolos a finale. Whiskey stands chewing his oats, he whinnies, he seems to smile. Blackout.*)

BRINGING IT ALL
BACK HOME

(1969)

THE PLAYERS

Son

Daughter

Mother

Father

Jimmy

Miss Horne

A *living room. Comfortably furnished, nice proportions. Front door, door leading off to kitchen, stairs leading up.*

SON. (*On the phone, smoking marijuana.*) Don't get so uptight, Margy, I just want to turn you on! Jeez, you'd think I'd asked you to do something really wild! . . . It's like . . . it's like flying! Sometimes you see all kinds of colors . . . Really! It's like a great big rainbow and you kind of just swim around in it . . . It is *not* habit forming . . . George Shirley's a queer. He's so freaked out on meth half the time he doesn't know where he's at . . . Come on, Margy, I wouldn't put you on anything that strong your first time. This is only grass . . . Rosemary Steber went to bed with guys before she ever *heard* of pot! . . . the whole ninth grade says! (*Catching sight of himself in a mirror.*) Hey, what's good for pimples? This keeps up I'm gonna ask mom to let me have my face sanded like Harry Butt. . . . Dena's pregnant? Oh cool! I wouldn't be surprised if Harry knocked her up, even if he *is* her brother. (*He's combing his hair.*) I can't come over . . . Aaaaw, I have to hang around this dump waiting for my brother . . . Mmmm, they're sending him home today . . . I'll ask her but it won't do any good. (*Yells up stairs.*) Mom! Hey, Mom! Can I go over to Margy's house? Mom!

DAUGHTER. (*Coming down stairs. Bathrobe, hair in rollers, drinking a coke.*) She's in the dryer.

SON. Who asked you? (*Calling again.*) Hunh, ma, can I? Please!

MOTHER. (*Off.*) I'm in the dryer!

DAUGHTER. I told you.

SON. Drop dead. (*Back into phone.*) She's in the dryer.

DAUGHTER. (*Sprawling in a chair.*) You talking to your . . . (*Good and loud.*) . . . ittle-wittle Margy with braces?

SON. Shove it, hunh? (*Into phone.*) I wasn't talking to *you.*

DAUGHTER. Junior high school brats!

SON. My sister the slut just walked in. (*To Daughter.*) Can't you do that stuff in your own room?

DAUGHTER. (*Buffing her nails.*) The living room belongs to all of us. And hurry up, I'm expecting a call.

SON. Fat Eddie. (*Into phone.*) This guy she goes with's so fat they use him for a goal post.

DAUGHTER. Eddie's first-string, all-state! That's how fat he is!

SON. He's as dumb as a goal post, too.

DAUGHTER. (*Wanting the phone.*) Come on, disaster area, get off the phone.

SON. Margy says maybe you could recommend Dena Butt a good abortionist.

DAUGHTER. (*Yelling upstairs.*) Momma! Momma! Johnny's starting about last winter again!

SON. Would you believe what I have to live with around here? (*Seeing Daughter on way to kitchen.*) That's right. Head for the kitchen. Fatten yourself up some more. (*Back to phone.*) I'll bring some stuff over with me tonight. . . . Stay around? What for? . . . Jimmy? Naaw, all that jazz is tomorrow. All we got today is some television interview. And listen, Margy, it's good stuff, too, Acapulco Gold, so don't chicken out. . . . From that guy at the filling station, who do you think? I wouldn't trust anybody else. Mikie's never burned me once. (*Daughter returns, eating potato chips.*)

DAUGHTER. (*Singsong.*) Johnny is a virgin.

SON. The whore just came back in.

DAUGHTER. Johnny is a virgin.

SON. You ought to go out for football. That way you could be *on* the team instead of *under* it.

DAUGHTER. Johnny is a virgin.

SON. She's already had the entire backfield. Now she's working her way across the line.

DAUGHTER. Johnny is a virgin.

SON. Talk about rigged elections for cheerleader.

DAUGHTER. Johnny is a virgin.

SON. I wouldn't be surprised if she's diseased.

DAUGHTER. Johnny is a virgin.

SON. It wouldn't be the first time!

DAUGHTER. Johnny is a virgin.

SON. I've gotta hang up. I'm gonna smack somebody's face open. I'll see you later. (*Bangs phone down.*) Now quit saying that.

DAUGHTER. Johnny is a—!

SON. I AM NOT!

DAUGHTER. Name one name.

SON. Why should I?

DAUGHTER. You can't.

SON. I'm a gentleman.

DAUGHTER. You're a virgin.

SON. Peggy Walsh.

DAUGHTER. Peggy Walsh?

SON. Peggy Walsh!

DAUGHTER. (*Leaping toward phone.*) What's her number?

SON. You gonna call her up and ask her?

DAUGHTER. What's her number?

SON. Come on, Susy, she's a nice girl.

DAUGHTER. What's her number?

SON. She'd kill me if she knew I'd—

DAUGHTER. Information?

SON. She's not there.

DAUGHTER. Do you have the number for a—?

SON. (*Cutting her off.*) No!

DAUGHTER. Johnny is a virgin!

SON. Well I almost did!

DAUGHTER. What happened?

SON. Never mind! Nothing!

DAUGHTER. That's more like it.

SON. She's only fourteen!

DAUGHTER. Name another name.

SON. What do you want from me? I'm only fifteen. Give me some time, hunh?

DAUGHTER. Is Billy Grey spending the night again this weekend?

SON. I don't know.

DAUGHTER. He's only fifteen, too.

SON. What does that crack mean?

DAUGHTER. As if you didn't know.

SON. As if I didn't know.

DAUGHTER. I hear things.

SON. Good for you.

DAUGHTER. Sounds.

SON. Big deal.

DAUGHTER. Noises.

SON. Just shut up.

DAUGHTER. Squeaks.

SON. He's my best friend.

DAUGHTER. You know there's a name for sub-human, sub-adolescent little boys like you.

SON. Billy's cooler than you'll ever be.

DAUGHTER. (*Spelling it out.*) F-A-I-R-Y.

SON. Godmother! It blows your mind out, hunh?

DAUGHTER. H-O-M-O

SON. Lots of guys my age fool around.

DAUGHTER. S-E-X

SON. Don't you watch those panel shows on TV?

DAUGHTER. U-A-L!

SON. I'm practically normal.

DAUGHTER. Fairy homosexual.

SON. What about when Patty Jackson used to spend the night with you?

DAUGHTER. That was different.

SON. I didn't hear things either, I saw.

DAUGHTER. Momma! Momma!

SON. There's a word for girls like you too!

DAUGHTER. I could just kill you.

SON. L-E-S

DAUGHTER. I was only fourteen.

SON. B-I

DAUGHTER. She started it.

SON. A-N.

DAUGHTER. Lots of girls do.

SON. Dike lesbian.

DAUGHTER. Well at least I grew out of it.

SON. You sure did. Now I've got the town pump for a sister. I'll probably grow up neurotic, thanks to you.

DAUGHTER. Grow up neurotic? You already are. A neurotic dwarf.

SON. I'm gonna grow.

DAUGHTER. When?

SON. Mom's getting me hormone shots!

DAUGHTER. Male ones, I hope! (*Doorbell rings.*) Get it.

SON. Get what?

DAUGHTER. The door.

SON. You.

DAUGHTER. I said get it.

SON. You make me sick the way you boss me around.

DAUGHTER. That's what little brothers are for.

SON. The raw end of the stick! (*Goes to door, opens it, admits two men carrying large box who bring it to center of room.*) Mom! It's Jimmy!

MOTHER. (*Off.*) I'm in the dryer.

SON. Jimmy's home!

MOTHER. (*Off.*) What?

SON. Jimmy, deafhead, he's home!

MOTHER. (*Off.*) I'll be right down.

DAUGHTER. (*Who has displayed herself attractively.*) Hello there! You want me to sign something? (*One of them has handed her a receipt.*)

SON. (*To the other man.*) Here you go. (*Flips him a coin.*)

DAUGHTER. And hi there to you!

SON. (*To both men.*) What are you standing there for? What kind of tip do you expect from a minor? (*The two men begin to leave.*)

DAUGHTER. Bye now! Bye now you two!

SON. Greedy bastards! (*After the men have gone.*) Well there's Jimmy.

DAUGHTER. There he is. (*They stand looking at the crate. They put their hands on it. It's like a foreign object to them. Pause.*)

SON. He was great.

DAUGHTER. Best big brother a sister ever had.

SON. That goes for me, too.

DAUGHTER. And now he's dead.

SON. That land mine tore his stomach right open, dad said. He never knew what hit him.

DAUGHTER. Do you remember what color his eyes were?

SON. Come *on*, I'm a guy. (*Silence, they keep their hands on the crate.*) Don't you?

DAUGHTER. (*After a long while.*) Well there's Jimmy.

SON. There he is.

DAUGHTER. He was a lot of laughs.

SON. You can say that again.

DAUGHTER. That goes for me, too.

SON. And now he's dead.

DAUGHTER. Poppa said that land mine tore his stomach right open. He never knew what hit him.

SON. Do you remember what color hair he had?

DAUGHTER. *Johnny!* I'm his sister! (*Pause.*) Don't you? (*They move away from the crate.*)

SON. Susy, have you tried LSD yet?

DAUGHTER. Of course I have.

SON. Good trip?

DAUGHTER. What do you think?

SON. Bad, hunh?

DAUGHTER. Terrible.

SON. You heard what happened to Sandy Seeger on his trip?

DAUGHTER. What goes on at Lakeview Junior High is of very little interest to seniors at Hamilton.

SON. He jumped off the Goodwin Tower building. He was naked, too.

DAUGHTER. Big deal.

SON. Ugh! Imagine doing something like that without any clothes on and the police finding you nude.

DAUGHTER. (*Who has found a record and put it on the phonograph.*) Come on, show me the Slip 'N Slide, will you?

SON. You're too spastic.

DAUGHTER. Be nice for a change. Put yourself out a little.

SON. I can't do it with my own sister.

DAUGHTER. There's a big dance after the game with Taft Friday night. Everybody'll know how but me. Please?

SON. If you tell me how many guys you've done it with.

DAUGHTER. Johnny!

SON. All right, get Patty Jackson to teach you the Slip 'N Slide.

DAUGHTER. Only nine! *Now* are you satisfied?

SON. Nine's a lot.

DAUGHTER. Wait'll you get to Hamilton. (*They dance. It's sexy. Mother comes downstairs in bathrobe and portable dryer.*)

MOTHER. IS THAT JIMMY??

SON. NO, IT'S RICHARD NIXON!!

MOTHER. I'M IN THE DRYER!!! (*She goes into kitchen.*)

SON. You've got it all wrong!

DAUGHTER. Well do it slower! (*Father enters in flashy bowling team shirt and windbreaker.*)

FATHER. Hello, peaches.

DAUGHTER. (*Running to him.*) Poppa!

FATHER. Hmm, you smell good.

DAUGHTER. So do you.

SON. Boy, if I don't grow up neurotic somebody's gonna have to rewrite the history of psychoanalysis!

FATHER. What's that smell in here?

DAUGHTER. He's been smoking that stuff again.

SON. I have not.

FATHER. Now, son, I've told you. I don't mind you smoking marijuana but not at home. I know all the kids are doing it but not at home. Got that?

SON. (*Militarily crisp.*) Yes, sir!

FATHER. Thatta boy!

SON. You bet!

FATHER. And what did I tell you about dancing with your sister?

SON. (*Thrown.*) Hunh?

FATHER. Don't do it. You should be on the street with the other boys playing football, knocking around, getting your nose bloodied. What are you, some kind of a sissy, hanging around girls all the time?

SON. I thought boys were supposed to like girls.

FATHER. Not at your age. When the time comes for girls I'll be the first one to let you know.

SON. I think it already has.

FATHER. Look, you fresh kid!

SON. I can't help it.

FATHER. You play with boys. Got that?

SON. Yes, sir!

FATHER. This country's raising a generation of faggots, but not in my house it's not.

SON. You bet!

FATHER. My boys are men.

SON. Your boy. Singular. (*Indicates crate.*)

FATHER. (*Going to it.*) So there's Jimmy.

SON. There he is.

FATHER. Most masculine son a father ever had.

DAUGHTER. You can say that again.

SON. Shut up, pig face!

FATHER. And now he's dead. You know, that land mine tore his stomach right open. He never knew what hit him.

SON. Do you remember how tall he was?

DAUGHTER. Stupid, daddy was his *father!*

FATHER. (*After a pause.*) Don't you? (*They move away from the crate.*)

SON. Dad, can I go to a shrinker, too?

DAUGHTER. Monkey see, monkey do!

SON. You don't need one.

DAUGHTER. With the strain I'm under?

SON. We all know what *that* is.

DAUGHTER. See, poppa, how he keeps bringing it up?

SON. Hunh, dad, can I?

FATHER. A boy your age seeing an analyst is just about the least masculine thing I can think of.

SON. Yes, sir!

FATHER. Just straighten up and fly right.

SON. You bet!

FATHER. Besides, the next person in this family to see an analyst is your mother.

SON. Roger!

FATHER. She's a deeply disturbed woman.

SON. Over and out!

FATHER. Now get upstairs and dress. They'll be here.

SON. You're wearing that?

FATHER. What's wrong with it?

SON. On television?

FATHER. Now look, you little snot . . . !

SON. Square!

FATHER. I'm proud of our bowling team. A bunch of men, real men, regular guys, drinking beer, horsing around. The cigar smoke gets so thick in there you can hardly see the pins for it. And oh brother, let me tell you our talk gets rough! Bowling's a man's sport. You ought to try it some time!

SON. Jeez! (*He goes upstairs.*)

FATHER. (*Yelling up the stairs.*) I'd like to see you try lifting those balls! You know how much some of them weigh? Hunh? Do you? And you know how many cans of beer I killed last night? Thirteen! A big one-three!

DAUGHTER. (*Coming to him.*) Poppa!

FATHER. (*Still muttering.*) Rotten little . . . (*She kisses him.*) Hello, peaches.

DAUGHTER. Poppa, you're wonderful!

FATHER. I try, I try.

DAUGHTER. You *are.*

FATHER. (*Patting her rump.*) Up you go now. You know what to put on.

DAUGHTER. Could I, poppa? Oh poppa, could I?

FATHER. That's what I like to see my little girl the best in.

DAUGHTER. Oh poppa, you're fabulous! (*She gives him another kiss, then starts up the stairs.*) All right, acne, you've been in there long enough! (*She is gone. Father makes sure the coast is clear, then gets out telephone directory. He clearly picks a number at random, dials it and waits impatiently for it to answer.*)

MOTHER. (*Enters from kitchen, nibbling food, still under her portable hair dryer.*) The Smiths' boy was arrested today.

FATHER. (*Startled, banging phone down.*) Turn that damn thing off. You can't hear yourself with it running.

MOTHER. Burned his draft card.

FATHER. Turn it off!

MOTHER. I'M IN THE DRYER! (*Father gives up, slumps in his chair. Mother goes right on talking.*) I told Betty letting him grow his hair so long was just the beginning. But no, she said all the boys were doing it and didn't Teddy look cute. Sure he'll look cute, I said to her, *cute behind bars.* I swear! Don't people read *Time* magazine anymore? Long hair is one of the seven danger signals.

FATHER. (*Shaking his head in despair.*) Mona, Mona, Mona.

MOTHER. Dirt and rampant liberalism are the other six!

FATHER. I'm sure they are.

MOTHER. WHAT'S A MOTHER TO DO?

FATHER. You'd better get ready. They'll be here any minute.

MOTHER. Did I see Jimmy?! I'll say I saw Jimmy! I'll probably trip over it and break my neck.

FATHER. You just do that.

MOTHER. (*As she stands looking down at crate, touching it with her hand.*) The most patriotic son a mother ever had. And now he's dead. They say he never knew what hit him. That dirty

Communist land mine tore his stomach right open. (*Pause.*) It's such a big box. I don't remember him being so long. Maybe he grew more over there. (*Turns to Father.*) I'M IN THE DRYER! (*She goes upstairs. The moment she leaves, Father is on the telephone again.*)

FATHER. TErminal 5-1461? . . . Hello, baby . . . never mind who . . . what are you wearing? . . . just out of the shower, hunh? . . . (*The lights on him are dimming and the sound of his voice is fading.*) . . . you sound like the kind of girl who knows what a good time is . . .

JIMMY. (*Sitting up in the crate.*) Well here's Jimmy. Here he is. (*Flashes a smile.*) Dad's making one of his obscene phone calls. This might be my only chance to talk. (*He climbs out of crate, steps forward.*) I'm really dead, you understand, but I can clear the air up a little bit. At least get the facts straight. I'm six foot one . . . *was*, I *was* six foot one, sorry about that . . . weighed one fifty-nine, had blue eyes and hair the color commonly called dirty blonde. Now don't feel too badly that they didn't remember all that. I couldn't answer the same questions about any of *them*. I mean *jeez*, I'm just their son and brother! But I can't understand half the things they've said about me. Like Susy. How can you call someone a good big brother when he took a brick and knocked your permanent front teeth out? That's a bridge she's flashing. Johnny's decided I was a load of laughs. What's an Italian pushing a baby carriage? That's the only joke I can remember, and even so I forget the punch line. And like everybody else I must have heard hundreds, thousands of jokes in my lifetime. I just never could remember them. And God only knows I never made one up. Dad's decided I was masculine all of a sudden and mom's gnawing the patriotism bone. I swear I don't know who they're talking about. And that bit about he never knew what hit him! At first I was just startled, I mean I never expected it to happen to me, but after a minute or two it hurt like hell. You have your guts hanging out and see how it feels! I'm sorry. I'm not meant to show any emotion. I'm dead. Thank you for your attention. (*He gets back into the crate.*) Is anybody wondering how it feels to be dead? I'll try to tell you. It's a . . . funny feeling. Funny because it's so hard to talk about. You see, there I was just kind of slopping around and I'd never really thought about what being alive meant and so now it's kind of hard to compare the two. But when I stepped on that mine I knew *something* had hit me, I can tell you that! Christ Almighty, it hurt! (*Flashes a smile.*) Well here goes Jimmy. Here he goes. (*He signals the peace sign and lies back down. Lights have come back up on Father on the phone.*)

FATHER. . . . tell me more, angel puss, tell me more! (*Noises from upstairs.*) I gotta go. I'll call again . . . Meet? Us? What are you, some kind of nympho! (*Bangs down phone as Daughter rushes down the stairs dressed in her cheerleader's outfit.*)

DAUGHTER. (*Waving pompoms.*)
<blockquote>Flying pig! Flying pig!
Oink! Oink! Oink!</blockquote>

(*Repeat several times. There is no stopping her, in fact. Father beams, egging her on. What he likes best about her outfit is the tight sweater.*)

SON. (*Banging down the stairs, dressed in mod clothes.*) The hair spray's so thick up there with those two, I'm getting cancer of the eyeballs. Wow! Are they red. (*Watches Daughter's performance.*) Boy, Jimmy cleared out of this house just in time! The neuroses around this dump are really getting to me. (*He goes to telephone.*)

MOTHER. (*Coming down stairs, suburban attire.*) Right before your very eyes and you don't even see it!

FATHER. Hunh?

MOTHER. One of the seven danger signals!

SON. (*On phone.*) Hello, Margy? It's your lover.

MOTHER. Look at his hair!

DAUGHTER. (*Trying to get phone.*) Do you have to monopolize that thing?

MOTHER. Well *do* something about it.

FATHER. Jimmy. I mean Johnny.

SON. They're on my back. I'll call you later. (*Hangs up phone.*)

FATHER. You heard your mother. Get a haircut.

SON. Yes, sir! (*Starts to leave.*)

MOTHER. Not now.

FATHER. Later.

SON. You bet!

FATHER. Roger!

SON. Over and out! (*Grins.*) You'll make a man out of me yet.

MOTHER. (*Peering out window.*) I wonder what's keeping them?

DAUGHTER. Can I do a cheer for the cameras?

FATHER. Anything you want, peaches.

SON. Sure, show everybody.

DAUGHTER. See how he starts on me?

SON. All I said was—!

DAUGHTER. Momma, Johnny's making cracks about what happened last winter!

MOTHER. (*Comforting her.*) Hush there, sshh! Well don't look at me, Sam. He's your son. Do something.

FATHER. You heard your mother.

SON. All I said was—!

DAUGHTER. (*Covering her ears.*) Don't let him talk about last winter, momma. Don't let him, don't let him, don't let him, don't let him! (*She has a tantrum right on the spot.*)

MOTHER. (*When she is quiet.*) You see what you've done.

FATHER. Good Lord, Mona, all the boy said was—!

DAUGHTER. Aaaaaaaaaaaaah!

MOTHER. (*With dignity.*) Lots of girls Susy's age get into trouble. They're nearly all doing it.

DAUGHTER. (*Between sniffles.*) Shelly Hines . . . Carrie Pope . . . Billie Lockwell . . .

MOTHER. Gretchen Heller.

FATHER. The little Herlihy girl.

SON. Dena Butt.

MOTHER. Dena Butt?

DAUGHTER. With Freddy Heller!

SON. Who told you?

DAUGHTER. I heard!

MOTHER. As you can see, Johnny, girls who get into trouble are no laughing matter.

DAUGHTER. Tell momma how much pot you've been smoking lately!

MOTHER. Some of the nicest girls in town have had abortions. They're no better than Susy.

DAUGHTER. And all those pills you've got hidden under your socks!

MOTHER. As far as this family is concerned, Susy never *had* an abortion. Willie Young never existed.

FATHER. You getting this all down, son?

DAUGHTER. Tell her about you and Billy Grey!

MOTHER. In fact, show me a girl Susy's age who *hasn't* been in trouble and I'll show you a girl who has something wrong with her.

FATHER. Your mother's right.

DAUGHTER. (*Drying her tears.*) Of course she is.

MOTHER. And to top it all off and bring this story to its happy ending, Susy, as we all know, has mended her ways.

SON. Hah!

DAUGHTER. (*Bawling again.*) You see? You see?

SON. All I said was hah! Everybody's so touchy in this house!

DAUGHTER. I'll kill him! I'll kill him! (*Nails bared, she's chasing him around the room.*)

SON. Whore! Slut! Strumpet!

MOTHER. (*Despairing now.*) What can we do with them?

FATHER. (*Defeated, too.*) I don't know . . . I don't know. (*Doorbell rings. Everybody freezes. Pause.*)

MOTHER. Get it.

FATHER. You.

SON. Not me again.

DAUGHTER. I can't. (*Doorbell rings.*)

FATHER. Mona!

MOTHER. It's your house.

DAUGHTER. Make Jimmy go.

SON. *There's* Jimmy!

DAUGHTER. I meant *you*, brat. (*Doorbell rings.*)

FATHER. Goddamnit, I won't go. Who's the man in this house anyway?

MOTHER. You're the one who made an issue of it. Women have pride, too, you know!

DAUGHTER. That's right.

SON. (*Who's looked out the window.*) They're leaving. (*There is a mass rush to the door. The room is empty. We hear voices off.*)

JIMMY. (*Sitting up in the crate.*) A dope pusher! I just remembered the punch line! "An Italian pushing a baby carriage is a dope pusher!" (*He makes the peace sign and lies back down as family returns with Miss Horne and two television cameramen. Miss Horne is a svelte, rather young Negro television reporter.*)

MOTHER. (*So affably.*) What's your first name, honey?

MISS HORNE. Fatima Beloved of Ali X.

MOTHER. Oh dear!

MISS HORNE. And none of you honkies better use it. It's Miss Horne to you. Where's the body? We'll do the interview over there.

FATHER. Smoke?

MISS HORNE. Why not? (*She rips off filter.*)

FATHER. Drink?

MISS HORNE. You been nipping at it?

FATHER. We've had a few, actually.

MISS HORNE. What the Muslims don't know won't hurt 'em. (*He fills her glass.*) Three fingers, honky!

FATHER. Sorry.

SON. (*To TV crew.*) Any of you cats got some grass on you? Aw come *on*, you're in show business.

DAUGHTER. (*To television men; provocatively seated.*) Hi there! And a hello to you!

MISS HORNE. Let's get this show rolling. They yours? (*Parents nod.*) All right, honky brats, over here. (*To Daughter.*) What are you smiling at?

DAUGHTER. (*Her standard answer, she loves giving it.*) I'm not smiling actually.

MOTHER. It's her eyes.

DAUGHTER. They twinkle all the time and that gives my face the appearance of a smile.

MISS HORNE. Get you! (*Son laughs.*) Cut it out.

SON. I thought *I* was a salty one!

MISS HORNE. It's not salt, sonny. Any bus I drive, you're in the back of it.

FATHER. Now just one minute—!

MISS HORNE. You're on the air. (*The family freezes, inane smiles. Miss Horne's voice assumes the cool, efficient tones of a professional broadcaster.*) Six o'clock news. Human interest feature. We're taping. (*The TV lights blaze, the camera whirs.*)

MOTHER. (*Terse whisper.*) Sit up, Susy. *Up!*

MISS HORNE. The war became a reality today for a family in exclusive Milford Haven. We spoke to them in their . . . (*With some sarcasm.*) . . . tastefully furnished living room.

MOTHER. Thank you.

MISS HORNE. Behind them . . . in a plain wooden crate . . . was the body of their oldest son.

MOTHER. That's our Jimmy.

FATHER. That's our Jimmy all right.

SON. A land mine ripped his stomach right open.

DAUGHTER. He never knew what hit him. (*From inside the crate, Jimmy raps in protest.*)

MISS HORNE. Tell us something about Jimmy. What kind of boy was he? We'll start with the youngest.

SON. He was . . . he was cool. (*Pause.*) I guess. (*Pause.*) I mean . . . no, he was cool.

DAUGHTER. Jimmy had a smile that could knock your eyes out. Girls were crazy for him.

MISS HORNE. What were some of his interests?

DAUGHTER. Oh, you know . . . usual stuff.

MISS HORNE. He was typical then?

FATHER. Very typical! Simple, good-natured, down to earth . . . (*Aside to Son who fidgets, yawns.*) Stop that, Jimmy!

SON. I'm not Jimmy.

FATHER. You know who I mean! (*Then.*) Excuse me. Where was I?

MISS HORNE. Run of the mill.

FATHER. That's Jimmy to a T! But above all . . . and this is how I'll most remember him . . . Jimmy was a real man. A man's man.

SON. Hah! That isn't what you used to say.

FATHER. He wouldn't be in that box, son, if he weren't anything *but* a man. The Army's gonna shape you up, too, one day. God bless it.

MOTHER. The main thing to say about Jimmy is that he was an American. A good American. I suppose the word "patriot" is old hat.

FATHER. Don't cry, mother.

MISS HORNE. Is this a moral war?

SON. Don't look at me.

DAUGHTER. I'm just in high school.

FATHER. Real men don't ask questions like that.

SON. She's not a man.

MOTHER. Neither do real Americans.

MISS HORNE. All right, then, and on a lighter note: How has Jimmy's death affected your routine of daily life?

SON. It hasn't.

DAUGHTER. It has too! We stayed out of school three whole days after we got the telegram. And we don't have to go tomorrow either because of the funeral.

SON. Really, ma?

MISS HORNE. Will you be on the field leading the student body for the Taft game Friday night?

FATHER. She certainly will.

MISS HORNE. I gather it's an important game for Hamilton?

DAUGHTER. I'll say it is. (*Directly to camera.*) Beat hell out of Taft!

FATHER. Could she . . . ? (*Motioning to Daughter.*) Go ahead, peaches.

DAUGHTER. (*In a flurry of pompoms.*)
Flying pig! Flying pig!
Oink! Oink! Oink!
(*She continues cheering.*)

SON. That's right, show everybody.

MOTHER. Susy, your skirt, keep it down!

SON. It's no secret what *she* is!

FATHER. Atta girl! Do the split now.

MISS HORNE. Thank you, Susy. Susy, that will do.

DAUGHTER. (*A final outburst before sitting.*) All the way to state, team, all the way to state!

FATHER. Isn't she terrific?

MISS HORNE. It seems then your life has been relatively unaffected by Jimmy's death?

FATHER. (*Reflectively.*) Well, you know, life continues. That's the beautiful thing about death, life continues.

MOTHER. Jimmy was as American as apple pie.

FATHER. (*Consoling her.*) Mother, mother.

MISS HORNE. Can you describe your emotions when you got the news about Jimmy?

SON. I cried.

DAUGHTER. Me, too. For days and days.

SON. Ella Exaggerater!

DAUGHTER. Oh shut up!

FATHER. It hit me pretty hard at first. But the more I thought about it . . . I hate to use this word . . . well, the happier I got. Thank God my son was a man. After all, how many American

fathers can say that? If you hadn't guessed it, I'm kind of a
virility nut. I even worry about my little Johnny here. Thank
God for the army, hunh? It really straightens these boys out.

SON. Yes, sir!

MOTHER. I was proud, Miss Horne, let me tell you. I was *proud*
of Jimmy. His father says he died like a man. I say he died like an
American. What more can a mother ask? You see this flag? It
came with the body. I thought that was very sweet of them.
Washington cares.

FATHER. We all do, Mona.

MOTHER. These are proud tears, America.

SON. It's a local show, ma.

MOTHER. I shed them with pride.

DAUGHTER. Momma, don't have an attack.

MOTHER. My son died an American! Mothers of the World, may
you live to see the day your sons die American!

SON. She thinks she's on Telstar.

MISS HORNE. One final question. *Why* did Jimmy die? (*Pause.*)

SON. Who wouldn't die if they stepped on a land mine and had
their stomach ripped open?

DAUGHTER. That's not what she means, stupid. Jimmy died defend-
ing the American way of life. Everything good, that's what he
died for. You and me. So we could go to school and football
games and dances in the gym just like he did. So we could have
color TV and our own rooms and live in a nice house in a nice
part of town. Jimmy died for you.

SON. (*Chastened.*) I didn't know that.

DAUGHTER. Don't you study civics? If people like Jimmy don't die
for the American way of life there won't *be* an American way
of life.

SON. Cripes!

FATHER. What your sister's trying to tell you, son, is that Jimmy
died so we could say to the world: This, this was a man. Dying,
you see, my son, is the real test of a man's masculinity. And
Jimmy passed it.

SON. And how he did! Wow.

MOTHER. And there's more to it than that, Johnny. Your brother
died because he was an American.

SON. I'm an American and I'm not dead.

MOTHER. You're too young. You'll get your chance.

SON. What about dad?

MOTHER. He's too old. He's had his.

FATHER. (*Aside.*) That's a lousy crack to make on television, Mona!

SON. What about you and . . . ?

DAUGHTER. We're *women!*

MOTHER. Right or wrong, Jimmy gave his life for his country and if that's not the American way of doing things, I'd like to know what is.

SON. *Who* right or wrong? Jimmy or his country?

MOTHER. Both. Both right. Jimmy *and* his country.

DAUGHTER. Boy, you're dumb.

FATHER. Live and learn, son, live and learn.

SON. Yes, sir!

MISS HORNE. Mrs. . . .

MOTHER. (*Head bowed.*) Mona, just Mona.

MISS HORNE. We can say then you're proud your son died as an American?

FATHER. As a man, too!

DAUGHTER. We all are!

MOTHER. Yes, that you can say, yes.

MISS HORNE. (*Slight change of tone.*) Did you know your son *did* know what hit him?

MOTHER. I'm sorry, I don't understand.

MISS HORNE. That it was forty-five minutes of pain and terror before he lost consciousness?

MOTHER. What do you mean?

MISS HORNE. That he sat under a tree holding his large intestine in the palm of his hand?

MOTHER. The telegram said he . . . I have it right here.

FATHER. Hey, what is this?

MISS HORNE. That your son never knew *why* he was over there or what he was fighting for?

MOTHER. The telegram . . . I can't find the telegram . . . !

DAUGHTER. Momma!

FATHER. Look, lady, take your left-wing politics somewhere else!

MOTHER. I had it somewhere. . . .

MISS HORNE. Do any of you know *anything*? (*Short pause, they all look at her in consternation.*) Or *want* to?

MOTHER. It was right here!

MISS HORNE. Six o'clock news. Human interest feature. Cut. (*TV lights are turned off.*)

FATHER. I want you people out there to know this is a *Negro* who's saying all this!

MISS HORNE. You're off the air.

FATHER. A black troublemaker!

MISS HORNE. All right, let's get out of here. (*TV crew begins to get ready to leave.*)

FATHER. Sure, just leave now! Look what you've done to my wife. She's upset.

SON. What channel are we gonna be on?

DAUGHTER. Will we be in color?

FATHER. I can't do anything for her when she gets like this.

SON. Hey, man, you sure you ain't got any grass?

DAUGHTER. Bye now. Bye now, you two!

FATHER. I hope you're pleased with yourself. (*Mother sits rigid, tears streaming down her face, not listening to anyone.*)

MISS HORNE. (*As the TV crew precedes her out.*) You can see yourself at six o'clock. (*She goes.*)

FATHER. I just hope you're *pleased!* (*Consoles Mother.*)

SON. What was all that about?

DAUGHTER. Beats me. (*Phone rings. Son and Daughter race for it. Daughter wins.*) Eddie? . . . Fine, how are you? . . . you're kidding! (*To Son.*) The Taft quarterback broke his leg at practice! (*Back to phone.*) Groovy! . . . I'll wait out in front . . . aaaw, they're hysterical as usual . . . okay, but hurry up. (*She hangs up.*) Tell mom I'm getting a coke with Eddie.

SON. You tell her.

DAUGHTER. Selfish! You wouldn't put yourself out for Jesus Christ if he came back. (*Picks up purse.*) I love my poppa! (*Runs out door. Son glowers, goes to phone.*)

SON. Margy? . . . I'm coming over now with some stuff. If you chicken out, I swear I'm gonna kill you . . . Hey, guess what? The show's in color! Bye. (*Hangs up.*) I'm going to Margy's.

FATHER. Please don't, mother, don't cry like that.

SON. Dad, I'm going to Margy's.

FATHER. You'll only upset yourself.

SON. I SAID I AM GOING TO MARGY'S!

FATHER. Communist propaganda, every word of it!

SON. Boy, I'm not only getting neurotic, I'm not even getting understood! (*He leaves.*)

FATHER. Mona, I'm going to have to leave you now. It's bowling night. Will you be all right? Just remember your own words, mother. You're proud your son died as an American. And I'm just as proud he died as a man. They can't take that away from us. You got that? Say it. I'm proud my son— (*Mother moves her lips, no sound comes out.*) Good girl. Just keep saying that to yourself over and over. Pretty soon you'll feel better. I bet you're not even awake when I get home! (*Nudges her playfully.*) Lazy bones I'm married to! (*Gets up.*) Don't stop! Over and over and over and over and over and . . . (*He is tiptoeing out the door.*) . . . over and over and over and over and . . . (*He is gone. Mother sits, reciting her soundless litany. The room is very still.*)

JIMMY. (*Sitting up in crate.*) I've figured something out while all that was going on. The main reason I wish I was alive is so I could figure out why I was dead. (*Puzzles a moment.*) Yeah, that's it. (*Lies back in crate. Pause. He sits up again.*) Do something for her, why don't you, hunh?

MOTHER. Jimmy.

JIMMY. Tell her . . . I don't know. Tell her she's right. Tell her you're proud I died as an American.

MOTHER. Jimmy.

JIMMY. Tell her you're proud I died as a man.

MOTHER. Jimmy.

JIMMY. You could even tell her I *was* a lot of laughs.

MOTHER. JIIIMMMMMYYYYY!

JIMMY. (*After a long pause.*) Then do us all a favor. Don't watch the six o'clock news. (*He starts to make the peace sign, decides not to this time and lies back slowly.*)

MOTHER. (*Emotions spent now, a little voice.*) Jimmy? (*Pause.*) Jimmy? (*Pause.*) Jimmy?